D1162413

THE BATTLE OF MIDWAY

THE BATTLE OF MIDWAY

The Naval Institute Guide to the U.S. Navy's Greatest Victory

EDITED BY
THOMAS C. HONE

Naval Institute Press
Annapolis, Maryland

Naval Institute Press
291 Wood Road
Annapolis, MD 21402

Library of Congress Cataloging-in-Publication Data
Hone, Thomas.
The Battle of Midway : the Naval Institute guide to the Battle of Midway / Thomas C. Hone.
pages cm
Includes bibliographical references and index.
ISBN 978-1-61251-126-9 (hbk. : alk. paper) — ISBN 978-1-61251-132-0 (ebook)
1. Midway, Battle of, 1942. 2. World War, 1939-1945—Naval operations, American. 3. World War, 1939-1945—Naval operations, Japanese. 4. World War, 1939-1945—Personal narratives, American. 5. World War, 1939-1945—Personal narratives, Japanese. I. United States Naval Institute. II. Title. III. Title: Naval Institute guide to the Battle of Midway.
D774.M5H65 2013
940.54′26699—dc23
2013004872

This paper meets the requirements of ANSI/NISO z39.48–1992 (Permanence of Paper).

Printed in the United States of America.

21 20 19 18 17 16 15 14 13 9 8 7 6 5 4 3 2 1

First printing

TO

Clayton E. Steele, R3C, USN

CDR E. P. Vollmer, USN

CAPT Gerard D. Roncolato, USN

CDR Robert Nazak, USN

CAPT George Thibault, USN

VADM William Bowes, USN

Contents

Illustrations

Photos

Maps

Acknowledgments

LCDR Thomas J. Cutler, USN (Ret.), editor, facilitator, and wise counselor. Paul Stillwell, for directing me to the articles that mattered. Norman Polmar, a careful student of aircraft carriers and carrier warfare. CDR Janis Jorgensen, USNR (Ret.), for help finding photographs. Frank Uhlig Jr., my best critic. And the staffs of the Navy Department Library and the National Archives.

Help for Readers

The different chronologies of the opposing forces

Japanese and American time-keeping differed during the battle, which can confuse readers. The Battle of Midway was fought across the international date line. The Japanese used east longitude dates and Tokyo time. The Americans used west longitude dates, and there was a two-hour difference between Midway clocks and clocks in TF-16 and TF-17 (the carriers were two hours ahead of Midway). This can be very confusing. The point to keep in mind is that 0130 for the Japanese was 0430 for the American defenders of Midway *the previous day*. What was often 4 June time for the Americans was 5 June time for the Japanese.

To simplify matters for readers, here is a brief chronology of events on 4–6 June in Midway time:

4 June 1942

0130: Midway-based PBY seaplanes begin attack on Japanese transports.

0405: Midway-based B-17s depart Midway to attack Japanese transports.

0430: Planes from the *kidō butai* launched to attack Midway.

0430: *Yorktown* sends 10 SBD scouts to search for Japanese carrier force.

0437: Dawn

0552: PBY reports sighting Japanese carriers.

0603: PBYs sighting received on the *Enterprise.*

0630: Marine antiaircraft guns open fire on Japanese planes attacking Midway.

0700–0705: The *Hornet* and *Enterprise* launch strike aircraft.

0705: Leader of the Japanese aircraft attacking Midway signals need for second strike.

0708: Midway-based attack aircraft begin attacks on the *kidō butai.*

0820: Scoutplane from the Japanese cruiser *Tone* signals that U.S. formation includes a carrier.

0838: The *Yorktown* launches a strike.

0918: The *Hornet* torpedo planes begin attack.

1020: American dive-bombers begin their attacks on the *Kaga, Akagi,* and *Soryu.*

1054: The *Hiryu* launches a strike against U.S. carriers.

1200: The *Hiryu* planes attack the *Yorktown.*

1320: The *Hiryu*'s second strike of attack planes sets off to attack U.S. carriers.

1445: SBD from the *Yorktown* locates the *Hiryu.*

1700: Planes from U.S. carriers attack the *Hiryu.*

5 June

0020: Admiral Yamamoto cancels cruiser attack on Midway.

0255: Admiral Yamamoto cancels Midway invasion.

0300 (approximately): The *Mogami* and *Mikuma* collide.

6 June

0945 (approximately): The *Hornet* aircraft attack the two cruisers. The *Enterprise* planes attack at 1230.

1331: The *I-168* attacks the *Yorktown* and *Hammann.*

1900: The *Enterprise* and *Hornet* recover aircraft and head east.

General Chronology

Events leading up to and including the Battle of Midway

11 January: The *Saratoga* torpedoed and damaged by a Japanese submarine. Sent to the mainland after temporary repairs at Pearl Harbor.

20 January: VADM William Halsey in the *Enterprise* arrives off Samoa.

23 January: The tanker *Neches* sunk by Japanese submarine.

24 January: The *Yorktown* arrives in Pearl Harbor after having escorted Marines to Samoa.

25 January: The *Enterprise* and *Yorktown* begin steaming toward the Gilbert and Marshall Islands.

31 January/February 1: Vice Admiral Halsey in the *Enterprise* (TF-8) and RADM Frank J. Fletcher in the *Yorktown* (TF-17) attack Japanese-held Wotje, Kwajalein, Jaluit, and Mili Islands.

5 February: The *Enterprise* returns to Pearl Harbor. The *Yorktown* returns on 6 February.

7 February and 9 February: Admiral Nimitz responds to Admiral King's order to take action with the carrier task forces. King wanted the carriers to take the offensive before Japanese forces then in the southwest Pacific could turn around and head east. He made this clear to Admiral Nimitz on 9 February.

14 February: *Enterprise* TF-16 leaves Pearl Harbor to attack Wake and Marcus Islands.

24 February: *Enterprise* planes attack Wake.

4 March: *Enterprise* planes attack Marcus.

10 March: TF-16 (*Enterprise*) returns to Pearl Harbor.

10 March: Aircraft from the *Lexington* and *Yorktown* attack Lae and Salamaua in New Guinea.

26 March: The *Lexington* returns to Pearl Harbor.

8 April: TF-16 (the *Enterprise* and *Hornet*) departs from Pearl Harbor on Tokyo raid.

18 April: U.S. B-25s from TF-16 bomb Tokyo.

25 April: Tokyo striking force (*Enterprise* and *Hornet* as TF-16) returns to Pearl Harbor.

30 April: TF-16 leaves Pearl Harbor for southwest Pacific.

4 May: Attack on Japanese forces on Tulagi by aircraft of TF-16.

7–8 May: Battle of the Coral Sea. The *Lexington* is lost and the *Yorktown* is damaged.

21 May: North Pacific Force established under RADM Robert A. Theobald to defend Alaska.

2 June: Task Force 17 (the *Yorktown*) joins Task Force 16 (the *Enterprise* and *Hornet*) northeast of Midway.

4–6 June: Battle of Midway. The *Yorktown* is damaged on 4 June and torpedoed and fatally damaged on 6 June.

Introduction

By LCDR Thomas J. Cutler, USN (Ret.)

The Battle of Midway is arguably the greatest battle in American naval history. It is a classic drama in which the underdog comes off the ropes to score a devastating knockout punch. It abounds with moments of phenomenal courage, inspirational sacrifice, clever deception, and fateful decisions. It has been studied in detail by great naval historians including Samuel Eliot Morison, Gordon Prange, and Craig Symonds because it is a rich case study, full of timeless lessons. It is a story that exemplifies how war brings out the best and the worst of humanity.

It is no surprise, then, that the U.S. Navy has chosen this battle—of all the battles it has fought over more than two centuries—as the one to commemorate annually, to reflect on it much as the Royal Navy has long celebrated its singular victory at Trafalgar, to draw from it a sense of those special qualities that define the American sailor.

It is fitting, too, that the U.S. Naval Institute—whose mission includes "the preservation of our naval history"—should provide this guide as a means of commemorating, researching, experiencing, and learning about this momentous battle. Within these pages, readers will find a unique collection of materials, all drawn from the Naval Institute's massive collections of intellectual content.

Over the years since June 1942, the Battle of Midway has been reported, analyzed, and discussed in the pages of *Proceedings* and *Naval History* magazines, in Naval Institute Press books, and as part of the Institute's ongoing oral history project. These have been collected, entirely or in part, in this useful and entertaining anthology.

Part I sets the stage for the upcoming battle; part II covers planning and preparations on both sides; part III describes the actual battle, including the first-hand accounts of both Japanese and American participants; part IV consists of postbattle events and analysis; part V includes the official battle report; part VI focuses on the senior commanders; part VII covers one of the most interesting aspects of the battle, the role of code-breaking; and part VIII concludes with numerous assessments of the battle. Three appendices round out the coverage with additional materials that provide further insight into the many facets of this important and gripping moment in history.

The result is a unique collection that only an organization as unique as the U.S. Naval Institute could provide. From general survey to detailed analysis, this book is a welcome addition to the vast literature on World War II, providing a superb reference collection as well as an aid to those who are searching for materials to enhance the annual commemoration of this awe-inspiring and historically significant battle.

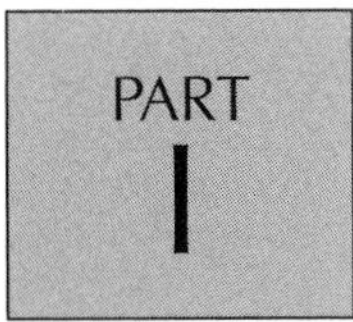

PART I

Midway Anthology

Part I contains four selections. The first, "*Akagi,* Famous Japanese Carrier" (chapter 1), is one of the first postwar accounts of the Battle of Midway to summarize the operations of the *kidō butai* up to and during the engagement off Midway. Published in 1948, it contains errors of detail that the author could not have known about when he wrote the article. It stands, however, as a succinct summary of events leading up to the battle and of the battle itself. The second selection, "Attacking a Continent" (chapter 2), explains how and why the Imperial Japanese Navy (IJN) came to appreciate large-scale carrier strikes and why Japanese carrier pilots were so skilled in 1941–1942. The third selection, "Time Is Everything (Japanese Side)" (chapter 3) from *Black Shoe Carrier Admiral,* puts the reader into the shoes of Admiral Yamamoto and shows why he insisted on a decisive battle with the U.S. Navy's Pacific Fleet. The last selection in part I, "Midway Island Operation Plan" (chapter 4), drawn from a widely read Japanese account of Midway, presents Admiral Isoroku Yamamoto from a Japanese perspective.

As the Royal Navy's official history, *War with Japan,* noted, Vice Admiral Chuichi Nagumo's *kidō butai* had, since 7 December 1941,

> operated across one-third of the globe, from Hawaii to Ceylon, conducting effective strikes against ships and shore installations at every important allied [*sic*] base out of reach of shore-based aircraft. . . . They had destroyed the United States battle fleets and driven the British out of the Indian Ocean. To their credit stood the destruction of thousands of tons of merchantmen, hundreds of Allied aircraft as well as docks, hangars and base facilities. All this Admiral Nagumo had accomplished without loss or damage to a single one of his ships—indeed, he was seldom sighted and never effectively attacked.[1]

The Battle of Midway would bring this naval triumph to an abrupt halt.

CHAPTER
1

Akagi, Famous Japanese Carrier

By Walton L. Robinson

Proceedings, May 1948: pp. 579–595

Few warships of World War II had as brief but spectacular a career as did His Japanese Majesty's Ship *Akagi,* one of the largest and finest aircraft carriers in Nippon's once proud and formidable Imperial Navy (*Teikoku Kaigun,* literally, the "Empire's National Sea Army"). Throughout the first six months of the Pacific War, or, as the Japanese liked to call it, "The Greater East Asia War," the *Akagi* played an unusually prominent role, spearheading nearly all of Japan's more important carrier operations. During this critical period, which ended with our victory at Midway, *Akagi* participated in operations ranging across 120 degrees of longitude—from Hawaii to Ceylon—and thereby demonstrated to the world, and to our Navy in particular, the full potentialities of carrier warfare.

Laid down in December, 1920, at the Kure Navy Yard as a 42,000-ton battle cruiser, part of Japan's famous "Eight-Four Program" (eight huge battleships and four battle cruisers), the *Akagi,* in conformity with the terms of the Washington Naval Limitation Treaty, was taken in hand in 1923 for conversion into a first-line aircraft carrier (*kokubokan*). She was launched in 1925 and commissioned two years later, a ship of 36,000 tons standard displacement, 763 feet in length, and capable of at least 28.5 knots speed. Reckoned on a tonnage basis *Akagi* was, therefore, somewhat larger than our *Lexington* and *Saratoga* (likewise converted from battle cruiser hulls), but was considerably slower and does not appear to have carried more than 60 planes. Her defensive armament comprised ten 8-inch guns, plus twelve 4.7-inch and numerous smaller anti-aircraft weapons. Originally four of the 8-inch guns were mounted forward in paired turrets, just below the upper flight deck, while the remaining six were mounted aft on either side of the main deck and quite close to the waterline.

A sister ship, the *Amagi,* was to have been similarly converted; but her hull received serious damage in the terrible earthquake of September 1, 1923. To replace her, the already launched hull of the 40,600-ton battleship *Kaga,* due to be scrapped under the Naval Treaty, was appropriated. Commissioned in 1928, the *Kaga* displaced 35,000 tons, but her shorter hull (715 feet), greater beam (11 feet more than *Akagi*) and weaker engines (91,000 horsepower instead of 131,000) gave her a *designed* speed of only 23 knots, according to pre-war Japanese statements. With her two enormous horizontal funnels (about 275 feet long, one on either side), the *Kaga* presented a most bizarre appearance.

In 1935–37 the *Akagi* and the *Kaga* underwent very thorough modernizations, emerging as near sisters in appearance. Alterations included the suppression of the lower flight deck (flying-off deck), extension forward of the upper flight deck, and removal of the 8-inch gun turrets and the mounting of their rifles aft along the side. The *Kaga* also lost her monstrous funnels, while both ships received small "island" superstructures—on the port side in the *Akagi* and on the starboard in the *Kaga.* It is likely, also, that the *Kaga*'s speed was raised by several knots—probably to between 28 and 30 knots.

In November, 1941, these two ships comprised Japan's "First Flying Squadron" (Car Div 1), the *Akagi* wearing the flag of Vice Admiral Chuichi Nagumo, Commanding the First Air Fleet, whose assigned mission was the surprise attack on Pearl Harbor. Two other Flying Squadrons, the Second and Fifth consisting, respectively, of the 17,500-ton carriers *Hiryu* and *Soryu* and the new 29,800-ton *Shokaku* and *Zuikaku,* were also attached to the Striking Force, as were the old but modernized 31,000-ton, 28-knot battleships *Hiei* and *Kirishima,* the new 12,000-ton heavy cruisers *Tone* and *Chikuma,* the old 5,700-ton light cruiser *Abukuma,* and nine of the newest and largest destroyers, the 1,900-ton *Kagero, Shiranuhi, Urakaze, Isokaze, Tanikaze, Hamakaze, Akigumo,* and the 1,850-ton *Arare* and *Kasumi.*

On November 17 the Striking Force departed from Saeki, on Kyushu's east coast, where for some weeks the carrier air groups had been undergoing intensive training. Five days later the ships anchored in Hitokappu Bay, in the bleak Kurile Islands, where they refueled and stood-by awaiting orders. These came on the 25th, from Admiral Isoroku Yamamoto, Commander in Chief of the Combined Fleet; and next morning the ships sortied on their secret mission, the nature of which was known only to Admiral Nagumo and senior members of his staff.

A week's slow steaming through the cold, gray mists of the North Pacific brought the force to a position about 800 miles south of the eastern Aleutians. Here on December 3, despite heavy seas, the ships fueled from five tankers; had this difficult operation failed, the carriers would have proceeded without their destroyer screen. On the 4th the Japanese altered course to 135 degrees. Two days later the pilots received their briefing for the attack. Next day, the 7th (Tokyo date), came the anxiously awaited code message: "Climb Mount Niitaka!"

Promptly the *Akagi* hoisted the flag signal, "Speed 24 knots. Course South." Even more inspiring to the Japanese crews was the dramatic appearance at the *Akagi*'s masthead of the huge battle ensign which had flown from Admiral Togo's flagship *Mikasa* at the Battle of Tsushima, and which had been carefully preserved during the intervening 36 years.

Dawn of December 8 (December 7, West Longitude Date) found the Japanese force 230 miles due north of Pearl Harbor. At 0600 all six carriers began launching the first attack wave. Led by Commander Mitsuo Fuchida, commanding the *Akagi*'s air group, this wave totalled 189 aircraft—54 dive bombers, 50 horizontal bombers, 45 fighters, 40 torpedo planes. These aircraft, which inflicted the major portion of the damage sustained by our warships and grounded planes, were followed an hour and fifteen minutes later by a second wave, consisting of 54 high level and 81 dive bombers escorted by 36 fighters. One pilot with this second wave reported enthusiastically, "Pearl Harbor in flame and smoke, gasping helplessly..." Actually, however, the Japanese did not learn—until it was too late—how badly they had hurt our Pacific Fleet.

After recovering all save 29 of their planes, the Japanese carriers turned northwest and steamed through heavy seas toward Japan, fueling once from a group of three oilers stationed along the retirement course. A planned strike against Midway Island, to have been made on December 11 by the *Hiryu* and *Soryu*, was cancelled because of severe weather conditions; but on the 16th these two carriers were detached at sea and, between the 21st and 23rd, made almost continuous strikes against Wake Island. In this operation the Second Flying Squadron was screened by the Eighth Cruiser Squadron (*Tone* and *Chikuma*) and part of the 17th Destroyer Group (*Urakaze* and *Tanikaze*).

On December 24 the *Akagi, Kaga,* and various screening units arrived at Kure, where they were joined next day by the *Shokaku* and *Zuikaku,* which had touched briefly at Saeki. Three days later the *Hiryu* and *Soryu,* delayed by their Wake Island mission, also reached Kure.

Following a brief period of rest and servicing at Kure, the *Akagi, Kaga, Shokaku,* and *Zuikaku* sortied from the Inland Sea on January 9 and, accompanied by the *Hiei, Kirishima, Abukuma,* and destroyers, proceeded to Truk. Three days later the *Hiryu* and *Soryu* also left Kure, but headed for Palau instead of the vaunted base in the Central Carolines.

Five days after departure from Kure the First and Fifth Flying Squadrons and screening units anchored at Truk, remaining there until January 17, when they sortied to support the operations in the Bismarck Archipelago. On January 20 planes from all four of the big carriers attacked Rabaul. Next day the *Akagi* and *Kaga* sent their air groups against Kavieng, while planes from the *Shokaku* and *Zuikaku* struck airfields at Lae, Salamaua, Madang, and Bulolo. On the 22nd *Akagi* and *Kaga* planes again attacked Rabaul, this time in support of landings which secured the place the next day. Then they headed for Truk, where they arrived on January 27 and were joined two days later by the *Shokaku* and *Zuikaku,* whose planes on the 25th had bombed the small airfield at Lorengau, in the Admiralties.

After an overnight stay at Truk the Fifth Flying Squadron left for Palau and Yokosuka. Two days later, while American carrier planes were attacking the Gilberts and Marshalls, the *Akagi* and *Kaga* left Truk for Palau, where they arrived on February 8 to find the Main Body of Vice Admiral Nobutake Kondo's Second Fleet, which had supported the Malay and Philippine invasions. Also in port were the *Hiryu* and *Soryu,* whose planes on January 23 and 24 had softened up the defenses of the small Dutch naval base on Amboina Island, captured a week later by Japanese landing forces.

Within a week of the *Akagi*'s arrival at Palau the combined forces, under Admiral Nagumo's overall command and totaling four battleships (the fast Kongos), four carriers (*Akagi, Kaga, Hiryu, Soryu*), at least six cruisers, and fifteen to twenty destroyers, sortied and, after steaming through the Molucca Passage and the Banda Sea, reached a position east of Timor by the morning of February 19. The carriers then launched their air groups against Port Darwin, wrecking its airfield and shore installations and sinking the old United States destroyer *Peary* and nearly all the Allied transports and supply vessels in the harbor. Japanese losses were two planes shot down: a bomber from the *Kaga* and a fighter from the *Hiryu.*

Two days after their Darwin strike the Japanese carriers anchored in Staring Bay, Kendari, whose seizure had been completed several weeks earlier. Four days were spent at this improvised base near the southeastern tip of the Celebes. Then, on February 25, Admiral Nagumo, with his flag still in the *Akagi,* took the entire force to sea. Skirting Timor's northwest coast, he passed into the Indian Ocean and steamed west to a position south of Java, upon whose northern shores Japanese troops began landing the night of February 28–March 1, following the Battle of the Java Sea.

On March 1 the carriers launched strikes against Allied warships and merchantmen fleeing toward Australia. One victim was our oiler *Pecos* (with the *Langley*'s survivors), which was first sighted at 1600 only thirty miles S.S.W. of the *Akagi.* Battleship, cruiser, and destroyer formations were also active that day, sinking, among other ships, the old United States destroyer *Edsall* and a large Dutch armed freighter. Two bombers from the *Hiryu* or *Soryu* (the accounts differ) assisted in the destruction of the *Edsall,* which went down at 1906 after a gallant but hopeless fight against overwhelming odds: *Kongo, Haruna, Tone,* and *Chikuma.* At 1747 these four ships had left the Main Body at 14° 34′ S; 106° 51′ E to engage the *Edsall* to the rear, the Main Body then steaming on a southeasterly course.

For the next several days Admiral Nagumo's powerful force steamed off Java's south coast to intercept Allied ships attempting to reach Australia. But his air groups appear to have been relatively inactive, limiting their efforts to searches which located various Allied ships for his surface units. In this manner our old gunboat *Asheville,* the four-stacker *Pillsbury,* and Britain's *Stronghold* were intercepted and sunk by Japanese warships. Details are still uncertain, but it seems likely that the *Asheville* and *Pillsbury* went down the night of March 2–3 in separate actions with heavy cruisers *Atago* (Admiral Kondo's flagship), *Maya,* and *Takao,* screened by two destroyers. In neither case did the Japanese tarry to rescue survivors, as they were anxious to expedite their next operation.

It is probable that Admiral Kondo's ships mistook the *Pillsbury* in the darkness for our light cruiser *Marblehead* (also a four-stacker), as only such an error could explain the Imperial Headquarters Communique [*sic*] of March 11, which jubilantly announced that "A Japanese cruiser formation, operating in the Indian Ocean west of Australia, on March 2 sank the 7,050-ton United States cruiser *Marblehead,* which was fleeing toward Australia." An earlier communiqué on March 5, had stated that "Japanese naval forces advancing in the Indian Ocean south of Java surrounded the British destroyer *Stronghold* . . . on March 2 and sank her," adding that "Other Japanese naval forces" sank the *Asheville* the following day.

The passivity of the Japanese carriers ended abruptly the morning of March 5, when the *Akagi, Kaga, Hiryu,* and *Soryu* sent their bombers and fighters against Tjilatjap, virtually wrecking the place and sinking nearly all the shipping which remained in the crowded little harbor. Air reconnaissance later reported that two gunboats and twenty-three merchant vessels (five large, three medium, fifteen small) had been sunk, beached, or set afire; and that over 200 buildings, including the railroad station, had been completely gutted by fire. The two "gunboats" presumably were the Dutch patrol vessel *Canopus* (773 tons) and surveying ship *Tydeman* (1,160 tons), while the merchant ship losses included the converted fleet repair ship *Barentsz* (4,819 tons, *gross,* formerly a K.P.M. freighter) and the unfinished auxiliary minelayer *Ram* (2,400 tons), launched in January and then towed to Tjilatjap.

Two days later, March 7, the South Java Operations virtually ended with a destructive surface bombardment of Christmas Island and anti-shipping strikes by *Hiryu* and *Soryu* planes, whose pilots reported sinking two merchantmen of 10,000 tons in the area south of Sunda Strait. Four days later the carriers and their screening units returned to the temporary base in Staring Bay.

On March 15 the *Kaga* was detached from the Striking Force and left for Sasebo, arriving there on the 22nd, five days after the *Shokaku* and *Zuikaku* had departed Yokosuka for Staring Bay. The reason for the *Kaga*'s return to the Empire is not clear. In any event, Japanese sources fail to confirm the war-time intelligence report that she had been damaged March 2 north of Lombok Strait by our submarine *Sailfish.* But the latter's claim of having successfully attacked a large Japanese naval unit off Lombok Strait was not unfounded, for it is now known that on March 2 her torpedoes sank the 6,440-ton aircraft ferry *Kamogawa Maru.*

On March 24 the *Kaga*'s place in the Striking Force was more than filled by the arrival at Staring Bay of the *Shokaku* and *Zuikaku.* Two days later Admiral Nagumo put to sea and again entered the Indian Ocean, steaming due west and then northwest, toward the great island of Ceylon. He now had with him five large carriers (*Akagi, Hiryu, Soryu, Shokaku, Zuikaku*), three old but fast battleships (*Hiei, Kirishima, Haruna*), about six cruisers, and nearly twenty destroyers—a force quite adequate to deal effectively with Admiral Sir James Somerville's hastily assembled Eastern Fleet, particularly under the new conditions imposed by carrier warfare, in which the Imperial Navy had shown such considerable ability.

Admiral Somerville's command at that time, so critical in the history of the "Greater East Asia War," consisted of five veteran battleships, three aircraft carriers (two modern, one old), two fairly modern cruisers, five old light cruisers, one modern anti-aircraft light cruiser, and some fifteen destroyers, plus five submarines (two British, three Dutch), one monitor, one armed merchant cruiser, and a few fleet auxiliaries and minor units: oilers, sloops, corvettes, and minesweepers. Several of these units, including the armed merchant cruiser *Hector* and the Dutch light cruiser *Sumatra,* were undergoing lengthy repairs and were, therefore, unready for sea.

As of April 1, the day on which Admiral Somerville received information that a strong Japanese force (estimated at three battleships, four or five carriers, and four or five cruisers) soon might launch attacks against Ceylon or India, the Eastern Fleet was organized into two task forces (one fast, one slow), as follows: Force "A"—the 24-knot battleship *Warspite* (flying the C-in-C's flag), fast carriers *Indomitable* and *Formidable,* the cruisers *Cornwall* and *Dorsetshire* (the latter under refit), the old light cruisers *Emerald* and *Enterprise,* and six destroyers; Force "B"—the old 21-knot battleships *Resolution* (flagship of Vice Admiral A. U. Willis, Commanding Third Battle Squadron), *Ramillies, Revenge, Royal Sovereign,* the old carrier *Hermes,* the light cruisers *Caledon* and *Dragon,* the Dutch anti-aircraft cruiser *Jacob van Heemskerck,* and eight destroyers. The aged battleships and cruisers were expected to suffer breakdowns at any moment, while many of the destroyers (some of them veterans of the First World War) were so worn-out that, in the words of Admiral Somerville himself, "it was a marvel that they still could keep running."[1]

By dawn of April 4 the *Akagi* and other Japanese carriers had steamed to within 500 miles of their first objective, Colombo, where they presumably hoped to surprise the Eastern Fleet at anchor. Around 1000, however, a Catalina flying boat approached part of the Japanese force (two battleships, two or three carriers, and two cruisers, plus destroyers). It was quickly shot down by six *Hiryu* fighters flying combat air patrol, its survivors being picked up by destroyer *Isokaze.* But the plane had succeeded in getting off a brief report of the sighting; Colombo's air defenses were accordingly alerted, while Admiral Somerville ordered the Eastern Fleet, then somewhat dispersed for refueling, to concentrate for the battle which appeared imminent.

At dawn of the following day, April 5, the Japanese Second and Fifth Flying Squadrons sent their bombers and fighters to attack Colombo, while the flagship *Akagi* apparently held her air group in reserve. The attackers encountered strong opposition over Colombo from the already air-borne defending fighter planes (a total of 33 Hurricanes and Fulmars) and from the alerted anti-aircraft batteries; but they succeeded in inflicting considerable loss and damage, though at relatively high cost to themselves.

According to the carrier pilots' original reports (greatly exaggerated), at least 38 and possibly 47 British planes were destroyed, while five large and "more than ten" small freighters were badly damaged or set afire, as well as several hangars, a repair shop, and some government buildings and piers. Actual British aircraft losses amounted to sixteen fighters, two Catalinas, and six Swordfish—the last intercepted on passage from Trincomalee to Colombo. One of the large "freighters" hit was the 11,198-ton armed merchant cruiser *Hector,* under repair. So completely was she gutted by fires that she became a total loss. Also hit was the old destroyer *Tenedos,* which sank in the harbor, the 5,800-ton submarine depot ship *Lucia,* and the 5,943-ton merchantman *Benledi,* while serious damage was inflicted on harbor installations and lesser damage on railway workshops. These successes, according to British claims, cost the attackers at least 24 planes definitely shot down, plus seven "probables" and nine planes damaged. But Japanese versions (possibly incomplete) admit the loss of only seven planes: one fighter from the *Soryu,* one bomber from the *Shokaku,* and five bombers from the *Zuikaku!* None of the *Hiryu*'s planes were lost, though nine received damage (again according to available Japanese records). The British claims are almost certainly much nearer the truth.

While the Colombo attack was at its height, about 0900, a striking force of ten Blenheim twin-engined light bombers took off to attack the Japanese Fleet, but they returned without having sighted it. Meanwhile, Admiral Somerville's old ships were steaming at their best speed to complete the planned concentration, Around noon, however, the cruisers *Cornwall* and *Dorsetshire,* proceeding from Colombo to a rendezvous at sea with Somerville's flag, were sighted in position 3° 01′ N, 77° 58′ E by several of the *Tone*'s float planes, which promptly called for carrier bombers. An hour or so later some 40 of these arrived over the British cruisers and at once pushed home determined and skillful attacks. Within less than a half hour both cruisers had slid beneath the surface. According to a Japanese account, the *Dorsetshire* disappeared in thirteen minutes after receiving seventeen direct hits from 550-pound bombs. Loss of life fortunately was not heavy, and next day the greater part of both ships' companies were picked up by British destroyers.

The strong attack launched against the *Cornwall* and *Dorsetshire,* coming as it did after the Japanese had suffered heavy aircraft losses over Colombo, convinced Admiral Somerville that more than "two or three" enemy carriers were operating off Ceylon. This realization induced him to act prudently—in marked contrast to the almost reckless daring he had displayed earlier when, as Flag Officer Commanding Force "H" (based at Gibraltar), he had unhesitatingly sought action with superior Italian forces. But Admiral Somerville, standing on the *Warspite*'s bridge off Ceylon, knew that he was now confronting a very different adversary, and his decision to order a general withdrawal was the only sensible one under the circumstances. So the Eastern Fleet, in the rhetorical words of Prime Minister Winston Churchill, "withdrew into the wastes of the Indian Ocean."[2] More accurately, Admiral Somerville's ships retired to the area between Ceylon and the Maldive Islands to the southwestward.

For the next three days the *Akagi, Hiryu, Soryu, Shokaku,* and *Zuikaku,* with their screening battleships, cruisers, and destroyers, milled about in the Indian Ocean, vainly trying to entice the Eastern Fleet to accept a decisive *daylight* battle, in which their air superiority could be used to advantage. But Admiral Somerville carefully avoided battle by day, meanwhile seeking an opportunity to launch night strikes with his carrier planes or to engage in a night surface action, in which latter case his superior gunnery strength (forty 15-inch guns against twenty-four 14-inch) would give him excellent prospects for victory. Unfortunately, no such opportunities developed.

Finally, on the morning of April 9, Admiral Nagumo ordered all his carriers to launch attacks against Trincomalee, the naval base on Ceylon's northeastern coast. These attacks, which apparently achieved some measure of surprise, inflicted considerable damage on the airfield, the naval dockyard, the 7,200-ton monitor *Erebus,* and the 7,958-ton S.S. *Sagaing* (set afire and beached, a total loss). Five British aircraft were shot down and eleven destroyed on the ground, compared with Japanese claims of 56 downed in combat and four destroyed on the ground! At least fourteen Japanese planes are believed to have been shot down.

While these attacks were in progress, one of the *Haruna*'s reconnaissance float planes sighted and reported the old British carrier *Hermes* south of Trincomalee. Accompanied by the corvette H.M.S. *Hollyhock* and Australia's veteran destroyer *Vampire,* the *Hermes* (minus her aircraft) had left Trincomalee several days before in obedience to Admiral Somerville's orders; it was hoped that once at sea she would have a better chance of escaping destruction. But at 0645 the *Hiryu* launched an attack group of dive bombers, which at 0822 sighted the *Hermes* in position 7° 26′ N, 81° 52′ E, about 70 miles south of Trincomalee. Twenty-eight minutes later the *Hermes* rolled over and sank as a result of nine direct hits and two near-misses. The destroyer *Vampire,* victim of several direct hits and one damaging near-miss, also went down as did the corvette *Hollyhock.* Sunk in other attacks, nearer Trincomalee, were the 5,868-ton tanker *British Sergeant* and the 5,571-ton auxiliary fleet oiler *Athelstone.*

At the very moment that the *Hermes* was sinking, a force of nine R.A.F. Blenheims approached the Japanese Fleet, which first sighted them at 16,000 yards. Several minutes later the Japanese screening ships opened fire on the Blenheims, while the carriers launched additional fighter planes (including six from the *Hiryu*). The Blenheims failed to score a single hit, and at 0900 turned for home, followed by the Japanese fighters, which claimed shooting down six of them during a 25-minute pursuit (actually, five Blenheims were shot down). Japanese losses apparently totalled four planes, including the leader of the *Hiryu*'s fighter unit, bringing their admitted losses for the day to eleven aircraft: five bombers and six fighters.

Four days later, to the immense relief of the British Admiralty, the *Akagi* and her four consorts, together with their supporting battleships and cruisers and destroyer screen, steamed through the Straits of Malacca, passed Singapore, entered the South China Sea, and then took a north-northeasterly course toward Bako, in the Pescadores.

Thus did the Imperial Navy conclude the "C" (Ceylon) Operation, which, had it been undertaken as support for a sea-borne invasion of India rather than as a mere raid-in-force, might well have altered the course of the war for many months and seriously delayed (though not changed) its final outcome. But Imperial Headquarters in Tokyo had long since formulated its war plans, and these did not contemplate waging an unlimited "global" war by coordinating Japan's strategy with that of Germany and Italy, whose African armies during most of 1942 offered a constant and serious threat to Alexandria, the Suez Canal, and the entire Middle East. Obsessed with the idea of a "limited" war, the objectives of which were the seizure, consolidation, and defense of the rich "Southern Resources Area" (Borneo, Malaya, Java, and Sumatra), the Japanese, though by no means unaware of the advantages to be obtained through close strategic cooperation with the European arm of the Axis, simply could not bring themselves to risk their precious and absolutely irreplaceable battle fleet in such distant waters as the Indian Ocean. Never again were any major Japanese warships to operate west of Singapore.

Accompanying Admiral Nagumo's force on the first leg of its homeward voyage through the South China Sea was the small carrier *Ryujo,* which on April 16 put in at Camranh Bay, on the Indo-China coast. With escorting cruisers and destroyers the *Ryujo* had arrived at Singapore on the 11th after completing a most successful anti-shipping sweep of the Bay of Bengal. This sweep, an integral part of the "C" Operation, resulted in the destruction or severe damaging by *Ryujo*'s air group of nine ships totaling some 45,000 tons. Additional merchant shipping was sunk by surface units (cruisers *Kumano, Mikuma, Mogami, Suzuya* and destroyers *Amagiri* and *Shirayuki*), bringing Britain's total losses in the Bay of Bengal for the week to nearly 100,000 tons.

On the morning of April 18, while Colonel Doolittle's bombers were taking off from the *Hornet* on their historic Tokyo raid, Admiral Nagumo's force arrived off the Pescadores. Here the Fifth Flying Squadron was detached and ordered into Bako, while the *Akagi, Hiryu, Soryu,* and most of the supporting and screening units continued on toward Japan. They had been on their way only a few hours when orders came to search for the American carrier force which that morning had been reported by the picket boats stationed in northern waters. This fruitless search was abandoned at 2200 of April 20, when the ships were ordered to proceed to their home ports, the *Akagi* arriving at Kure on the 22nd.

Meanwhile, on the 20th, the *Shokaku* and *Zuikaku* had left Bako for Truk. They arrived there on April 25 and began final preparations for the "MO" (Moresby) Operation, which culminated in the Battle of the Coral Sea—a strategic defeat for the Imperial Navy and its first major setback. Sunk in this battle, with heavy loss of life, was the new light carrier *Shoho* (converted from a submarine tender), while the *Shokaku* almost capsized from her heavy damages and the *Zuikaku* received enough punishment to keep her out of action for several critical weeks.

Following her return to Kure the *Akagi* was taken in hand for routine repairs, her air group being sent to Kagoshima for continued training. Early in May the Commander in Chief Combined Fleet outlined to Admiral Nagumo his plans for the gigantic "MI" (Midway Island) Operation, upon which he had apparently determined immediately after the Doolittle raid. It seems that Admiral Yamamoto, never dreaming that the B-25's could have taken off from a carrier, reasoned that they had somehow managed to fly from Midway. Another equally important motive for launching the Midway Operation was the desire to force the U.S. Pacific Fleet into decisive action before it could be strengthened by new construction and the repair of damaged units.

Shortly after this conference Admiral Nagumo transferred his flag to the *Kaga,* which, as his only operational carrier, was constantly engaged in flight training exercises, sorely needed by the new pilots assigned as replacements for many of the seasoned veterans of Pearl Harbor and Ceylon. Later, upon the *Akagi*'s arrival at Hashira anchorage, in Hiroshima Bay, Admiral Nagumo's flag was returned to her. The ships assigned to his command, now known as the "First Mobile Force," were the *Akagi, Kaga, Hiryu,* and *Soryu,* the battleships *Haruna* and *Kirishima,* the heavy cruisers *Tone* and *Chikuma,* and the newly formed *Dai Juu Kuchiku Sentai* (DesRon 10)—twelve destroyers led by the light cruiser *Nagara.* They began arriving at

Hashira Shima in early May, but the entire force was not assembled there until a few days before the scheduled sortie.

Meanwhile four more carriers were being readied for the ambitious offensive. Two of them, the *Hosho* (Japan's oldest and smallest) and the *Zuiho* (sister ship of the ill-fated *Shoho*), were assigned to provide air cover for Yamamoto's "Main Body" of seven battleships—the modernized *Fusos, Ises,* and *Nagatos,* led by the huge fleet flagship *Yamato.* The remaining carriers (*Ryujo* and the recently commissioned *Junyo*) formed the nucleus of Rear Admiral Kakuji Kakuta's "Second Mobile Force," whose mission was to attack Dutch Harbor, partly to divert American attention from Midway and partly as support for landings in the Aleutians.

On May 22 the *Ryujo,* Kakuta's flagship, and the *Junyo* left Tokuyama for Ominato, arriving there on the 25th and sortieing next day for the "AL" (Aleutian) Operation. At 0600 of the 27th Admiral Nagumo departed from Hashira Shima and passed through the Bungo Channel with his four carriers and seventeen screening ships. Finally, on the 29th, the *Hosho* and *Zuiho* sortied from the Inland Sea with Yamamoto's battleships, screened by three light cruisers and twelve destroyers. Accompanying the Main Body the first two days of its voyage was Vice Admiral Kondo's Second Fleet, consisting of the battleships *Kongo* and *Hiei,* several heavy cruisers, one light cruiser, and destroyers. On May 31 these ships left the Main Body (First Fleet) and headed for a scheduled rendezvous with the Landing Force (transports and escort) proceeding from Saipan.

After negotiating the defensive mine fields in Bungo Channel, the *Akagi* led the First Mobile Force toward the southeast (Course 128 degrees) at a speed of fourteen knots. Rigid radio silence was observed, while the twelve destroyers maintained a strict anti-submarine guard. Additional protection against submarine attack was provided by a patrol of four Type 97 attack (torpedo) planes, searching to a distance of 45,000 yards.

At dawn of May 28 the Mobile Force, then in position 28° 30′ N, 137° 35′ E, turned due east and at noon rendezvoused with the First Supply Group (five "*Maru*" oilers). At dusk the *Akagi* set the fleet course at 71 degrees, which was maintained with only minor variations until 1030 of June 3 (1330 of June 2 by American reckoning). Between May 31 and June 2 all ships refueled from the five oilers, this task apparently being accomplished while underway at nine knots. Just as refueling had been completed, at about 1000 of June 2, visibility began to decrease, steadily deteriorating to the point where the ships became completely invisible from one another.

As the use of visual signals had become impossible in the prevailing visibility, radio silence was finally broken at 1030 of the 3rd, when *Akagi* ordered course changed to 125 degrees, thereby placing the Mobile Force almost on a direct course for Midway Island. At 1300, an hour after the destroyers started fueling again from the oilers, visibility began to improve somewhat, and in the afternoon visual signaling became possible once more. By midnight the fog had completely lifted, though scattered clouds remained overhead. At 0307 of June 4 the Supply Group was detached with destroyer *Akigumo* as escort, and the Mobile Force increased speed to twelve knots. At noon Admiral Nagumo called for double this speed and, in obedience to the *Akagi*'s signal, the Mobile Force was soon steaming at 24 knots. Its task organization and cruising disposition at this time were as follows:

TASK ORGANIZATION

Air Attack Force: CarDiv 1: *Akagi* (FF), *Kaga*
CarDiv 2: *Hiryu* (F), *Soryu*

Supporting Force: CruDiv 8: *Tone* (F), *Chikuma*

BatDiv 3 (2nd Section): *Haruna*, *Kirishima*
(Note : BatDiv 3 under tactical command of ComCruDiv 8)

Screening Force: DesRon 10: *Nagara* (CL) (F)
DesDiv: 4: *Arashi*, *Nowake*, *Hagikaze*, *Maikaze*
DesDiv 10: *Makigumo*, *Yugumo*, *Kazegumo*
DesDiv 17: *Urakaze*, *Isokaze*, *Tanikaze*, *Hamakaze*

At 1630 the *Tone* suddenly opened fire on what she mistook for about ten American planes, whereupon the *Akagi* promptly launched three fighters. They could find nothing, of course, and at 1654 returned to the carrier. Still jittery, the *Akagi*'s lookouts twice reported, around midnight, brief sightings of American planes among the clouds.

At 0100 of June 5 (0400 of June 4 by American reckoning) the Mobile Force, then making 20 knots, went to General Quarters. Thirty minutes later the *Akagi* and the other carriers began launching their planes for the attack on Midway. The flagship sent out eighteen bombers and nine fighters, as did the *Kaga,* while each of the carriers in the Second Flying Squadron launched eighteen attack planes (torpedo planes armed with bombs) and nine fighters, making a total of 108 aircraft (36 VB, 36 VT, 36 VF).

Just after departure of this strike the *Akagi* and *Kaga* each launched a torpedo plane for reconnaissance, while five float planes were catapulted for the same purpose by three other ships: the *Tone* and *Chikuma* (two planes each) and *Haruna* (one plane). These seven aircraft had scarcely left on their important mission when the Mobile Force sighted "two or three" of our patrol bombers, which proceeded to maintain continuous contact.

Meanwhile, the Midway strike had also been sighted by one of our ubiquitous PBY's, which promptly alerted Midway's air and ground defenses. Thirty miles from their objective the Japanese attackers encountered Marine Corps fighter planes, but their overwhelming numbers enabled them to penetrate this defense, inflicting heavy losses on it, and to bomb Midway with considerable effect. Of the loss and damage inflicted, the *Akagi*'s striking group was credited with shooting down nine fighters, probably shooting down two more, strafing a grounded B-17, and setting fire to three buildings on Eastern Island. Only six Japanese aircraft failed to return from this strike: three attack planes (level bombers), two fighters, and one dive bomber.

While the Midway holocaust was at its height, about 0400, the Mobile Force, then steaming on course 140 degrees at 28 knots, received its first attack from our aircraft: four B-26's (armed with torpedoes) and six Navy torpedo planes (Avengers). At 0407 the *Akagi* opened fire to starboard and four minutes later turned to head into the attack. Sixty seconds later she was maneuvering violently to avoid three torpedoes, one of which passed to starboard and the others to port. Between 0410 and 0417 the *Akagi*'s anti-aircraft gunners must have shot down something, though their claim of "three twin-engined torpedo planes" is patently inaccurate, or at least exaggerated as to numbers, only two B-26's having failed to return from this attack. But the *Akagi* had not escaped entirely unscathed, for strafing had damaged her Number Three 4.7-inch anti-aircraft gun and seriously wounded two of its crew.

At 0415, just after these gallant but ineffective attacks had been repulsed, Admiral Nagumo received a radio report from the leader of the Midway strike that a second attack on the island would be necessary. Orders were therefore issued to rearm with bombs the 45 torpedo planes which the *Akagi* and *Kaga* had held in readiness. This work was being feverishly pressed when, at 0456, the Mobile Force was subjected to a furious attack by U.S. Marine Corps dive bombers. This attack, made in two waves, lasted a half hour, during which bombs fell harmlessly about the *Haruna* and *Kaga,* though at 0508 the *Hiryu* received some damage from four near-misses, which killed four men and wounded many others. Japanese sources fail to confirm the reputed suicide crash of Major Lofton Henderson's plane into a carrier, but they have stated that at 0512 one dive bomber, apparently hit by A.A. fire from the *Hiryu,* crashed into the sea close aboard the ship and near her island superstructure (port side). At 0535, five minutes after the Marine bombing attack ended, sixteen Army B-17's appeared, flew over the Mobile Force, and dropped their bombs without scoring so much as a single hit or damaging near-miss.

About the time that the Marine dive bombers began their attack, one of the *Tone*'s float planes, scouting to the northeast, reported having sighted at 0428 some ten American warships 240 miles north of Midway. At 0520 this plane, in reply to the *Akagi*'s order to "Advise ship types," reported that a carrier (obviously the *Yorktown*) appeared to be in company with the group. This report, received aboard the *Akagi* at 0530, was the first definite knowledge the Japanese had of the presence of American carriers.

After considering the new situation for some minutes, Admiral Nagumo at 0555 sent the following radio dispatch to Admiral Yamamoto: "Enemy composed of one carrier, five cruisers, and five destroyers sighted at 0500 in position bearing 10 degrees, distance 240 miles from Midway. We are heading for it." Simultaneously, he had the *Akagi* inform the Mobile Force by blinker that "After taking on the returning planes, we shall proceed north to contact and destroy the enemy task force."

At 0559 the last of the Midway dive bombers returned to the *Akagi* and *Kaga,* seven minutes later the twelve remaining fighters landed on the four carriers, while by 0618 the *Hiryu* and *Soryu* had taken aboard the last of their attack planes. At 0617, therefore, the *Akagi* turned to the northeast (course 70 degrees) and called for maximum battle speed. Within a few minutes the Mobile Force had worked up to 30 knots (most interesting in view of the fact that the *Kaga*'s original *rated* speed, as given by the Japanese before the war, was only 23 knots, while the *Akagi*'s was 28.5 knots, and that of the two battleships only 26 knots).

The turn toward the northeast had barely been completed when the *Chikuma* sighted fifteen hostile planes (the *Hornet*'s VT 8) to starboard, 35,000 yards distant and coming in low. At 0619, the *Akagi* began evasive action and soon all ships were twisting violently, meanwhile firing furiously with their anti-aircraft and machine guns to supplement the defense being put up by the fighter planes of the combat air patrol. This aerial defense was most effective and succeeded in bringing down all fifteen planes, many of them before they could launch their torpedoes.

Following this attack there was a lull of about fifteen minutes, which the *Akagi* and the other carriers utilized in feverish efforts to complete preparations for launching a large-scale strike against the *Yorktown.* A total of 93 planes (36 VB, 45 VT, 12 VF) were to participate in this attack, of which total the *Akagi* was to provide eighteen torpedo planes and three fighters. At 0640, while these preparations were still incomplete, more American torpedo planes appeared, and at 0702 still more (a total of 26 VT-3 and VT-6 from the *Yorktown* and *Enterprise*). Despite its fighter escort, this torpedo attack also encountered effective resistance from the Japanese combat air patrol, which brought down about twenty of the torpedo planes. Again, no hits were scored, though the *Kaga* at 0658 had a close call.

Although the four Japanese carriers were still undamaged, they had been thrown into some confusion by these last torpedo attacks, delaying their preparations for launching the planned strike against the *Yorktown,* while the combat air patrol had not only taken serious losses from our fighters with the torpedo squadrons, but its attention had been so occupied that it was not in position to intercept another and different kind of strike which had been developing and was now to burst with sudden fury. At about 0725 the dive bombing squadrons of the *Enterprise* and *Hornet* roared down to attack the Mobile Force.

In five hectic minutes the tide of battle turned decisively. Despite violent evasive tactics, the flagship *Akagi* was hit by two bombs at about 0727, the *Soryu* received three hits, and the *Kaga* took four hits and, like the other carriers, burst into flames. Only the *Hiryu* escaped unscathed through this tempest. The crisis at Midway was over.

One of the two bombs which struck the *Akagi* hit just behind her midships elevator, and the other farther aft, on the port side of the flight deck. Neither hit *in itself* was fatal; but as the *Akagi* was then engaged in rearming and refueling her planes for the strike against the *Yorktown,* the fires started by the second hit spread rapidly throughout the hangar and set off violent explosions among the crowded, partially armed planes. At 0729 some of the torpedoes stored in the hangar exploded, whereupon orders were given to flood the ammunition and bomb storage rooms. The forward groups were promptly flooded, but valve damages in the after sections prevented their being flooded for over two hours.

At 0742, just as the *Akagi* stopped her engines temporarily because of damage to them and to her steering gear, all hands were ordered to fire-fighting stations. The pump system, however, had been damaged, so there was little that could be done to check the fires. These, their intensity steadily mounting, gradually had moved forward until they were raging near the bridge. The only guns remaining in action by this time were the two foremost machine-gun groups and Number One anti-aircraft gun (4.7-inch).

At 0743 the flames set fire to a fighter plane near the bridge and then spread to the bridge itself. Realizing that his flagship was crippled, if not doomed, Admiral Nagumo decided to transfer his flag to the light cruiser *Nagara,* flagship of DesRon 10. The destroyer *Nowake,* therefore, was ordered to come alongside, and at 0746 Admiral Nagumo and his staff abandoned the *Akagi*'s bridge and prepared to board the destroyer. While this transfer was in progress the undamaged *Hiryu,* flying the flag of Rear Admiral Tamon Yamaguchi, ComCarDiv 2, launched her first attack against the *Yorktown:* eighteen dive bombers escorted by five or six fighters.

At 0830 Admiral Nagumo boarded the *Nagara* from the *Nowake* and promptly sent two radio dispatches, one to Admiral Yamamoto and one to the Mobile Force. The first advised the Commander in Chief Combined Fleet of the crippling damage to the three carriers, of Nagumo's transfer to the *Nagara,* and of his plan to seek a decisive surface engagement. The second dispatch ordered the Mobile Force to assemble for the attack, forming in order of DesRon 10, CruDiv 8, and BatDiv 3 on course 170, speed 12 knots. A quarter of an hour later, after having ordered the *Nowake* to return to the assistance of his erstwhile flagship, Admiral Nagumo formally hoisted his flag in the *Nagara.*

Meanwhile, the *Akagi*'s fires were burning more fiercely than ever, and at 0820 Captain Taijiro Aoki and his officers had to leave the bridge and move to the forward flight deck. Ten minutes later the *Akagi*'s air personnel and wounded were ordered transferred to the destroyers *Arashi,* standing by, and the *Nowake,* returning from the *Nagara.* At 0835 the *Akagi* was shaken by fresh explosions in her torpedo and bomb storage rooms, after which the fires crept so far forward that the captain had to leave the flight deck for the safety of the forward anchor deck. Here, at 0850, the chief engineer arrived to report on the condition of the ship's engines. A few minutes later the *Akagi* suddenly came to life and began turning to starboard, whereupon an ensign managed to contact the engine room, only to learn that most of its personnel had been killed. At 0930 Captain Aoki had the *Nowake* radio this message to Admiral Nagumo: "All safe except on flight deck. Every effort being made to fight fires."

But these fire-fighting efforts were of no avail, and the flames continued to devour the once proud carrier. At 1038, therefore, His Imperial Majesty's portrait was transferred to the *Nowake,* which shortly thereafter reported: "Fires still raging in *Akagi.* The Emperor's portrait has been safely brought aboard this ship." At 1050 the *Akagi* came to a stop, her engines at last completely finished. An hour later communication with the after section of the ship was temporarily restored, but at noon an induced explosion in the *Akagi*'s hangar destroyed the forward hangar bulkheads and started fresh fires.

At 1208 the *Nowake* received a radio message from Admiral Yamaguchi in the *Hiryu.* It read, "Please relay the following to *Akagi:* If any of your planes can take off, have them transfer to *Hiryu.*"

Far from being able to fly off any planes, the *Akagi* was then engaged in transferring her air personnel to the destroyers, which transfer she completed at 1300. Two hours later the *Arashi* and *Nowake,* still standing by, thought they detected the presence of a submarine, but nothing came of this supposed contact. At 1520 some men attempted to go below to determine the condition of the engines, but fumes and heat prevented their carrying out this mission; and at 1615 the chief engineer reported to Captain Aoki that there was no possibility of the *Akagi*'s steaming under her own power.

Realizing at last that his ship could not be saved, Captain Aoki decided to order "Abandon Ship," and advised Admiral Nagumo to that effect, at the same time requesting permission to have a destroyer sink the *Akagi* with torpedoes. Five minutes later the 700 officers and men still on board were ordered to assemble to hear the abandon ship order, and at 1700 all hands began transferring to the destroyers, 500 to the *Arashi* and 200 to the *Nowake.*

The other carriers damaged in the morning attack, the *Kaga* and *Soryu,* had meanwhile been experiencing even more serious difficulties. The latter, hit by three bombs between 0725 and 0728, promptly burst into flames from stem to stern. At 0740 both engines stopped and five minutes later Captain Ryusaku Yanagimoto gave the "Abandon Ship" order. While the officers and men were gathering on deck a terrific explosion occurred, blowing many of them overboard. The transfer of survivors to the destroyers *Hamakaze* and *Isokaze* was completed about 1600, at which time the flames died down somewhat. A fire-fighting party was accordingly organized to reboard the ship, but at 1613 she was torpedoed by a lurking submarine (the U.S.S. *Nautilus*) and plunged to the bottom, taking with her Captain Yanagimoto, last seen on the bridge, where he could be heard shouting "Banzai, banzai, banzai!"[3] Of the *Soryu*'s complement of some 1,400 officers and men, approximately half (718) perished with her.

The big *Kaga,* hit by four bombs, one of which destroyed the bridge and killed all its occupants (including Captain Okada), quickly became a blazing, unmanageable hulk. Attempts to put out the fires were completely unavailing, and as there seemed little possibility of saving the ship, the Emperor's portrait was transferred at 1025 to the destroyer *Hagikaze.* Thirty-five minutes later the *Kaga* was hit by a submarine's torpedo, but it failed to detonate. By 1340 the situation had become hopeless and the approximately 1,000 survivors began transferring to the *Hagikaze* and *Maikaze.* At 1625, just as the *Akagi* a few miles to the northeast was preparing to abandon ship, the *Kaga*'s fires reached the fuel tanks, fore and aft, causing two tremendous explosions which completely destroyed the ship. Her dead totaled some 800 officers and men.

Meanwhile the *Hiryu,* undamaged in the morning attack, had launched two effective strikes against the *Yorktown,* the first at 0758 and the second at 0906. Sixteen aircraft participated in the second attack: ten torpedo planes and six fighters, one of the former belonging to the *Akagi*'s air group and two of the latter to the *Kaga*'s. This final, desperate strike, pushed home with great determination, obtained two torpedo hits on the *Yorktown,* already badly hurt by the earlier dive bombing attack.

About two hours later the *Hiryu* herself was furiously attacked by dive bombers from the *Enterprise* and *Hornet,* which at 1403 scored four direct hits and two damaging near-misses. Fierce fires broke out at once, but the *Hiryu* continued steaming at high speed until 1803, when she finally stopped to permit the *Chikuma* to assist her in firefighting work.

After several hours it appeared that the *Hiryu*'s fires might be brought under control, but at 2058 an induced explosion rekindled the flames. It gradually became evident that nothing could save the ship, and at 2330 all hands were ordered to prepare to abandon ship. Twenty minutes later Admiral Yamaguchi and Captain Tomeo Kaki delivered stirring addresses to the crew, after which, amid thunderous "Banzais," the battle flag and command flag were ceremoniously lowered. At 0015 of June 6 (0315 of June 5 by American reckoning) "Abandon Ship" was ordered, the Emperor's portrait was removed, and the transfer of personnel to destroyers begun.

Despite the effective loss of three carriers that morning, followed by the crippling of the *Hiryu* in the early afternoon, Admiral Yamamoto did not at once decide to abandon the Midway Operation. On the contrary, he was determined to push on even though his Combined Fleet had now lost control of the air. But he apparently did not regard this control as irretrievably lost, for he still had the *Hosho* and *Zuiho* with his Main Body, while far to the northward were the *Ryujo* and *Junyo,* comprising Admiral Kakuta's Second Mobile Force, which that afternoon attacked Dutch Harbor for the second consecutive day. At 0920 Admiral Yamamoto actually ordered this distant force to rendezvous as soon as possible with the remnants of the First Mobile Force.

Until shortly before midnight the flagship *Yamato*'s radio transmitter was busy sending out orders directing the First Mobile Force and Vice Admiral Kondo's Second Fleet to continue the operation and prepare for decisive surface action. At 2355, however, after protracted discussions with his staff officers, headed by Rear Admiral Matome Ugaki, the Commander in Chief Combined Fleet reluctantly cancelled, by radio dispatch, the occupation of Midway Island and ordered the First Mobile Force and the Second Fleet to rendezvous with his Main Body (First Fleet) next morning, while the Landing Force (transports and escort) was to retire westward out of Midway's air range.

While the staff discussions aboard the *Yamato* were at their height, the end was rapidly approaching for the stricken *Akagi* and *Hiryu.* At 1925 Admiral Yamamoto radioed the *Arashi* and *Nowake,* standing by the *Akagi,* to "Delay disposition." At midnight, however, ComDesDiv 4, aboard the *Arashi,* reported that "She (*Akagi*) is still burning. There is danger of her sinking." The destroyers continued to stand by until 0150, when the Commander in Chief ordered: "Dispose." Ten minutes later the *Akagi,* having been torpedoed by the *Arashi,* slid beneath the surface; her position then was 30° 30′ N, 178° 40′ W. Eight officers and 213 men, out of a complement of some 1,800, had perished. Among the survivors was Captain Aoki, who retired from active service following a brief period as Commanding Officer of the Kure Naval Arsenal.

A half hour before the *Akagi* went down, the *Hiryu*'s personnel completed their transfer to the destroyers *Kazegumo* and *Makigumo.* Two men, however, remained aboard the blazing ship—Admiral Yamaguchi and Captain Kaki. They were last seen waving their caps in farewell to the survivors aboard the destroyers. At 0210 the *Hiryu* was disposed of by a single torpedo from the *Makigumo,* going down some 60 miles north and west of the *Akagi*'s grave. Her dead totaled 29 officers and 387 men.

The destruction of the *Akagi* and the other carriers was a terrible blow to the *Teikoku Kaigun*—a blow from which it never fully recovered. Reckoned on a tonnage basis they represented 43 per cent of Japan's total carrier strength at that time; on the basis of all-round fighting value they represented somewhat more—perhaps a full 50 per cent. Most important of all, however, the loss of these four veteran carriers meant that the Imperial Navy could no longer launch ambitious offensive operations, but would have to adopt a defensive or, at the very best, a cautious, limited offensive strategy, relying primarily for its air cover and support on land-based planes rather than on highly mobile carrier-borne aircraft.

— *AUTHOR* —

An associate member of the Naval Institute since 1929, Mr. Robinson has had more than 200 articles published in naval magazines in the United States and England, including nine previous articles in *Proceedings*. For the past five years, he has been the Foreign Naval News Editor of *Our Navy Magazine*.

CHAPTER
2

Attacking a Continent

By Mark R. Peattie

Sunburst, The Rise of Japanese Naval Air Power: 1909–1941 (Annapolis, MD: Naval Institute Press, 2007): chap. 5 Attacking a Continent, pp. 124–125

Despite the deeply rooted fixation of the Imperial Japanese Navy on warships as the decisive weapons of naval war, the navy's air war in China brought home to nearly all its leadership the tremendous offensive potential of aerial weapons. . . . Just as important, the China War was of tremendous value to the Japanese navy in demonstrating the way in which aviation could contribute to the projection of naval power ashore. . . .

A corollary to the navy's recognition of the enormous potential, if not the primacy, of air power was the effect on navy thinking of the sudden increase in the scale of aerial warfare. The air operations over China showed the tactical advantage of employing considerably larger units than had been contemplated before the conflict. . . . the navy came to recognize the effectiveness of scale: the air group system had increasingly given way to the formation of combined air groups, and combined air groups brought about the concept of air fleets, with which the navy was able to launch the massive hammer blows against Allied naval forces and facilities in the first months of the Pacific War. . . .

Vital, too, was the tactical proficiency that the navy's fighter pilots gained during the China War. Before the conflict, the navy's air service was an organization without practical experience in air combat. . . . [In China] the Japanese naval air service had pioneered new roles for fighter aircraft. It was the world's first air force to use fighter planes as escorts on long-range bombing missions, a role not assumed by Allied fighter aircraft until 1943. . . . It was the skill of Japanese fighter pilots honed in air combat over China, 1937 to 1941, as much as the excellence of Japanese air weapons, such as the Mitsubishi Zero, that provided the confidence behind the aggressive Japanese air operations in the first six months of the Pacific War.

回想の航空母艦"加賀"
写真提供ならびに解説：福井静夫
Recollection of the Aircraft Carrier KAGA
Shizuo Fukui

The IJN's *Kaga* under construction at Yokosuka Naval Shipyard in 1927. As built, the *Kaga*—like the *Akagi*—had three aircraft decks. The "landing on" deck is clearly visible in this photograph, as is the long smoke pipe needed to carry her stack gases clear of it. The other two decks—for "flying off"—opened out of her two main aircraft hangars. The three decks were created to speed up flying operations. The idea was to be able to recover aircraft while others were taking off. The two flying off decks were eliminated during the *Kaga*'s reconstruction in 1934–1935, and the ship was given one flight deck that ran from bow to stern. At Midway, the *Kaga* was 812 feet long and had a beam of almost 107 feet. She could steam at over 28 knots, carried 72 planes, and had a complement of 1,708 officers and men. The *Kaga* suffered more casualties than any other Japanese carrier at Midway.

U.S. Naval Institute Photo Archive

— AUTHOR —

Dr. Mark R. Peattie is emeritus professor of history at the University of Massachusetts (Boston) and the co-author (with the late David C. Evans) of *Kaigun: Strategy, Tactics and Technology in the Imperial Japanese Navy, 1887–1941* (1997).

CHAPTER

3

Time Is Everything (Japanese Side)

By John B. Lundstrom

Black Shoe Carrier Admiral (Annapolis, MD: Naval Institute Press, 2006): chap. 16 Time Is Everything, pp. 218–221

The MI Operation

Admiral Yamamoto permitted no deviation from his plan to destroy the Pacific Fleet in one huge battle. Deep embarrassment over the Doolittle raid only hardened his resolve. That insult also brought the army on board, not only for the MI and AL (Aleutian) operations, but also for the eventual invasion of Hawaii. From 28 April to 4 May chart maneuvers and critiques laid out the strategy for the Second Operational Phase. The MO operation would terminate on 10 May with the capture of Port Moresby. Midway and the western Aleutians would fall in early June, followed in July by Fiji and Samoa (FS Operation). Assaults against the Hawaiian Islands could start perhaps in October. "As a result of the smooth progress of the first-phase operations," Yamamoto explained, "we have established an invincible strategic position" that "cannot be maintained if we go on the defensive." Instead, "in order to secure it tenaciously, we must keep on striking offensively at the enemy's weak points one after another." Now was the perfect time to draw out what was left of the enemy's battleships, carriers, and cruisers and finish them off before numerous warships under construction could intervene. Imperial General Headquarters formally approved the MI Operation on 5 May.

To the concurrent MI and AL operations the Combined Fleet committed more than two hundred ships (including ten carriers) and air units with an authorized

Admiral Yamamoto Isoroku was the charismatic, aggressive commander of the IJN's Combined Fleet. Though not a pilot, he had created a powerful naval aviation force, and he audaciously challenged the IJN's General Headquarters staff in Tokyo for control of Japanese naval operations. It was Yamamoto who insisted on and led the planning for the attack on Pearl Harbor, and it was Yamamoto who insisted on the Midway operation as a means of drawing out and then defeating what was left of the U.S. Navy in the Pacific. But to get the support of the General Headquarters staff, Yamamoto had to agree to the invasion of the Aleutians and to a Japanese offensive in the Solomon Islands. He believed correctly, however, that the forces available to him were nevertheless strong enough to defeat the remaining U.S. Navy's carriers—if his subordinate, Vice Admiral Nagumo Chuichi, could catch them by surprise.

U.S. Naval Institute Photo Archive

strength of more than eight hundred aircraft. At their head was, as Walter Lord quipped, "A dazzling army of twenty admirals." The Northern Force (Vice Adm. Hosogaya Boshiro, Fifth Fleet commander) was to invade Adak, Kiska, and Attu in the Aleutians. Rear Adm. Kakuta Kakuji's 2nd *Kido Butai* (2nd Striking Force) would provide carrier support with sixty-three planes of light carriers *Ryujo* and the new *Junyo.* To capture Midway itself, Vice Adm. Kondo Nobutake's Attack Force, built around his Second Fleet, received two fast battleships, eight heavy cruisers, light carrier *Shoho* (twenty planes), a seaplane carrier, a converted seaplane carrier, and two destroyer squadrons, as well as numerous transports and auxiliary ships. Admiral Nagumo's elite First Air Fleet (1st *Kido Butai*) included carriers *Akagi, Kaga, Soryu, Hiryu, Shokaku,* and *Zuikaku,* screened by two fast battleships, two heavy cruisers, and a destroyer squadron. Its authorized strength of 387 carrier planes would overwhelm Midway's air strength, reduce its ground defenses, and open the way for the invasion. In line with his quest for victory through decisive battle, Yamamoto for the first time committed his entire battle line. The Main Force comprised the seven First Fleet battleships (including the

Yamato), two destroyer squadrons, light carrier *Hosho* (fifteen planes), and two fast seaplane carriers crammed with midget submarines and torpedo boats. The Main Body under Yamamoto would back up the attack on Midway, while the Guard Force, led by Vice Adm. Takasu Shiro (Commander, First Fleet), initially covered the Aleutians operation. Vice Adm. Tsukahara Nishizo's Base Air Force (Eleventh Air Fleet) would furnish shore-based aircraft.

On 8 May Combined Fleet planners made the changes necessary due to losses suffered in the Coral Sea and announced the timetable of events for the MI and AL Operations. [Rear Admiral] Fletcher's victory [at the Coral Sea] cost the MI Operation the *Shoho* and *Shokaku*. Light carrier *Zuiho* (twenty-four planes) would replace her sister *Shoho* in Kondo's Attack Force. Midway was to be invaded early on N-Day, 7 June (Tokyo time; 6 June, Midway local time), the last significant moonlight for nearly a month. Inspired by Fletcher's surprise 4 May carrier strike on Tulagi, the opening gambit now included a reprise of Operation K, the night reconnaissance and bombing of Pearl Harbor by flying boats in March. The object of the Second Operation K was to determine if Pearl Harbor contained the U.S. carriers and battleships. If they were not present, Combined Fleet could operate under heightened alert ready for any ambushes. A refueling rendezvous between the two flying boats and submarines was to take place the evening of 30 May (Hawaii local time) at French Frigate Shoals, northwest of the Hawaiian Islands. The flight could be rescheduled up to 2 June if necessary. Other subs from the Advance Force would scout ahead of the attack forces. On N-5 (2 June, Tokyo time; 1 June, Midway local time), a dozen subs were to assemble along two deployment lines positioned five hundred miles northwest and west of Oahu to watch for and attack U.S. heavy ships expected to hasten north from Pearl Harbor after the offensive began.

The 8 May Combined Fleet message also specified *simultaneous* carrier strikes at dawn on N-3 (4 June/3 June) by Kakuta against Dutch Harbor in the Aleutians and Nagumo against Midway. That would awaken the clueless Pacific Fleet to its danger and provoke the desired response. Nagumo's prime objective was to surprise Midway's aircraft on the ground. Later on N-3 Day, the lead element of the Midway assault force, coming east from Saipan, would penetrate Midway's air search range from the southwest. Nagumo was to press his attacks the next two days until he destroyed Midway's air force and softened up the island for invasion. On N-1 Day (6 June/5June) Kondo would set up a seaplane base on tiny Kure Island fifty-five miles west of Midway, while Hosogaya landed troops on Adak and Kiska in the Aleutians. The Adak foray was merely a raid in force. The men were to withdraw and occupy Attu on N+5 (12 June/11 June). Before dawn on N-7 Day (7 June/6 June) five thousand elite naval and army troops would storm Midway. If things went as planned, special pioneer troops would restore the airstrip to operation yet that day for the first of thirty-six Zero fighters being transported on the carriers, and nine land attack planes staging in from Wake. Six flying boats would also deploy there.

With the fall of Midway, the "decisive fleet battle" phase (the vital aspect of the MI Operation) would commence. The huge train of oilers could support the Combined Fleet for an additional week in the eastern Pacific. Japanese forces would regroup to deal with the U.S. Fleet that would only just be flushed out of Pearl. The decisive battle force was to deploy in a giant rectangle. Yamamoto's Main Body (the three most powerful battleships [*Yamato, Nagato,* and *Mutsu*]) would take station six hundred miles northwest of Midway, with Nagumo's six carriers three hundred miles east. Scurrying down from the Aleutians to form the northern corners of the box, Takasu's four Guard Force battleships were to move five hundred miles north of Yamamoto, while Kakuta's 2nd *Kido Butai* (reinforced by the *Zuiho* from Kondo) took the corresponding slot five hundred miles north of Nagumo. The balance of Kondo's Attack Force would cover Midway and serve as bait. The staff drew up specific responses depending on exactly where the U.S. ships showed up, either to the south, north, or east. If as hoped, the Pacific Fleet drew up in full array off Midway, Kakuta was to race south to join Nagumo and attack, while Takasu linked up with Yamamoto. After subs and carrier aircraft wore down the Americans, Yamamoto's big guns would finish them off.

Following the inevitable annihilation of the Pacific Fleet, Yamamoto's battleship force would return to Japan. Planning would start in earnest for the invasion of Hawaii, possibly late that year. Meanwhile, the isolation of Australia through the conquest of the South Pacific would be complete. On 15–20 June Kondo's Attack Force and Nagumo's five 1st *Kido Butai* carriers were to assemble at Truk to regroup for the invasions of Fiji and Samoa, set for July by the troops of the newly activated 17th Army. Inoue and the 17th Army would also seize New Caledonia and Port Moresby. In the northern Pacific, Hosogaya would hold onto Midway, the gateway to Hawaii and also the Aleutians. To foil more desperate lunges against the homeland, the Northern Force would wield the four fast *Kongo*-class battleships, eight heavy cruisers, carriers *Ryujo, Junyo, Zuiho,* and later the repaired *Shokaku.*

On 14 May [Rear Adm. Hara Chuichi's] summary of air group casualties in the Coral Sea demonstrated not even the *Zuikaku,* undamaged but minus 40 percent of her aviators, could participate in the MI Operation. She required time to work up a new, properly trained air group. The absence of supernumerary carrier squadrons left Nagumo no other alternative. Even the sight of torn-up *Shokaku* when she limped in on 17 May did not alter Yamamoto's supreme confidence, although chief of staff Ugaki thought her "very lucky to have got off lightly with such damage." Repairs would take three months. The *Zuikaku* showed up on the twenty-first. Hara was to bring her out in mid June after the victory to join the forces concentrating at Truk for the FS Operation. The absence of the Fifth Carrier Division reduced Nagumo to four carriers and 250 planes, including twenty-one Zeroes meant for Midway. Yamamoto judged them more than sufficient. Japanese intelligence believed both the *Yorktown* and *Saratoga* succumbed in the Coral Sea; the *Lexington* had either gone down in the January sub attack or was still under repair. Thus the Pacific Fleet could defend Midway with at most two or three big carriers (*Enterprise, Hornet,* and possibly *Wasp*), two or three converted carriers, two battleships, four or five heavy cruisers, seven or eight light cruisers, thirty destroyers and twenty-five subs. To Yamamoto the big challenge was to coax these meager forces out to fight. The two U.S. carriers sighted on 15 May off Tulagi had ample time to return to Hawaiian waters. Yet the [seaplane tender] *Tangier*'s adroit radio deception and the 28 May Tulagi raid by her PBYs, which Inoue misinterpreted as a carrier strike, led to doubts on that score.

At the final Midway planning conference on 25 May, Nagumo unexpectedly informed Yamamoto that he could not sail on the twenty-sixth as planned. The carriers desperately needed another day to complete necessary preparations for battle. Therefore the 1st *Kido Butai* must postpone the initial Midway strike from N-3 Day (4 June/3 June) to N-2 Day (5 June/4 June). Yamamoto reluctantly approved. He refused at that late date to reschedule N-Day (7 June/6 June), delay the Aleutians attack, or otherwise alter the timetable. He took the calculated risk that on N-3 Day, Midway's air search would not patrol west far enough to sight the lead elements of Kondo's Attack Force scheduled to close within six hundred miles of Midway that afternoon. That last-minute change fostered the mistaken impression that the AL Operation was always intended to serve as a diversion for Midway. On 26 May Kakuta's 2nd *Kido Butai* left Ominato in northern Japan bound for the foggy Aleutians. Nagumo's 1st *Kido Butai* departed the Inland Sea on 27 May, the anniversary of the glorious 1905 Battle of Tsushima and Japan's Navy Day, to the cheers of Yamamoto's Main Force and the big ships of Kondo's Attack Force. The Midway invasion convoy sailed from Saipan on 28 May, and Yamamoto and Kondo left Japan on 29 May.

By 30 May, however, two more components of Yamamoto's plan unraveled. Nearly all the Advance Force submarines failed to sail on time from Kwajalein and consequently reached their picket lines between Midway and Oahu up to two days late. Moreover, the sub detailed to refuel the flying boats in the Second Operation K found U.S. ships guarding French Frigate Shoals. That forced the cancellation of the Pearl Harbor reconnaissance flight. Had the flying boats gone forth on the night of 30–31 May as planned, they would have found no heavy ships at Pearl. That might have given Yamamoto pause to reflect.

— AUTHOR —

John B. Lundstrom is Curator Emeritus of History at the Milwaukee Public Museum and the award-winning author of *The First Team, Pacific Naval Air Combat from Pearl Harbor to Midway* (1984) and *The First Team and the Guadalcanal Campaign* (1994).

CHAPTER

4

Midway Island Operation Plan

By Mitsuo Fuchida and Masatake Okumiya

Midway, The Battle That Doomed Japan
(Annapolis, MD: Naval Institute Press, 1955):
chap. 5 Midway Operation Plan

Yamamoto—The Guiding Spirit (pp. 73–77)

The final Combined Fleet plan for the Midway operation, officially designated "Operation MI" by Imperial General Headquarters, was the composite product of many minds. The basic outline was largely the work of the Senior Operations Officer, Captain [Kameto] Kuroshima. A theoretician given to spending long hours in meditation in his darkened cabin, he was the author of a manual laying down Combined Fleet tactical doctrine for fleet-versus-fleet decisive battle with battleships in the key role. Other members of the staff elaborated detailed parts of the plan, each within his special sphere of competence. Over-all supervision of the drafting activities was performed by the aggressive and resourceful Chief of Staff, Rear Admiral [Matome] Ugaki, a consistent proponent of offensive fleet action against Hawaii.

But, above all, the Midway plan reflected the ideas and personality of the Navy's dominant figure and Combined Fleet's Commander in Chief, Admiral Isoroku Yamamoto. The task of assessing this forceful leader must necessarily be left to others more competent and better informed than myself. I only wish to put down here some random impressions and thoughts about the man as I, one of thousands of officers who served under his command, saw him.

If, at the start of the Pacific War, a poll had been taken among Japanese naval officers to determine their choice of the man to lead them as Commander in

Chief Combined Fleet, there is little doubt that Admiral Yamamoto would have been selected by an overwhelming majority. I am confident, too, that his supporters would have included every flying officer in the Navy. After the war, in fact, American historical investigators put such a hypothetical question to a number of ex-officers of the Japanese Naval Air Corps, including myself. Our unanimous reply was, "Admiral Yamamoto."

The tremendous following which Yamamoto enjoyed among the Navy's fliers stemmed from the fact that he was one of the foremost promoters of naval aviation. Though not a career aviation officer himself, he was appointed Executive Officer of the Kasumigaura Naval Air Training Corps when still a Captain, and he thereafter held a succession of important air posts. The Naval Air Corps was then in its infancy and sorely needed a strong leader and champion. Yamamoto stepped into this role with enthusiasm, bringing to the task his extraordinarily keen foresight and warm-hearted human understanding.

In these early days a flying career was not particularly attractive in view of the frequency of fatal accidents. Indeed, many of the Navy's high-ranking officers would not even set foot in an airplane if they thought that it was going to leave the ground. As recently as the late thirties, Admiral Zengo Yoshida, a classmate of Yamamoto's and then Commander in Chief Combined Fleet, adamantly refused to board a plane which his staff had made ready to fly him on an official trip.

Other high-ranking officers paid lip service to the importance of naval aviation and urged young men starting their careers in the Navy to go into that branch, but their enthusiasm ended abruptly when it came to having their own sons become flying officers or even to having their daughters marry fliers. Admiral Yamamoto was no such part-way enthusiast. His belief in aviation was sincere, and he demonstrated it by encouraging a number of his younger relatives to join the Naval Air Corps.

Yamamoto's fondness for fliers did not extend to sharing one of their common failings, a weakness for alcohol. He was a teetotaler. He did, however, like games of chance and was known to be a highly competent and daring player of bridge and poker. He would have been a gifted gambler, for he had the gambler's all-or-nothing spirit. If it were true, as many said, that the Pearl Harbor attack represented an all-or-nothing strategy, it was in keeping with Yamamoto's character, and perhaps the gambler-like boldness which inspired it was one of the chief reasons for its success.

Besides his capacity to take bold, imaginative decisions, another thing that earned Yamamoto the respect and admiration of the Navy's younger officers was the fact that he exercised strong, unequivocal leadership. In this respect he was an exception rather than the rule among the Navy's admirals. Perhaps influenced by British naval traditions, the Japanese Navy from its early days had laid great stress on instilling gentlemanly qualities in its officers. Unfortunately, however, a tendency arose to equate a lack of assertiveness and an easygoing affability with gentlemanliness, with the result that there were many bright and likable flag officers, but few real leaders and fighting commanders.

The lack of real leadership manifested itself on many occasions. For example, when a fleet command or naval district held maneuvers or battle exercises, the officers usually assembled afterward for a critique. The fleet or naval district commander presided at such conferences, but it was seldom that he actively guided the discussions or offered any incisive comments. The officers consequently had little idea whether they were on the right track or not.

Admiral Yamamoto was quite different. In the study conferences following Combined Fleet maneuvers, he took a leading part in the discussions. If some movement had been carried out improperly, he pointed it out and explained how he wanted it done in the future. He did not employ his staff officers as a brain trust but rather as aides for executing his own policies and decisions. His clear-cut guidance left no doubt as to what these policies were, so that when his subordinates were obliged to make independent decisions, they knew exactly what course of action would correspond to the thinking of their Commander in Chief.

It was these strong qualities of leadership which caused the Navy as a whole to look upon Yamamoto as the man best fitted to be its supreme commander. For in war the fate of the nation may be staked upon the outcome of a single battle, and in turn victory or defeat in battle hinges largely on the character and ability of a single individual, the Commander in Chief. This is necessarily so because only by concentrating the power of decision can unified action be assured, and without unified action victory is impossible. It is so also because moves in battle cannot be debated around the conference table and decided by majority rule; they must be decided swiftly by the commander on the basis of his own judgment and with full realization that each move, once made, is irrevocable. To make such decisions requires extraordinary courage and self-confidence. Yamamoto had both.

Yet, with all the qualities which seemed to make him an incomparable supreme commander, the test of war showed that Admiral Yamamoto also had his failings. These, it seems to me, were clearly evidenced by his hasty and uncompromising insistence upon the Midway operation in the face of all the cogent arguments against it. It is difficult to avoid the conclusion that his judgment in this instance was warped by his obsession about keeping Tokyo immune from air attack and by his sense of injured pride caused by the Doolittle raid. Had these feelings not unduly swayed him, he surely would have shown greater flexibility in his thinking about future strategy.

Undoubtedly, too, the haste with which Yamamoto plunged into the Midway venture was inspired by his conviction that the balance of military strength between Japan and the United States would shift in the latter's favor within two years at the most from the start of hostilities. Because of this pressing time factor, he felt that Japan's only hope lay in seeking a quick decision which might induce the enemy to come to terms. The move on Midway, he hoped, would force such a decision. He confided to Rear Admiral Yamaguchi and other trusted subordinates that, if he succeeded in destroying the United States Pacific Fleet in the Midway operation, he intended to press the nation's political leaders to initiate overtures for peace.

Yamamoto was unquestionably correct in his judgment that it was essential to engage the enemy fleet in decisive battle at the earliest possible opportunity. Indeed, if any criticism is to be made on this score, it must be directed at his failure to act earlier toward this objective by keeping the powerful Japanese Carrier Striking Force operating to the east after the initial assault on Pearl Harbor. At all events, the destruction of the United States Pacific Fleet was certainly a top-priority task in the spring of 1942. What is open to serious question, however, is whether the occupation of Midway was either the only or the most feasible way to accomplish this goal.

From the tactical standpoint, the Midway plan evidenced an adherence to the outmoded doctrine of the battleship advocates, which was difficult to reconcile with Yamamoto's supposed understanding of the role of air power. It seems strange, to say the least, that the man who conceived the carrier strike on Pearl Harbor was not quicker to institute sweeping changes in fleet organization and tactics so as to make air power the central core of the combat forces. Perhaps Yamamoto himself was afflicted with the characteristic Japanese tendency to cling to the past. Or perhaps he found traditional concepts so firmly entrenched that he was powerless to effect any radical overnight change.

It is often said that warfare is a succession of errors on both sides and that victory goes to the side which makes fewer. Admiral Yamamoto and his subordinates certainly made their share of mistakes, including some for which it is hard to find any logical explanation. But rather than place blame, it is more important for us to ponder the lessons of such mistakes and of the defeat that followed.

PART

II

Approach to Midway

Part II covers planning and preparations on both sides as their forces assembled for what became the Battle of Midway. The first selection in this part, "Sortie from Hashirajima," from *Midway, The Battle that Doomed Japan,* by Mitsuo Fuchida and Masatake Okumiya (chapter 5), describe the feelings of Fuchida as the Japanese *kidō butai* weighed anchor and headed for sea, Fuchida's memory of war games before Midway, and Fuchida's memory of Vice Admiral Nagumo. In planning major operations, there are three key variables: time, space (geography), and force. Admiral Yamamoto believed he had to hurry, and Fuchida's account reveals the consequences of planning in a hurry and then acting quickly. Moreover, the *kidō butai* had maneuvered and fought over a huge area for six months. Is it any wonder that at least some of *kidō butai*'s personnel were fatigued and therefore less capable as planners?

The next selection, "Mobile Force Commander's Estimate of the Situation," from a translation of *The Japanese Story of the Battle of Midway* (chapter 6) is very revealing. What is missing is a discussion of the "enemy's" (the U.S. Navy's) likely and best (from the U.S. perspective) courses of action. Vice Admiral Nagumo assumed that U.S. forces would be on the defensive, reacting constantly to his force's attacks. But what if U.S. forces were able to take the offensive? What if U.S. forces were not surprised? What if the U.S. commander could maneuver his carriers in coordination with the land-based aircraft at Midway and surprise the *kidō butai?* Proper planning requires a thorough assessment of the enemy's courses of action, including those thought not likely but still possible. That assessment is missing from Nagumo's report.

Nimitz took good advantage of the work of the Navy's code-breakers. He knew when the Japanese forces would appear, what their objectives were, and what ships and air units they would deploy against him. As historian John Lundstrom shows in

"Time Is Everything (American Side)" (chapter 7), Nimitz "made Midway his personal battle." The Japanese wanted a decisive battle. Nimitz would deny it to them while clipping their wings.

In "Prelude to Midway" (chapter 9), Captain Fuchida argues that a major weakness of the Japanese plan was its reliance on a one-phase form of air reconnaissance. He also argues that the *kidō butai* had no way of knowing that the U.S. Navy was aware of its presence. This is arguing back from events—the *kidō butai* was defeated, and here, therefore, are the reasons. However, there were warnings that the U.S. Navy might be aware of the approach of the Japanese, and Fuchida cites them. Moreover, there is always a trade-off between scouting (reconnaissance) and strike. There were never enough planes to do both missions adequately in the early months of World War II. As Fuchida notes, Japanese doctrine emphasized strike. That placed responsibility for scouting on planes flying from cruisers and battleships. And there was the fatal weakness—relying on noncarrier aircraft to conduct a critical mission.

Several selections detail the carrier aircraft and their organizations: "Soaring," "Opening Shots," "Forging the Thunderbolt," "Preparing to Defend Midway," and "Lest We Forget: Civilian Yard Workers" (chapters 8, 10, 11, 12, and 13). The IJN had the majority of the finest carrier aviators in the world and some excellent aircraft. But an ace up the sleeve of Admiral Nimitz was the Pearl Harbor Navy Yard, which readied the *Yorktown* for battle in record time. Professional military planners know that logistics—including both supply and maintenance—is a key factor to any campaign or battle plan. Both navies were far from major bases, but Pearl Harbor was closer.

CHAPTER

5

Sortie from Hashirajima

By Mitsuo Fuchida and Masatake Okumiya

Midway, The Battle That Doomed Japan (Annapolis, MD: Naval Institute Press, 1955): chap. 1 Sortie from Hashirajima, pp. 18–21, chap. 6 Preparations for Battle, pp. 88–92, chap. 7 Heading for Battle, pp. 107–109

Sortie from Hashirajima (pp. 18–21)

As day broke over the western Inland Sea on 27 May 1942, the sun's rays slanted down on the greatest concentration of Japanese fleet strength since the start of the Pacific War.

The setting was at the island of Hashirajima, which lies to the south of the well-known city of Hiroshima and southeast of the lesser-known coastal town of Iwakuni. The anchorage at Hashirajima is surrounded by hilly little islands, most of which are cultivated from water's edge to summit. Camouflaged antiaircraft batteries atop almost every hill belied the peaceful appearance of these islands. The anchorage was large enough to accommodate the entire Japanese Navy and was well off the ordinary routes of merchant ships. It was a wartime stand-by anchorage for Combined Fleet, whose headquarters had been functioning in safety from a battleship group stationed there since the start of the war. It had remained there so long, in fact, that naval officers had come to speak of Combined Fleet Headquarters simply as "Hashirajima."

Within the anchorage Commander in Chief Combined Fleet Admiral Isoroku Yamamoto's 68,000-ton flagship, *Yamato*, was moored to a red buoy. Underwater cables to shore permitted instant communication with Tokyo. Gathered around *Yamato* were a total of 68 warships, constituting the greater part of the surface strength of the Combined Fleet.

Admiral Yamamoto's Battleship Division 1 consisted of the *Yamato, Nagato,* and *Mutsu* [the last two with eight 16-inch guns each], which with *Ise, Hyuga, Fuso,* and *Yamashiro* [each with twelve 14-inch guns] of Battleship Division 2 made the total of seven battleships. Torpedo nets were extended around each of these giants. Pearl Harbor had impressed on us the importance of protecting ships against torpedo attacks, even in home waters. The other ships were disposed around the battleships as further protection against attacks by planes or submarines. There were light cruisers *Kitakami* and *Oi* of Cruiser Division 9, flagship *Sendai* and 12 destroyers of Destroyer Squadron 3, eight destroyers of Destroyer Squadron 1, light carrier *Hosho* with one destroyer and two torpedo boats, and seaplane carriers *Chiyoda* and *Nisshin,* each of which had six midget submarines on board [instead of the twenty-four catapulted aircraft normally carried].

All these ships and units except Battleship Division 1 belonged to the First Fleet commanded by Vice Admiral Shiro Takasu, whose flag flew in *Ise.* Both the First Fleet and Battleship Division 1 had remained at Hashirajima since the outbreak of war, awaiting an opportunity for decisive surface battle. Aviators of the Carrier Force sarcastically referred to them as the "Hashirajima Fleet."

The 21 ships of our force, commanded by Vice Admiral Chuichi Nagumo, were anchored to the north of the so-called "main strength" just described. To the west of us was a force under Vice Admiral Nobutake Kondo, commander of the Second Fleet. Here were heavy cruisers *Atago* (Kondo's flagship) and *Chokai* of Cruiser Division 4, *Myoko* and *Haguro* of Cruiser Division 5, fast battleships *Hiei* and *Kirishima* of Battleship Division 3, light cruiser *Yura* and seven destroyers of Destroyer Squadron 4, and light carrier *Zuiho* with one destroyer.

This massive gray armada swung silently at anchor, each ship riding low in the water under a full load of fuel and supplies taken on board at Kure in preparation for the sortie. The only traffic in the whole area consisted of chugging yellow Navy tugboats which emitted heavy black smoke from their tall stacks. On board the warships there was little evidence of activity other than the occasional fluttering of signal flags as messages were exchanged. But despite the general quiet of the anchorage, one felt the excitement permeating the entire fleet.

It was Navy Day, the anniversary of Admiral Togo's great victory over the Russian Fleet in the Battle of Tsushima. Japan's achievements during the first six months of the war in the Pacific seemed to rival that triumph 37 years earlier. Spirits were high—and why not? Now we were embarking on another mission which we confidently thought would add new glory to the annals of the Imperial Navy.

At 0800 *Akagi*'s ensign was raised. Then on her signal mast went up a single flag which gave the tensely awaited order, "Sortie as scheduled!"

Standing at the flight deck control post, I turned to watch the ships of Destroyer Squadron 10. White water splashed from the anchor cables of each destroyer, washing mud from the heavy links as they dragged through the hawseholes. The destroyers soon began to move, and they were followed by Cruiser Division 8, the second section of Battleship Division 3, and Carrier Divisions 1 and 2, in that order. The Nagumo Force was on its way toward the scene of one of the most significant naval actions in history.

As we steamed out of the anchorage the ships of the other forces, which would sortie two days later, gave us a rousing send-off. The crews lined the rails and cheered and waved their caps as we passed. They seemed to envy our good fortune in being the first to leave. We waved back a farewell, and a general gaiety prevailed. Every man was convinced that he was about to participate in yet another brilliant victory.

Two hours later we were halfway across the Iyonada and before long would enter the Bungo Strait. Beyond the strait it was expected that we might encounter enemy submarines. Combined reports on their activities were sent out daily from Imperial General Headquarters. Latest reports indicated that a dozen or more of them were operating close to the homeland, reporting on ship movements and seeking to destroy our lines of communication. Occasionally they would send radio reports to Pearl Harbor, and it was at such times that our scattered radio direction finders would endeavor to spot them.

Akagi, the sleek aircraft carrier flagship of Admiral Nagumo, headed westward through Kudako Strait, cruising easily at 16 knots on her course toward Bungo Channel and the broad Pacific. Through scattered clouds the sun shone brightly upon the calm blue sea. For several days the weather had been cloudy but hot in the western Inland Sea, and it was pleasant now to feel the gentle breeze which swept across *Akagi*'s flight deck.

The fleet had formed a single column for the passage through the strait. Twenty-one ships in all, and they cruised along at intervals of 1,000 yards, resembling for all the world a peacetime naval review. Far out in front was Rear Admiral Susumu Kimura's flagship, light cruiser *Nagara,* leading the 12 ships of Destroyer Squadron 10. Next came Rear Admiral Hiroaki Abe's Cruiser Division 8—*Tone,* the flagship, and *Chikuma*—followed by the second section of Battleship Division 3, made up of fast battleships *Haruna* and *Kirishima.* (The first section of Battleship Division 3, *Hiei* and *Kongo,* had been assigned to Admiral Kondo's Invasion Force for this operation.) Behind *Kirishima* came large carriers *Akagi* and *Kaga,* comprising Carrier Division 1, under Admiral Nagumo's direct command. Rear Admiral Tamon Yamaguchi's Carrier Division 2—*Hiryu* and *Soryu*—brought up the rear, completing the Nagumo Force.

Presently a dozen or so fishing boats waiting for the tide hove into sight to starboard, and their crews waved and cheered as we passed. To port the tiny island of Yurishima appeared to be floating on the surface of the sea, its thick covering of green foliage set off against the dim background of Aoshima. Beyond, the coast of Shikoku lay hidden in mist.

As the fleet steamed on, three seaplanes of the Kure Air Corps passed overhead, their pontoons looking like oversized shoes. The planes were on their way to neutralize any enemy submarines which might be lying in wait for us outside Bungo Strait.

Yashirojima soon appeared to starboard. Wheatfields, cultivated high up the mountainsides, were lightly tinged with yellow, proclaiming the nearness of summer. Offshore a small tug belched black smoke as she struggled to pull a string of barges. We soon left them far behind as the tiny islands of Ominasejima and Kominasejima came into view, lying peacefully on the sea.

Belated Consultations (pp. 88–90)

[At the end of April] Vice Admiral Nagumo and Vice Admiral Kondo, neither of whom had previously been consulted regarding the Midway operation, now had their first opportunity to study the Combined Fleet plan. So far as the First Air Fleet commander and his staff were concerned, the reaction was almost one of indifference. . . . The Nagumo Force had run up a brilliant record of achievement in the first-phase operations, and the headquarters was fully confident of its ability to carry out any mission which Combined Fleet assigned. . . .

The attitude of Vice Admiral Kondo and his staff, however, was quite different. On 1 May, the Second Fleet commander boarded *Yamato* for his first meeting with Admiral Yamamoto since the start of the war. After a brief discussion of the first-phase operations, the conversation turned to the Midway plan. Vice Admiral Kondo frankly voiced misgivings, emphasizing in particular that the assault on Midway would have to be carried out without shore-based air support, while the enemy would be able to employ not only substantial shore-based air strength but also carrier forces which as yet had not been seriously damaged. . . .

Admiral Yamamoto, however, brushed aside Kondo's objections with the assertion that the Midway plan had been agreed upon between Combined Fleet Headquarters and the Naval General Staff after careful study on both sides, and could not be changed. He added that in spite of the risks involved in the Midway operation, there was no reason to fear defeat if surprise were successfully achieved.

Vice Admiral Kondo then turned to the Combined Fleet Chief of Staff, Rear Admiral [Matome] Ugaki, and asked if the Fleet Headquarters was not concerned over the difficulty of keeping Midway supplied after its capture. Unless this could be done, he asserted, its occupation would be pointless. To this, Ugaki's far from reassuring reply was that if it eventually became impossible to continue supplying the occupation forces, they could be evacuated after completely destroying military installations.

Testing the Battle Plan (pp. 90–92)

On the same day that Vice Admiral Kondo communicated his doubts concerning the Midway venture to Admiral Yamamoto, Combined Fleet Headquarters initiated a four-day series of war games designed to test various operations already planned or tentatively contemplated for the second phase of the war. Staged on board flagship *Yamato* under the direction of Combined Fleet Chief of Staff Rear Admiral Ugaki, the games were attended by a majority of the commanders and staff officers of the forces which were to take part in the Midway operation. Those who had returned only a short while earlier from the southern area were conspicuous by the deep tan of their complexions, a result of six months spent under the tropic sun. Their eyes sparkled with excitement as they assembled to study the roles they would play in the forthcoming operations.

The invasion of Midway was the starting point of the games, but it was only the beginning. Not since the war games of November 1941, which had rehearsed the Pearl Harbor attack and the southern invasions, had such a grandiose program of offensive operations been tested. The over-all hypothetical plan formulated by Combined Fleet Headquarters as a basis for the games was briefly as follows:

1. In early June the main strength of Combined Fleet will capture Midway, and a part of its strength will seize the western Aleutians.
2. After completion of these operations, most of the battleship strength will return to the homeland and stand by, while the remainder of the Midway invasion naval forces will assemble at Truk to resume operations early in July for the capture of strategic points in New Caledonia and the Fiji Islands.
3. The Nagumo Force will then carry out air strikes against Sydney and other points on the southeast coast of Australia.
4. Following the above, the Nagumo Force and other forces assigned to the New Caledonia-Fiji Islands operations will reassemble at Truk for replenishment. Sometime after the beginning of August, operations will be launched against Johnston Island and Hawaii, employing the full strength of Combined Fleet.

Except for the staff of Combined Fleet Headquarters, all those taking part in the war games were amazed at this formidable program, which seemed to have been dreamed up with a great deal more imagination than regard for reality. Still more amazing, however, was the manner in which every operation from the invasion of Midway and the Aleutians down to the assault on Johnston and Hawaii was carried out in the games without the slightest difficulty. This was due in no small measure to the highhanded conduct of Rear Admiral Ugaki, the presiding officer, who frequently intervened to set aside rulings made by the umpires.

In the tabletop maneuvers, for example, a situation developed in which the Nagumo Force underwent a bombing attack by enemy land-based aircraft while its own planes were off attacking Midway. In accordance with the rules, Lieutenant Commander Okumiya, Carrier Division 4 staff officer who was acting as an umpire, cast dice to determine the bombing results and ruled that there had been nine enemy hits on the Japanese carriers. Both *Akagi* and *Kaga* were listed as sunk. Admiral Ugaki, however, arbitrarily reduced the number of enemy hits to only three, which resulted in *Kaga*'s still being ruled sunk but *Akagi* only slightly damaged. To Okumiya's surprise, even this revised ruling was subsequently cancelled, and *Kaga* reappeared as a participant in the next part of the games covering New Caledonia and Fiji Islands invasions. The verdicts of the umpires regarding the results of air fighting were similarly juggled, always in favor of the Japanese forces.

Admiral Nagumo (pp. 107–109)

My first acquaintance with Admiral Nagumo dated back to 1933. I was then a Lieutenant and Chief Flying Officer of heavy cruiser *Maya,* assigned to Cruiser Division 4, Second Fleet. Besides *Maya,* the division comprised flagship *Chokai,* [and] *Takao* and *Atago*, Japan's newest heavy cruisers. Nagumo, then a captain, was commanding officer of *Takao.*

My duties brought me into frequent contact with Captain Nagumo, a capable, intelligent and energetic officer who was rated high among the many able captains in the Fleet. He belonged to what Navy officers called the "Red Brick Group." This meant that he had already served a tour of duty in the Navy Ministry, the curious designation coming from the fact that the Navy Ministry building was made of red brick. He had also served in the Naval General Staff, on the staff of Combined Fleet, and as an instructor at the Naval War College. His command of a heavy cruiser followed the normal course of promotion to flag rank. He would get a battleship the following year and eventually would become a Fleet Commander.

In the Combined Fleet tactical organization prevailing at that time, the Second Fleet constituted the Advance Force. Consequently, the emphasis in our training was primarily on torpedo attacks and night engagements. Captain Nagumo, an expert in torpedo warfare, was the right man in the right place. As a junior officer whose job was simply to fly planes, I looked up to him with a feeling of awe and admiration because of the outstanding way he discharged his exacting duties. Every aspect of his leadership impressed me. His speeches at maneuver conferences were always logical and enlightening, and one could not help respecting his extraordinary ability. Candid, yet open-hearted and considerate, he was always willing to assist the younger officers. We held him in high esteem and placed complete confidence in him.

At this time sentiment in favor of abrogating the Washington Naval Limitation Treaty was rapidly mounting in the Navy. In our eyes, the attitude of the central authorities seemed weak-kneed, and Captain Nagumo was leading an active movement against it. He busily visited the commanding officers of other ships and urged them to join in pressing for an early abrogation of the treaty. As a result of his efforts, a recommendation was drafted and, after being signed by many officers, was forwarded to the central authorities through Fleet Headquarters as representing the opinion of the Fleet. This particularly pleased the young officers who always favored a firm policy, whatever it might be. My impressions of Captain Nagumo at that time convinced me that he would be a great naval leader.

Our paths did not cross again until 1941, by which time Nagumo had risen to Vice Admiral in command of First Air Fleet. I was assigned as a wing leader on carrier *Akagi.* In the intervening years Nagumo's reputation had continued to rise, especially during his command of Destroyer Squadron 1 as a Rear Admiral. Serving under him again revived my memories of seven years earlier, and I was happy to be a member of his command.

It was not long, however, before I noted that Nagumo had changed, and I began to feel dissatisfied with his apparent conservatism and passiveness. It might have been because he was now commanding an air arm, which was not his specialty. Personally he was as warmhearted and sympathetic as ever, but his once-vigorous fighting spirit seemed to be gone, and with it his stature as an outstanding naval leader. Instead he seemed rather average, and I was suddenly aware of his increased age.

In directing operations he no longer seemed to take the initiative, and when plans were being developed, he most often merely approved the recommendations of his staff. Commander [Minoru] Genda, his operations officer, once summed up the situation to me in these words:

"Whenever I draft a plan, it is approved almost without consideration. This might appear to make my job easier, but it doesn't. On the contrary, it is disquieting to see my own plans approved without any check from above, and then issued as formal orders. I am self-confident, but not so self-confident that I don't realize that anyone can make mistakes. Often I am puzzled over how to resolve an important problem. When I consider that a stroke of my pen might sway the destiny of the nation, it almost paralyzes me with fear.

"If I were serving under a commander like Admiral Onishi or Admiral Yamaguchi, my plans would be thoroughly studied from every possible angle and returned to me with comments and opinions. I would then feel more sure and more free to propose ideas that might be extreme."

CHAPTER 6

Mobile Force Commander's Estimate of the Situation

Translator: Fred Woodrough Jr., Office of Naval Communications

The Japanese Story of the Battle of Midway (translation), Office of Naval Intelligence, OPNAV P32–1002 (Washington, DC: GPO, June 1947)

Part I, Existing Conditions and Trends

3. Mobile Force Commander's Estimate of the Situation

(a) Although the enemy lacks the will to fight, it is likely that he will counter attack if our occupation operations progress satisfactorily.

(b) The enemy conducts air reconnaissance mainly to the West and to the South but does not maintain a strict vigil to the Northwest or to the North.

(c) The enemy's patrol radius is about 500 miles.

(d) The enemy is not aware of our plans. (We were not discovered until early in the morning of the 5th at the earliest.)

(e) It is not believed that the enemy has any powerful unit, with carriers as its nucleus, in the vicinity.

(f) After attacking Midway by air and destroying the enemy's shore based air strength to facilitate our landing operations, we would still be able to destroy any enemy task force which may choose to counter attack.

(g) The enemy's attempt to counterattack with use of shore based aircraft could be neutralized by our cover fighters and AA fire.

Vice Admiral Nagumo Chuichi commanded the IJN's First Mobile Striking Force, or *kidō butai*, at the Battle of Midway. He was selected for that command because of his seniority, not because Admiral Yamamoto wanted him. In fact, Yamamoto had criticized Nagumo for not destroying any U.S. carriers during the raid on Pearl Harbor. After Pearl Harbor, however, Nagumo's force had spearheaded Japan's conquest of Southeast Asia, ranging from the Central Pacific to the Bay of Bengal. It was an impressive display of the strategic mobility of naval forces. Though the *kidō butai* was reduced to a four-carrier force by June 1942, Vice Admiral Nagumo still believed that his carriers would probably catch any defending U.S. carriers by surprise during the assault on Midway. After Midway, Vice Admiral Nagumo stayed in command of the IJN's surviving carriers through the battles of the Eastern Solomons and the Santa Cruz Islands in August and October 1942.

U.S. Naval Institute Photo Archive

CHAPTER

7

Time Is Everything (American Side)

By John B. Lundstrom

Black Shoe Carrier Admiral (Annapolis, MD: Naval Institute Press, 2006): chap. 16 Time Is Everything, pp. 226–229

The Midway Plan

At dinner [on 27 May] Nimitz reconvened the conference that now included Fletcher, Spruance, [RADM Leigh] Noyes, [RADM Milo] Draemel, and [CAPT William] Smith, along with important staff. Having briefed senior army and navy commanders that morning, Nimitz again elucidated his ideas regarding the offensive against Midway and the Aleutians. He was superb in these prebattle conferences. Fletcher thought Nimitz was "rather shocked by the enormity of it all, but still he remained calm and imperturbable. These were his best characteristics." Spruance admired Nimitz's "intelligence, open-mindedness, approachability for anyone who had different ideas, and above all, his utter fearlessness and his courage in pushing the war." To Spruance, "an offensive fighting spirit is of the utmost importance in the top commanders." Nimitz encouraged his subordinates through quiet confidence laced with humor not cheerleading histrionics or the coercion of a taskmaster.

Nimitz distributed Cincpac Operation Plan 29–42 that [CAPT Lynde] McCormick's War Plans Section just compiled. Against the Midway-Hawaii line, Japan could employ four or five big carriers, two to four fast battleships, and seven to nine cruisers with commensurate numbers of destroyers, up to two dozen submarines, and a powerful landing force. (Actual strength was even greater because of the participation of the First Fleet's battleships, hints of which the code breakers

RADM Chester W. Nimitz as chief of the Navy's Bureau of Navigation in 1940. Nimitz commanded surface ships and submarines in his early career, and he developed at-sea refueling techniques during World War I. After the war, he was a member of the Board of Submarine Design, served as the executive officer of the battleship *South Carolina*, and attended the Naval War College, where he created an innovative steaming formation for the fleet. The late VADM Lloyd Mustin, who served as a junior officer under Nimitz when Nimitz commanded the heavy cruiser *Augusta* in the Asiatic Fleet in 1933–1935, said that Nimitz was the finest teacher in the 1930s Navy. After leaving the *Augusta*, Nimitz commanded cruiser and battleship divisions and was then made chief of the Bureau of Navigation in Washington. He was pulled out of that position and promoted to full admiral; he relieved VADM William Pye, who had temporarily succeeded ADM Husband Kimmel as commander in chief of the Pacific Fleet after the Japanese attack on Pearl Harbor.

U.S. Naval Institute Photo Archive

detected but which, for unexplained reasons, the analysts discounted.) Smaller but powerful forces, including carriers, threatened the Aleutians. The two offensives would commence shortly. Subs would first reconnoiter U.S. fleet dispositions and form blocking lines to catch ships that sortied to succor Midway. There might even be another night bombing of Pearl Harbor by flying boats, as in March. The carriers would close swiftly to overwhelm Midway's defense and open the way for invasion. [Admiral] King believed that "N-Day," when the Midway and Aleutian landings would take place, was 3 June, but Nimitz leaned toward 5 June (one day prior to the real N-Day). The initial carrier air attacks could begin on 3 or 4 June, likely from northwest of Midway, while heavy ships pounded the defenses at night. The landings themselves might occur at night. Should Midway fall, the Japanese would immediately rush in aircraft and base defenses to consolidate their hold. As for the Aleutians, Nimitz elected only to reinforce its shore-based aircraft and form TF-8 under Admiral [Robert] Theobald, with two heavy cruisers, three light cruisers, and four destroyers. Nimitz made Midway his personal battle. Exercising "general tactical command" from Pearl, he positioned all the forces and approved the search patterns.

What was available for Midway? Nimitz wisely ruled out the seven old, slow battleships of [ADM William] Pye's TF-1 based at San Francisco. They still lacked the vital air support and screening ships essential when battling forces supported by carriers. As usual King hoped to use the battleships, but Nimitz declared on 24 May that he would hold them on the West Coast "until objectives for their striking power are more definite." He thought in the back of his mind they could pummel Midway should he have to retake it. Eventually he hoped to use converted auxiliary carriers to protect the battleships, but now he had only the *Long Island,* the first U.S. auxiliary carrier. The *Saratoga* was far more valuable with the carrier striking force than shepherding old battleships. Such a passive role did not sit well with a restive Pye, who thought he should take an active role in the defense of Midway or at least the Hawaiian Islands.

Having dispensed with the battleships, Nimitz reckoned on four basic assets. Spruance's TF-16 (*Enterprise* and *Hornet*) would be in position off Midway by 1 June; TF-17 (*Yorktown*) would join the next day. Fletcher received tactical command of both task forces, which totaled 230 planes. Fitch's TF-11 (*Saratoga*) should depart San Diego on 5 June, too late to fight at Midway unless the Japanese were considerably delayed. [RADM Patrick] Bellinger (CTF-9, shore-based aircraft) was to deploy as many navy, marine, and army aircraft onto Midway as the small atoll could comfortably hold. That ultimately numbered 125 planes under Capt. Cyril T. Simard, the island commander. Long-range searches by PBYs from Midway and Johnston would locate suitable targets, both for the carriers and land-based bombers that included B-17s shuttling in from Hawaii. Simard's marine fighters must defend the air base against certain fierce and unremitting air attack. A proud wearer of the submariner's dolphin insignia, Nimitz anticipated a stellar performance from Rear Adm. Robert H. English's Pacific Fleet subs (TF-7). A dozen boats would form a scouting line west of Midway, patrol their sectors until contact was made, then swarm in. All available subs would reinforce them. Finally, more than two thousand resolute, well-armed marines would defend Midway itself.

Weaker than his opponents in most categories, Nimitz could no longer simply meet them head-on. McCormick put it well. "Not only the directive from [Cominch] but also common sense dictates that we cannot now afford to slug it out with the probably superior approaching Japanese forces." Instead, "We must endeavor to reduce his forces by attrition—submarine attacks, air bombing, attacks on isolated units." Thus, "If attrition is successful the enemy must accept the failure of his venture or risk battle on disadvantageous terms for him." McCormick took notice of King's all-too-accurate fear that the Japanese intended to trap the surface forces but thought the extensive air reconnaissance should forestall that calamity. It was vital to get the maximum effect out of Midway's air, "Without exposing our carriers to danger of destruction out of proportion to the damage they can inflict. We must calculate the risk and must accept the danger when our prospects of frustrating or destroying the enemy carriers are sufficiently good."

Nimitz looked carefully into the deployment of his carriers, the key to success at Midway. As excellent as radio intelligence was in predicting Japanese strategic intentions, he had relatively little actual information, other than his own common sense, as to how the enemy might go about reducing Midway. An important clue from a decrypt appeared in [LCDR Edwin] Layton's scorecard on 21 May. "Staff member 1st Air Fleet request [*sic*] weather data from 3 hrs. prior to take off on 'N'-2day. Asked to be informed of any BLUE activity that area. Planes will be launched 50 miles N.W. of Midway attacking from N-2 days until N-day." Thus Nimitz deduced that for two days prior to the invasion the whole carrier force would strike Midway "from short range, say 50 to 100 miles," to pulverize its air defenses. Midway's own planes "must try to inflict prompt early damage to Jap carrier flight decks if recurring attacks are to be stopped." Nimitz tasked [CAPT Arthur] Davis, his fleet aviation officer, to "visualize as closely as possible [the Japanese] method of operation and OUR best counter tactics" [emphasis in original]. He wanted Davis to keep in mind, "Where does Halsey best fit into this picture, remembering we can ill afford loss of carriers." It was vital to determine the best initial position for the U.S. carriers. . . .

Nimitz agreed that the sector northeast of Midway was the best initial location for his carrier striking force. From there the carriers could "seize opportunity to obtain initial advantage against carriers which are employing their air groups against Midway." The goal was to "inflict maximum damage on enemy by employing strong attrition tactics," but "not accept such decisive action as would be likely to incur heavy losses in our carriers and cruisers." Cincpac's separate letter of instruction to Fletcher and Spruance directed them to "be governed by the principle of calculated risk which you shall interpret to mean the avoidance of exposure of your forces to attack by superior enemy forces without good prospect of inflicting, as a result of such exposure, greater damage to the enemy. This applies to a landing phase as well as during preliminary air attacks." Spruance's flag lieutenant, Robert J. Oliver, recalled that Nimitz told Spruance no matter what not to lose his carriers. If things got too tough, he was to withdraw and let Midway fall. Any enemy foothold so far east could be recaptured later. Fletcher doubtless received the same instructions.

The defense of Midway posed a daunting task. The Japanese "have amply demonstrated their ability to use their carrier air with great ability," and "we can no longer underestimate their naval air efficiency." That is a rather surprising admission that showed that prior to the loss of the *Lexington*, Japanese prowess was not recognized. Nimitz's decision to fight at Midway was all the more courageous. Japan held the initiative. The Combined Fleet outnumbered the Pacific Fleet in all classes of combat ships. Its carrier aircraft enjoyed longer range and the fighters possibly superior performance. Its amphibious forces were experienced and highly efficient. The weaker Pacific Fleet must resort to attrition tactics rather than direct confrontation. Yet Nimitz had strong reason for optimism at Midway. The situation certainly warranted taking a "calculated risk." His men were "just as brave, and those who have been properly trained are believed to be better than their opposite Jap number." The remarkable radio intelligence gave him sufficient warning to gather his forces in secret. Japan must expose its precious carriers to counterattack vastly abetted by the element of surprise. The enemy would confront a "fairly strong" land-based air force beyond supporting range of his own shore-based aviation. "Our submarines have demonstrated considerable superiority." The assault on Midway would prove costly to the attackers. The battle is far from the desperate gamble that is often portrayed. Although the odds still favored Japan, Nimitz had devised a careful plan where victory would pay enormous dividends.

CHAPTER 8

Soaring

By Mark R. Peattie

Sunburst, The Rise of Japanese Naval Air Power, 1909–1941 (Annapolis, MD: Naval Institute Press, 2007): chap. 4 Soaring, pp. 91–97

The [Zero's] lightness, indeed its near fragility of structure, which helped to give the aircraft unprecedented maneuverability, meant that it contained too many single-point failure points (points at which structural failure would cause destruction of the entire aircraft), a weakness compounded by the fact that it possessed virtually no armor protection for either its pilot or its fuel tanks. . . . While the Zero was a marvel of maneuverability below 4,500 meters (15,000 feet), its performance fell off sharply above that altitude, even though it had a flight ceiling of 10,000 meters (33,000 feet). . . .

Even before . . . 1940, the navy had issued specifications for a new carrier torpedo bomber, since none of the prototypes for such an aircraft developed in the early 1930s had proved satisfactory. . . . Specifications had been issued as early as 1935, calling for a three-seat single-radial-engined aircraft of monoplane design, capable of a speed of 180 knots at 2,000 meters (about 7,000 feet), able to carry an 800-kilogram (1,764-pound) torpedo or an equivalent bomb load, and an endurance of four hours when carrying its full payload, or of seven hours for unarmed reconnaissance missions. Nakajima's entry, the B5N . . . was a cleanly designed aircraft. It was equipped with such novelties as a variable-pitch propeller, a retractable undercarriage, and a hydraulically operated mechanism that folded the wings up and inward at approximately their halfway point for storage aboard a carrier. . . .

Combat experience in China and normal technological evolution led to a new version of the aircraft, the B5N2, driven by a more powerful engine (the 1,000-horsepower Nakajima Sakae 11). The B5N2 went into production early in 1940 as the Type 97 Model 12 and by 1941 had replaced the earlier version as the navy's front-line carrier attack bomber. . . .

By the years of the Pacific War, seaplanes—both flying boats and floatplanes—came to occupy a significant place in Japanese plans for amphibious operations in the southern Pacific. Advance seaplane bases to supply reconnaissance and air cover for invasion convoys were seen as easy to establish, given the large number of quiet lagoons and sheltered harbors of the tropical Pacific. For great distances, the flying boat was still the navy's principal reconnaissance aircraft, and the navy continued to depend on Kawanishi to produce this type. The Kawanishi H6K had proved to be an outstanding aircraft, but in 1938 the navy was already thinking of a successor . . . [which became] the H8K1, a clean but sturdy-looking high-wing monoplane with cantilevered wings . . . [that] had undertaken its maiden flight in January 1941 . . . an outstanding representative of its type. . . .

For shorter-range reconnaissance, as well as operations, the navy came to acquire two workhorse floatplanes for the fleet. Despite its obsolete configuration, the singular maneuverability of the Mitsubishi F1M1/2 Type 0 ("Pete") observation seaplane, a single-engined two-seat single-float biplane that went into production in 1940, led to its use not only as a catapult-launched aircraft aboard battleships and cruisers but also as an interceptor, a dive bomber, and a coastal patrol aircraft. Similarly useful was the Aichi E13A1 Type 0 ("Jake") reconnaissance seaplane, a single-engined three-seat twin-float monoplane that went into production in 1940. Operating from cruisers and seaplane tenders, it saw service in 1941 both in attacks along the China coast and in reconnaissance over Hawai'i.

CHAPTER
9

Prelude to Midway

By Mitsuo Fuchida and Masatake Okumiya

Proceedings, May 1955: pp. 504–513

The Midway operation had two central objectives. The first and more limited one was the seizure of Midway as an advance air base to facilitate early detection of enemy carrier forces operating toward the homeland from Hawaii, with the attack on the Aleutians as a diversion. [The attack on the Aleutians would also sever any direct link in the Pacific between the United States and the Soviet Union.] *The second, much broader objective was to draw out what was left of the United States Pacific Fleet so that it could be engaged and destroyed in decisive battle. Were both these objectives achieved, the invasion of Hawaii itself would become possible, if not easy.*

To carry out the invasion plan, Combined Fleet mustered the mightiest force in Japanese naval history. The task organization embraced more than 200 ships, including eleven battleships, eight aircraft carriers, 22 cruisers, 65 destroyers and 21 submarines, and almost 700 planes, carrier and shore-based. These forces were organized as follows:

Main Force—Admiral I. Yamamoto
First Carrier Striking Force—Vice Admiral C[huichi] *Nagumo*
Midway Invasion Force—Vice Admiral N[obutake] *Kondo*
Northern (Aleutians) Force—Vice Admiral M[oshiro] *Hosogaya*
Advance Submarine Force—Vice Admiral T[eruhishi] *Komatsu*
Shore-Based Air Force—Vice Admiral N[ishizo] *Tsukahara*

Between May 26 and 29 these forces sortied from three widely separate take-off points: Ominato, on northern Honshu, Hashirajima in the western Inland Sea, and Saipan and Guam in the Marianas. All cleared port uneventfully, evading the prying eyes of enemy submarines, and headed for the battle areas.

On May 29, 1942, at the end of the day, the various Japanese forces were forging ahead toward their objectives without any hitch other than the fog still plaguing the [Rear Admiral Kakuji] Kakuta Force [accompanying Vice Admiral Hosogaya]. On the 30th, however, the weather also began to deteriorate over that part of the Central Pacific now being traversed by the Yamamoto and Kondo Forces. In the afternoon the Yamamoto Force encountered rain and increasingly strong winds which caused the destroyers and cruisers to ship occasional seas over their bows. The formation cut its speed to fourteen knots, and zigzagging was discontinued.

It was not only the weather that was ominous. *Yamato*'s radio crew, which was keeping a close watch on enemy communications traffic, intercepted a long urgent message sent by an enemy submarine from a position directly ahead of the Japanese Transport Group. The message was addressed to Midway. It was in code, and we could not decipher it, but it suggested the possibility that the Transport Group had been discovered. If so, it would be logical for the enemy to surmise that the transports were heading for Midway for the purpose of an invasion attempt, since so large a convoy sailing east-northeast from Saipan could hardly be taken as merely a supply force destined for Wake Island. Admiral Yamamoto's staff officers, however, were not greatly concerned. They nonchalantly took the view that if the enemy had guessed our purpose and now sent his fleet out to oppose the invasion, the primary Japanese objective of drawing out the enemy forces to be destroyed in decisive battle would be achieved.

Bad weather continued in the central Pacific on May 31. Not only the Yamamoto and Kondo Forces, but also Vice Admiral Nagumo's carriers, which were a few hundred miles farther east, encountered strong winds and occasional rain. Meanwhile, *Yamato*'s radio intelligence unit observed further signs of enemy activity, especially of aircraft and submarines, in both the Hawaii and Aleutians vicinities. Admiral Yamamoto and his staff surmised that the activity around Hawaii might presage a sortie by an enemy Task Force, and they waited eagerly for reports of the flying boat reconnaissance which was to have been carried out over Hawaii.

The two Type-2 flying boats assigned to this mission, designated the second "K" Operation, had duly moved up to Wotje and were scheduled to take off at 2400 May 30 (Tokyo time) to reach French Frigate Shoals by 1430 (1730 local time) shortly before sunset, refuel there from submarines, and take off within an hour and a half for Hawaii. If all went well, they would arrive over Hawaii at 2045

(0115 May 31, local time). After completing their reconnaissance, they would fly non-stop back to Wotje, reaching there about 0920 (Tokyo time) on June 1. Vice Admiral [Teruhishi] Komatsu, Commander Submarine Force, had assigned six submarines to the operation. Three of them were to refuel the flying boats at French Frigate Shoals. Another was to take station on a line between Wotje and French Frigate Shoals, about 550 miles from the latter, to serve as a radio picket ship. The fifth was to lie off Keahole Point, Hawaii, as a rescue boat in case of mishap, and the sixth was to be stationed eighty miles southwest of Oahu for patrol and weather observation.

The carefully laid plan, however, had already gone awry. On May 30, one of the fueling subs (I-123) reached French Frigate Shoals and, to its dismay, found two enemy ships lying at anchor. It urgently radioed this information back to Kwajalein, adding that there appeared to be little prospect of carrying out the refueling operation at the Shoals as planned. Vice Admiral Goto, 24th Air Flotilla commander at Kwajalein, who was responsible for directing the second "K" Operation, accordingly ordered a 24-hour postponement, instructing I-123 to keep watching the Shoals in the hope that the enemy ships would depart.

This forlorn hope was blasted the following day when I-123 reported that she had sighted two enemy flying boats near the entrance to the Shoals. This made it apparent that the enemy was already using the Shoals as a seaplane base, and there consequently was no alternative but to abandon Operation "K" altogether.

These disappointing developments were promptly communicated to Admiral Yamamoto in *Yamato.* The failure of Operation "K" meant that there was no way of ascertaining what enemy strength actually was present at Pearl Harbor. Nevertheless, Combined Fleet Headquarters still hoped that, if an enemy force did sortie from that base to oppose the Midway invasion, the submarine cordons scheduled to be established by Vice Admiral Komatsu's command between Hawaii and Midway by June 2 would suffice to provide advance warning as well as knowledge of the enemy's strength.

The first of June found the Yamamoto Force still surrounded by dark, forbidding weather, although the rain had ceased. Low-lying clouds made visibility so poor that it was barely possible from *Yamato*'s bridge to make out the phantom shapes of the destroyer screen 1,500 meters away.

It was now time for the Main Force to rendezvous with its tanker train and refuel. The oilers were not found at the prearranged rendezvous point, however, and *Hosho* launched planes to look for them. The search proved unsuccessful because of the poor visibility, but at this point the tanker train radioed its position to *Yamato,* making it possible to effect a rendezvous. At the same time, because radio silence had been broken, it had to be assumed that the enemy was now aware of the position of the Main Force.

Evidence that the enemy had already discovered or, at the very least, strongly suspected the Japanese advance toward Midway, mounted sharply during the day. Radio intelligence disclosed a marked intensification of communications traffic out of Hawaii, and 72 out of 180 intercepted messages were "urgent," indicating an unusually tense situation. A chance encounter 500 miles north-northeast of Wotje between a Japanese patrol plane from that island and an American flying boat, which exchanged brief machine-gun bursts, also showed that the enemy had extended his Midway-based air patrols out to a radius of 700 miles. There were still further reports to the effect that enemy submarines had been sighted about 500 miles northeast and north-northeast of Wake Island, which indicated the existence of an American submarine patrol line about 600 miles southwest of Midway.

By this time the Midway transport convoy had reached a point about 1,000 miles to the west of Midway and was proceeding on a northeast course. Advancing at a rate of 240 miles in 24 hours, the convoy would enter the 700-mile patrol radius of American planes from Midway on June 3, two days before the date set for the pre-invasion air strike on the island by the Nagumo Force. It looked as if the transports were advancing too fast for their own safety.

Cloudy weather, with occasional rain, persisted in the vicinity of the Yamamoto Force on June 2. Fueling operations, which had started the preceding day after the delayed rendezvous with the tanker train, were resumed in the morning but had to be discontinued again when visibility became so poor that the ships could no longer maneuver safely.

Still another hitch now developed in the operation plan. Owing to overhauls which had delayed their departure from the homeland, the submarines of SubRon 5 assigned to the "B" cordon line scheduled to be established on this date to the northwest of Hawaii failed to reach their assigned positions. Boats of SubRon 3 assigned to the "A" cordon line to the west of Hawaii were also unable to reach their stations because of delays resulting from the miscarriage of Operation "K." Actually it was not until June 4 that the submarines arrived on station.

With the submarine cordons not yet established, Admiral Yamamoto and his staff remained completely in the dark regarding enemy task force activities. During June 2, however, submarine I-168, reconnoitering the Midway area, sent in a few bits of information regarding the situation there. The report stated that no ships had been observed other than a picket ship south of Sand Island; that the enemy appeared to be flying intensive air patrols to the southwest, probably to a distance of 600 miles; that a strict alert seemed to be in force, with numerous aircraft on defensive patrol day and night; and that many cranes were visible on the island, suggesting that the installations were being expanded. This eventually turned out to be the only significant reconnaissance report sent in by a submarine during the Midway operation.

During the 2nd the Nagumo Force, cruising some 600 miles ahead of the Yamamoto Force, entered an area enveloped in thick mist. Clouds hovered low over the ocean, and light rain began to fall. Fog seemed likely to follow. Already visibility was so restricted that neighboring ships in the formation could scarcely see each other.

Vice Admiral Nagumo in flagship *Akagi* was as much in the dark about enemy fleet movements and intentions as Combined Fleet Headquarters. Indeed, because of *Akagi*'s limited radio-receiving capacity, coupled with the radio silence being observed by the advancing Japanese forces, he lacked much of the information which had been received by Admiral Yamamoto in the Fleet flagship and which strongly suggested that the enemy was already aware or highly suspicious of a Japanese advance toward Midway and was preparing to counter it. This was precisely the situation which Rear Admiral [Ryunosuke] Kusaka, Nagumo Force Chief of Staff, had feared might develop. Prior to the sortie, he had repeatedly requested that *Yamato* relay all important radio intelligence information to *Akagi*, but it was apparent that Admiral Yamamoto and his staff still hoped that surprise had not been lost and felt it advisable to continue radio silence.

Thus, as June 2 ended, the Japanese forces were steadily approaching their objectives through adverse weather. Thus far there was no certain indication that any of them had actually been detected by the enemy, and every man from Admiral Yamamoto on down hoped that the precious advantage of surprise was still in Japanese hands.

By dawn on June 3 the mist which the Nagumo Force had encountered the previous afternoon had become a heavy blanket of fog. Steaming at fog navigation quarters, adjoining ships in the formation were often unable to see each other across their scant 600-yard intervals. Powerful searchlights were turned on, but they scarcely showed through the gloom.

The task of maintaining zigzag courses through this endless veil, with only momentary and infrequent glimpses of consorting ships, was arduous and nerve-wracking. Yet it had to be done, for we were entering waters patrolled by enemy submarines. While the fog was advantageous in keeping us hidden from prying scout planes, this benefit was canceled by the increased hazards of navigation. And the enemy's radar-equipped submarines would be little affected by the fog which at the same time prevented us from launching antisubmarine patrol planes. To cope with these and other problems that beset us, all ships were at full alert and double watches were posted at submarine lookout stations.

The starboard side of *Akagi*'s bridge was occupied by Admiral Nagumo and his entire staff. They stared silently at the impenetrable curtain surrounding the ship, and each face was tense with anxiety. Captain [Taijiro] Aoki and his navigation officer, Commander [Gishiro] Miura, on the other side of the bridge, devoted their entire energies to keeping the ship on course and maintaining position in the formation. From time to time they leaned out of the window in an effort to peer through the all-encompassing fog.

A change in course was scheduled for 1030, and it had to be executed if our timetable was to be carried out. Yet, prior to execution of such a course change in heavy fog, confirmation would have to be communicated to all ships in the formation lest some stray and become lost. With visibility so limited, flag signals obviously could not be employed, and even searchlights would be ineffective to transmit the required orders. Nothing remained but to use radio, which was sure to reveal our presence to the enemy.

This distressing situation served to bring out the fact that the Nagumo Force had been assigned two tactical missions which were essentially incompatible. The assignment to attack Midway on June 5 in preparation for the landing operation put the Task Force under rigid limitations of movement. The other mission—to contact and destroy enemy naval forces—required that Nagumo be entirely free to move as the situation required, and it also made it absolutely essential to keep our whereabouts secret while searching for the enemy.

A decision obviously had to be made as to which of these missions should be given precedence. Nagumo's staff had pondered this problem hypothetically for a long time, but now the Task Force Commander faced a situation requiring a definitive choice. And still there was not a scrap of information about enemy naval forces. In this critical situation the senior member of the staff, Captain [Tomatsu] Oishi, was the first to speak up.

"The Combined Fleet operation order gives first priority to the destruction of enemy forces. Co-operation with the landing operation is secondary. But the same order specifically calls for our air attack on Midway Island on June 5. This means that the air attack must be carried out exactly as scheduled, provided that nothing is heard about enemy Task Forces by the time we are ready to launch.

"If we do not neutralize the Midway-based air forces as planned, our landing operations two days later will be strongly opposed and the entire invasion schedule will be upset."

With his usual directness Admiral Nagumo voiced the question in everyone's mind, "But where is the enemy fleet?"

In answer Oishi continued, "We know nothing of the enemy's whereabouts because we failed to reconnoiter Pearl Harbor. But if his forces are now in Pearl Harbor, we shall have plenty of time to prepare to meet them should they sortie following our strike at Midway. They will have over 1100 miles to cover.

"Even if they are already aware of our movements and have sortied to meet us, they cannot be far out from base at this moment and certainly can't be near us. I think the first thing for us to do is to carry out the scheduled raid on Midway."

At this, Chief of Staff Kusaka turned to the Intelligence Officer and asked if radio intercepts had given any indication of enemy movements. Informed that nothing had been picked up, Kusaka asked if any information had been received from Combined Fleet flagship *Yamato*. Receiving another negative response, he addressed a suggestion to Admiral Nagumo. "Since we must maintain the schedule at all cost, would you approve the use of our low-powered, inter-fleet radio for sending the order to change course?"

The Commander assented to this as the only feasible solution and the order was sent accordingly by medium-wave transmitter. A reduced-power transmission would reach out to the fringe of our force and, it was hoped, not farther. This method was not entirely safe, but it had worked on occasion in the past, thanks to enemy carelessness. In this case, however, the message was received clearly even by *Yamato,* which was 600 miles to the rear. Inasmuch as an enemy Task Force was then only a few hundred miles distant—a fact of which we were totally unaware—it was highly probable that it, too, intercepted this signal. [However, the Americans had not.]

From the first, the planners of the Midway operation calculated that the enemy naval forces would be lured out by the strike at Midway Island and not before. We had not the slightest idea that the enemy had already sortied, much less that a powerful enemy Task Force was lying in wait, ready to pounce upon us at any moment.

Dense fog still hung over the Nagumo Force throughout the afternoon and on into the night. In contrast to the tenseness prevailing on *Akagi*'s bridge, her wardroom hummed with the lusty chatter and laughter of carefree flyers whose only job was to jump into their planes and roar off at a moment's notice. Everything was ready for the scheduled air raid two days hence, and no flight missions had been ordered because of the adverse weather.

Meanwhile, the weather around the Yamamoto Force, 600 miles astern, improved somewhat in the afternoon, and refueling, which had been suspended on the preceding day, was resumed.

The worst thing about the persistent fog was that it cloaked enemy movements in complete secrecy. As previously mentioned, the plan for a flying boat reconnaissance of Pearl Harbor on May 31, using French Frigate Shoals as a refueling point, had been thwarted. Nor did our submarines provide any information. The sole remaining source of information was radio intelligence. As early as May 30, such intelligence picked up by Admiral Yamamoto's flagship *Yamato* had pointed to brisk enemy activity in the Hawaii area, especially of patrol planes. This strongly suggested the possibility of a sortie by an enemy force from the Hawaiian base, but Combined Fleet sent no warning whatever to Admiral Nagumo!

Admiral Nagumo and his staff were deeply chagrined when they learned after the battle that Combined Fleet Headquarters had suspected an enemy sortie because of this radio intelligence. Why did Combined Fleet not transmit this vital information to the Carrier Striking Force so that any danger of its being taken by surprise might be averted?

There were two reasons behind this unfortunate failure. Firstly, Combined Fleet Headquarters thoughtlessly believed that *Akagi,* closer to the enemy than *Yamato,* would naturally have obtained the same information, and that Admiral Nagumo was formulating his decisions accordingly. Secondly, they feared that radio communication between the two forces would reveal their positions to the enemy.

At any rate, Admiral Yamamoto's failure to issue necessary precautionary instructions to the forces under his command was an important cause of the Midway fiasco. He was to blame for being too much preoccupied with the idea of "radio silence." It is easy to imagine what angry and bitter emotions must have welled up inside Rear Admiral Kusaka when he went on board *Yamato* after the battle to report on the near annihilation of the Nagumo Force and there learned for the first time of Combined Fleet's negligence. Well might he have said, "How often I told them not to let this happen!"

Combined Fleet Headquarters, however, was not alone to blame. The Naval General Staff back in Tokyo was also partially responsible, for it again sent a radio [message] to Combined Fleet concerning enemy fleet activity in the Solomon Islands area. The message carried the strong implication that the movement of the Japanese forces toward Midway was not yet suspected by the enemy.

The Naval General Staff had originally opposed the Midway operation, but once having given its approval, it was responsible for the whole operation even more than was Combined Fleet Headquarters. With the decisive battle only a few days off, it was engaged in gathering all available intelligence regarding enemy activity. What particularly attracted the attention of the intelligence staff were indications that an American Carrier Task Force still was operating in the Solomons area. If this was true, as the Naval General Staff believed, it constituted powerful evidence that the enemy did not yet suspect our intention, for, if he did, he would obviously have called all his scarce remaining carriers back from the Southwest Pacific. Even after intercepting a number of "Urgent" calls from American radios in the Hawaii-Midway area, the Naval General Staff still stuck fast to its first conclusion.

The storm of battle was about to break, and for the first time in six months, Fate did not seem to be smiling upon us. No change, however, was made in the operational plan. All forces plunged on through the boundless fog like stagecoach horses driven blindly forward by a cracking whip.

At about 0300 on the morning of June 4 the noisy drone of plane engines warming up roused me from slumber. I got out of bed and attempted to stand, but my legs were still unsteady. The sound of engines alternately hummed and then rose to a whining roar. *Akagi* was preparing to launch her planes for the attack on Midway.

Unable to resist the desire to be topside at take-off time, I slipped out of the sick bay. The watertight doors of every bulkhead had been closed, leaving only a small manhole in each door open for passage. It was an arduous task to squeeze through these small openings in my weakened condition, and cold sweat soon ran down my forehead. I frequently felt exhausted and dizzy and had to squat on the floor to rest.

The passageways were empty. All hands were at their stations. Lights were dimmed for combat condition, and one could see a distance of only a few feet. With great effort I finally climbed the ladders up to my cabin just below the flight deck, clutching the handrails every step of the way. There I paused long enough to catch my breath and put on a uniform before going on to the flight control post. The first-wave attack planes were all lined up on the flight deck. The warm-up was completed, and the roar of the engines subsided. I found Commander [Shogo] Masuda, Air Officer of *Akagi,* in charge of flight preparations.

My colleagues expressed concern over my leaving bed, but they understood when I explained that I could not bear to hear the sound of the engines and remain below in sick bay. I looked up at the dark sky. The dawn still seemed far off. The sky was cloudy, and the weather, while not good, was not bad enough to prevent flying. The sea was calm.

I asked Lieutenant Furukawa when sunrise would be.

"At 0500, Sir," was the reply.

"Have search planes already been set out?"

"No, Sir. They will be launched at the same time as the first attack wave."

"Are we using the single-phase search system?"

"Yes, Sir. As usual."

I recalled the attacks on Colombo and Trincomalee in the Indian Ocean, two months earlier, when single-phase search had been employed. It had not been a wise tactic. In both instances, the searches had spotted enemy surface forces while our attack groups were away hitting the enemy bases, and this had caused our carriers some anxious moments. With this in mind, I inquired what plans had been made for the eventuality that our search planes might sight an enemy fleet during the Midway attack.

"No need to worry about that," Lieutenant Commander [Shigiharu] Murata replied. "After the first attack wave departs, the second wave, consisting of Lieutenant Commander [Takashige] Egusa's dive bombers, my torpedo bombers, and Lieutenant Commander [Shigeru] Itaya's Zeros, will be available to attack an enemy surface force, if discovered."

"I see. Well, that's a good team, and we can just hope that the enemy fleet does come out so we can destroy it. What searches are scheduled?"

Furukawa explained them to me on the map board. "There are seven lines extending east and south, with Midway lying within the search arc. We are using one plane each from *Akagi* and *Kaga*, two seaplanes each from *Tone* and *Chikuma*, and one from *Haruna*. The search radius is 300 miles for all planes except *Haruna*'s, which is a Type-95 and can do only half that."

Although the coverage appeared adequate, I still felt that a two-phase search would have been wiser. A single-phase search might be sufficient if we wished only to confirm our assumption that no enemy fleet was in the vicinity. However, if we recognized the possibility that this assumption might be wrong and that an enemy force might be present, our searches should have been such as to assure [*sic*] that we could locate and attack it before it could strike at us. For this purpose a two-phase dawn search was the logical answer.

As the term indicates, a two-phase search employs two sets of planes which fly the same search lines, with a given time interval between them. Since our planes were not equipped with radar at this time, they were completely reliant on visual observation and could search effectively only by daylight. Consequently, to spot an enemy force as soon as possible after dawn, it was necessary to have one set of planes (the first phase) launched in time to reach the end of their search radius as day was breaking. This meant that the areas traversed in darkness on their outbound flight remained unsearched. Hence, a second-phase search was required over these same lines by planes taking off about one hour later.

Men assigned to the first phase of such a search obviously had to be well trained in night flying. Nagumo had such pilots and could have used this method, but it would have required twice as many planes as a single-phase search. Despite the importance of conducting adequate searches, our naval strategists were congenitally reluctant to devote more than a bare minimum of their limited plane strength to such missions. Ten per cent of total strength was all they were willing to spare for search operations, feeling that the rest should be reserved for offensive use. But such overemphasis on offensive strength had proven detrimental to our purposes before this, and it would again.

Naturally enough, Admiral Nagumo was eager to devote maximum strength to the Midway attack and did not want to use any more planes for search than seemed absolutely necessary. Since he had no reason to suspect the presence of an enemy force in the area, he was satisfied that a single-phase search was adequate precaution.

Search planes from *Akagi* and *Kaga* were launched at 0430, simultaneously with the departure of the first Midway attack wave. *Haruna*'s seaplane was also catapulted at this time. But the *Tone* and *Chikuma* planes, which were covering the center lines of the search pattern, were delayed. Watching the two cruisers, I noticed that the last of their search planes did not get off until just before sunrise, nearly half an hour behind schedule. It was later learned that *Tone*'s planes had been held up by catapult trouble, while one of *Chikuma*'s planes had a balky engine. This last plane was forced to turn back at 0635 when the engine trouble recurred and it ran into foul weather.

Although poorly advised, a one-phase search dispatched half an hour before sunrise would still have been helpful if everything had worked out as planned. But the delay in launching *Tone*'s planes sowed a seed which bore fatal fruit for the Japanese in the ensuing naval action. Reviewing the full story of the battle on both sides, we now know that the enemy task force was missed by *Chikuma*'s search plane which, according to the plan, should have flown directly over it. The enemy force was discovered only when the belated *Tone* plane, on the line south of the *Chikuma* plane, was on the dog-leg of its search. Had Admiral Nagumo carried out an earlier and more carefully planned two-phase search, had the observer of the *Chikuma* plane been more watchful on the outward leg of his search, or had the seaplanes been on schedule, the disaster that followed might have been avoided.

The fundamental cause of this failure, again, lay in the Japanese Navy's overemphasis on attack, which resulted in inadequate attention to search and reconnaissance. In both the training and organization of our naval aviators, too much importance and effort were devoted to attack. Reconnaissance was taught only as part of the regular curriculum, and no subsequent special training was given. Also, there were no organic reconnaissance units of any appreciable size in the Japanese Navy. When reconnaissance missions were required, attack planes were usually refitted and assigned to perform them. There were no carrier-borne planes designed solely for search. In the Pearl Harbor attack, every carrier-borne bomber of Nagumo's six carriers was assigned to the attack, leaving for search only some ten-odd float planes from the accompanying battleships and cruisers. This had been perhaps the basic reason for Admiral Nagumo's decision to withdraw upon that occasion without exploiting his advantage. At the critical moment, when he had to decide whether to launch another attack on Pearl Harbor, he did not have the vital information which reconnaissance planes could have provided. The Nagumo Force continued to suffer from this same lack of aerial reconnaissance in every action that followed.

While searching for the British Fleet in the Indian Ocean earlier in the year, our search planes often lost their way and the carriers had to send out radio signals on which they could home. This, however, also alerted the enemy to our positions, and the result was an understandable reluctance on the part of Admiral Nagumo and his staff to send out search planes if it could possibly be avoided. This reluctance was still present in the Midway operation and, coupled with the erroneous estimate of the enemy situation, was responsible for the inadequate search dispositions ordered by Admiral Nagumo.

One small step toward remedying the search weakness of the Nagumo Force had been taken prior to the sortie for Midway. After prolonged negotiations with the authorities, Nagumo had succeeded in getting two carrier-based reconnaissance planes of a new type, on which experiments had just been completed. This type had been designed originally as a dive bomber, but was altered for use as a search plane. It was later designated the Type-2 carrier-borne reconnaissance plane or *Suisei* ("Judy") dive bomber, and there were high expectations for its success in reconnoitering powerful enemy Task Forces. Two of these planes had been loaded on board *Soryu*.

At the time his search and attack groups took off from the carriers on June 4 Admiral Nagumo was unaware that the Japanese Transport Group had already been sighted and attacked by planes from Midway. *Akebono Maru,* the only ship hit, was not damaged enough to hinder her progress, but the important thing was that the enemy was fully alerted to the presence of Japanese ships approaching in the direction of Midway. And we did not know that they knew.

— *AUTHORS* —

Mitsuo Fuchida served twenty-five years in the IJN and was a captain at the end of World War II. An aviator with three thousand hours of flight time, he served as commander of the air groups of Cardiv 1 from August 1941 to July 1942, in the *Akagi.* Wounded during the Battle of Midway, he was hospitalized for about one year. In June 1943 he was made senior staff officer of the First Air Fleet at Kanoya, and later at Tinian when the First Air Fleet was moved to the Marianas. In April 1944 he was transferred to the *Oyodo* as air operations officer of the Combined Fleet. When fleet headquarters moved ashore to Hiyoshi in September 1944, he continued in this same position until the end of the war.

Masatake Okumiya entered the Imperial Japanese Naval Academy in 1927, was commissioned an ensign in 1932, and joined the naval air corps in 1933. After duty in China during 1937, he was test pilot for divebombers until September of the next year when he suffered a serious air accident. Active again in 1941 as an air staff officer, he joined Cardiv 4 in April 1942, under Rear Admiral Kakuji Kakuta in the flagship *Ryujo* for the AL Operation. He was with Admiral Kakuta in Cardiv 2 on the flagship *Junyo* during the Battle of Santa Cruz and the Battle of Guadalcanal. He saw duty at Wewak in December 1942, in the Guadalcanal withdrawal operation of January–February 1943, and at Rabaul and Buin in April 1943; he was with the last of the air forces at Rabaul in February 1944. In June 1944 he was air officer to Rear Admiral Takaji Joshima, ComCardiv 2, in the flagship *Junyo.* He was at Okinawa in July and August before joining the naval general staff as air staff officer with the rank of commander, where he remained until the end of the war. As a member of the Second (Navy) Demobilization Board after the war, he had access to what naval records survived.

CHAPTER 10

Opening Shots

By John B. Lundstrom

The First Team, Pacific Naval Air Combat from Pearl Harbor to Midway (Annapolis, MD: Naval Institute Press, 1984, 1990): chap. 10 Opening Shots, pp. 182–186

The Inscrutable Enemy

In most respects, Japanese naval aviation evolved in similar fashion to its great trans-Pacific rival, the United States Navy, but there was one important exception. The Imperial Navy's Air Arm (*Kaigun Koku Butai*) developed into a complete air force well before the Pacific War by creating a strong, land-based air contingent flying medium bombers as well as carrier planes and other aircraft of a more nautical nature. After World War I, the Imperial Navy had assumed the task of defending the sea approaches to Japan and her possessions. Concomitant with this responsibility was the necessity of expanding from a purely naval into a major land-based air force as well, a strategically more complex role than that of the U.S. Navy even including aircraft serving with the U.S. Marine Corps. During the China Incident (1937–41), the *Kaigun Koku Butai* demonstrated it could wage a major land-based air offensive right alongside (and in competition with) the Imperial Japanese Army Air Force. In no conceivable way did the use of strong naval air contingents deep within China fulfill purely naval requirements. The Imperial Navy's Air Force had become a complete counterpart to the Japanese Army Air Force. That was why from February 1942 to well within 1943 the United

States Pacific Fleet could rampage the length of the Great East Asia Co-Prosperity Sphere's eastern flank without encountering a single Japanese Army aircraft.

In May 1942, the Imperial Navy wielded a mighty fist of six fleet carriers and a similar number of light or converted flattops. The First Air Fleet (*koku kantai*) under Vice Admiral Nagumo Chuichi was the principal carrier command. In battle, Nagumo usually led between four and six fleet carriers with their escorts, his operational command being known as the *Kido Butai* (literally, "Mobile Force," better rendered as "Striking Force"). The carriers themselves comprised carrier divisions (*koku sentai*), corresponding to the land-based air flotillas (also *koku sentai*). With the fleet carriers, each division contained two flattops. In the Imperial Navy, the concept of the carrier division was much more important, as opposed to its purely administrative function in the U.S. Navy. Before the war, the Japanese adopted multi-carrier formations as a means of massing carrier air power into one or two coordinated strikes, epitomized by the attack on Pearl Harbor. They initiated "group training," meaning that the aircraft from one carrier division trained closely together, underscoring the fact that the aircraft within a carrier division formed a coherent unit, a "wing" to borrow a foreign term. In 1941–42, the Japanese achieved a far higher level of coordination in integrating aircraft from different carriers than did the Americans.

Japanese carrier aviation paralleled the organization of the land-based naval air units already described. In place of the land-based air group or *kokutai* was the aircraft carrier herself. The aviators, mechanics, armorers, radiomen, and other aviation personnel all served as an integral part of the ship's company with the rest of the flattop's crew. They did not belong to separate, independent squadrons like those in the U.S. Navy. Consequently the flying units could not switch from carrier to carrier with the ease of American squadrons, nor could they operate independently ashore. To replace losses, it was necessary to transfer individuals from other aviation units instead of assigning a new air group. Thus heavy losses could cripple a Japanese carrier.

The carrier air unit (*hikokitai*—U.S. equivalent, "air group") took its name from its parent ship and made up the actual flying element operating off the ship. Aloft, the air unit was commanded by a *hikotaicho* (group leader), one of the two flight command ratings within the naval air system. Usually lieutenant commanders or very senior lieutenants, *hikotaicho* were qualified to lead air strikes made up of aircraft from their own carrier divisions and from others as well. They also retained direct command over a portion of the strike group, depending on the type of aircraft they flew. Japanese carrier pilots early in their career specialized in one of the three types of carrier aircraft: dive bomber, torpedo plane, and fighter, and they retained this specialty even as *hikotaicho.* On the vertical tail surfaces of their personal aircraft, three broad stripes denoted their command rating. A fleet carrier could have on board more than one *hikotaicho* (the flagship *Akagi* for example, had three); if so, the senior *hikotaicho* led the *hikokitai* or carrier air unit.

Within their air units, the fleet carriers featured three types of flying units or squadron equivalents: one equipped with dive bombers, the second with torpedo planes, and the third with fighters. Like the air units themselves, these squadron equivalents bore the same name as the parent carrier. At this time, light carriers usually had only one type of strike plane (either torpedo planes or dive bombers) in addition to the carrier fighters. These squadrons all existed only as tactical organizations within their respective *hikokitai.* They were not autonomous and did not serve away from their ships. Within the squadrons, two basic subunits appeared for flight operations: the *chutai* (division) of six or nine aircraft and the *shotai* or section of three aircraft. Commanding the squadrons and divisions were officers, usually lieutenants, with the command rating of *buntaicho* or division leader. In most cases on board light carriers, the senior *buntaicho* also led the carrier air unit. Within the squadrons were usually two or three *buntaicho,* at least one per *chutai.* In air strikes, senior *buntaicho* occasionally led aircraft from other carriers as well as their own. As their command insignia they sported two stripes on the vertical tail surface of their aircraft.

Imperial Japanese Naval Aviation Organization

U.S. Navy Equivalent	Rank of CO	Japanese Carriers	Japanese Land-Based
Aircraft, Battle Force (later: Carriers, Pacific Fleet)	Vice Admiral	*Kido Butai* (Striking Force)	*Koku Butai* (Base Air Force)
Carrier Division	Rear Admiral	*Koku Sentai* (Carrier Division)	*Koku Sentai* (Air Flotilla)
Aircraft Carrier (ship)	Captain	*Kuko Bokan* (Aircraft Carrier)	*Kokutai* (Air Group)
Carrier Air Group	Commander or Lt. Cdr.	*Hikokitai*	
Squadron: Fighting (VF) Bombing (VB) Scouting (VS) Torpedo (VT)	Lt. Commander or Lieutenant	*Kanjo:* *Sentokitai* (VF) *Bakugekikitai* (VB) *Kogekikitai* (VT)	
Division		*Chutai*	*Chutai*
Section		*Shotai*	*Shotai*

Its dive bombers, the Imperial Navy called "carrier bombers" (*kanjo bakugekiki,* abbreviated *kanbaku*). Thus the carrier bomber unit was known as the *kanjo bakugekikitai.* The standard carrier bomber was the Aichi D3A1 Type 99 carrier bomber [VAL]. A graceful, trim airplane sporting elliptical wings and neatly spatted fixed landing gear, the two-seat Type 99 *kanbaku* sported a payload of one 250-kilogram bomb. In performance it was roughly equivalent to the Douglas SBD Dauntless, but less rugged. Nominal strength for a carrier bomber unit was twenty-one airplanes (eighteen operational and three spares), organized tactically into two *chutai* of nine planes each.

The other type of strike aircraft operating from Japanese carriers was the so-called carrier attack plane (*kanjo kogekiki,* conveniently shortened to *kanko*). Operating as either a torpedo plane or a horizontal bomber, the carrier attack plane offered dual strike capability. The carrier attack unit (*kanjo kogekikitai*) had a paper strength of eighteen operational aircraft and three spares (except in the *Kaga* with twenty-seven operational *kanko* and three spares) organized into three *chutai* of six aircraft each. The basic torpedo plane was the Nakajima B5N2 Type 97 carrier attack plane [KATE]. Adopted in 1937, the big, three-seat Type 97 was superior to the U.S. Navy's TBD-1 Devastator in such criteria as speed, climb, and range. Even more important, Japanese aerial torpedoes proved much more rugged and reliable than their American counterparts, allowing much higher release speeds and altitudes.

The Japanese term for carrier fighter was *kanjo sentoki* (abbreviated *kansen*); hence the carrier fighter unit was the *kanjo sentokitai.* On board fleet carriers, carrier fighter units had a nominal strength of twenty-one aircraft (eighteen operational and three spares), while most light carriers shipped between twelve and sixteen fighters on board. The normal twenty-one plane units consisted of two *chutai* (divisions) each with nine fighters. The unit commander (usually a *buntaicho*) led the 1st *Chutai* personally, while the junior *buntaicho* took the 2nd *Chutai.* Usually the fighter squadrons had only two *buntaicho,* as officer pilots were scarce. Each *chutai* in turn comprised three *shotai* (sections), made up of [a] *shotaicho* (section leader) and two wingmen. The three spare fighters more often than not were conspicuous by their absence due to shortages in aircraft and pilots. However if they were present, the unit could form a seventh *shotai* or, more likely, distribute them among the other *shotai,* making some four rather than three planes. Under certain conditions, Japanese fighters also operated in pairs.

The standard Japanese carrier fighter was the Mitsubishi A6M2 Type O carrier fighter, Model 21 [ZEKE], known popularly as the Zero fighter (in Japanese, *Reisen*) from the last digit of its year of adoption, 1940 or 2600 in the Japanese calendar. The Zero fighter became the pride of the Imperial Navy and served almost as a symbol of the empire's fighting spirit. . . .

Late in 1940, the factory redesigned the wingtips so they could fold back one meter to permit easier stowage on board carriers. This modification became the Model 21, put into quantity production in February 1941. In 1940–41, Zero fighters literally swept the Chinese Air Force from the skies, suffering in return only the lightest losses.

Sleek and smooth, with long, tapering wings and a large, streamlined cockpit canopy, the Zero looked every inch a fighter. Powered by a 950-hp Sakae-12 fourteen cylinder radial engine, the Model 21 registered a top speed of about 288 knots (331 mph) at 14, 930 feet. Climb rate was exceptional, initially 2,750 feet per minute, but the airplane required only five minutes, 55 seconds to reach 16,400 feet (average 2,770 feet per minute) and 7 minutes, 27 seconds to attain 19,685 feet (average 2,642 feet per minute). The aircraft was light, only 5,313 lbs. loaded, and it was exceptionally maneuverable with quick acceleration. Internal fuel comprised 137.25 gallons of gasoline, with provisions in the original design for a specially streamlined drop tank holding up to 87.5 gallons more. The Japanese used their drop tanks extensively, even for [combat air patrol] missions. Normal fuel load, including drop tank, was 182 gallons. Consequently, range and endurance were excellent, 1,010 miles without auxiliary fuel and up to 1,675 miles with a full drop tank. This gave the Zero fighter a combat radius of up to 300 miles from a carrier and well over 500 miles from a land base.

In the criteria of protection and armament, the Zero differed radically from American fighter designs. Always offense-minded, Japanese pilots did not feel the need for pilot armor, not wishing to encumber their machines with excessive weight. They desired a highly maneuverable, agile fighter that, if properly employed, could fly out of trouble. In 1939–40 as the fighter worked up for service, few in the Imperial Navy realized the potential of leak-proof fuel tanks, and they did not pursue the concept. Thus the Zero became vulnerable to gunfire if an opponent could score, creating a great fire hazard. In May 1942, U.S. naval fighter pilots began using incendiary bullets which increased the risk of fire. . . . Light losses in aerial combat over China had lulled [Japanese] naval analysts into thinking their crack pilots (among the best-trained in the world) and magnificent fighter aircraft were nearly invulnerable. . . .

The Mitsubishi designers chose a mixed armament of rifle caliber (7.7-mm) machine guns and big 20-mm cannons for the new Zero fighter. They styled such armament as "all purpose" believing that it could deal with bombers as well as single-seat targets. Mounted in the fuselage decking behind the engine were two Type 97 7.7-mm machine guns synchronized to fire through the propeller. . . . With 680 rounds per gun, there was plenty of shooting time. Fitted in each wing was one Type 99 20-mm cannon. . . . Lightweight, reliable, and firing explosive shells, the cannon was thought capable of bringing down enemy aircraft with minimal hits. Its cyclic rate of fire was 520 rounds per minute, but there were only 60 rounds per gun. . . . A selector switch on the control stick permitted the machine guns to be fired with the cannons or separately. Common procedure was to open with the machine guns for sighting, then cut in with the 20-millimeters when the bursts were on target. The Japanese soon discovered their armament was not as effective as they hoped. Unaided, the 7.7 bullets were rarely enough to bring down rugged American planes, but it took great skill to score consistently with the cannons. Because of the [20-mm's] low muzzle velocity, the trajectory was high. With only 60 rounds per cannon, Japanese pilots could not afford to waste their shots. Because of aiming difficulties, the effective range was perhaps 200 meters. On the whole, Japanese were fairly good gunners, often riddling their targets with 7.7-mm bullets. Trouble was, the 7.7s usually failed to penetrate armor plate or defeat self-sealing fuel tanks, whereas the 20-mm explosive shells could do the job, but owing to the nature of the weapon such decisive hits were rare.

CHAPTER
11

Forging the Thunderbolt

By Mark R. Peattie

Sunburst, The Rise of Japanese Naval Air Power, 1909–1941 (Annapolis, MD: Naval Institute Press, 2007): chap. 6 Forging the Thunderbolt, pp. 130–156

For the Japanese navy the guiding objective that drove the training of its aircrews, the development of the aircraft they were to fly, the design of the carriers from which those aircraft were to operate, and the positions those carriers were to take in any fleet action remained the midocean destruction of the U.S. carrier forces and battle fleet. . . .

It was during the China War . . . that the navy's fighter and bomber squadrons perfected the basic tactical formation, the three-aircraft *shotai* composed of a leader and two wingmen. When not actually engaged, the three aircraft usually formed an equilateral triangle with about a 50-meter (160 foot) interval between the section leader and his wingmen with all three flying at the same altitude. When anticipating combat, Japanese navy pilots usually adopted a looser formation, . . . [often] with one aircraft trailing the leader at about 200 meters (650 feet) higher altitude and the third flying about 300 meters (1,000 feet) higher than the leader to provide top cover. . . .

Success for these formation tactics in the wild chaos of combat required an aircraft of exceptional maneuverability, which the navy had in the Mitsubishi Zero, and pilots of consummate skill whose teamwork was the result of hours of relentless training and practice. . . . Indeed, so familiar with each other's combat tactics were the fliers in a three-man *shotai* that some navy pilots claimed to have developed an almost sixth sense (*ishin denshin*) by which they could communicate with their two comrades flying with them. . . .

[T]he dive bombers [were] to approach [their target] on a course opposite to the target, in one of a number of possible formations, beginning their attack at an altitude of probably 3,000 meters (10,000 feet) and about 20–30 nautical miles from the target. At that point, forming in echelon, the bombing aircraft would go into a shallow dive of about 10 degrees at full throttle. In succession, the aircraft would plunge in a dive of about 65 degrees, aiming at a point in advance of the target's intended course and releasing their bombs at a height of 600 meters (2,000 feet) above the target. After releasing its payload at the bottom of its dive, each aircraft would retract its air brakes, pull sharply up, and, at low altitude, use all possible speed to avoid antiaircraft fire and get away. In certain circumstances, the lead dive bombers were to be sacrificed in an attempt to suppress such fire with their own bombs. The navy anticipated that losses would be severe among dive-bombing squadrons in such operations. . . .

By the beginning of the Pacific War, . . . the navy was armed with powerful torpedoes of unrivaled speed and range. The configuration of the Type 91 aerial torpedo, when it was first developed in 1931, had enabled the navy's torpedo bombers to launch from a height of 100 meters (330 feet) while maintaining an airspeed of 100 knots. . . . By 1937, navy torpedo bombers were able to release their torpedoes at heights of up to 200 meters (660 feet) and speeds of up to 120 knots. By 1938, Japanese tactical doctrine called for releasing them at approximately 1,000 meters (3,300 feet) from the target. . . .

[Commander] Genda Minoru, then [1940] serving as assistant naval attaché in London . . . was sitting in a London movie theater and watching a newsreel that showed a concentration of American carriers steaming together in a box formation. It immediately occurred to him that not only could carriers operate together in a single formation in order to mass air groups for offensive operations, but the risk of discovery and subsequent attack on such a formation would be more than offset by the ability of the concentrated carriers to launch a larger combat air patrol. It also meant that massed carriers should be able to throw up a greater concentration of antiaircraft fire than could be achieved by any single carrier . . .

As early as 1939, various Combined Fleet maneuvers had demonstrated that success in preemptive attack [against an enemy's carriers] was usually a matter of only a few minutes' advantage. In this, much depended not only upon the time required for [Japanese] carriers to launch their attack squadrons but, even before that, upon finding the enemy first. . . .

The problem of a preemptive strike by carrier air power on an enemy carrier force also raised questions of fleet air defense. In considering such a strike, Japanese tacticians had to assume that the two strikes—one's own and the enemy's—would be launched about the same time. This being the case, considerable study on the eve of the Pacific War was devoted to two questions: first, how to preserve part of the strike force to finish off the enemy after reciprocal aerial attacks had caused reciprocal losses, and second, how to increase the defensive capabilities of one's own carrier force to deal not only with the enemy's first strike but also with his second . . . the Japanese navy was still wrestling with these questions as it plunged into war . . .

[A] Japanese fleet carrier [such as the *Akagi*] usually embarked about eighteen Zero fighters. These were divided into two groups: nine fighters to provide escort to the outgoing carrier attack aircraft, and nine to stay above the Japanese carrier and thus contribute to the combat air patrol. But this number of patrolling fighters was far too small to provide for an adequate defense in all directions. Without radar, moreover, those directing the carrier group's air defense in combat were obliged to work out a system of standing patrols with only a few planes in the air at a time: one three-plane *shotai* aloft per carrier; another spotted for launch; and a third in a lesser state of readiness. Standard duration of a patrol was about two hours. If during that time an enemy flight was detected approaching the carrier group, the remaining six aircraft could be scrambled to join the CAP [combat air patrol]. Each individual fighter pilot was responsible for a sector of air space adjacent to his carrier, and theoretically other aircraft in the patrol could be vectored to any threatened sector.

[However], the poor quality of the navy's voice radio made it almost impossible to control CAP aircraft already aloft. . . . [In addition], there were serious organizational problems in Japanese fleet air defense. Chief among these was the fact that responsibility for this activity was invariably divided among a number of officers aboard one of the carriers. The position of air defense officer was not permanent; rather, it was assigned on an ad hoc basis to any one of a number of carrier pilots who were otherwise unoccupied.

CHAPTER 12

Preparing to Defend Midway

By E. B. Potter

Nimitz (Annapolis, MD: Naval Institute Press, 1976): chap. 6 Preparing to Defend Midway, p. 78

Admiral Nimitz's visit to Midway Atoll in early May 1942 was the result of a hunch based on a study of the map. If the Japanese were about to launch an offensive in the Pacific Ocean, as Commander [Joseph] Rochefort was predicting, they were going to have either to seize or bypass the armed U.S. outpost at Midway, which stood squarely in their way. And, thus far, the Japanese juggernaut had shown no tendency to bypass strong points. Busy as he was, the commander in chief decided that he had better fly out and have a look at the atoll's defenses.

Nimitz and members of his staff spent May 2 inspecting thoroughly the fortifications of the atoll's two islets, Eastern and Sand. The admiral crawled into gun pits, let himself down into underground command posts, examined the hangars, questioned the marine defenders, and observed the operations of the communication facilities, especially the priceless cable connection with Honolulu. By means of this cable, a segment of the old transpacific cable system, Midway and Pearl Harbor could communicate in plain English without having to worry about static or enemy interception and traffic analysis.

Nimitz liked what he saw, and was particularly pleased with the obviously close liaison between Commander Cyril T. Simard, the atoll commander, and Lieutenant Colonel Harold Shannon, USMC, commander of the ground forces. At the end of the day he asked them what they would need if they had to defend

This photo shows the reef surrounding most of the atoll. The atoll itself is about six miles in diameter. The term "Battle of Midway" is somewhat inaccurate. The correct term is "Battle of Midway Atoll." Eastern Island, with its three runways, is nearest the camera. The seaplane base and radio station were located on Sand Island. Pan American Airways established its seaplane station on Sand Island in 1935. The Navy built its own installations after 1938. In June 1942 both islands were heavily defended by the Marines, with 7-inch and 5-inch guns to ward off surface ships, 3-inch guns, 37-mm weapons, and heavy machine guns to defend against air attack, and radar to warn of Japanese air strikes. These defenses were complemented by the 6th Defense Battalion and by units from the 4th Defense Battalion and the 2nd Raider Battalion.

Navy Department, National Archives

Midway against a powerful attack from the sea. Shannon, who had already given the problem much thought, reeled off a list.

"If I get you all these things you say you need, then can you hold Midway against a major amphibious assault?"

"Yes, sir," replied Shannon.

Nimitz smiled and appeared to relax. He asked Shannon to put his list in writing and to add to it any other supplies and reinforcements that he or Simard thought would ensure the defense of the atoll. The next morning he and his staff boarded his PBY-5A and flew back to Pearl Harbor. In his usual quiet way he had thoroughly alerted the defenders of the atoll and at the same time instilled confidence in them.

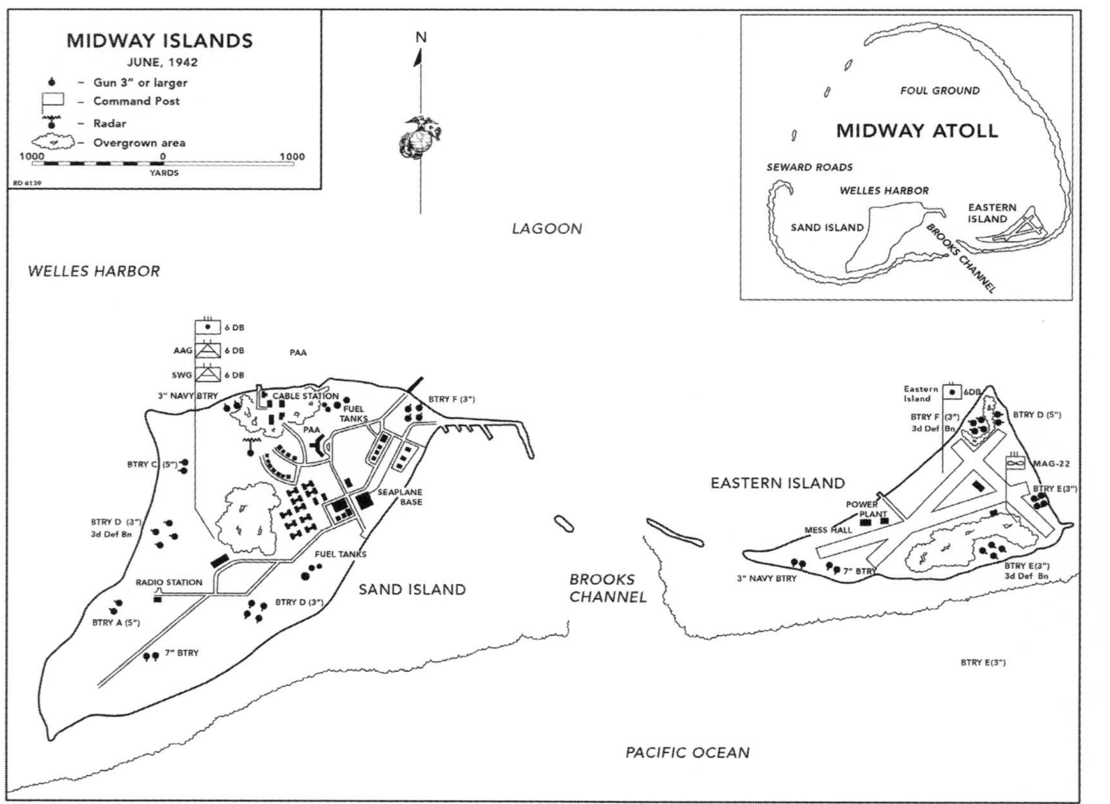

Map 1. Midway Atoll, June 1942

Marines at Midway, LTCOL Robert D. Heinl Jr., Marine Corps Historical Section, 1948

Admiral Nimitz on the beach during his trip to Midway on 2 May. During his daylong tour of Midway, Nimitz asked LTCOL Harold N. Shannon what the Marine defenders needed to ward off a Japanese assault from the sea. The Marines had already transformed Sand and Eastern Islands into a working and strongly defended base, but Shannon wanted reinforcements, including additional antiaircraft guns, two rifle companies, five light tanks, and sixteen SBD-2 dive-bombers. He got them all by 26 May—just in time.

U.S. Naval Institute Photo Archive

Midway's defenders were dug in, but Sand Island was mostly what the name implied, and much of the digging of emplacements for defensive positions was done by hand. Eastern Island was even lower to the sea. The Marines had been shelled by two Japanese destroyers on 7 December 1941, and Japanese submarines had shelled the atoll on 25 January, 8 February, and 10 February 1942, so the Midway garrison was not new to combat. But most of the Marines lived, ate, and slept in reinforced dugouts like those used by soldiers in World War I. This photo shows Admiral Nimitz emerging from an aid station during his visit on 2 May. To encourage and reward Lieutenant Colonel Shannon and CDR Cyril T. Simard, Nimitz promoted both—to colonel and captain, respectively.

U.S. Naval Institute Photo Archive

CHAPTER
13

Lest We Forget: Civilian Yard Workers

By LCDR Thomas J. Cutler, USN (Ret.)

Proceedings, July 2005, pp. 94

Though *Yorktown* was the focus of the Pearl Harbor Naval Shipyard after she arrived at berth 16 on 27 May, it's important to remember that the Shipyard's work force was busy with salvaging ships sunk on 7 December 1941 and with repairs required by ships needed for immediate operations. So while *Yorktown* was being repaired in Dry Dock Number 1, salvage and repair crews were—to mention only a few of their efforts—removing 14-inch shells and wreckage from *Arizona,* pumping water from the badly damaged hull of *West Virginia* prior to raising her, overhauling the Coast Guard buoy tender *Kukui,* replacing the starboard propeller of destroyer *Morris,* repairing pumps on the old destroyer *Allen,* and replacing part of the fire fighting piping system on light cruiser *Honolulu.* The Navy Department had invested large sums in the Shipyard in 1940 and 1941, and the investment paid off.

Lest We Forget: Civilian Yard Workers (p. 94)

USS *Yorktown* limped up the Pearl Harbor channel. Two near misses and a direct hit from Japanese aircraft had done considerable damage to this aircraft carrier and it seemed certain that she would have to sit out the war for a number of weeks—perhaps months—for repairs.

But huge forces were at work. A Japanese armada was headed for an island north of Hawaii—an atoll diminutive in area but gigantic in strategic significance. Should Midway fall, the U.S. Navy might well be driven into a retreat all the way back to the West Coast of America.

Only three aircraft carriers—including *Yorktown*—and a handful of cruisers and destroyers were left to meet this gargantuan enemy force. If the U.S. fleet was to have any chance at all, this limping carrier would have to be included.

As she entered a dry-dock, Admiral Chester Nimitz, Commander of the Pacific Fleet, wearing hip boots like the others, sloshed around in seawater deep in the ship's innards, dodging hanging cables and peering at the damage as the repair experts tallied up the weeks of work needed. Nimitz turned to the supervisor and quietly but firmly said, "We *must* have the ship back in three days."

Civilian yard workers swarmed aboard armed with a different arsenal of war—hammers, acetylene torches, and the like—and soon the ship echoed with a cacophony of frantic but purposeful activity. Working around the clock in temperatures sometimes reaching 120°, these workers labored in an eerie world of pulsating light, choking smoke, pungent fumes, and a racing clock. Men collapsed from exhaustion, were hauled topside for some air and a quick sandwich, and then returned to the hell below. One man was found asleep on a scaffold, his cutting torch still in hand.

Three days later, the resurrection was complete. *Yorktown* steamed down the channel, headed for sea and a "rendezvous with destiny," civilian workers spilling from her insides into small boats alongside as she went.

The courage and sacrifice of the men who fought the battle of Midway is legendary, but the miracle began when others fought exhaustion and the clock to do the seemingly impossible. The victory is theirs as well.

— AUTHOR —

LCDR Thomas J. Cutler is a former member of the faculty of the U.S. Naval Academy and the Acquisitions Editor at the Naval Institute Press. He is the author of *Brown Water, Black Berets, Coastal and Riverine Warfare in Vietnam* (1988) as well as *The Battle for Leyte Gulf, 23–26 October 1944* (2001) and *The Bluejacket's Manual* (24th edition).

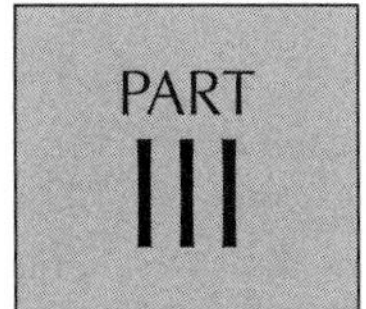

The Battle

The selections in part III cover the actual battle, especially the aircraft engagements and attacks of 4 June 1942. Tactically, Midway was mostly a battle between aviators, and the aviators on both sides were young men who loved to fly and their somewhat older and more seasoned commanders, like "Jimmy" Thach and Mitsuo Fuchida. Few saw the big picture. They were too busy with the details of preparing for and then performing missions. Though young, pilots in both navies were professionals; they followed orders and did their duty. Their sacrifices were often extraordinary.

But those who were not pilots also did their duty, including the sailors manning the U.S. Navy's torpedo boats at Midway, the IJN's submarine commander who torpedoed the U.S. carrier *Yorktown,* the Marine gunners who put up a barrage against Japanese air attacks on Midway, and the U.S. Navy's sailors who manned their service's carriers, cruisers, and destroyers. Part III presents some of their experiences and tells their stories—often in their own words.

As veterans will tell you, battles usually involve minutes of adrenaline-charged excitement and fear coupled with hours of anxious waiting and even boredom. Few of the individuals engaged in fighting actually can perceive the whole battle. Each survivor gets his own personal view, and even that intensely felt and remembered view may be mistaken. If you examine a number of accounts, however, you can come to sense what a battle was like for those who fought it and survived.

The following selections were chosen for different reasons. There are, for instance, two memoirs from the pilot and crewman from just one U.S. Navy torpedo bomber: "Out in Front at Midway" (chapter 14) and "Torpedo Squadron 8, the Other Chapter" (chapter 15). Taken together, they give the reader a sense of what many other pilots and aircrew must have encountered on 4 June, and how they must have felt. The report of the actions of the PT boat squadron highlights a little-known aspect of the battle ("Report of Incidents in Connection with Participation of Motor Torpedo Boat Squadron One in the Battle of Midway Island, June 4–6, 1942," chapter 17). The accounts of signalman Peter Karetka ("'Flags' at Midway," chapter 23) and communicator Frank Fabian ("We Weren't Going to Go Off and Leave the Ship: Oral History of Frank Fabian," chapter 24) present the story of the battle "from the deckplates." By contrast, historian John Lundstrom's account of RADM Raymond Spruance's decision to launch the planes of the *Enterprise* and *Hornet* on the morning of 4 June reveals the factors behind Spruance's decision—a major factor in the American victory ("Mounting the TF-16 Strike," chapter 18). Admiral Thach's account of his fighter squadron's clash with Japanese Zeros takes the reader right back into the furious action in the skies above the Japanese carriers ("Flying into a Beehive," chapter 20).

"Five Fateful Minutes at Midway" (chapter 19), Mitsuo Fuchida's account of how the Japanese carriers suffered at the hands of attacking U.S. Navy dive-bombers the morning of 4 June, contains a major error. Captain Fuchida's 1955 account said that the decks of the Japanese carriers were loaded with strike aircraft when the dive-bombers struck. That was not true. Instead, the Japanese carriers had lowered their returning strike aircraft to their hangars and were cycling fighters through their CAP stations. Photographs that are in the collection of the U.S. Navy's History and Heritage Command taken by attacking B-17s on 4 June show clearly that the only aircraft on the decks of the Japanese carriers were fighters. However, Captain Fuchida's memory of the *Akagi*'s hangars being crowded with both bombs and torpedoes is correct. The hangars of the Japanese carriers were conflagrations waiting to happen.

Captain Fuchida's flawed account shaped most subsequent histories of the Battle of Midway. For example, LCDR Thomas E. Powers, USNR, writing in 1967, accepted Fuchida's claim that the Japanese carriers' decks were loaded with armed and fueled strike aircraft (dive-bombers and torpedo bombers) when the U.S. dive-bombers first attacked. Powers also believed that the antiaircraft fire of the *kidō butai* was effective, when a careful reading of the accounts (admittedly few) of the surviving U.S. attackers did not suggest this was the case. Powers' article also described the Japanese attacks in the Aleutians as a "feint" ("Incredible Midway," chapter 26). This was also incorrect, but it is important to point out that it was what was accepted as true at the time. Finally, Lieutenant Commander Powers could not understand why the Japanese could not include the carrier *Zuikaku* in the order of battle for the Midway operations. In making this point, Powers was assuming that the IJN produced carrier squadrons the way that the U.S. Navy did—but the Japanese did not. Their carrier squadrons were an integral part of each carrier, not independent units that could shift from carrier to carrier as the need arose.

Two comments on the essay by Lieutenant Commander Powers have been included—*not* in order to highlight his errors, but rather to show that details matter in telling the story of a battle ("Comment and Discussion: 'Incredible Midway,'" chapter 27). The task of historians and those told to prepare after-action reports is difficult. Details matter, but what if the details are not available—hidden, destroyed after the engagement, or lost on a sunken ship (as then–Rear Admiral Fletcher's papers were lost when the *Yorktown* sank)? What if one side's total account of a battle is available but the other side's is not? Captain Fuchida was an experienced and important officer in the IJN. Who could have had good reason in the 1950s to question his recollections?

It took more than sixty years to get a full and accurate Japanese account of the Battle of Midway—Jonathan Parshall and Anthony Tully's *Shattered Sword, The Untold Story of the Battle of Midway.* Parshall and Tully acknowledged that their book was, "in a sense, a vast collaborative effort on the part of the wider Japanese naval history community."[1] The Naval Institute, through its publishing, book reviews, and "Comment and Discussion" section of *Proceedings,* has encouraged this sort of collaboration and has helped bring to light the changing assessments of the Battle of Midway and of World War II in the Pacific.

Rounding out part III of the anthology is a brief excerpt by historian John Lundstrom describing the participation of a Royal Navy liaison officer in the battle and of the contribution of that officer and his service to the later success of the U.S. Navy in its campaign against the IJN ("The Battle of Midway I: The Most God-Awful Luckiest Coordinated Attack," chapter 22). The article on VADM Stanhope Ring's unfortunate decision to turn in the opposite direction from the *kidō butai* on 4 June needs to be supplemented by the mention of Ring's service in 1940 with the Royal Navy carrier *Ark Royal.* It was the Royal Navy that pioneered central control and coordination of CAPs while the *Ark Royal* was serving in the Mediterranean. U.S. Navy liaison officers, serving as observers, reported on the Royal Navy's achievements and stimulated a thorough review of carrier defenses that was undertaken by the forces commanded by VADM William Halsey in the summer of 1941.

CHAPTER 14

Out in Front at Midway

Compiled by Dr. Fred H. Allison

Naval History, June 2004: pp. 51–53

Hours before U.S. Navy pilots staggered the powerful Japanese fleet bearing down on Midway Island on 4 June 1942—changing the course of World War II—25 U.S. Marine Corps pilots of Marine Fighter Squadron 221 (VMF-221) sortied to meet the first thrust of the Japanese, a 108-plane strike force inbound to blast the island. Only 15 Marines survived the brief encounter. One, then-Captain John F. Carey . . . , was perhaps the first American to draw Japanese blood in the war's most important Pacific battle. In two interviews, one in 1982 and one in 2001, Carey recounts his experiences at the Battle of Midway.

Q: Why were you and your squadron on Midway and what were conditions there?

Carey: We started out on the USS *Saratoga* [CV-3] to go to Wake [Island], part of the Wake relief force. The task force got about 200 miles from Wake, and Wake fell. The relief force turned around and went back, and they decided to put us off on Midway. We flew on up to Midway on Christmas Day of 1941. We had two Christmases, one on board ship and another one on [Midway] because we crossed the International Date Line. Things were quiet at the time. A civilian force was building up the island. We were pretty perturbed because they didn't want to unload ships on overtime. Anyway, we ended up on Eastern Island, which had the airfield. Construction work went on, revetments were built for the aircraft, dugouts were built in which we would sleep, and routine training went on.

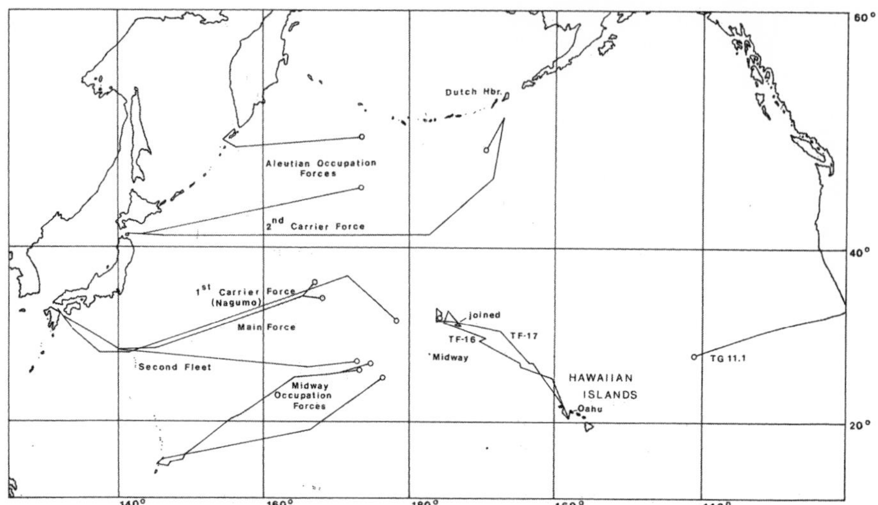

Map 2. This map clearly shows the degree to which Japanese naval forces were dispersed as they closed on Midway and the Aleutians. In separating his forces, Admiral Isoroku Yamamoto ran the risk that one of them could be attacked before the other forces could come to its rescue. By contrast, ADM Chester Nimitz concentrated his most effective naval units in one force, ready to strike the Japanese *kidō butai* as soon as it was located.

Lundstrom, *The First Team*, p. 321

Q: Was VMF-221 the only squadron on the island?

Carey: No, VMSB-241 [Marine Scout Bombing Squadron 241] had the SB2U-3s [Vindicator aircraft]. They had flown out from Hawaii previously, escorted by a PBY [Catalina aircraft].

Q: What type of flying did you do, and what were the living conditions at the time?

Carey: At that time no one knew an attack was imminent. We were just an outpost. It was really a communications and refueling station. Submarines would come in and go out on patrol. We took our hats off to those guys. They were the ones fighting the war at the moment.

Life in these dugouts was not the greatest. You did the best you could to make them comfortable. The mess hall provided good food. There was no alcohol on the island, no clubs or anything like that. We amused ourselves watching the gooney birds.

During this time we ran routine patrols around the island. We were flying two-plane sections and six-plane divisions. On normal training flights, we would patrol around the island and then we would run tactics and dogfights to try to keep everyone in shape.

Periodically a Japanese submarine would surface and lob a few shells onto the island. About the second time this happened we put up an evening patrol. We alternated with the other squadrons. We had two 100-pound bombs on the fighters, which were F2A Brewster Buffaloes. One night, in about February 1942, [CAPT] Phil White and I were on patrol and a little sub popped up. There was a ceiling of about 1,200 feet that evening. We saw the sub and went after it, dropped our bombs, and missed. We didn't have enough altitude. But we came around and strafed the sub and it immediately submerged. If we had had depth charges on instead of bombs it would have been duck soup; we would have had a sub.

Q: The Buffaloes weren't real good planes, were they?

Carey: No, but they were a lot of fun to fly. A bunch were lost at Midway. They just didn't compare to the Japanese Zero.

Q: When did you first get any idea that the Japanese might attack?

Carey: Things went on pretty normally until May 1942, and then we began to get progressive reports that something was about to happen. At the time we didn't know that the Japanese communications code had been broken. We thought the intelligence people were really good. They were talking about the Japanese coming up, and reporting, "Midway is about to be attacked." We began to train more intensely and reinforcements began to come in—[Army Air Forces] B-26s, Martins, and B-17s. We objected to the B-17s being out there because we had to pump gas for them by hand from barrels. It was a heck of a job. The Marines were helping the Army Air Forces; mostly they just came out with an aircrew, and we provided support for them. The Navy sent in I think it was six TBFs [Avenger aircraft], the first TBFs that got into action.

At that time VMF-221 was augmented by seven F4Fs [Wildcat aircraft]. Interestingly, we threw away our life vests to lighten the plane; but we did have parachutes. At that time I had in my division more pilots qualified in the F4F than any other division in the squadron, so I got the Grummans [F4Fs] instead of the F2A. [CAPT] Marion Carl was my second section commander, [CAPT Francis P.] McCarthy was my third section leader, and I led the division.

Q: What do you recall of that fateful day?

Carey: As we got closer to 4 June, everybody was getting more and more nervous. Intelligence was saying a big Japanese force was due on 3 June. They didn't know where it was going to hit, just that it was coming. Then we were told it was delayed, that it wasn't due in until 4 June. We said, "Geez, we must have some damn good intelligence out there. There must be submarines or something watching this force." We were just amazed they knew the size of the force and when they were going to hit us.

Sure enough, that morning we were on the alert on the predawn patrol. For some reason, McCarthy and the last section did not join up with us. I never did find out what happened to him. The call came in to land and refuel. McCarthy didn't get the word on that either—four of us landed and he was still flying around with two planes. We landed, refueled, and were ready. Just before we were about to take off again, McCarthy's section came in, for low fuel.

And then the siren went off and the scramble came in. My wingman's airplane fell off the planks in the dugout and got stuck in his revetment. It ended up that, out of the six planes I should have had with me, I was alone as the leader of the division, with Marion Carl and his wingman behind me.

You can imagine the confusion that morning. Boy, we had all the fighters taking off; the B-26s were getting off and the B-17s. The people running the radar, even though it was an early version, vectored us to the enemy formation and even had the altitude right. They had no altitude readout, but however they figured it, they vectored us right to them. By the time they all got squared away and ready to go, the squadron was pretty well split up into divisions.

We circled for altitude. I think we were typical young aviators, ready to go into battle; we'd been waiting for it, trained for it. We cleared our guns and, boy, here we go! Marion sent his wingman up to fly on my wing. We were the first ones to contact the enemy, to see them. I saw this flight coming in and it was below us. We were at 14,000 feet.

Q: Was the sun behind you?

Carey: Yes, we went out to the northwest. I gave the tally-ho to the rest of the squadron. There were 17 or 19 planes in the formation. I rolled into an overhead attack on the first of this group of Japanese dive bombers that was coming in. I went down through the formation and got the leader. It just exploded into a fireball—I had to push over even more to avoid flying through all the debris. [2nd Lt. Clayton M.] Canfield was on my wing at the time and he stayed with me, and I think he picked off one of them. The Zeros were at 14,000 feet and the attacking bomber force was at 12,000 feet. Marion went through the fighter protection, which was behind the bombers. We never could understand why they were that far behind the aircraft they were supposed to be protecting. Marion pulled a bunch of them back with him, and that gave us a chance to come back and make a second pass at this formation.

On that initial attack, once you started getting shot at it awakened you to reality in a hurry. I no sooner rolled over into that first attack than I got one in my windshield, which was a thick, bulletproof windshield, and I thought, "Geez, these boys are serious." But Canfield and I came back up to make a second pass at them, and I got hit in both legs coming down through. With neither leg operable, I thought the best thing to do was to go home. I got back to the island as best I could.

Q: Could you feel the rudders?

Carey: No, not at all. This black cloud would come in and get about to the instrument panel, and I'd shake it off and go on. I couldn't use either leg, but I didn't know how badly I was hurt. I was headed back to the island, and this wave [of blacking out] again would come in, and I'd push it off. Evidently, it was a strong human instinct to survive.

Q: What was your altitude?

Carey: I came all the way down to about 1,000 feet and my windshield was glazed over, spidered up. But it was always in the back of my mind that I was passing out, and I fought that thing back enough that I could control the plane with the stick. I flew the routine to get back to the field, circling, letting them know I was a friendly and so on. I got in there, and my wingman was still with me. Besides my legs, one of the tires had been shot out, so when I landed and it was rolling out, I started to ground loop [a sharp, out-of-control pivot around one of the main landing gear, quickly reversing direction] and I couldn't control it because I couldn't use either leg. One of the last things I remember is the two guys walking along beside the runway. I reached out and yelled and waved to them, "Get away, get away!" because I was starting to ground-loop into them. The last I saw they disappeared under the wing—I didn't know if I hit them or not. Apparently, the wing went over them. I ended up ground-looping into one of the revetments. I know when I hit the revetment my head went forward and hit the gun sight. I waved and yelled at some of the ground Marines there in the defense battalion. They came and pulled me out of the plane and into one of the machine-gun revetments.

Just about then the Japanese wave hit. Bombs were falling, then Zeros were strafing the field at low altitude. This was the first engagement many of these antiaircraft gunners had ever been in, and you could see the tracers and they just weren't leading enough. Boy, I wanted to get ahold of those guns and move it out in front. They got some, but they just weren't giving enough lead.

When it settled down, they took me into the hospital. Our flight surgeon came in and looked at me and shook his head and said, "He'll never walk again." I'm happy to have proved him wrong. This was early in the morning, and they evacuated me and Herby [CAPT Herbert M.] Merrill. He was burned and his fighter had been shot up, but he landed just off the lagoon and was picked up by a PT boat. Herby and I were flown back that night to the hospital on Pearl. I remained there until the end of the month and then was evacuated back to the States. I ended up in San Diego. When I landed at North Island, some of the Marines from the other side of the field came over and said, "Hi, how are you doing? I heard about you." Then I went into the San Diego naval hospital.

Q: What is your final assessment of that day?

Carey: We took a tremendous licking of course, but obviously it was worth it. We took it less than they did—but [it] was a turning point.

> Captain Carey served a full career as a Marine aviator and retired as a colonel. He is best known for pioneering helicopter tactics. For his action at the battle of Midway, Colonel Carey was awarded the Navy Cross.

— *AUTHOR* —

Dr. Allison researched and edited these interviews—one conducted by Dr. David Thompson, administrator of the Sandhills Community College (Pinehurst, North Carolina) Oral History Project and a volunteer with the Marine Corps' Oral History program—as part of his duties as an oral historian at Marine Corps History and Museums Division, Marine Corps University. He is a retired Marine Corps major and served as an F-4 radar intercept officer.

CHAPTER 15

Torpedo Squadron 8, the Other Chapter

By LT H. H. Ferrier, USN

Proceedings, October 1964: pp. 72–76

The gallant but little-known role of a six-plane all-volunteer TBF detachment, of which the author and his pilot were members, adds further to the record of the terrible, yet triumphant, sacrifices made during the Battle of Midway.

Torpedo Squadron Eight was commissioned at Norfolk, Virginia, in the late summer of 1941 as an element of carrier Air Group Eight, better known then as the *Hornet* Air Group. The ceremony took place in front of an old World War I hangar at Chambers Field on the Naval Air Station. East Field, which is now the operating portion of NAS, Norfolk, had not been completed. The first commanding officer of Torpedo Eight, who also led the squadron in their fateful flight, was Lieutenant Commander John C. Waldron, U.S. Navy, a veteran of more than 20 years of naval service.

The first aircraft assigned to the squadron were SBN-1s. These planes were a mid-wing design of the Brewster Aircraft Company, manufactured by the Naval Aircraft Factory, Philadelphia. They were used to provide pilot training for our newly commissioned squadron as there was a shortage of TBD-1 Douglas Devastators and the TBF-1 Grumman Avenger had not yet reached the production stage. The rest of the Air Group was little better equipped; the bombing and scouting squadrons were assigned SBC-4s, a mid-1930 biplane scout bomber built by the Curtiss Aircraft Company.

I first reported to the squadron on 7 September 1941, a green but enthusiastic radioman striker fresh from the Aviation Radio School at NAS, Jacksonville, Florida. My first flight involved an attempt to locate a mobile direction finder station which was somewhere in the Dismal Swamp area. We then had only manual direction finders which required some skill to operate. Since the pilot and I were both new at this challenging exercise our success was something less than spectacular. It was not long, however, before gunnery, torpedo tactics, bombing, and Field Carrier Landing Practice were familiar and meaningful terms to me.

Our training was progressing satisfactorily, and finally, in October, we received a few TBD-1 aircraft. The Japanese attack on Pearl Harbor that December and our immediate entry into a state of war caused a rapid acceleration of training, culminated by a month-long shakedown cruise by the *Hornet* and her embarked air group in January 1942.

Shortly after our return to Norfolk, it was decided to form a detachment of approximately 80 officers and men who would remain in Norfolk and take delivery of the first TBF-1s. The *Hornet,* with the main portion of the squadron, left immediately thereafter for the Pacific. In March 1942, members of our detachment were sent to the Grumman factory on Long Island to learn as much as possible about the airplane from the engineers and builders-this was in the days before the Naval Air Technical Training Command mobile trainers and the Fleet Indoctrination Program. It was an interesting experience, but the knowledge we gained was very limited.

In the latter part of March we received and flew our first of 21 shiny new Grumman Avengers. (Actually, the Avenger tag was given to the airplane after the Battle of Midway to exemplify the mission and dedication of all torpedo squadrons-to avenge the heroic sacrifice of their predecessors.) We were all impressed with the Avengers' speed, maneuverability, and ruggedness.

At Quonset Point, Rhode Island, we made our first high-speed torpedo drops of a newly designed torpedo which was capable of surviving drop speeds of 125 knots and 125–150 feet of altitude. This, we knew, would give us an advantage over the TBDs and their 100-knot, 100-foot attack capability. After only a few days of the test program had been completed, we were recalled to Norfolk and told to fly our planes across the country and join the *Hornet* and our shipmates in the Pacific.

After an uneventful crossing from San Diego to Pearl Harbor in the USS *Kitty Hawk* (AKV-1), a converted railroad car transport, we unloaded our TBFs at Ford Island and started preparing them for shipboard duty. The *Hornet* was then at sea. Within hours after our arrival a call went out for volunteers to fly six planes to Midway Island. The mission was not stated, but there was little doubt that some action was in the offing. There was no difficulty in obtaining volunteers, and I counted myself lucky to have been one of those chosen.

Bright and early on the morning of 1 June we took off from Ford Island on our eight-hour, 1,300-mile flight to Midway—a little dot in the ocean, northwest of Hawaii. We were guided by two navigators from Patrol Squadron 44, since none of us had ever been to Midway before, and our flight out was uneventful to the point of monotony. The detachment was led by Lieutenant Langdon K. Fieberling, U.S. Navy. I was assigned to fly with Ensign Albert K. Earnest, U.S. Naval Reserve as his radioman and tunnel gunner; our turret gunner was J. D. Manning, AMM3. We flew wing on Lieutenant Fieberling in the first section of three airplanes.

As soon as we arrived we could feel a tension in the air. We were all sure that a meeting with the enemy was not far off. Many planes of all types were in evidence—Brewster F2As, Grumman F4Fs, Douglas SBDs, and Chance Vought SB2Us, all flown by Marines; and Boeing B-17s, Consolidated B-24s and Martin B-26s being flown by the Army Air Corps. Incidentally, the B-26s were equipped as torpedo planes, carrying their "fish" externally below the bomb bay. And, of course, the venerable Consolidated PBYs were present.

We quickly prepared our planes for combat, which included loading six of the new type of torpedoes which we had been testing so recently. They had been flown to Midway under the wings of the PBYs. We all felt exhilarated at the prospect of meeting the enemy. I'm not sure now why we did it, but we put patches of masking tape on the leading edges of our wings and painted black circles on them to simulate gun ports. I know we were not particularly impressed with the effectiveness of the single .30-caliber machine gun which was synchronized to fire through the propeller arc. We had much greater confidence in the .50-caliber gun turret, and .30-caliber tunnel gun which covered our rear.

That evening Lieutenant Fieberling called us all together and quickly confirmed our suspicions that something momentous was about to happen. He said the Navy believed that a Japanese thrust in the direction of Hawaii was imminent and that Midway Island was most certainly a target of that thrust. We were also told that the Navy expected the Japanese to attack the Aleutian Islands but that this attack would be merely a diversionary tactic to draw our ships away from the sea around Midway and Hawaii.

For the next two mornings, we were up at 0400, warming up our engines and then standing by in an alert status until 0700. The rest of the time was spent in exploring the island and chasing the Gooney birds. We were camped on Eastern Island which was then nothing more than a long, low strip of sand, with the runway taking up almost its entirety. What little space remained was occupied by aircraft parking revetments, tents and a scattered collection of wooden buildings.

On the morning of 4 June, we were up and manning our planes at 0400, as usual. About an hour after we had shut down, a Marine officer came running to our plane and told us to start our engine. He stated that unknown planes had been sighted about 100 miles away by a patrol plane. We started up and joined the other planes of our group taxiing out to the take-off spot.

Immediately after taking off, we joined up with the others in two sections of three planes each, climbed to 2,000 feet, and headed out on a course of 320 degrees True at 160 knots. Very shortly after the take-off, a single pass was made at us by two or three Japanese planes, one of which Ensign Earnest tentatively identified as a Messerschmitt-109, a plane which was reputedly being flown by the Japanese. In all probability, the enemy planes were Zeros or Vals from the force that was heading in to attack Midway. After this brief encounter, we climbed to 4,000 feet and continued on our original course.

We sighted the enemy carrier force at approximately 0700 about 15 miles away. In his post-battle report Ensign Earnest had reckoned their numbers at ten ships. In reality there were 21 ships in the formation, including four carriers. Almost simultaneously with our sighting of the enemy we were attacked by their combat air patrol.

It was evident at once that we were outnumbered.

The pilots immediately pushed over into a dive and applied full throttle to the engines. On the second firing pass of the attacking Zeros, the turret gunner, Manning, was hit and his turret put out of action. I remember looking over my shoulder to see why he had stopped firing. The sight of his slumped and lifeless body startled me. Quite suddenly, I was a scared, mature old man at 18. I had never seen death before, and here in one awesome moment my friends and I were face to face with it. I lost all sense of time and direction but huddled by my gun hoping for a chance to shoot back.

I recall that, at one point in the battle, I glanced out of the small window on my left and saw an airplane streak by on fire and enter a cloud. The glance was so fleeting that I had no chance to identify it. Unfortunately, it later proved to have been one of ours.

The attacking fighters outnumbered us by at least three to one and it soon became evident that they did not intend that any of us should survive. Another pass and I was out of the fight—our hydraulic system had been hit and the tail wheel was now blocking the field of fire of my gun. My left arm felt a searing pain as a bullet grazed my wrist. It was shortly after this that I was struck a stunning blow on the head and lost consciousness. I shall always remember coming to and viewing through bleary eyes a stream of blood that was rapidly coloring my gun an ugly red. Gingerly I fingered my scalp. After some moments I decided that maybe I was not going to die after all, but I was still unable to contribute anything to the battle.

I was never aware of just how precarious our position was until after the battle. Some few miles short of the enemy carriers, our elevator control cables were severed, and our plane began rapidly plunging toward the water. With foresight,

Ensign Earnest had opened the bomb bay doors at the first attack. Thinking that we were now out of control, he released our torpedo in the direction of a light cruiser and hoped for the best.

Just before we hit the water, he regained altitude control by using the trim tab. Our salvation was by no means assured as two Zeros continued to press home their attacks. About ten minutes later, apparently having run out of ammunition, our two tormenters finally turned away and returned to their carrier. As he glanced back towards the force, Ensign Earnest was unable to see any damage to the Japanese ships, as indeed there was none. Ours was the first of many futile attacks by a total of 51 torpedo planes. Only nine of these planes survived the suicidal assaults.

There still remained the problem of returning to Midway which had not been made any easier by the loss of our compass system as well as the previously recounted control difficulties. No provisions had been made for a standby compass. Ensign Earnest's sole means of navigation now was the sun, and the knowledge that we had departed from Midway on a generally westerly course.

Sometime later when we were heading back towards Midway I crawled up over the bomb bay compartment and sat in the seat immediately behind the pilot. Much later I saw a huge column of black oil smoke seemingly rising from the sea. This proved to be Midway Island with the fuel dump ablaze. It was a most welcome sight to us.

Compared to the battle, our landing was fairly smooth even though it was made on only one main wheel without flaps, the bomb-bay doors open, and only limited elevator control available. At least we were able to walk away from it. A TBF-1 had survived its baptism of fire and had proved itself a rugged, worthy replacement for the TBDs which had been almost completely eliminated from the Navy inventory on the day of the battle. I have made a deliberate effort to remember the Bureau number of the plane in which I saw so much of this battle. It was TBF-1 BUNO 00380, the first plane delivered to the squadron; it bore the side number 8-T-1. I have often wondered since then if our attackers made any greater effort to get us because of our side number, or if they were aware of it and its significance.

Our TBF-1 had been the only plane of the detachment to survive the battle. But the ordeal was not yet ended for us, since we still had to accept the irrefutable loss of our companions. It was our sad task to take inventory and pack their few personal possessions, a treasured book of poems, letters and pictures of sweethearts and families—all of them mirrored somehow their owners.

We did not know until much later just how terrible, yet triumphant, the sacrifices had been that day. The futile attacks of Torpedo Squadrons Three, Six and Eight, and the work of the four Army Air Corps B-26s had unalterably sealed the fate of the Japanese carriers. Our fellow fliers in the bombing and scouting squadrons were thereby enabled to attack the Japanese when they were most vulnerable—while rearming and refueling their aircraft.

— *AUTHOR* —

Following his assignment to Torpedo Squadron 8 (1941–1942), Lieutenant Ferrier served briefly in Torpedo Squadron 3 and then, for sixteen months, in Bombing Squadron 5 on board the USS *Yorktown.* Commissioned as an ensign in January 1945, he was assigned to Composite Squadron 33 at the war's end. He was attached to the Field Command, Armed Forces Special Weapons Project, Albuquerque, New Mexico, from 1952 to 1955. Selected for permanent commission as a limited duty officer in June 1955, he served in Heavy Attack Squadrons 6 (1955 to 1957) and 123 (1959 to 1962) and in Heavy Attack Wing 2 (1957 to 1959). He is now V-3 division officer in the USS *Princeton* (LPH-5).

CHAPTER 16

The Lone Avenger

By Rich Pedroncelli

Naval History, June 2001: pp. 26–29

A young Bert Earnest flew into combat at Midway in the Navy's newest torpedo plane with five of his squadron mates. At the end of the day, he was the only one to come home.

Ensign Bert Earnest was straining to see through the haze in which he was flying. Then an image began to take shape in the distance. "At first I thought it was a Japanese transport, and I told myself, this is going to be like duck soup," he recalls. "But then I looked again, and there was the whole Jap fleet with two carriers."

Sitting in the den of his Ocean Beach, Virginia, home almost 60 years later, retired Captain Albert "Bert" Earnest recalls vividly his role as a young pilot, flying the new Grumman TBF torpedo plane on its first combat mission during the Battle of Midway. Leaning forward in his chair, Earnest points to a large photograph of his plane taken just after he returned from the attack on the Japanese fleet. "They counted over 64 bullet holes," he says. "We lost a lot of good men that day."

A native of Richmond, Earnest graduated from the Virginia Military Institute in 1935 with a degree in civil engineering and a second lieutenant's commission in the field artillery. "I didn't like the artillery. I wanted to fly and tested to get into the Army Air Corps," he says.

He failed the eye exam because of a weak eye muscle, which prevented him from qualifying for flight training. In October 1940, however, the Navy came to Richmond in search of aviation recruits. A friend decided to take the Navy flight test and talked Earnest into accompanying him.

"I took the exam, and they found the same eye problem that the Army had found. But they said it was easy to fix. They gave me some eye exercises and told me to come back in a month," says Earnest. A month later he returned and was reexamined. "They couldn't tell I had a problem." In February 1941, Earnest began naval flight training.

When he finished the following November, he was surprised and dismayed about receiving orders to report to Torpedo Squadron 8 (VT-8). "I had wanted to fly fighters," recalls Earnest. "I had never flown torpedo planes before, not even during flight school, but I knew what they did and it sounded pretty hairy to me."

On 10 December, three days after the Japanese attacked Pearl Harbor, Earnest went to Norfolk, Virginia, and reported for duty to VT-8, stationed on board the recently completed carrier *Hornet* (CV-8).

When Earnest joined VT-8, the ship and her air group were preparing for their shakedown cruise. Lieutenant Commander John Waldron, skipper of VT-8, decided that instead of taking the new pilots along for the shakedown, he would send Earnest and several other new pilots, including Ensign George Gay, to the Advanced Carrier Training Group until the ship returned. While there, Earnest flew mostly SNJ trainers, but he finally got a chance to fly the TBD-1 Devastator that VT-8 was flying. "The TBD was a very easy plane to fly. It had a low wing and it handled beautifully."

On 3 February 1942, the *Hornet* returned, and Earnest and the others rejoined VT-8. With the ship preparing to sail for the Pacific in early March, Waldron worked his squadron continuously, practicing bombing and torpedo runs, along with field carrier landings.

During this time the pilots learned that VT-8 was to get the first of new Grumman TBF-1s to replace their aging TBDs. But with the *Hornet* set to sail soon, it was clear the squadron was not going to be ready to fly the new planes before the ship's departure.

Navy officials decided to split the squadron in half, with Waldron and the most experienced pilots going to war with the *Hornet* in the TBDs. The remainder of the squadron remained at the Norfolk Naval Air Station to receive the new TBFs. When the *Hornet*'s departure was delayed a week, Earnest was left behind with the VT-8 receiving detail.

The first TBFs arrived in mid-March, and the pilots began the task of getting checked out in the new planes. "The TBF was a much better aircraft," recalls Earnest. "It was much faster; the first ones we got were almost as fast as the F4F Wildcat fighters. You could drop a torpedo at a faster speed. It had heavier control forces, and you had to use the tab a lot for the elevators, which saved my life later on." By 1 May, when 21 TBFs had been delivered, the receiving detail was ordered to the Pacific to rejoin the *Hornet* and the rest of the squadron.

After a cross-country flight, the group eventually arrived at Alameda Naval Air Station, where they were loaded on board the *Hammondsport* (APV-2). They were ferried to Pearl Harbor, which they reached on 28 May. But the *Hornet* and her air group, including the remainder of VT-8, already had sailed for Midway the previous day.

It was decided to send six of the new TBFs to Midway to help with the island's defense. "We all volunteered to go. We had been trained to go to war, and we thought this was something exciting," recalls Earnest.

On 1 June, the six TBFs—led by Lieutenant Langdon K. Fieberling, the executive officer of the receiving detail—took off from Ford Island and headed for Midway. To make the 1,200-mile flight, the planes were fitted with extra fuel tanks, and two patrol plane pilots flew with the TBFs as navigators. Accompanying Earnest in the three-man TBF were Radioman Third Class Harry Ferrier, who manned the radio and tunnel gun, and Seaman First Class Jay Manning, the turret gunner. "We'd never trained as a squadron and had no regular crewmen assigned. I had seen them around the squadron before, but didn't know them. They were both fine young men."

The six TBFs made the flight uneventfully and landed on Eastern Island, already crowded with planes preparing to meet the expected Japanese attack. "Everywhere you looked there were planes," recalls Earnest. "I was impressed there were so many B-17s; they were parked all over the place. There were so many airplanes there was almost no place to park."

Fieberling went and met with the Marines. When he returned, he explained the situation. "He told us a Japanese attack was imminent and the island had to be defended. He also told us that we would join with the Marine dive-bombers and make a joint attack on any enemy forces," said Earnest.

In the early morning of 4 June, Earnest, Ferrier, Manning, and the other TBF crews manned their planes before dawn. As they had done since their arrival at Midway, they warmed their engines in anticipation of action. After a half-hour, Earnest cut his engine and waited. "We stayed with the plane until the morning search planes reported in," recalls Earnest. As he sat silently in the cockpit, Earnest watched the sunrise in the eastern sky.

At around 0600, Earnest saw a jeep pull up to Fieberling's plane. A Marine officer climbed out, scrambled up the wing, and talked with him. Another Marine went over to Earnest and shouted, "Enemy forces at 320°, 150 miles," Earnest recalls. He quickly restarted his plane and prepared to take off. Fighters already were taking off as the six TBFs rolled to the runway. The torpedo planes fell into line behind the fighters and lifted off, climbing through the scattered cloud layer.

Forming into two three-plane sections, Earnest took his position in the first section on the left wing of the flight leader, Fieberling. Taking the position on the right of Fieberling was Earnest's close friend, Lieutenant Charlie Brannen.

They climbed to about 4,000 feet, but instead of waiting to form up with the dive-bombers as planned, Fieberling led the group alone toward the enemy on a north easterly course. As Midway began to fade in the distance, Manning, in the turret, said he could see guns firing from the island.

The formation continued on its way, and after about an hour the pilots sighted the Japanese fleet. "I saw a large force ahead of us with at least two carriers. It was the first fleet I had ever seen."

As Earnest spotted the carriers, Manning's voice filled his earphones as he called out, "Here come the Zeros," and began firing his gun.

Zeros swarmed over the torpedo planes, firing away as they passed through the group. Immediately, Fieberling led the formation in a dive toward the water, leveled off at about 200 feet, and headed for the nearest carrier. "When the fighters attacked, we held formation pretty well. The first thing we did as we dove was open our bomb bay doors."

The Zeros continued their attacks as the TBFs bore down on the Japanese carrier. "There were so many of them they were getting into each others' way. You couldn't help but be impressed by how maneuverable they were."

Bullets tore into Earnest's plane as he pressed his attack. As the fighters pulled up after their third pass, Earnest heard the turret gun go silent. From his tunnel gun position in back, Harry Ferrier looked up and saw Manning hanging in his safety harness, obviously dead.

The plane continued to be racked by bullets and cannon shells. "I saw cannon shells exploding along the edge of the wing and could feel bullets hitting the armor plating behind my seat. It was a very frightening thing."

Earnest's problems were only beginning. A Zero made another attack that sent bullets into his plane and severely crippled the TBF. "Suddenly, my elevator control went out and the plane gently began to nose down toward the water. My hydraulics also went out—and then I heard Ferrier's gun fall silent."

As Earnest fought to keep his plane aloft, a shell fragment burst through the canopy and struck him on the side of his cheek, cutting the chin strap on his flight helmet. "Blood spurted all over the place, covering the control panel. I could feel blood going down my neck. All I knew was that I was still alive."

With his plane crippled and losing altitude, his two crewman [*sic*] apparently dead, and himself bleeding from a wound, Earnest knew he probably had no chance of launching his torpedo at the carrier. But he was determined to launch his torpedo at one of the Japanese ships.

He looked around quickly for the closest target, and spotted what appeared to be a Japanese light cruiser just to the left. Earnest broke formation and headed for the ship.

"My ailerons and rudder were okay, so I kicked the plane around and headed for the Japanese ship that happened to be fairly close. I dropped the torpedo at it but doubt if I got a hit. I didn't get much of a lead on it."

Despite dropping the 2,000-lb torpedo, Earnest's TBF continued to descend, and he readied the plane for a water landing. "Instinctively my hand went down to the elevator tab, which I always did during landing to get the tail down. Suddenly the airplane jumped back into the air. I realized I could fly the plane with the elevator tab! I should have known this, but I didn't."

As the plane began to gain altitude slowly, Earnest attracted the attention of two Zeros that immediately focused on the crippled plane. "They just peppered me," he recalled. "I did everything I ever had heard of to throw them off. I kept trying to turn into them-I heard this might work. It didn't seem to bother them a bit; they pounded me at will. They chased me for what seemed like hours but could have been only a few minutes."

After several minutes of dodging and turning with machine guns blazing away at him, the only sound he heard was the drone of his plane's engine. "I didn't hear guns firing anymore. I scanned the sky and there we [*sic*] no fighters. They had left me. They were gone. They had headed back to the carriers."

Alone, Earnest took stock of his situation. His efforts to escape the Zeros had caused him to fly to the northwest, and the Japanese fleet stood between him and Midway. To compound matters, his hydraulics had been shot out, so he could not close his bomb bay doors or lower his flaps, and his compass had been damaged. "Not many things were working in the cockpit," says Earnest. He decided the simplest thing to do was "fly south until I thought I was opposite Midway, then turn back to the east."

"I looked back at the Japanese fleet and couldn't see any signs of damage. I didn't see any airplanes burning on the water or anything. I didn't know what happened to the other guys."

Earnest began flying a southerly course, then was shocked to hear the voice of Harry Ferrier in his earphones. Ferrier had been hit earlier when a bullet pierced the baseball cap he was wearing, grazed his head, and knocked him out. "I had called to him earlier but hadn't gotten an answer," Earnest says.

"I asked Ferrier if he could see if the torpedo had been launched. He said the window was covered in blood and he couldn't see. He asked to move up to the center seat. I said okay."

After settling on his course, Earnest's heart skipped a beat when he sighted another plane in the distance. "I couldn't tell if it was ours or theirs. It was flying in the opposite direction—toward the Japanese—so I figured it was theirs and I ducked into a cloud."

Earnest continued on a southerly course until he thought it was time to turn east. He then flew on an easterly course for more than an hour.

"I decided to climb up through the broken clouds to about 4,000 feet to see if I could see anything. When I broke through the cloud cover, I saw a huge black plume of smoke off to the east." Earnest dove back under the clouds to see if he could spot where the smoke was coming from and saw Kure Island, which he knew was 50 miles to the west of Midway. In his battered TBF, Earnest homed on the plume of smoke, which was coming from a burning fuel tank.

As he neared Midway, he tried to lower the landing gear in preparation for landing. But with the hydraulic system shot out, he had to use the emergency release. "I pulled the release and only one wheel, the left one, came down." Earnest gained altitude, tried to shake the right wheel down, and headed in for a landing. As he made his approach, he was waved off. Earnest pulled the plane up and once again tried to shake the right landing gear loose, then made a second attempt to land.

Again he was waved off. "After the second time I just said the hell with this and came in and landed. I landed nicely on the one wheel . . . until the right wing dropped to the runway. The plane spun around and parked just off the side of the runway. I couldn't have parked it any better. I found out later that during the wave-offs they had been telling me on the radio to bail out, but my radio had been shot out."

As soon as the plane came to a stop, Earnest unbuckled his harness, climbed out of the cockpit, and started to run around to the back of the plane to check on the condition of his gunner, Manning. "A big Marine grabbed me and said, you don't want to go there, you don't want to see that, and led me away."

As he left the field the air raid alert sounded, but instead of enemy planes, the SBD dive bombers of the *Hornet*'s Bombing Squadron 8 (VB-8) came in to land. "This is the first time I knew that U.S. carriers were in the vicinity."

"I reported in to the operations tent and told them what I did and what I had seen. I volunteered to fly dive bombers, but they said they had plenty of dive-bomber pilots and didn't need me." He left the operations tent and went for treatment of his wound.

After he was treated, Earnest wandered back to the airfield, looking to see if any other planes from his flight had returned. Still, none of the other five TBFs had come back. Instead, Earnest ran into some of the pilots from the *Hornet*'s VB-8. They told him of the U.S. carrier task force that had been lying in wait for the Japanese, and of their fruitless search for the enemy carriers that found them landing on Midway almost out of fuel. "They were pretty impressed," recalls Earnest. "After all, I had been in combat and they hadn't. They were anxious to hear about our attack on the Japanese carriers."

As the day drew to a close, Earnest learned of the great U.S. victory. But it soon was evident to him there might have been a high cost in lives, as none of the other TBFs returned. "I hoped they would find some of the others, but as the days passed, they didn't." PBY Catalina flying boats patrolling from Midway picked up survivors of the battle, including George Gay, who had flown a TBD from the *Hornet*'s VT-8, but none of the other TBF crewmen were recovered. Earnest learned later that of the two groups of aircraft from Torpedo 8, only he, Harry Ferrier, and George Gay had survived.

As the days passed, Earnest, Ferrier, and Machinist's Mate J. Coffey, a VT-8 mechanic who had flown from Pearl Harbor to Midway with the TBFs, had the duty of inventorying and packing up their squadron mates' personal belongings. In the meantime, Jay Manning was buried at sea in the lagoon between Eastern and Sand Islands.

Five days after his flight, Bert Earnest returned to Pearl Harbor. When the *Hornet* returned, he rejoined VT-8. "My plane was also taken back to Pearl Harbor where they counted at least 64 7.7-mm machine-gun bullets and 9 20-mm cannon shells."

For his actions at Midway, Earnest received the Navy Cross for his attack on the Japanese task force. He was awarded the Purple Heart and another Navy Cross for getting his badly damaged aircraft back to Midway. Earnest eventually returned to action and made five more torpedo attacks during the war. They included his being credited with hitting the Japanese carrier *Ryujo* in the Battle of the Eastern Solomons, which earned him a third Navy Cross. "I don't really know if I hit it," he recalls. "I didn't claim a hit, but someone said I did and I was given credit."

Thinking back, Earnest questions some of the events surrounding the TBFs attack at Midway, including the fact the group headed alone against the Japanese. "One of the great mysteries of my life," recalls Earnest, "is why Fieberling decided to head straight for the Japanese instead of waiting for the dive-bombers as planned."

"We didn't help hardly a damn thing, but lost quite a few people. We didn't pull the fighters away like the torpedo squadrons from the carriers did. We did waste a lot of their gas and ammunition. I would like to think we had an effect, but I don't think [we] did."

— *AUTHOR* —

Mr. Pedroncelli is an Associated Press photojournalist based in Sacramento, California.

CHAPTER

17

Report of Incidents in Connection with Participation of Motor Torpedo Boat Squadron One in the Battle of Midway Island, 4–6 June, 1942

By LTJG H. S. Parker Jr., USNR

Naval War College Archives

June 7, 1942

From: Executive Officer, Motor Torpedo Boat Squadron One

To: Commander, Motor Torpedo Boat Squadron One

Subject: Report of incidents in connection with participation of Motor Torpedo Boat Squadron One in battle of Midway Island, June 4–6, 1942.

0600 June 4, 1942, PT's [*sic*] 20, 21, 22, 24, 26, 27, 28 & 42 were moored alongside dock at Midway Island, T.H., PT 29 & PT 30 being on patrol at Kure Island, some sixty miles to the west. Air raid alarm sounded, and all boats cleared the dock. At 0620 a large formation of aircraft was sighted to the northwest, proceeding in an easterly direction. At 0630, a tight formation of Japanese level bombers came in from the north, altitude about 8000 feet. These were engaged by Marine AA batteries from shore and by PT 42 with caliber .50 machine gun fire. One aircraft from this formation burst into flames and crashed into the lagoon, her bomb falling separately also into the lagoon, both narrowly missing PT boats in that area.

Motor Torpedo Boat Squadron 1, consisting of ten fast torpedo boats, was formed at Midway in 1942 and was very active during the battle. Eight of the boats were based at Midway. Two were stationed at Kure Island during the battle, and the rest were sent to Kure Island in order to reach farther to the west in search of Japanese stragglers after 6 June. The PT boats carried torpedoes and depth charges, along with a defensive armament of machine guns. This is one of their number in March 1942, exercising in Hawaiian waters.

Navy Department, National Archives

The first wave was immediately followed by another and by one over East Island, immediately after which approximately 18 dive bombers dived on East Island from the North East, all of which pulled out near the vicinity of the PT boats scattered about the lagoon and were engaged by all caliber .50 (four per boat) and caliber .30 (one per boat) machine guns, and in some cases by rifle and Thompson sub-machine gun fire of all boats while aircraft were within range. Immediately thereafter Sand Island was subjected to dive bombing attacks and strafing, and all dive bombers and fighters within range were likewise engaged by PT boats. One of these, a zero type fighter flying west, altitude about 500 feet was seen to crash in trees on Sand Island after having been engaged for some seconds by PT's [*sic*] 21 & 22, tracers from both boats indicating perfect shooting. Meanwhile the whole area was being strafed by both dive bombers and a large numbers [*sic*] of zero type fighters. . . .

Near the end of the raid a fighter plane, thought to be one of ours, probably a Brewster Buffalo, was seen to crash just outside the reef to the north, followed by two of what apparently were zero type fighters. The pilot escaped by parachute, . . . but was followed down by the two opposing aircraft, which each dived over the spot where he had landed. It was not seen if any bullets were fired at him, . . . but from the manoeuvers over the spot it was indicated that he was strafed in the water. Two PT boats attempted to reach the spot, but were prevented by the reef, and then PT 26 was sent out the channel and around the island to search the area. Nothing was found. . . .

Also every officer and man aboard the PT boats is commended for his coolness and bravery. Although the PT boat personnel were the only exposed personnel anywhere in the area, every man carried out his assignment with coolness and the utmost enthusiasm and the utmost disregard for his own safety. Fire was held until the range was closed to a sure chance for hits, and in only one case was fire opened on our own aircraft, and then only for an instant, despite the extreme difficulty of identification at some attitudes during the mellee [*sic*]. . . .

At about 0730, Japanese aircraft having disappeared, PT's [*sic*] 20, 22 & 28 returned to Sand Island dock and sent fire and rescue parties ashore. . . .

At 0815 The [*sic*] air raid alarm sounded again; all boats cleared dock for lagoon. PT 20, 22, 26 and 42 got underway for waters outside the island to rescue pilots of planes thought to be down. [Five pilots and two aircrew were rescued.] . . .

At about 1730 orders received to fuel all boats to capacity and proceed to a point 170 miles bearing 338 [deg.] T from Midway, there to contact and attack enemy main body.

All boats underway at 2115 with 200 gallons of extra fuel carried in drums on deck, for designated spot at 30 knots. A great deal of difficulty was experienced by all boats due to considerable quantities of salt water in fuel, causing repeated failure of main engines, generators, and consequently, in some cases, radios.

PT 29 and PT 30 arrived at reported position at 2315 and saw no signs of enemy vessels, remaining boats in squadron arriving at location at about 0300. Entire area was searched until daylight by all units with no contacts being made. Units started independently for Midway at 0430. PT 20 and PT 21 sighted column of smoke—distance about 15 miles to the west. Closed at 40 knots, but smoke disappeared. Nothing further seen except large area fuel oil and wreckage, apparently Japanese.

At 0730 Enemy [*sic*] observation seaplane (biplane) attacked PT 20, strafing twice and dropping 2–50 lb. bombs, one of which landed only 10 yards astern of PT 20. All hands were thrown down by concussion, but no damage was done. Aircraft was engaged throughout but escaped. At 1230 PT's [*sic*] 20, 21, 25 and 42 encountered task force (US) consisting of two carriers and escort ships. . . .

By 1720 all units had returned to Midway. The lack of contact by any unit was due to fact that contact spot was designated from position of main body on afternoon of June 4th, while during the hours of darkness as PT's [*sic*] were headed for that spot, enemy was heading south-westerly, being, at time when PT's [*sic*] were at supposed contact area, about 100 to 150 miles to the southwest of them, or west of Midway, distance 60 to 150 miles. It is thought that PT's [*sic*] 29 and 30 would have had excellent chance of contact if they had remained at Kure Island. It is believed that if PT boats had been sent out early enough to have proceeded to contact location during daylight, taking advantage of subsequent aircraft contact reports, in order to arrive at a location recently verified shortly after darkness, there would have been excellent chance of success.

On June 6, 1942, eleven casualties of marine [*sic*] detachment defending Midway, killed in air raid of June 4th were buried at sea from PT boats.

CHAPTER

18

Mounting the TF-16 Strike

By John B. Lundstrom

Black Shoe Carrier Admiral (Annapolis, MD: Naval Institute Press, 2006): chap. 17 The Battle of Midway I: "Give Them the Works", p. 244

[RADM Raymond] Spruance's role in the initial phase of the battle was carefully circumscribed, with little discretion on his part. When he thought TF-16 was within range of one of the enemy carrier groups he was to dispatch every *Enterprise* and *Hornet* strike plane (seventy-one dive bombers and twenty-nine torpedo planes, plus twenty escort fighters) in a coordinated surprise assault. In truth he could do little else, given his flight decks were configured not only with attack aircraft but also combat air patrol fighters. The limiting factor for range was the maximum accepted radius of 175 miles for the TBDs and escort fighters, the new F4F-4 Wildcats. In contrast, the SBD dive bombers could go well beyond two hundred miles. Spruance's task appeared straightforward. However, few aspects of the Battle of Midway are less understood than the circumstances behind the launch of the U.S. strike groups.

At 0615 [on 4 June] Spruance reckoned the target, if correctly reported (a big "if," which was why Fletcher added "as soon as definitely located" [to his direction to Spruance]), to be about 175 miles away. Should he launch immediately? Mitscher [captain of the *Hornet*] thought so. He directed the *Hornet* aircrews, less group and squadron commanders, to man planes, but stood down when the *Enterprise* did not turn into the wind. In truth the relative position of the opposing forces, the wind direction and velocity, and tactical considerations made the decision of when and how to launch the strikes much more complex than it might first appear. TF-16 opened the battle poised on the enemy's left flank, an admirable

Eleven aircraft of Torpedo Squadron 6 (VT-6) on the *Enterprise* on the morning of 4 June. The aircraft are TBD Devastators, and the torpedoes slung under the aircraft are visible. The *Enterprise* sent fourteen Devastators against the *kidō butai* that day. Only four of LCDR Eugene E. Lindsey's squadron returned, and Lindsey did not survive their attack on the Japanese carriers. Astern of the *Enterprise* is her plane guard destroyer, assigned the task of picking up any aviators who had to ditch their aircraft.

U.S. Naval Institute Photo Archive

A Midway-based PBY patrol bomber flies above the *Yorktown* early on 4 June as her attack aircraft await news on the location of the Japanese carriers. U.S. Navy carrier doctrine was to launch a carrier's whole strike force in order to send a pulse of attacking planes against an enemy carrier's defenses. IJN doctrine was to send half of a carrier's strike aircraft in an attack but to normally operate two, four, or six carriers together so that the offensive pulse would still overwhelm an opponent's defenses.

U.S. Naval Institute Photo Archive

tactical position, but one that meant the track of the enemy carriers crossed ahead at nearly a right angle to the incoming U.S. strike planes. Finding them was no sure thing. There must be some margin for error if the target did not appear at the expected intercept point and the strike must search for it. However, an immediate launch at 0615 actually translated to an outbound leg of well over 175 miles, too much under the chancy circumstances for the TBDs and F4Fs. That was because the breeze blew from the southeast at a modest six knots, so little that the carriers had to steam above twenty-five knots to generate enough wind velocity over the deck for flight operations. Diverging southeast would take them on a tangent away from the target and substantially increase the distance their planes must fly to get there. If the launch, as expected, lasted forty-five minutes, the target would be twenty miles farther away, closer to two hundred miles, when the groups could actually depart. Fletcher's TF-17 faced different circumstances in the Battle of the Coral Sea, when on both days the Japanese obligingly steamed toward the U.S. carriers. When [ADM Aubrey] Fitch launched at two hundred miles he counted on the target being thirty miles closer when his planes arrived. Spruance had no such assurance. [CAPT Miles] Browning suggested the launch begin at 0700, when the enemy should be 155 miles away. When the strike planes actually departed, that distance should have increased to 175 miles. Eager to attack as soon as good judgment would permit, Spruance readily agreed. At 0638 he ordered the *Enterprise* and *Hornet* to commence launching at 0700.

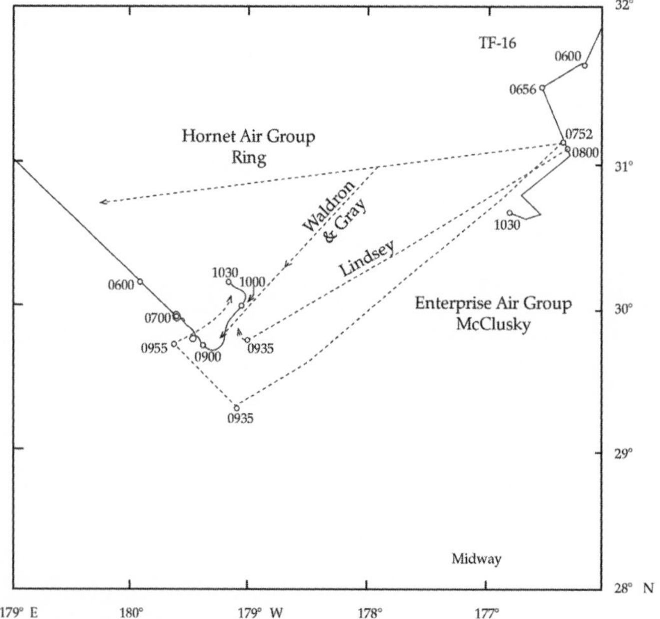

Map 3. The *Hornet* and *Enterprise* attacks

Lundstrom, *Black Shoe Carrier Admiral*, p. 259

CHAPTER

19

Five Fateful Minutes at Midway

By Mitsuo Fuchida and Masatake Okumiya

Proceedings, June 1955 (pp. 660–665)

This article is an excerpt from the book *Midway, The Battle That Doomed Japan, The Japanese Navy's Story* (Annapolis, MD: Naval Institute Press, 1955).

Preparations for a counter-strike against the enemy had continued on board our four carriers throughout the enemy torpedo attacks. One after another, planes were hoisted from the hangar and quickly arranged on the flight deck. There was no time to lose. At 1020 Admiral Nagumo gave the order to launch when ready. On *Akagi*'s flight deck all planes were in position with engines warming up. The big ship began turning into the wind. Within five minutes all her planes would be launched.

Five minutes! Who would have dreamed that the tide of battle would shift completely in that brief interval of time?

Visibility was good. Clouds were gathering at about 3,000 meters, however, and though there were occasional breaks, they afforded good concealment for approaching enemy planes. At 1024 the order to start launching came from the bridge by voice-tube. The Air Officer flapped a white flag, and the first Zero fighter gathered speed and whizzed off the deck. At that instant a lookout screamed: "Hell-divers!" I looked up to see three black enemy planes plummeting toward our ship. Some of our machine guns managed to fire a few frantic bursts at them, but it was too late. The plump silhouettes of the American "Dauntless" dive bombers quickly grew larger, and then a number of black objects suddenly floated eerily from their wings. Bombs! Down they came straight toward me! I fell instinctively to the deck and crawled behind a command post mantelet.

The terrifying scream of dive bombers reached me first, followed by the crashing explosion of a direct hit. There was a blinding flash and then a second explosion, much louder than the first. I was shaken by a weird blast of warm air. There was still another shock, but less severe, apparently a near-miss. Then followed a startling quiet as the barking of guns suddenly ceased. I got up and looked at the sky. The enemy planes were already gone from sight.

The attackers had gotten in unimpeded because our fighters, which had engaged the preceding wave of torpedo planes only a few moments earlier, had not yet had time to regain altitude. Consequently, it may be said that the American dive bombers' success was made possible by the earlier martyrdom of their torpedo planes. Also, our carriers had no time to evade because clouds hid the enemy's approach until he dove down to the attack. We had been caught flatfooted in the most vulnerable condition possible—decks loaded with planes armed and fueled for an attack.

Looking about, I was horrified at the destruction that had been wrought in a matter of seconds. There was a huge hole in the flight deck just behind the amidship elevator. The elevator itself, twisted like molten glass, was drooping into the hangar. Deck plates reeled upward in grotesque configurations. Planes stood tail up, belching livid flame and jet-black smoke. Reluctant tears streamed down my cheeks as I watched the fires spread, and I was terrified at the prospect of induced explosions which would surely doom the ship. I heard [Commander Shogo] Masuda yelling, "Inside! Get inside! Everybody who isn't working! Get inside!"

Unable to help, I staggered down a ladder and into the ready room. It was already jammed with badly burned victims from the hangar deck. A new explosion was followed quickly by several more, each causing the bridge structure to tremble. Smoke from the burning hangar gushed through passageways and into the bridge and ready room, forcing us to seek other refuge. Climbing back to the bridge I could see that *Kaga* and *Soryu* had also been hit and were giving off heavy columns of black smoke. The scene was horrible to behold.

Akagi had taken two direct hits, one on the after rim of the amidship elevator, the other on the rear guard of the portside of the flight deck. Normally, neither would have been fatal to the giant carrier, but induced explosions of fuel and munitions devastated whole sections of the ship, shaking the bridge and filling the air with deadly splinters. As the fire spread among planes lined up wing to wing on the after deck, their torpedoes began to explode, making it impossible to bring the fires under control. The entire hangar area was a blazing inferno, and the flames moved swiftly toward the bridge.

Because of the spreading fire, our general loss of combat efficiency, and especially the severance of external communication facilities, Nagumo's Chief of Staff, Rear Admiral Kusaka, urged that the Flag be transferred at once to light cruiser *Nagara*. Admiral Nagumo gave only a half-hearted nod, but Kusaka patiently continued his entreaty; "Sir, most of our ships are still intact. You must command them."

The situation demanded immediate action, but Admiral Nagumo was reluctant to leave his beloved flagship. Most of all he was loath to leave behind the officers and men of *Akagi*, with whom he had shared every joy and sorrow of war. With tears in his eyes, Captain Aoki spoke up: "Admiral, I will take care of the ship. Please, we all implore you, shift your flag to *Nagara* and resume command of the Fleet."

At this moment Lieutenant Commander Nishibayashi, the Flag Secretary, came up and reported to Kusaka: "All passages below are afire, Sir. The only means of escape is by rope from the forward window of the bridge down the deck, then by the outboard passage to the anchor deck. *Nagara*'s boat will come alongside the anchor deck port, and you can reach it by rope ladder."

Kusaka made a final plea to Admiral Nagumo to leave the doomed ship. At last convinced that there was no possibility of maintaining command from *Akagi*, Nagumo bade the Captain good-bye and climbed from the bridge window with the aid of Nishibayashi. The Chief of Staff and other staff and headquarters officers followed. The time was 1046.

On the bridge there remained only Captain Aoki, his Navigator, the Air Officer, a few enlisted men, and myself. Aoki was trying desperately to get in touch with the engine room. The Chief Navigator was struggling to see if anything could be done to regain rudder control. The others were gathered on the anchor deck fighting the raging fire as best they could. But the unchecked flames were already licking at the bridge. Hammock mantelets around the bridge structure were beginning to burn. The Air Officer looked back at me and said, "Fuchida, we won't be able to stay on the bridge much longer. You'd better get to the anchor deck before it is too late."

In my condition this was no easy task. Helped by some sailors, I managed to get out of the bridge window and slid down the already smoldering rope to the gun deck. There I was still ten feet above the flight deck. The connecting monkey ladder was red hot, as was the iron plate on which I stood. There was nothing to do but jump, which I did. At the same moment another explosion occurred in the hangar, and the resultant blast sent me sprawling. Luckily the deck on which I landed was not yet afire, for the force of the fall knocked me out momentarily. Returning to consciousness, I struggled to rise to my feet, but both of my ankles were broken.

Crewmen finally came to my assistance and took me to the anchor deck, which was already jammed. There I was strapped into a bamboo stretcher and lowered to a boat which carried me, along with other wounded, to light cruiser *Nagara*. The transfer of Nagumo's staff and of the wounded was completed at 1130. The cruiser got under way, flying Admiral Nagumo's flag at her mast.

Meanwhile, efforts to bring *Akagi*'s fires under control continued, but it became increasingly obvious that this was impossible. As the ship came to a halt, her bow was still pointed into the wind, and pilots and crew had retreated to the anchor to escape the flames, which were reaching down to the lower hangar deck. When the dynamos went out, the ship was deprived not only of illumination but of pumps for combating the conflagration as well. The fireproof hangar doors had been destroyed, and in this dire emergency even the chemical fire extinguishers failed to work.

The valiant crew located several hand pumps, brought them to the anchor deck, and managed to force water through long hoses into the lower hangar and decks below. Firefighting parties, wearing gas masks, carried cumbersome pieces of equipment and fought the flames courageously. But every induced explosion overhead penetrated to the deck below, injuring men and interrupting their desperate efforts. Stepping over fallen comrades, another damage control party would dash in to continue the struggle, only to be mowed down by the next explosion. Corpsmen and volunteers carried out dead and wounded from the lower first aid station, which was jammed with injured men. Doctors and surgeons worked like machines.

The engine-rooms were still undamaged, but fires in the middle deck sections had cut off all communication between the bridge and the lower levels of the ship. Despite this the explosions, shocks, and crashes above, plus the telegraph indicator which had rung up "Stop," told the engine-room crews in the bowels of the ship that something must be wrong. Still, as long as the engines were undamaged and full propulsive power was available, they had no choice but to stay at General Quarters. Repeated efforts were made to communicate with the bridge, but every channel of contact, including the numerous auxiliary ones, had been knocked out.

The intensity of the spreading fires increased until the heat-laden air invaded the ship's lowest sections through the intakes, and men working there began falling from suffocation. In a desperate effort to save his men, the Chief Engineer, Commander K. Tampo, made his way up through the flaming decks until he was able to get a message to the Captain, reporting conditions below. An order was promptly given for all men in engine spaces to come up on deck. But it was too late. The orderly who tried to carry the order down through the blazing hell never returned, and not a man escaped from the engine-rooms.

As the number of dead and wounded increased and the fires got further out of control, Captain Aoki finally decided at 1800 that the ship must be abandoned. The injured were lowered into boats and cutters sent alongside by the screening destroyers. Many uninjured men leapt into the sea and swam away from the stricken ship. Destroyers *Arashi* and *Nowaki* picked up all survivors. When the rescue work was completed, Captain Aoki radioed to Admiral Nagumo at 1920 from one of the destroyers, asking permission to sink the crippled carrier. This inquiry was monitored by the Combined Fleet flagship, whence Admiral Yamamoto dispatched an order at 2225 to delay the carrier's disposition. Upon receipt of this instruction, the Captain returned to his carrier alone. He reached the anchor deck, which was still free from fire, and there lashed himself to an anchor to await the end.

Stand-by destroyer *Arashi* received word at midnight that an enemy Task Force was ninety miles to the east of *Akagi*'s and her own position. One hour later a lookout sighted several warships through the darkness, and the commander of the destroyer division, Captain K. Ariga, gave chase with all four of his ships, *Arashi, Nowaki, Hagikaze,* and *Maikaze.* He failed to catch up with or identify these shadows, however, and returned to stand by the carrier. It later turned out that the mysterious ships belonged to Rear Admiral Tanaka's DesRon 2.

When Admiral Yamamoto ordered the delay in disposing of *Akagi,* it was because he saw no need for haste in this action since his force was then proceeding eastward to make a night attack on the enemy. Now, however, as defeat became apparent and the prospect of a night engagement grew dim, a quick decision became necessary. At 0350 on June 5, Admiral Yamamoto finally gave the fateful order to scuttle the great carrier. Admiral Nagumo relayed the order to Captain Ariga, directing him to rejoin the force when his mission had been accomplished. Ariga in turn ordered his four destroyers to fire torpedoes at the doomed ship. *Nowaki*'s skipper, Commander Magotaro Koga, later described how painful it was for him to fire the powerful new Type-93 torpedo into the carrier, which was his first target of the war. Within twenty minutes all four destroyers had fired. Seven minutes later the sea closed over the mighty ship, and a terrific underwater explosion occurred, sending out shocks that were felt in each destroyer. The carrier's final resting place was at latitude 30° 30′ N, longitude 179° 08′ W. The time was 0455, just minutes before the sun rose on June 5.

All but 263 members of the carrier's crew survived this last of her great battles. Before the fatal torpedoes were fired, *Akagi*'s navigator, Commander Y. [*sic*] Miura, had boarded the carrier and persuaded Captain Aoki to give up his determination to go down with the ship. Both men finally moved safely to one of the destroyers.

Kaga, which had been hit almost simultaneously with *Akagi* in the sudden dive-bombing attack, did not last as long as the flagship. Nine enemy planes had swooped down on her at 1024, each dropping a single bomb. The first three were near-misses which sent up geysers of water around her without doing any damage. But no fewer than four of the next six bombs scored direct hits on the forward, middle, and after sections of the flight deck. The bomb which struck closest to the bow landed just forward of the bridge, blowing up a small gasoline truck which was standing there and spreading fire and death throughout the bridge and surrounding deck area. Captain Jisaku Okada and most of the other occupants of the ship's nerve center were killed on the spot. The senior officer to survive the holocaust was Commander Takahisa Amagai, the Air Officer, who immediately took command of the carrier.

Furious fires broke out, seemingly everywhere. During the succeeding hours damage control crews fought desperately to check the spreading flames, but their efforts were largely unavailing, and there was scarcely a place of shelter left in the entire ship. Commander Amagai was forced to seek refuge on the starboard boat deck, where he was joined by many of the men. The carrier's doom seemed imminent.

Some three and a half hours after the bombing attack, a new menace appeared. The flame-wracked carrier now lay dead in the water and had begun to list. Commander Amagai, scanning the adjacent sea, suddenly discerned the telltale periscope of a submarine a few thousand meters from the ship. Minutes later, at 1410, Lieutenant Commander Yoshio Kunisada, a damage control officer, saw three white torpedo wakes streaking toward the carrier. They seemed sure to hit, and Kunisada closed his eyes and prayed as he waited for the explosions. None came. Two of the torpedoes barely missed the ship, and the third, though it struck, miraculously failed to explode. Instead, it glanced off the side and broke into two sections, the warhead sinking into the depths while the buoyant after section remained floating nearby. Several of *Kaga*'s crew, who were swimming about in the water after having jumped or been blown overboard when the bombs struck the carrier, grabbed onto the floating section and used it as a support while awaiting rescue. Thus did a weapon of death become instead a life-saver in one of the curious twists of war.

Kaga's protecting destroyers, *Hagikaze* and *Maikaze,* were unaware of the submarine's presence until the torpedo attack occurred. Immediately they sped out to its suspected location and delivered a heavy depth-charge attack, the results of which were not known. The submarine failed to reappear, so the destroyers turned back to the crippled carrier and resumed rescue operations.

Meanwhile, uncontrollable fires continued to rage throughout *Kaga*'s length, and finally, at 1640, Commander Amagai gave the order to abandon ship. Survivors were transferred to the two destroyers standing by. Two hours later the conflagration subsided enough to enable Commander Amagai to lead a damage-control party back on board in the hope of saving the ship. Their valiant efforts proved futile, however, and they again withdrew. The once crack carrier, now a burning hulk, was wrenched by two terrific explosions before sinking into the depths at 1925 in position 30° 20′ N, 179° 17′ W. In this battle 800 men of *Kaga*'s crew, one third of her complement, were lost.

Soryu, the third victim of the enemy dive-bombing attack, received one hit fewer than *Kaga,* but the devastation was just as great. When the attack broke, deck parties were busily preparing the carrier's planes for take-off, and their first awareness of the onslaught came when great flashes of fire were seen spouting from *Kaga*, some distance off to port, followed by explosions and tremendous columns of black smoke. Eyes instinctively looked skyward just in time to see a spear of thirteen American planes plummeting down on *Soryu*. It was 1025.

Three hits were scored in as many minutes. The first blasted the flight deck in front of the forward elevator, and the next two straddled the amidship elevator, completely wrecking the deck and spreading fire to gasoline tanks and munition storage rooms. By 1030 the ship was transformed into a hell of smoke and flames, and induced explosions followed shortly.

In the next ten minutes the main engines stopped, the steering system went out, and fire mains were destroyed. Crewmen forced by the flames to leave their posts had just arrived on deck when a mighty explosion blasted many of them into the water. Within twenty minutes of the first bomb hit, the ship was such a mass of fire that Captain Ryusaku Yanagimoto ordered "Abandon ship!" Many men jumped into the water to escape the searing flames and were picked up by destroyers *Hamakaze* and *Isokaze*. Others made more orderly transfers to the destroyers.

It was soon discovered, however, that Captain Yanagimoto had remained on the bridge of the blazing carrier. No ship commander in the Japanese Navy was more beloved by his men. His popularity was such that whenever he was going to address the assembled crew, they would gather an hour or more in advance to insure [*sic*] getting a place up front. Now, they were determined to rescue him at all costs.

Chief Petty Officer Abe, a Navy wrestling champion, was chosen to return and rescue the Captain, because it had been decided to bring him to safety by force if he refused to come willingly. When Abe climbed *Soryu*'s bridge, he found Captain Yanagimoto standing there motionless, sword in hand, gazing resolutely toward the ship's bow. Stepping forward, Abe said, "Captain, I have come on behalf of all your men to take you to safety. They are waiting for you. Please come with me to the destroyer, Sir."

When this entreaty met with silence, Abe guessed the Captain's thoughts and started toward him with the intention of carrying him bodily to the waiting boat. But the sheer strength of will and determination of his grim-faced commander stopped him short. He turned tearfully away, and as he left the bridge he heard Captain Yanagimoto calmly singing "Kimigayo," the national anthem.

At 1913, while her survivors watched from the nearby destroyers, *Soryu* finally disappeared into a watery grave, carrying with her the bodies of 718 men, including her Captain.

Not one of the many observers who witnessed the last hours of this great carrier saw any sign of an enemy submarine or of submarine torpedoes. There was a succession of explosions in the carrier before she sank, but these were so unquestionably induced explosions that they could not have been mistaken for anything else. It seems beyond doubt, therefore, that American accounts which credit U.S. submarine *Nautilus* with delivering the *coup de grace* to *Soryu* have confused her with *Kaga*.

CHAPTER

20

Flying into a Beehive

By ADM John S. "Jimmie" Thach, USN (Ret.)

"Fighting Three at Midway," *Naval History,* June 2007

Six Grumman F4FA Wildcat fighters of Fighting Squadron 3 (VF-3) were the sole protection for the USS *Yorktown's* twelve torpedo planes and seventeen dive bombers that attacked the Japanese First Carrier Striking Force early on 4 June 1942. Launching nearly two hours after their compatriots on board the USS *Enterprise* and USS *Hornet,* the F4Fs were led by then–LCDR Jimmie Thach; they were the only fighters to engage the Japanese over their ships that morning. The following account is adapted from Thach's U.S. Naval Institute oral history.

Flying into a Beehive (pp. 24–31)

Before leaving Pearl Harbor, I was given very brief indications that we expected an attack, and there was obviously a big battle coming up in the middle of the Pacific. That's about all I was told before I landed aboard the *Yorktown* (CV-5) on May 30. That night, the air group met in the wardroom where Commander Murr Arnold, the air officer, gave us a complete briefing on everything they knew about the opposing Japanese forces and their probable intentions. So we had a day or so to think before we arrived in position. After this briefing, it was obvious a very serious and crucial engagement was coming up. If we could win this one, we might be able to stop the Japanese advance.

LCDR John S. Thach, leader of the *Yorktown*'s fighter squadron at Midway and the creator of the Thach weave. Thach survived the war and eventually became an admiral, retiring from the Navy in 1967.

Navy Department, National Archives

Lieutenant Commander Maxwell Leslie, commanding officer of the *Yorktown*'s dive-bomber squadron who was going to lead VB-3 and part of VS-5, and Lieutenant Commander Lance "Lem" Massey, commanding officer of Torpedo Squadron (VT)-3, suggested that we have a conference. I'd talked a bit to Lem before that and told him I thought the fighter escort should go with him instead of with the dive bombers. He said, "I think you ought to get up with the dive bombers because that's where the Zeros are going to be. That's where they were in the Coral Sea battle." We knew we weren't going to have enough fighters to send with each.

I had a plan to take eight planes because I wanted two divisions—that was the basic tactical breakdown we developed—and I couldn't believe that anybody would try to break this up. If you're going to send any number of airplanes, it's got to be divisible by four, otherwise you've left two planes without wingmen.

Max Leslie said he thought that I should go with the torpedo planes. I said, "How about letting me decide?" because they were playing Alphonse and Gaston, trying to give the fighters to the other squadron. I decided that, since in the Coral Sea battle the torpedo planes had gotten in pretty much unopposed and done the work in sinking these ships, the Japanese would be more concerned about them. They were going to be very concerned about a torpedo attack, and they're going to try to knock it out. So we all agreed that I would go with VT-3.

The torpedo planes were old fire traps that were so slow—those old TBDs would go about 80 knots, with the nose down maybe 110-awkward and had no self-sealing tanks. They needed protection more than anyone else, so that governed our decision.

I don't know how many people slept very well the night of the 3rd of June.

I was very concerned about whether the torpedo planes could get in or not, and I knew that if the Japanese were together in one formation and had a fighter combat air patrol from all the carriers, we would very likely be outnumbered. We were also quite concerned that the Zero could outperform us in every way. We felt we had one advantage in that we could shoot better and had better guns. But if you don't get a chance to shoot, better guns matter little. I was thinking about all this and which pilots I would take with me. I didn't sleep much that night, but we were all pretty optimistic because we felt that we were going to get tactical surprise. We didn't think the Japanese knew that we were anywhere near there, and this was a great morale builder, when you think you're going to have one of the basic principles of warfare—surprise—on your side.

I was a little appalled that we were in two separate task forces, with the *Yorktown* the only carrier in one of them. Captain Elliott Buckmaster, commanding the *Yorktown,* or Rear Admiral Frank Jack Fletcher, tactical commander of all the carriers and commander of Task Force 17, I guess, made the decision the next morning before we launched that we would have only six fighters go. I didn't have time to work my way up to talk to either one about it, but I did go to Murr Arnold. I said I was appalled that the *Yorkton* [*sic*] was separated from the *Enterprise* (CV-6) and *Hornet* (CV-8), but wasn't too worried because I thought they would stick close together, enough for mutual defensive support. He said, "And, another thing, you'd better bring your planes back because I think we're in for one hell of a fight."

I held a last-minute briefing and emphasized that I wanted the formation to stick together, that nobody was going to be a lone wolf, because lone wolves don't live very long under the circumstances we were going into, and that was the best way to survive and protect the torpedo planes.

I had to quickly revise the formation that we were going to fly over the torpedo planes because six isn't divisible by four. I had Ensign Robert A. M. "Ram" Dibb as my wingman with Lieutenant (junior grade) Brainard Macomber, of VF-42, as my other section leader, and his wingman was Ensign Edgar Bassett, also of VF-42. That left two, Machinist [machinist's mate] Tom Cheek and Ensign Daniel Sheedy. So I decided that we would put them just astern of the 12 torpedo planes, down at a slightly lower altitude than I would fly, 1,000 or 1,500 feet above the torpedo plane formation, which would be a formation in the shape of a triangle, a sort of a V of Vs. That's the way they would fly up to the target until they had to split and spread out to make the torpedo attack.

We had to do S turns, to slow down so we wouldn't run away from the TBDs because they were so slow, and we didn't want to be stalling along with no ability to maneuver in case something hit us before we anticipated it. We were flying our standard combat formation that I'd developed, with a section leader and only one wingman, in a combat division of four planes, two two-plane sections. I was leading. Ram Dibb was right in under my wing, and Macomber had Bassett on his wing.

I'd made that standard before the war. I recommended, after I'd developed this weave business, that all the squadrons accept this as a standard fighting formation. I got a message back from commander, Aircraft, Battle Force, that since the two-plane section was such a radical change he wouldn't force all the squadrons to do it, but that I had authority to do it in my squadron. Actually, by this time the idea was catching on anyway. VF-2 was doing it, and so were some of the others. They'd thrown away the third plane and were flying two-plane sections, but they had not adopted the weaving tactics.

The *Hornet* was rather new in the Pacific, and I hadn't seen her pilots, but I tried to circulate this around. Lieutenant Commander James Flatley, executive officer of the *Yorktown*'s VF-42 at the Battle of the Coral Sea, and I had discussed it—sometimes late into the night—and he helped me for a while. He said: "I think the four-plane division is good, but I think we shouldn't all try the same thing. Why don't I try six planes in a formation, and you try four, and we'll see which one makes out the best." Later he sent two messages, a personal one to me saying the four-plane division is the only thing that will work, and "I am calling it the Thach Weave, for your information." Six planes don't work. The two extra ones get lost. He sent an official message describing this and saying that they were convinced that it was the only way for our fighters to fight, especially against superior enemy fighters.

We took off later than the planes from the *Enterprise* and *Hornet*. They started a little after 0700 and we didn't begin launching until around 0840. By 0900 I was in the air. It was a beautiful day. There were little puffy clouds up around 1,000 feet to 1,500 feet that sometimes would get a little thicker and other times they'd open up and be very scattered. It was that way all the way into the enemy formation.

A strange thing happened on the way. We were flying along and, all of a sudden, ahead of us and a bit to the side, two big explosions threw water way up high. There didn't seem to be anybody around, but I wondered if someone hadn't inadvertently dropped a couple of bombs. That's exactly the way it turned out. In arming the bombs—the arming device worked in a way that also released the bomb. Max Leslie and three others in his squadron lost theirs.

So we went in. All of us were, of course, highly excited and admittedly nervous. I think most other people did pretty much what I did—kept going over my check-off list, and as soon as we had gotten in the air I had each section test their guns so they'd be ready, and all the switches on and not on safety, and in we went.

Lem Massey made a small change of course to the right. We took off on a heading of about southwest, and I wondered why he did that. Looking ahead, I could see ships through the breaks in the clouds, and I figured that was it. We had just begun to approach about ten miles from the outer screen of this large force, looked like it was spread over the ocean, and several colored antiaircraft bursts appeared out in our direction, one red and another orange, and then no more. I wondered why they'd be shooting at us because we weren't even nearly in range. We'd been sighted from the surface screen and they were alerting the combat air patrol. A very short time after, before we got near antiaircraft range, Zero fighters came down on us. I tried to count them. We'd always been trained to count things at a glance, and I figured there were 20.

The first thing that happened was that Bassett's plane was burning. He pulled out, and I didn't see him any more. He was shot down right away; I didn't see the Zero that got him. I was surprised that they put so many Zeros on my six fighters. I had expected they would go for the torpedo planes first. They must have known we didn't have the quick acceleration to catch them the way they were coming in at high speed in rapid succession and zipping on away. But then I saw they had a second large group that was now streaming in right past us and into the poor torpedo planes.

Macomber's position was too close to me to permit an effective weave, and I was not getting very good shots at the Zeros. I called him on the radio and said: "Open out more. About double your present distance and weave." No acknowledgment. His radio must have been dead. (He has since stated it was.) How ironic this situation had become! I had spent almost a year developing what I was convinced was the only way to survive against the Zero, and now we couldn't seem to do it. I kept wondering why Macomber was so close instead of being out in a position to weave. Of course, he had never practiced the weave. He was one of the VF-42 pilots during the Coral Sea battle and had tangled with some Zeros then. But he had reported to VF-3 just before we flew out to land aboard the *Yorktown* enroute to Midway.

I had assumed that my exec, Lieutenant Commander Donald Lovelace, had briefed them or required them to read the *Squadron Tactical Doctrine*. I suddenly realized Don didn't have much time to brief anyone before he had his head chopped off [in an accident on *Yorktown*'s flight deck]. I had tried so hard to wipe that ghastly accident out of my mind that I forgot Don was no longer with us. Then I remembered telling my flight during the last-minute briefing to stick together. Macomber must have thought I meant for him to fly a closed-up formation. What I actually meant was I wanted no lone-wolf tactics.

Too late to correct that misunderstanding now. I couldn't see Cheek and Sheedy so I called Ram Dibb, my wingman, and said, "Pretend you are a section leader and move out far enough to weave." He said, "This is Scarlet Two, wilco." His voice sounded like he was elated to get this "promotion" right in the middle of a battle.

Several Zeros came in on a head-on attack on the torpedo planes and burned Lem Massey's plane right away. It just exploded in flames. And, beautifully timed, another group came in on the side against the torpedo planes. The air was like a beehive, and I wasn't sure at that moment that anything would work. It didn't look like my weave was working, but then it began to work. I got a good shot at two of them and burned them, and one of them had made a pass at my wingman, pulled out to the right, and then came back. We were weaving continuously, and I got a head-on shot at him, and just about the time I saw this guy coming, Ram said, "There's a Zero on my tail." The Zero wasn't directly astern, more like 45 degrees, beginning to follow him around, which gave me the head-on approach.

I probably should have decided to duck under this Zero, but I lost my temper. He just missed me by a few feet with flames coming out of the bottom of his airplane. This is like playing chicken with two automobiles on the highway except we were both shooting as well. That was a little foolhardy; I didn't try it any more.

They kept coming in and, by this time, we were over the screen, and more torpedo planes were falling, but so were some Zeros. At least we're keeping a lot of them engaged. We could see the carriers. They were steaming at very high speed and launching airplanes. The torpedo planes had to split in order to make an effective attack. We thought we were doing pretty well until they split. Then, of course, they were extremely vulnerable, all alone with no mutual protection. The Zeros were coming in on us, one after the other, and sometimes simultaneously from above and to the side. We couldn't stay with the torpedo planes, except for one or two that happened to be under us.

I kept counting the number of airplanes that I knew I'd gotten in flames going down. You couldn't bother to wait for them to splash, but you could tell if they were flaming real good and you saw something besides smoke. If it was real red flames, you knew he'd had it. I had this little knee pad and would mark down every time I shot one that I knew was gone. This was sort of foolish. Why was I marking my pad when it wasn't coming back? I was utterly convinced then that we weren't coming back. There were still so many Zeros, and they'd already gotten one of our fighters, and looking around, I couldn't see Cheek or Sheedy anymore, so there were just two others that I could see of my own; Macomber over on my left and Ram Dibb, and me.

Pure logic would convince anyone that with their superior performance and the number of Zeros they were throwing into the fight, we could not possibly survive. "Well," I said, talking to myself, "we're going to take a lot of them with us if they're going to get us all." We kept on working this weave, and it seemed to work better and better. How much time this took, I don't know, but ever since then I haven't the slightest idea how many Zeros I shot down. I just can't remember, and I don't suppose it makes too much difference. It only shows that I was absolutely convinced that nobody could get out of there, that we weren't coming back, and neither were any of the torpedo planes.

Then it seemed that the attacks began to slack off a little bit. I called and said: "Hell, they don't like it as well as they used to. Stick together and we'll get home yet." The torpedo planes went on in. I saw three or four of them that got in and made an attack. I believe that at least one torpedo hit was made. All the records, and the Japanese, and Sam[uel Eliot] Morison's book said that no torpedoes hit. I'm not sure that the people on board a ship that is hit repeatedly really know whether they got hit by a torpedo or a bomb. I was aboard the *Saratoga* (CV-3) when she was torpedoed and the *Yorktown* when she was bombed and I couldn't tell the difference. I think I saw at least one hit, but it occurred either during or very shortly before the dive bombers came in.

Being pretty busy, I couldn't more than every now and then get a glance. Then I saw this glint in the sun—it looked like a beautiful silver waterfall—these were the dive bombers coming down. I could see them very well, because that's the direction the Zeros were, too. They were above me but closer, not anywhere near the altitude of the dive bombers.

I'd never seen such superb dive bombing. It looked to me like almost every bomb hit. Of course, there were some very near misses. There weren't any wild ones. Explosions were occurring in the carriers, and about that time the Zeros slacked off. We brought out two torpedo planes and then went back and picked up another one we saw [and stayed] right with him and over him, hoping that the Zeros wouldn't have him all to themselves. Of course, the TBDs may have been badly hit and some of them were in the water and we didn't see them after the torpedo attack. I know more than two attacked. We had come in a little earlier than the dive bombers by a matter of just minutes, and drew most, if not all, of the enemy combat air patrol. They were ready and waiting for us as we came in a full 30 minutes after the VT-8 and VT-6 attacks.

I could only see three carriers. I never did see a fourth one. One of them, probably either the *Soryu* or the *Kaga,* was burning with bright pink and sometimes blue flames. I remember looking at the height of the flames [and] noticing that it was about the height that the ship was long—the length of the ship—just solid flame going up and a lot of smoke on top of that. I saw three carriers burning pretty furiously before I left, picked up one torpedo plane, and flew on back toward the *Yorktown* with it. I was over the Japanese fleet a full 20 minutes.

Was the decision to cover the torpedo planes the right one? Oh, yes. These torpedo pilots were all my very close friends, Lem Massey especially, and he was lost. I felt pretty bad about that, just sort of hopeless. I felt we hadn't done enough, that if they didn't get any hits this whole business of torpedo planes going in at all was a mistake. But, of course, you couldn't fail to send them, and in thinking about it since then I realize that this classic, coordinated attack that we practiced for many years, with the torpedo planes going in low and the dive bombers coming in high, pretty much simultaneously, that's what we tried to do, although it's usually better if the dive bombers hit first, then the torpedo planes can get in better among the confusion of bombs bursting.

I realized that here was the reverse of the Coral Sea battle, that these people hadn't given their lives in vain, they'd done a magnificent job of attracting all the enemy combat air patrol, all the protection that the Japanese carriers had were engaged and were held down. So we did do something, and maybe far more than we thought at the time. We engaged the enemy that might have gotten into the dive bombers and prevented them from getting many hits.

The six *Yorktown* Wildcats were the only fighters that got any combat over the Japanese fleet—no other fighters. And VF-3 was the only fighter squadron in the Battle of Midway that had any significant aerial combat later in defense of our carriers.

Working the Weave (pp. 28–29)

I developed the "weave" before the war, in the summer of 1941 on my kitchen table in Coronado. I've read that I studied the combat reports of the Coral Sea battle and figured it out just before the Battle of Midway. This is not true at all. We'd been practicing it for a long time.

In the spring of 1941 we received an intelligence report of great significance out of China. It described a new Japanese aircraft, a fighter, that had performance that was far superior to anything we had. It had more than 5,000-feet-per-minute climb, very high speed, and could turn inside of any other aircraft. I felt we should give the report some credence because whoever wrote it talked like a fighter pilot, like he knew what he was talking about.

If you have somebody who's faster than you are, you have to trap him somehow so that he can't use his superiority, whatever it is. I believed we had one advantage: We had good guns, and could shoot and hit. We must do something to entice the opponent into giving us that one all-important opportunity. It was the only chance we had. So every night I worked on this problem. I used a box of kitchen matches on the table and let each represent an airplane. I would work on this every night until about midnight.

For years the formation we flew with, three-plane sections, a leader and two wingmen, irked me. If you're going to fight and do radical turns, this was an unwieldy formation. It was obvious that if we were going to be able to do something sudden to fool an enemy, we ought to throw away one of those planes and just have a two-plane section, which is what I did. At that time, everybody was flying three-plane sections, both in our country and Europe.

Thach envisioned the basic combat unit as a four-plane division consisting of two two-plane sections. The right pair would watch the tails of the left section and vice versa. With the two sections split wide apart, an enemy plane would have to choose one over the other. If the right section saw its fellows about to be attacked, it would break into a 90 [degree] turn toward the left section. That section, always watching to the right, would see the break and instinctively know they were under attack and immediately break to the right. The enemy would follow the left section, but be subject to a head-on attack by the right section.

So, the weave looked like it was, maybe, the only thing to do. I was very excited about this discovery and presented it to the squadron. To simulate the Zero's superiority I told Butch O'Hare, one of the squadron's top pilots, to take four aircraft and use full power, and I would take four and never advance the throttle more than half way. That gave him at least superior performance. Maybe double, maybe not. I told Butch, "You attack from any direction you want."

He made all sorts of attacks, quite a few from overhead and coming down, this way and that. After we landed he said, "Skipper, it really worked. It really works. I couldn't make any attack without seeing the nose of one of your half-throttle airplanes pointed at me. So at least you're getting a shot, even though I might also have got a shot, at least it isn't one sided. Most of the time that sudden turn, although I knew what you were going to do, it always caught me a little bit by surprise. When I was committed and about to squeeze the trigger, here he went and turned and I didn't think he saw me."

Of course, he didn't. That's the beauty of this, and you didn't need a radio. So we felt a little better about the situation. Now we had something to work on, to keep us from being demoralized.

Jimmy Flatley gave it the name "Thach Weave." I didn't.

— AUTHOR —

After a forty-year career, Admiral Thach retired as CominCh of U.S. naval forces in Europe in 1967. The 1927 U.S. Naval Academy graduate commanded two aircraft carriers and was an antisubmarine warfare expert. Among other awards, he received the Navy Cross with Gold Star and the Distinguished Service Medal. He died in 1981.

CHAPTER

21

Moment at Midway: McClusky's Decision

Proceedings, April 1975: pp. 64–65

For the pilots of the two squadrons of SBD Dauntless dive bombers, and most especially for their group commander, Lieutenant Commander Clarence McClusky, the 50-mile visibility on this cool and beautiful June morning served only to emphasize the emptiness of the ocean, 20,000 feet below. Where were the Japanese carriers?

At daybreak on the morning of 4 June 1942, Vice Admiral Chuichi Nagumo had launched an air strike against Midway which was aimed at softening up this westernmost U.S. base preparatory to its seizure by naval forces under the command of Isoroku Yamamoto. Now Nagumo was confronted with the decision of whether to send his aircraft for a follow-on strike on Midway or to rearm all of the aircraft on his four carriers, *Akagi, Kaga, Soryu,* and *Hiryu,* for an attack against the American carrier whose presence had just been reported by his scouts.

At this time the Japanese carrier force (Midway Attacking Force) was some 150 miles northwest of Midway (Admiral Yamamoto with the main body . . . was following well behind). The American carrier force was north of Midway; approximately 150 miles separated the two carrier forces.

Even as Nagumo pondered his decision, he was successfully fending off attacks by Midway defending aircraft, including Navy torpedo planes, Army B-17s, and Marine dive-bombers, all of which failed to inflict any damage. Nagumo elected to

Taken on 1 April 1942, this photo shows the two quadruple 1.1-inch antiaircraft mounts forward of the island on the *Enterprise.* Above and behind the guns is the protected battle look-out station (with the small square windows), the pilothouse, and the antiaircraft director for the ship's dual purpose 5-inch guns. The ship's tripod mast towers over the director. The ship's air-search radar is the bedspring antenna atop the tripod mast, and above the radar is the homing beacon designed to guide returning aircraft to the carrier. The *Yorktown*'s island was almost identical. The newer *Hornet* had a small but visible armored conning tower in front of her bridge.

Navy Department, National Archives

forego [*sic*] his second attack on Midway in order to launch a combined strike on the enemy carrier. He then ordered a course change, from southwest to northeast.

Meanwhile, [Rear] Admiral Frank Fletcher, the U.S. force commander, directed Rear Admiral Raymond Spruance to proceed southwesterly and attack the Japanese carriers which were reported approaching Midway from the northwest.

The *Enterprise* and the *Hornet* launched their air groups first, followed by the *Yorktown,* and the strike elements proceeded on separate courses to intercept the enemy carriers at an estimated point of advance. The *Hornet*'s dive-bombers reached the point of intercept but, because of Nagumo's abrupt course change, found no targets and were forced to return when fuel reached a low state.

The *Yorktown*'s dive-bombers, although actually departing an hour later than those of the *Enterprise,* followed a more direct route to the enemy force. The *Enterprise* bombers, 33 SBDs under McClusky, searched on a southwesterly course.

Now, airborne over two hours as he arrived at the expected point of contact, McClusky scanned the sea with increasing concern as he continued some 35 miles further [*sic*] with still no sighting. Although he could not know of all the confusing events which were acting to focus an enormous significance on his own actions, he nevertheless was aware that much, if not most, of the U.S. striking power was represented in the bombs slung beneath the SBDs. Posed for him was the question: where had the Japanese gone? Such profound importance of the *correct* answer to that question for McClusky and the U.S. Navy has rarely been encountered elsewhere in either fact or fiction.

Confident of his own navigation and of his estimate of the speed of the Japanese carriers, McClusky concluded that the enemy might have reversed course, and so he turned his formation to a northwesterly course to overtake. Then, for half an hour he searched anxiously for the glimpse of wakes of ships or smoke which might reveal the location of his quarry.

There was only the sea. Then, as, surely, anxiety must have begun to give way to mounting frustration, there appeared on the surface ahead the thin but unmistakable wake-trace of a ship traveling at high speed. As he closed the ship, McClusky identified her as a Japanese destroyer that was in an obvious hurry.

And it was at that moment, if indeed one moment may be singled out for recording, that there occurred the decision which changed the fortunes of a war and thrust U.S. naval aviation to its highest peak of effectiveness in its 30 years of existence.

McClusky reasoned that the enemy destroyer was racing to rejoin its parent formation—which most likely was the carrier force—and once again he led his formation in a turn, to parallel the destroyer's course, northeast. Within a quarter of an hour McClusky sighted the Japanese force on the horizon, where Nagumo was even then repelling the ill-fated attacks of the torpedo planes which had found the carriers and were attacking independently and without support cover.

What followed is, indeed, history, well-recorded in detailed accounts of how McClusky's aircraft arrived for the attack even as the *Yorktown*'s dive-bombers closed from another quarter, each group unaware of the other's presence as they dove on the box formation of four carriers and their escort units.

For the Japanese, exultant over their successful defense against the torpedo attacks, their world was turned upside down in the space of five devastating minutes. In that brief span, the *Kaga, Akagi,* and *Soryu* became the focal points of destruction that was as appalling to the Japanese as it was satisfying to the attackers. Only the *Hiryu,* fleeing under cloud cover, escaped for the moment. She would also be sunk within hours, to complete a victory which established, for the first time since Pearl Harbor, a balance of naval air power which would enable the United States to continue the Pacific war [*sic*] to the final victory.

For the Japanese Empire, Midway marked the end of the major naval victories it had amassed for three and a half centuries.

For America, Midway gave the first encouragement in the years of prewar uncertainty and the months of dismaying wartime experiences.

For the U.S. Navy, Midway meant the turning point which opened the way to success in the long campaigns still ahead.

For naval aviation, Midway was both the hour of reckoning and the time of fulfillment for a force which could not be ignored again, for any reason. On the results of one decision, by one naval aviator, in one moment, naval aviation had come of age.

CHAPTER
22

The Battle of Midway I: The Most God-Awful Luckiest Coordinated Attack

By John B. Lundstrom

Black Shoe Carrier Admiral (Annapolis, MD: Naval Institute Press, 2006): chap. 17 The Battle of Midway I, pp. 258–261

The Most God-Awful Luckiest Coordinated Attack

Six days elapsed before Fletcher learned more details of the high drama, sacrifice, and glory of the past two hours [on 4 June], when U.S. carrier aviators fatally damaged three carriers and won the Battle of Midway. The actual sequence of events was stranger than anyone could have imagined; as [RADM Murr] Arnold wrote in 1965, it was "the most god-awful luckiest coordinated attack." Two powerful formations of SBDs, one launched ninety minutes before the other, converged simultaneously to catch the 1st *Kido Butai* at a highly vulnerable moment. That vulnerability arose after other squadrons, both from Midway and the carriers, gallantly pressed their attacks at enormous cost in the teeth of fierce fighter opposition.

The first U.S. carrier planes found the target because of a highly unusual personal decision. During the first half hour after the departure of the *Hornet* strike group, Lt. Cdr. John C. Waldron, commanding officer of VT-8, grew more frustrated and angry after [CDR Stanhope] Ring, the group commander, set the westerly course for his fifty-nine planes (thirty-four SBDs, ten F4Fs, and fifteen TBDs). To Waldron that was a serious blunder. He preferred attacking the two carriers already located southwest of TF-16, rather than seek others thought to be somewhere to the west. After a vehement exchange with Ring, who demanded that Waldron just follow him, Waldron swung VT-8 left at about 0825 to head southwest. [LT James S.] Gray's ten VF-6 escorts, cruising twenty thousand feet above, stayed with Waldron. Ring's strong force moved westward completely out of the picture and eventually disintegrated. First the VF-8 escort fighters broke off for lack of fuel, and all ten ditched in a vain effort to find TF-16. Then VB-8 with half the SBDs turned southeast, vainly seeking the enemy along the reported Japanese track. Most ended up at Midway, but three returned to the *Hornet.* Meanwhile, Ring with the VS-8 SBDs proceeded all the way to 225 miles, found nothing, then reversed course straight to the *Hornet.* [The *Hornet*'s captain Marc] Mitscher's great gamble to find the second enemy carrier group ended in disaster.

Waldron's instincts proved uncannily accurate, as he aimed directly toward Nagumo's force. At 0910 the VF-6 F4Fs from their lofty height sighted distant ships almost dead ahead beyond a low cloud bank. Near the water, Waldron noticed smoke on the horizon. The 1st *Kido Butai* first espied the low-level intruders at 0918, just after turning northeast. As the ships evaded at high speed, thirty Zeroes tore into the new wave of attackers. Waldron bravely bored straight toward the nearest carrier, the *Soryu,* but by 0936 all fifteen lumbering TBDs, likened by one VT-8 pilot to "flying freight cars bearing the white star," fell to fighters. Only Ens. George H. Gay survived. The few torpedoes that VT-8 managed to fire missed their targets. Perched high over the eastern edge of the carrier force, Gray never saw the actual torpedo attack through the clouds. Although the *Enterprise* SBDs were his primary responsibility, he previously arranged with [LCDR Eugene

LCDR John C. Waldron, commanding officer of the *Hornet*'s torpedo bomber squadron. On 4 June Waldron deliberately ignored the orders of his strike group commander, CDR Stanhope C. Ring, and led his Devastator torpedo planes right to the *kidō butai*'s carriers. But Waldron's decision took his torpedo bombers away from *Hornet*'s covering fighters, and all fifteen of Waldron's TBDs were shot down by defending Japanese Zero fighters. They failed to get a hit on any Japanese carrier.

U.S. Naval Institute Photo Archive

E.] Lindsey's VT-6 to descend if they radioed they were in trouble from enemy fighters. Gray heard no such call for assistance (Waldron never knew to ask) and patiently awaited [LCDR Clarence Wade] McClusky's SBDs.

At 0938 Nagumo's lookouts sighted more enemy planes coming in low over the water. Lindsey's fourteen VT-6 TBDs went down alone on the 240-degree track and nearly missed the 1st *Kido Butai* to the north. At 0930 he sighted smoke thirty miles northwest. Steaming northeast at high speed, the Japanese carriers forced VT-6 to close from astern, a poor angle for the slow TBDs. Zeroes swarmed the prolonged approach. Far above, Gray did not know VT-6, too, fought and died nearby. Worried about fuel, he . . . at 1010 left for home without firing a shot. Valiant VT-6 split to try to catch one of the carriers in an anvil attack. Around 1000 one element drew near enough to the *Kaga* to fire torpedoes but missed the swiftly moving flattop. The other element chased the *Hiryu* but never got close enough to score. Only five TBDs escaped the vicinity of the 1st *Kido Butai,* and one soon ditched.

Even as VT-6 completed its gallant attack, the *Yorktown* aviators shed their blood in the pending Japanese disaster. Only the *Yorktown* strike established group integrity. The running rendezvous went well, and by 0945 [LCDR "Jimmy"] Thach's six VF-3 F4Fs eased into covering position over the twelve TBDs of [LCDR Lance] Massey's VT-3 cruising at fifteen hundred feet. Flying at fifteen thousand feet, [LCDR Maxwell] Leslie's VB-3 sighted the TBDs far below. Due to an electrical glitch four SBDs (including Leslie's) inadvertently jettisoned their 1,000-pound bombs but stayed in formation. Bomb or no, Leslie was leading his attack. So accurate was the estimate of [*Yorktown* air officer] Arnold and [fighter director] Pederson, the *Yorktowners* did not even have to fly to the end of their navigational leg before finding the enemy. At 1003 VT-3 discerned smoke to the northwest and discovered ships twenty to twenty-five miles off. Thach and Leslie followed Massey's turn. Japanese lookouts spotted the torpedo planes easily enough but missed the dive bombers above. While Massey assaulted the *Hiryu,* the combat air patrol grew to forty-one fighters. The Zeroes chasing the remnants of VT-6 ran straight into Massey and Thach. Like a reluctant pied piper, VT-3 enticed Zeroes down to the wave tops. The relentless interceptors prevented the escort F4Fs from protecting the TBDs. Torpedo Three's sacrifice (ten of twelve shot down) opened the skies over the carriers at exactly the right instant. Closing from the southeast, Leslie discerned two carriers relatively close together, with possibly a third to the west. Unaware VS-5 had not made the mission, he radioed [LCDR Wallace] Short at 1015: "How about you taking the one to the left [evidently the *Hiryu*] and I'll take the one on the right [the *Soryu*]? I'm going to make an attack." Somewhat puzzled at not receiving a reply, he stalked the *Soryu,* northernmost of the three carriers, and still hoped to attack in concert with VT-3. Leslie thought it a great shame no one else was around to take on the other juicy targets.

Unknown to Leslie, other dive bombers already drew a bead on the flotilla of flattops. McClusky's *Enterprise* SBDs undertook quite an odyssey since their hasty departure at 0745. He anticipated contact at 0920 about 142 miles out. Nothing was there, so he flew southwest for fifteen more minutes, then pivoted northwest on the reciprocal bearing of the original Japanese course toward Midway. He planned to hold that heading until 1000 and venture northeast for a short time, before finally turning east for home. Fuel became a real problem. Finally at 0955 he reaped the lucky break his careful reasoning deserved. Below, the long white wake of a destroyer beckoned northeastward. McClusky believed she must be rejoining the main body. In fact the *Arashi* had remained behind to keep the *Nautilus* down while Nagumo cleared the area. Paralleling her track, McClusky was supremely gratified at 1002 to sight the carrier force far to the northeast. If he sent a contact report, Spruance and Fletcher never monitored it.

Nagumo's time was up. The torpedo attacks that consumed the last hour (and still continued) disrupted preparations for the "grand scale air attack" originally scheduled to launch at 1030. Busy handling fighters, no carrier yet spotted any carrier bombers or torpedo planes. The combat air patrol Zeroes either circled at low altitude low on gas and ammunition, chased VT-3 while it desperately closed the *Hiryu,* or tangled with VF-3 Wildcats. The 1st *Kido Butai* was momentarily defenseless against a surprise dive bombing attack. At 1022 McClusky, closing from the west, confronted two carriers. An ex-fighter pilot unfamiliar with dive bombing procedure, he erred by pushing over against the *Kaga,* the nearer carrier. Instead, he should have taken the lead squadron to the more distant target and allowed the trailing SBD squadron to attack the first carrier. Some twenty-eight SBDs, nearly the entire force, followed McClusky down and soon smothered the *Kaga* with perhaps ten hits. Realizing the neighboring carrier was not being attacked, Lt. Richard H. Best, commanding officer of VB-6, tried to round up his men, radioing: "1st div., 2nd div., stay with me and come on over. Don't let this carrier escape." In the end only he and his two wingmen broke off after the *Akagi.* In perhaps the most splendid single performance of the battle, they secured two 1,000-pound bomb hits and a damaging near miss. At the same time, Leslie led VB-3 against the *Soryu* off to the north. Nine pilots plastered her with three 1,000-pound bombs. Seeing that carrier was doomed, the other four attacked screening ships.

Seven decisive minutes (1022–1028) saw Nagumo lose three-quarters of his carrier strength, and with it the Battle of Midway. On all three stricken flattops, heavy bombs shattered flight decks and penetrated into the hangars. Fierce flames torched fueled and armed aircraft, as well as ordnance left lying around after the hasty rearming. Fire-fighting systems were either destroyed by the blast or incapable of dealing with the intense flames.

CHAPTER

23

"Flags" at Midway

By Thomas B. Allen

Naval History, June 2002: pp. 26–29

A signalman—[Peter E.] "Flags" Karetka—at battle stations on board destroyer *Hughes* (DD-410) in what has been called the greatest sea battle of World War II kept notes as Japanese dive bombers attacked the aircraft carrier *Yorktown.* . . . To commemorate the sixtieth anniversary of the battle, he recalls what he witnessed that day.

On 4 June, in the epic 20-minute carrier battle that changed the Pacific War, U.S. dive bomber pilots sank three Japanese aircraft carriers, the *Soryu, Kaga,* and *Akagi.* The fourth, the *Hiryu,* still lived. From her deck, heading for the *Yorktown,* flew a vengeful force of 18 Val dive bombers and 6 Zero escorts. U.S. fighters protecting the *Yorktown* got ten Vals. Antiaircraft fire shot down two more.

The surviving Japanese dive bombers flew on, three coming in from astern the *Yorktown,* the others off to starboard. Dozens of guns ripped one of the planes into three pieces. But its bomb hurtled on, tumbling through the air and heading for the flight deck of the *Yorktown.*

At that moment, the *Hughes* was close in on the port beam of the *Yorktown.* Flags Karetka, at his battle station on the starboard wing of the *Hughes*'s bridge, saw that bomb hit. Against regulations, Karetka kept notes on what he saw:

14:02 enemy sighted.

14:10 dive bombers attack.[1]

Two of the surface ships screening the carrier *Hornet.* The camouflaged ship to the left is the light cruiser *Atlanta,* with sixteen 5-inch dual-purpose guns. Closest to the camera and releasing a cloud of steam is the destroyer *Balch.* The *Atlanta* was later fatally damaged at Guadalcanal, sinking on 13 November 1942 after being wrecked by a torpedo and dozens of shells fired at her by Japanese warships.

U.S. Naval Institute Photo Archive

The bomb exploded on the flight deck, tearing it open and wiping out 19 of the 20 men at the 1.1-inch gun mount astern of the smokestacks on the starboard side. Other men nearby also were killed. Red-hot shrapnel touched off fires in the *Yorktown*'s hangar deck, where Lieutenant A. C. Emerson switched on sprinklers and water curtains that snuffed out the flames.

A second bomb pierced the flight deck near the island and exploded in a fire-room, knocking out five of the six boilers. The carrier, which had been twisting evasively at 30 knots, slowed abruptly to 6 knots. Another bomb hit the Number 1 elevator forward of the island, plunged deep into the ship and exploded.

The *Yorktown* lost all headway. But her damage-control crews were serving her well. By 1350 the fires were under control and refueling of the fighters began on deck. At 1402, Karetka saw the *Yorktown*'s yellow breakdown flag lowered. And he let out a cheer when he read the new hoist: "My speed 5." In minutes the speed was 12 knots, then 15 knots.

On board the *Hiryu,* torpedo planes were taking off for another raid on the *Yorktown.* Her radar picked up the planes from the *Hiryu* when they were 37 miles away. From Karetka's personal log:

> Torpedo planes attack, hitting carrier. Some of the torpedoes were dropped from such a height they nose-dived straight down into the water.

> I can see their cockpits open, grinning faces and leather headgear flapping. Watching them fly off, I noticed two of our fighter planes jump them. The results: two splashes, flights terminated.

Two torpedoes slammed into the *Yorktown*'s port side. Fuel tanks exploded. Her rudder jammed. She began to list to port. The rim of her flight deck almost touched the sea. At 1500, Captain Elliott Buckmaster, fearing his ship would capsize, ordered the hoisting of the blue-and-white signal, "Abandoning ship."

From Karetka's log: " . . . listing heavily to port, abandoned."

(Some of Karetka's notes are not intact; words along the left sides of pages are missing. "We were told that anybody caught with diaries or notes would be subject to court martial," he says. So he tore the pages out of his log, threw some overboard and stashed others. "Also we were told not to talk about the Midway battle. One day I was sitting at a bar next to a soldier. After a few minutes he is telling me the great victory of the U.S. Navy.")

The *Hughes* and other destroyers pulled alongside to rescue the 2,270 men still alive. Some were scrambling down cargo nets. Others managed to reach boats or life rafts. Able-bodied men got the wounded out of sick bay, sometimes dragging them across a listing deck too steep for carrying stretchers. The *Hughes* picked up about 20 survivors.

On board the destroyer, Karetka grabbed a pair of binoculars and scanned the water for two sailors he knew were on board the *Yorktown*—brothers James and Marty Quinn, Karetka's boyhood chums. Later he learned that another destroyer had saved them both. Later also came the news that 24 dive bombers from the *Enterprise* (CV-6)—ten of them flown over from the *Yorktown*—had taken off to kill the *Hiryu,* then about 110 miles away. They sank her with four direct hits.

The *Hughes* was ordered to stay with the *Yorktown* until she sank. All through the night, the men on board the destroyer, both ship's company and the rescued of the *Yorktown,* expected that the carrier would slip beneath the sea. But she would not die. During that night, Karetka felt a bond between himself and the doomed *Yorktown.* It would be a bond that the passage of time has not dissolved. For Karetka, the *Yorktown* has been an enduring passion. He remembers: "The rest of the task force left the area. It did not make sense to keep the task force there, with a doomed carrier and the Japanese fleet still in the area. Losing a single destroyer and damaged, sinking carrier was acceptable, but not several ships. The *Hughes* was chosen to be the expendable one."

The destroyer was ordered, he says, to prevent anyone from boarding the *Yorktown* and to sink her "if necessary to prevent capture" or if a serious fire broke out. "We spent the night of June 4th alone with the *Yorktown,*" he says. "We stood close in for protection. Some lights were showing aboard and we could hear items sliding off the carrier, hitting the water."

At 0626 on 5 June, the *Hughes*'s radar picked up a target, apparently an aircraft about 20 miles to the west. Lieutenant Commander Donald Ramsey, commanding officer of the destroyer, ordered his crew to stand by to defend against air attack. But the blip faded away. No one realized that the blip was a scouting aircraft from a Japanese cruiser. It had spotted the stricken *Yorktown*, and orders had gone out to the Japanese submarine 1–168 to attack the carrier.

About an hour later, the *Hughes* was patrolling on the port side of the *Yorktown* when crewmen heard gunfire coming from the carrier. Karetka, on the bridge wing, saw a string of little waterspouts between the *Yorktown* and the *Hughes*. "I thought a Jap plane was firing at us," he says. Another crewman thought that flying fish might have made the splashes.

What Happened Next?

One way to tell what happened next is to skip ahead 58 years to a story in *The Sunday Republican*, a newspaper published in Springfield, Massachusetts. Jani Fox steps out of a store in Greenfield and happens to see the word "Yorktown" on a poster over a display of World War II memorabilia. Karetka was there, helping to raise funds for a World War II memorial. She knew her great-uncle had served on a ship by that name. She walked up to Karetka and asked him, "Did you know Norman Pichette?"

With sudden tears in his eyes, Karetka nodded and told her how he knew Norman Pichette. Jani Fox's question had taken him back to that day that began with the string of little waterspouts in the water.

When the *Yorktown* was being abandoned, two men in the sick bay had been given up for dead. One was Norman Pichette. The other was George K. Weise. In a letter to Karetka, Weise once wrote, "So many things happened to me out there that they seem very hard to believe."

The happenings began on 4 June 1942, when Weise, a leading seaman, was firing a 50-caliber machine gun mounted near the *Yorktown*'s stack. A battle legend has the explosion of the day's second bomb throwing him so high that he grazed the wing of the Japanese plane. But in reality he slammed his head against the gunsight, fractured his skull, and then flew into the air, landing on the flight deck. Half-conscious, his right side paralyzed, he lay in sick bay, under eerie blue battle lights. He remembers hearing the battle horn blaring with the signal to abandon ship. Then:

> The third class pharmacist's mate had his arm behind me, holding me up while asking the first class mate, "What about him?" The first class said, "Leave him. He's gonna die anyway." The third class was crying during the entire ordeal. He didn't want to leave me.[2]

After a while, in the stillness, Weise heard someone weakly call his name. It was Norman Pichette, another seaman, on a nearby bunk. Suffering from a stomach wound, he, too, had been left to die.

"What can we do?" he asked Weise.

"I told him to wrap a sheet around his waist and stomach and try to get on deck to fire a machine gun, and perhaps someone would know we were still on board."

Pichette did as Weise suggested. Bleeding and staggering, he made his way up to the listing port side of the hangar deck, where he found a machine gun, its barrel aiming at the sea. With failing strength he fired the gun and collapsed.

The *Hughes* sent over a motor launch and took the unconscious Pichette back to the destroyer. He regained consciousness long enough to say, "There's another live man in sickbay." Then he died and was buried at sea.

That is what Karetka told the woman he had chanced to meet outside a store where she happened to stop for wrapping paper on the way to a bridal shower. She finally had learned how her great-uncle had died.

As for Weise, the motor launch went back, found him, and brought him to the *Hughes*. "I remember being on a mess table on the *Hughes*," Weise says. "I got a blood transfusion from a doctor. It was his blood." Weise and Karetka still keep in touch.

Another 5 June note from Karetka's torn pages reads as follows: "*Yorktown* being towed by tug *Verio* [*sic*]."

The oceangoing tug was the Vireo (AT-144), a veteran of the Japanese attack on Pearl Harbor. While she was towing the carrier to Pearl Harbor at about two knots, a 170-man salvage team went aboard. They jettisoned aircraft, cut loose an anchor, and tried to trim the carrier by pumping seawater into empty fuel tanks. "*Yorktown* was dark and dead and silent," one of the salvagers said later. But she was rallying. Counterflooding had reduced her list, and the weight reduction had raised her higher in the water, making towing easier.

On the morning of 6 June the destroyer *Hammann* (DD-412) came alongside the *Yorktown*. The submarine I-168 was about 550 yards away.

Commander Yahachi Tanabe, captain of the I-168, raised his periscope and saw the *Yorktown*, looming large. Too close, he thought; torpedoes fired from that distance might go under the carrier. He backed off until he was about 1,300 yards away.[3] He knew that several destroyers were guarding the *Yorktown*, and when he heard silence rather than sonar "pings" above him, he wondered if the sonar operators above him were all at lunch.

Tanabe fired two torpedoes, waited three seconds, and fired two more. Karetka remembers:

> I was standing watch on the starboard wing. I noticed torpedo wakes heading for both ships. I ran to the pilothouse to warn the destroyer over the TBS,

> but a call was already going out warning them of the torpedoes approaching. I rushed back to witness the hits.
>
> The *Hammann*'s crew was prepared for such an emergency, but the alarm came too late. I watched as a crewman on the focs'le [*sic*] was chopping away at a mooring line. The destroyer must have gone into emergency astern, reacting to the call. With some mooring lines still attached to the carrier, this caused the stern to dig in, creating a backwash of water onto the stern.

One torpedo struck the *Hammann*, almost breaking her in half. Two passed under the destroyer and hit the *Yorktown*. Moments later, the *Hammann*'s depth charges exploded. An officer on board the *Yorktown* watched the men in the water disappear—the way a "windshield wiper erases the droplets" from your windshield. "We were in so close to the *Hammann*," Karetka says, "that when her depth charges went off, it raised our stern."

While the *Vireo* and three destroyers rescued survivors from both torpedoed ships, the *Hughes* and two other destroyers went after the submarine. They hunted for hours, dropping a number of depth charges. (Tanabe counted 61.) Some came close enough to the I-168 to damage her severely. Her batteries knocked out and her forward torpedo room flooded, she surfaced and was smoking. The *Hughes* and another ship fired at her. Karetka wrote: "*Hammann* alongside *Yorktown* hit by torpedo and sunk, *Yorktown* also hit. Had surface fight with same sub reported possibly sunk."

As night fell, the *Hughes* headed back to the foundering and once again abandoned *Yorktown*. Karetka still bristles over his ship's withdrawal from the hunt, for he discovered long after the war that the I-168 made it back to a hero's welcome in Japan.

When the *Hughes* reached the *Yorktown*, a light signal came from a ship in the carrier group, which was heading for Pearl Harbor. Karetka read the flashes: "Stay with the carrier. Do not let her fall into enemy hands. Sink her if necessary. Good luck."

Karetka said to himself: "Thanks a lot, you bastards. Another night alone with the carrier."

Karetka saw the *Yorktown* go down at 0659 on 7 June. He remembers:

> She slid gracefully, like a lady, beneath the waves, no dive, no gurgle, no foamy froth, no plume of water or screws showing—a sad but proud moment for me. The battle flag of my country was fully unfurled, proudly showing her colors, as she picked up speed in her final moments. At this point, tears flowed down my cheeks. I looked around and thought to myself, "This is a goddamn big ocean." To this day, when I see an American flag fully unfurled, flying stiffly out, I see the USS *Yorktown* beneath it.

In the years that followed the war, Karetka frequently read accounts that said the *Yorktown* had rolled over before she disappeared. He even saw a U.S. Navy photo claiming that the carrier had capsized and then sunk. The claims angered him, for they spoiled the majestic image he carried in his memory. He even found a *Yorktown* survivor and brought him to a notary public to swear that, while standing on the deck of the *Hughes*, he watched the carrier "go down bow first with a slight list to port."

[The *Yorktown* in fact rests upright on the ocean bottom near Midway.]

— AUTHOR —

Mr. Allen is the author of books on a variety of subjects, from shark attacks and exorcism to espionage and the Gulf War. He has teamed with *Naval History*'s "Historic Aircraft" columnist Norman Polmar on several books, including *Rickover: Controversy and Genius* (New York: Simon & Schuster, 1982), *Merchants of Treason* (New York: Delacorte, 1988), *World War II: America at War 1941–1945* (New York: Random House, 1991), *Code-Name Downfall* (New York: Simon & Schuster, 1995), and *Spy Book: The Encyclopedia of Espionage* (New York: Random House, 1996). A former writer–editor and associate chief of the National Geographic Society's Book Division, Mr. Allen accompanied Robert Ballard on his expedition to find the *Yorktown* at Midway and wrote about it in the April 1999 issue of *National Geographic Magazine,* to which he contributes regularly. His most recent appearance in *Naval History* was as editor of a detailed report on the 1898 sinking of the USS *Maine,* which appeared in the April 1998 issue.

CHAPTER 24

"We Weren't Going to Go Off and Leave the Ship": Oral History of Frank Fabian

Interview with Dr. Evelyn Cherpak, Naval War College Archivist

Oral History Collection of the Naval War College (No. 435) of Frank Fabian (Naval War College Archives): pp. 16–23

Enlisted sailor Fabian had abandoned *Yorktown* on 4 June and had been picked up by a destroyer. His story begins the next day.

Thursday was the first day of the battle. On Friday, the heavy cruiser *Astoria* came alongside of the destroyer I was on. Who was aboard but Captain Buckmaster. . . . He was looking for volunteers to go back to the *Yorktown*. . . . She was afloat and there was a fair chance of saving or salvaging the vessel.

The fellows that were with me on that destroyer. There was a number of them from my division—K division—which was Communications. We looked at each other and I finally said, "Well, okay. I'll go back." The other fellows . . . kept saying, "Don't do it, Frank. Don't do it. You haven't got a chance of saving the ship. You'll lose your life." I said, "Well, somebody has to go back. The captain can't do what he has to do all by himself." . . .

We rigged up a breeches buoy and swung me and half dozen of other fellows over to the *Astoria*. . . . By the time we got back to the *Yorktown*, it was Saturday morning [6 June]. . . . My job, being in communications . . . was to destroy all the classified material, coding machines, you name it. So, Saturday morning . . . at

Smoke from fires set by three bomb hits covers the *Yorktown* after the Japanese dive-bombing attack of 4 June. It was this smoke that led Japanese aviators to believe that they had mortally wounded the *Yorktown*. This photo shows how the sides of the hangar decks on the *Yorktown, Enterprise,* and *Hornet* could be opened to allow aircraft to warm up their engines there instead of just on the flight deck above.

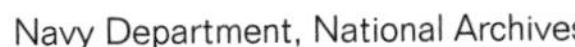

Navy Department, National Archives

dawn they put us in a launch from the *Astoria* and . . . about twenty-five or thirty of us . . . went over to the *Yorktown*. Now she was laying on her portside, like a sailboat. I stepped from the launch onto the hangar deck on the portside, which would normally be twenty-five or thirty feet above the waterline. You couldn't hold your balance because of the incline of the vessel, so we had to run lines all around the hangar deck, hand over hand to keep from going back into the ocean.

My job was to go up to Radio Central to get some big mail sacks that we always had aboard, fill them up with all different kinds of classified paraphernalia . . . everything I could get my hands on . . . and drop them off the side. The first couple of bags I dropped from the flight deck, but because of that angle it was difficult to get near the edge of that flight deck and push the bags over to make sure they [went] to the bottom. . . . So after a while I started going from Radio Central down the ladders to the hangar deck, which was difficult. I had on a kapok life jacket, which was cumbersome, and . . . going down those steep ladders and trying to hang on to the ladder with one hand and the sack with the other hand, until I got to the hangar deck, then drop them over, which was much easier. Well, I did that all morning until around noon time. . . .

[When the *Yorktown* was attacked again that afternoon, Fabian recalled the hit on the destroyer *Hammann*.] I'm standing on the hangar deck looking right at that. . . . She broke in two. . . . It went so quick, I couldn't believe it. . . . [T]he bow section went under within about a minute, I would say. But the stern section stayed up longer and there were two men—I can still see them—working on the depth charges on the stern of that vessel trying to evidently put them on safety. And when that stern section went under after two minutes, they went under with it. Shortly thereafter, the depth charges went [off] under the *Yorktown*. So between

A chief petty officer, with his socks pulled up over his pants to shield his legs from possible burns, walks forward past the number IV 1.1-inch antiaircraft gun on the *Yorktown* after the morning dive-bombing of the ship on 4 June. The first bomb to strike the *Yorktown* killed or injured almost all the men manning this gun and number III gun, which was partly protected by the large crane seen to the left of this photograph. LT Joseph P. Pollard, one of the *Yorktown*'s medical officers, was manning Battle Dressing Station Number 1, and he and his assistants were suddenly faced with the need to treat dozens of severely wounded men. As he later recalled, blood and body fragments covered the two gun mounts. Splinters from this bomb started fires on planes in the *Yorktown*'s hangar, but hangar officer LT Alberto C. Emerson triggered the hangar sprinkler system and doused the blaze.

U.S. Naval Institute Photo Archive

the torpedoes, and the bombs, and the depth charges that poor vessel took an awful beating. . . .

It dawned on me that I had left my life jacket up at Radio Central. Coming down those ladders to the hangar deck was so cumbersome, I took the life jacket off after a while and left it at Radio Central. So I'm saying to myself, "Will I have time to go up to Radio Central to get it? Is the ship going to capsize? If she does, I'm gone." I decided I'd better not. . . . I made my way in a scrambling fashion all the way back to the stern of the vessel, and not a damn life jacket to be seen anywhere. I didn't know what to do. I couldn't jump in the water. I'd drown. Then I realized that we had an ocean going tug that had come out from Midway Island, the *Vireo*. She had put a line on the *Yorktown* . . . and was to the stern of the *Yorktown*.

The *Yorktown*'s damaged funnel emits a pillar of dark smoke after the ship was hit by three bombs on 4 June. Members of the crew are repairing damage to the flight deck. Visible to the left are two 5-inch dual-purpose guns, multiple 50-caliber machine guns, and the two forward 1.1-inch gun mounts. Also visible are arresting gear wires stretched athwart the flight deck forward. They gave the *Yorktown* the ability to land planes over her bow while she steamed in reverse.

U.S. Naval Institute Photo Archive

[The *Vireo*] was picking up the other fellows that had gone back with me that had survived, and hauling them aboard . . . I couldn't swim from the stern of the *Yorktown* to where she was, . . . [but] fortunately, in an area suspended between the flight deck and the hangar deck on the *Yorktown*, was an area we called the Hollywood Deck. I don't know where the name came from. Up there was a lot of tarpaulins and other Navy gear . . . I got out one of the planks . . . and threw it over the side, jumped in, came up beside it, got on it.

I laid down on it and paddled all my way over to where the *Vireo* was. Just as I came alongside the *Vireo* she was lying dead in the water as she picked up the other fellows that had gone back to the *Yorktown* with me. They were all aboard by this time. By the time I got over there, somebody aboard the *Vireo* thought they saw more torpedo wakes and with that they started up . . . the engine on the vessel and the propeller, of course. All of a sudden I realized as I came alongside the *Vireo* I was heading towards the propeller. I let out a devilish scream. One of the fellows that was on the *Vireo* threw me a line, which I grabbed and they all pulled me aboard. . . .

We stayed aboard overnight on the *vireo*. . . . We weren't going to go off and leave the ship.

CHAPTER
25

I Sank the *Yorktown* at Midway

By Yahachi Tanabe, formerly Lieutenant Commander, IJN, with Joseph D. Harrington

Proceedings, May 1963: pp. 59–651

The tension in *I-168*'s conning tower had been steadily building up for six and a half hours. In the cramped command post, I stood, palms out, waiting to grip the rising periscope's handles. We were all perspiring heavily. My torpedo petty officer was scanning his switch panel, and a nervous helmsman wiped clammy hands frequently on his pants. Lieutenant (jg) Nakagawa, pencil in hand, mopped his damp brow between looks at the compass and speed indicator. But my gunnery officer, Ensign Watanabe, seemed almost unconcerned. Of the five, his job was by far the simplest. Our submarine was creeping straight toward the crippled American aircraft carrier *Yorktown.* There were no ballistics problems for Watanabe to work out—the range was point-blank, and target speed was nearly zero.

The whine of the periscope's lift motor died away as I sighted through the eyepiece. I had been allowing myself a maximum of five seconds on each sight check and I didn't intend to change the tactic. One quick glance would give me the range, and I could give the order to fire torpedoes.

The periscope stopped. I looked and then stepped back. "Down periscope! Right, twenty degrees rudder! Maintain full silence! Maintain speed of three knots!"

My navigator and gunnery officer were astounded. "What has happened, Captain?" they asked, "Aren't we attacking?" They knew we were at that moment so close to *Yorktown* that we could not possibly miss.

"We are going around again." I told them, knowing full well that four, and maybe as many as seven, American destroyers were prowling overhead. "The range is too short! I'm going to open the range and try again. I want to be sure of this kill!"

An odd series of events had put *I-168* where she was on 6 June 1942, deep inside the *Yorktown*'s protective circle of American destroyers whose crews were listening for a Japanese submarine. Although I would soon write a last line in that bloody chapter of Japanese history called the Midway Island Battle, the portion I had originally been scheduled to carry was small, indeed. Of the 160-odd ships that gathered from all parts of the Empire to strike at Midway, and the Aleutians, *I-168* had the simplest assignment of all—scouting.

I-168's task was to scout to the southward of Midway, and report on as much of the enemy's activities as we could observe. According to the basic plan, we were

This Norman Bel Geddes painting shows the *Hammann* and the *Yorktown* as both were torpedoed on the afternoon of 6 June by the Japanese submarine *I-168*. Lieutenant Commander Tanabe Yahachi, skipper of the submarine, spent many hours stalking the *Yorktown* and managed finally to slip inside the *Yorktown*'s protective destroyer screen. The torpedo that hit the *Hammann* damaged the destroyer so severely that she sank quickly—so quickly that at least some of the depth charges on her stern could not be disarmed, and they exploded under water, killing or injuring a number of swimmers. The carrier sank the next day, 7 June.

U.S. Naval Institute

to see no action at all. We would be near when the troops landed, but by then, our job would have been done.

We were the van ship of the entire operation, coming in sight of Kure Island, west of Midway, on 31 May 1942. Part of the over-all strategy called for seizing this island, too. It was to be a seaplane and midget submarine base. After radioing a report that nothing appeared to be happening on that island, I proceeded to Midway, and spent the first three days of June making observations there. We would spend daylight hours on periscope watch, on Midway's southern horizon. After dark each night, we moved in within five miles, and continued to watch through powerful binoculars. Our observations made us think that the Americans were expecting imminent attack. I radioed the information that 50 to 100 planes were making landings daily. This meant that American forces on Midway were getting ready to fly extensive patrols, or else were bringing in air protection from Hawaii.

The four carriers of our striking force, although detected at the last, got near enough to launch planes against the island. *I-168* had a front seat, or at least I did, at the day periscope, when 108 of our planes hit the island. Divided into equal numbers of fighters, dive bombers, and torpedo bombers, the last of which operated as level bombers and carried a 1,770-pound bomb each, this force did heavy damage. My crew grew more and more excited as I described the action to them, and a great cheer went up as I described some fuel tanks being blown sky high.

This portion of the attack appeared to be successful, even though Midway's airplanes had been warned. We saw them take off before ours arrived, and watched them land after that first attack ended. At this point Japan was doing very well. More than 100 of our 108 planes made it safely back to their carriers, while our Zeros shot down or badly damaged two dozen American fighters.

Readers are aware of what transpired after that. The Americans counterattacked, with Grumman torpedo bombers, Martin bombers, and Boeing Flying Fortresses, as well as Douglas and Vultee dive bombers. A total of 52 planes attacked our striking force. All were either shot down or driven off, none of them able to do more than get a few machine gun bullets into one Japanese ship. The American aircraft carriers had slipped into the battle area before our submarine scouting lines had gotten into position. Their planes came next. They sent in an additional 41 planes, 32 of which were shot down. At that point, practically no damage had been done to our side. The 4th of June seemed to be a great day for Japanese arms.

Then the tide of battle turned. While our Zeros were at low level, defending against torpedo bombers, 54 American dive bombers plunged out of the sky against loaded flight decks. They made a shambles of *Kaga*, *Akagi*, and *Soryu*. No hits were made on *Hiryu*. She soon got away two strikes. They put three bombs and two torpedoes into USS *Yorktown,* but a return attack by the Americans hurt *Hiryu* so badly that her crew had no choice but to abandon and sink her.

By midnight of 4 June, the Midway Battle was lost, though we did not know it yet. Admiral Yamamoto still had hopes of finding the American ships and sinking them in a surface engagement. It was only the cautiousness of America's Admiral Spruance that prevented this. Having lost one carrier, Spruance decided it was better to fight again another day, and he turned his ships eastward after a short run westward. Comparison of ships' logs after the war showed that, had he continued westward, his two carriers, eight cruisers, and 15 destroyers would have run into a Japanese force that included seven battleships!

While Yamamoto's main body was steaming eastward, hoping to catch the American striking force, *I-168* was given orders to close in on Midway and open fire with her 4-inch deck gun. I was to continue this until joined by the cruisers *Mikuma, Mogami, Suzuyu,* and *Kumano.* These were the world's most powerful heavy cruisers then. Their 40 big guns might easily have smashed Midway's defenses with a bombardment in the early hours of 5 June, paving the way for an easy landing of the 5,000 troops in the transport force.

I obeyed orders, taking *I-168* in. We surfaced about 0130 on 5 June but got off only six rounds before a pair of shore searchlights picked us out. We submerged immediately. Meanwhile, the four cruisers had their order changed, and were withdrawing. In the morning we were sighted by planes and attacked by them, suffering no damage. We were pursued for a short while by an American ship.

I-168 slipped back onto station as soon as I thought it was safe. We were supposed to watch the enemy and I intended to do so.

The next time our radio antenna poked above the waves frightening news came through it. *Soryu* and *Kaga* had gone down the evening before. *Akagi* and *Hiryu* had followed them not long before the American planes attacked *I-168.* One of the messages gave *I-168* a new role to play. Scout planes from Japanese cruisers had sighted the American aircraft carrier *Yorktown* lying dead in the water about 150 miles northeast of Midway. My orders came through quite clearly: "Submarine *I-168* will locate and destroy the American carrier."

We set off at once, running submerged in daylight hours at the best speed we could make and still nurse our batteries. After dark I ran on the surface, but could not use top speed for fear of missing our target in the blackness. So it was that, at 0530, on 6 June, the 12-mm. binoculars of my best-trained lookout picked up *Yorktown.* She was a black shape on the horizon, about 11 miles distant.

It was the easiest intercept a submarine commander ever made. My course had not changed, from beginning to end.

I ordered a dive, a course change to 045 degrees, and then reduced speed to six knots, leveling off *I-168* at 90 feet. As we shortened the range, I reduced speed until we were never doing more than three knots. At intervals I moved *I-168* up to 60 feet and took sightings. It required only a few course adjustments to set her heading straight for *Yorktown*'s beam.

Our screws were barely turning over, and I hoped they were not giving off enough turbulence for the American ships to detect us. I had sighted one destroyer ahead of the carrier with a towline out to her, and another destroyer nestled close to *Yorktown*'s side. Three more kept station on the side I was approaching, which made me feel certain there must be at least two more on the opposite side. This meant seven of them against one of us.

It never occurred to me to do anything except continue my approach and attack, in spite of the odds. Our intelligence said the American Fleet had seven carriers. Two of them, *Ranger* and *Wasp,* were reported in the Atlantic, and we had word that *Saratoga* was on the U.S. West coast. One more, and perhaps two, had been sunk in the Coral Sea Battle a month before. That left the United States with no more than three carriers operating against us, and one of them was dead ahead. Sinking her would mean that the enemy would be left with no more than two to use against us for some time, a vital point now that we had just lost four of our first-line aircraft carriers.

Each time I took a sight, the sun was higher in the sky. *Yorktown* appeared to be making just a little headway. I kept making minor changes of course to keep *I-168* headed at her amidships section. We might get sunk in this action, but before that happened, I meant to do the maximum possible damage to this ship. I wanted my torpedoes to plow into her midsection, not her bow or stern.

In those moments, a lot of faith was being placed by my crew in shrine charms previously given to each *I-168* man by Lieutenant Gunichi Mochizuki, my chief electrical officer. Mochizuki, a deeply religious man, spent much time at shrines ashore, praying. My crew fervently hoped that his piety had given him some extra influence with the gods. When there was time to turn my thoughts in that direction, so did I.

All *I-168* men limited their movements to the most necessary ones only, fearing to create some sound which the American detectors might pick up. By 1100, I had decided that the enemy equipment was not very sensitive. This gave me confidence as the range shortened; I kept moving in. Suddenly my sound operator reported that the Americans had stopped emitting detection signals. I couldn't understand this but, since it was now nearly noon, I tried to make my voice light and told my crew, "It appears the Americans have interrupted their war for lunch. Now is our chance to strike them good and hard, while they are eating!" There were small jokes made about what to give them for dessert. Shortly thereafter I raised the periscope again.

Abaft my beam, each about 1,000 yards distant, were a pair of American destroyers, one to port, one to starboard. *I-168* had safely pierced the protective screen of escorts; I could now give the order to fire.

Then I took another look. *Yorktown* and her hugging destroyer filled my periscope lens. I was too close! At that moment I estimated my range at 600 yards or less. It was necessary to come around and open up the range.

What I had to do now was try to escape detection by those destroyers above us and get far enough away so that my torpedoes, fired from a 60-foot depth, would have enough running space to stabilize themselves at a 19-foot depth for hitting. Whatever was the reason, enemy sound detectors could no longer be picked up by our equipment. I knew the destroyermen above were not asleep.

I kept *I-168* in a right-hand circle, easing the rudder a little so that I could return to my original track at a point about one mile from *Yorktown.* I didn't dare put up the periscope until the compass showed us back on our original course. So I concentrated instead on a torpedo tactic I wanted to use. Though some submarines in 1942 had Model 95 torpedoes—underwater versions of the very powerful Model 93 "Long Lance" used on surface ships—my torpedoes were an older type. Model 95's had 991-pound warheads, mine had 446-pound ones. So I planned to make two torpedoes into one.

If I followed the usual procedure and fired my four torpedoes with a two-degree spread, they would cover six degrees. But I wanted very badly to deprive the Americans of this carrier. I intended to limit my salvo to a two degree spread. I would fire No.1 and No.2 first, then send No.3 and No.4 in their wakes, on the same courses. That way, I could achieve two large hits instead of four small ones. I could thus deliver all my punch into the carrier's midsection, rather than spread it out along her hull.

When I was back on my approach course, I took another look, and wagged my head at how the destroyers still seemed unaware of us. Either they were poor sailors, had poor equipment, or *I-168* was a charmed vessel. At a range of 1,200 yards, my periscope up, I sent my four torpedoes away as planned. I did not lower the periscope then, either. The wakes of my torpedoes could be seen, so their source could be quickly established. And, if *I-168* was going to die, I at least wanted the satisfaction of seeing whether our fish hit home.

Less than a minute later we heard the explosions. "Banzai!" someone shouted. "Go ahead at full speed!" I ordered, then, "Take her down to 200 feet!" My conning tower officers were surprised when I ordered speed cut back to three knots a short time afterward, but by that time we were where I wanted to be, directly beneath the enemy carrier. I didn't think she would sink at once, so had no fear of her coming down on us. And one of our torpedoes had run shallow and hit the destroyer alongside *Yorktown.* There would be men in the water. Her destroyers wouldn't risk dropping depth charges for awhile, for fear of killing their comrades. Meanwhile, I hoped to creep out of there. I ordered left rudder, and tried to ease away at three knots.

My plan didn't work. The American destroyers were on us in no time, dropping depth charges. They had *I-168* pinpointed, and took turns making runs, according to my sound operator. We had torpedoed *Yorktown* at 1330. By 1530, the enemy had dropped 60 depth charges at us, one or two at a time. They were much more sparing with these than they were later in the war, and I took advantage of this by trying to keep an opposite course to whichever destroyer attacked us. The tactic worked a number of times, many depth charges dropping well astern of us as the enemy passed directly overhead.

One of the destroyer captains must have estimated that I was doing this, though. The last depth charge of the two-hour barrage landed just off my bow, putting out all lights, springing small leaks in many places, and causing the danger of chlorine gas forming in my forward battery room.

This was serious. *I-168* had only ten gas masks for a crew of 104 men. But Lieutenant Mochizuki took a small group of men into the forward battery room, closed it behind them to protect the rest of us, and began disconnecting damaged batteries. Before long they had the situation under control, but more trouble was occurring in the bow. Both the outer and inner doors of No. 1 Torpedo Tube were sprung. *I-168* was partly open to the sea; water was entering the bow section.

We couldn't work on the outer door, of course, so men tried to seal off the inner one, that last depth charge having distorted it. Instead of lying flat in its seal, it bulged into the torpedo room, while water jetted from leaks around its edge. Torpedomen finally plugged the leaks with wedges, however, and everything came under control.

By now we had taken on enough water to weigh the bow down considerably. I ordered all crewmen possible to move aft as a counterweight. This did not remedy the situation, so I employed a tactic used by other Japanese submarines in the war. Every man walked forward again, picked up a sack of rice from our supplies, and carried it aft. This helped considerably, and *I-168* was on an even keel by the time full electrical power was restored.

Now we had been operating nearly 12 hours submerged. The destroyers had continued to fire depth charges after 1530, but only sporadically. That sixtieth one had hurt us, and made us bob up from 200 feet nearly to 60 feet. A few more like it, and we might have broached, a perfect target for the searchers. But it seemed as if they were hoarding charges for a final attack, knowing we would have to surface and charge batteries before long.

There were five pistols and ten rifles in *I-168*'s armory. I ordered these issued and told my deck gun crew to stand by near the tower. Sunset was not far off. If we could surface then, and run long enough to charge our batteries, *I-168* might have a chance to reverse the situation, for we still had six torpedoes and five usable tubes left. We might even be able to dive and counterattack, using the darkness to our advantage.

It was still daylight when I ordered "Surface!" There had been a long lull in the firing, and I thought the enemy destroyers might have given up when no sounds could be heard on our detectors. When I got to the open bridge, there was no sign of *Yorktown* on the eastern horizon. I was sure she was somewhere beyond it, sinking, for I had seen the torpedoes hit. Between myself and the horizon, I could see three American destroyers, running in line abreast to the east, on an opposite course from my own. I guessed they were looking for other possible submarines, or else had been summoned back to help with survivors of the carrier.

We were not long on the surface before two of the three ships swung about in pursuit. I estimated their distance at about 11,000 yards. We ran west at 14 knots, the best speed I could make while charging batteries and taking in air. I ordered smoke made, using the heavy black clouds for cover. It helped for a while, and the enemy ships did not appear to be gaining on us very much during the first 30 minutes. I couldn't understand this at all, because of the speed I knew they could make.

When they closed to about 6,500 yards, they opened fire and not long afterward *I-168* was straddled. All a good gunnery officer had to do now was "walk" across me a few times and all would be over.

I can remember the moment of the straddle most vividly. My lookouts began darting quick looks at me, their faces strained and pale. They were anxious to be back in the hull, and diving. I could also detect a high note in the voices below as reports on the progress of the battery charge were called up to me. The men above wanted to dive, though they dared not say so, and the men below wanted to remain surfaced as long as possible while dials and gauges made higher readings. Finally, the enemy silhouettes growing ever larger, I called down, "Do you have enough air and power for short time operations?"

A reluctant "Yes, sir," came up.

"Stand by to dive!" I shouted, and cleared the bridge. I followed all hands into the hatch, ordering *I-168* swung about for a dive into her own smoke. The tactic worked. Both destroyers over-ran us. They soon had our location fixed again, but dropped only a few charges before breaking off the action and making toward the east at high speed.

I looked at my watch. Only a few minutes until sunset. Whether the enemy ships departed because they feared a night encounter with us, or whether they had no more depth charges, I did not know. In either case, *I-168* was going to get out of this now.

We surfaced a little while after sunset. Assuming that patrol planes from Midway would be seeking us out, we headed north. I hoped they would think I had set a course for Truk, and thus be thrown off the scent. After a few hours, we changed course for Hokkaido, our northernmost island, it then being the nearest to us on a great circle course. *I-168* cruised at her most economical speed, for we were not out of trouble yet. Oil was the Imperial Navy's lifeblood and strictly rationed. *I-168* had been given only enough for cruising to Midway and operating there for a few days. All submarines were supposed to have refueled from captured stores when the island was taken. By practicing severe economies, however, we were able to set Yokosuka, then Kure, as our final destination.

A great crowd greeted our arrival. There were cheers, music, congratulations, and speeches in abundance as we tied up. A special news broadcast had told earlier how *I-168* had torpedoed the carrier *Yorktown,* and that she had sunk the following morning. A special report of the exploit was rendered His Majesty, The Emperor—something done only when the war news was of great magnitude.

I was given command of a new submarine, *I-776,* at once and granted special permission to hand-pick only men who had factory and machine experience as civilians. This guaranteed me a crack crew.

There were to be other exciting times in the war for me. In *I-776,* I made the first submarine reinforcement of Guadalcanal after the Americans landed there, and with one torpedo knocked out the heavy cruiser *Chester* for a year. Later, after surviving a tenacious attack on *I-776* in the Solomons, I was received in audience by the Emperor himself.

But all I could think of that day at Kure, while being hailed as a hero, was that as yet no news of *Kaga, Akagi, Hiryu,* and *Soryu* had been released to the public. All the Japanese people thought we had scored another Pearl Harbor at Midway. They didn't know that four of our fighting carriers, together with hundreds of Japan's best planes and pilots, were gone forever. My sinking of the USS *Yorktown* was small revenge for that loss.

— *AUTHOR* —

LCDR Yahachi Tanabe entered the submarine service of the Imperial Japanese Navy in 1934. At the end of World War II, he acted as the Imperial Naval Representative at Atsugi, Japan. Chief Journalist Joseph D. Harrington, USN, assisted LCDR Tanabe in preparing this article.

CHAPTER

26

Incredible Midway

By LCDR Thomas E. Powers, USNR

Proceedings, June 1967: pp. 64–73

A sophisticated reader would reject as absurd a work of fiction the plot of which hinged on circumstances and events similar to those surrounding the Battle of Midway. That reader doubtless would dismiss the story as too contrived, too bizarre to have ever happened. Yet, of course, it did happen. Can it have been a quarter of a century ago?

Midway atoll is a speck of coral barely jutting out of the blue Pacific some 1,300 miles west-northwest of Pearl Harbor. Except for smaller Kure Island some 60 miles beyond, Midway is the final link in the sprawling Hawaiian chain. Its essential parts are few, consisting of two tiny islands, Sand and Eastern, enclosed in a forbidding reef.

Two considerations aroused Japanese interest in this remote piece of real estate. First, Japanese strategists calculated that if the "Sentry of Hawaii," as Midway was known, were threatened, those ships which had escaped the Pearl Harbor catastrophe—particularly the aircraft carriers—would be drawn to her defense, only to be crushed in a showdown battle. Second, Midway itself would strengthen Japan's eastern defense perimeter and would serve as a base from which aircraft and submarines could more easily detect U.S. ship movements.

Admiral Isoroku Yamamoto, Commander-in-Chief of the Japanese Combined Fleet, was in over-all command of the Japanese forces which participated in the Midway engagement. His intricate plan called for the deployment of some 200 ships, divided mainly among four distinct operating forces. A Northern Force of two light carriers accompanied by cruisers and destroyers was to feint at Dutch Harbor in the Aleutians on 3 June 1942, with the purpose of drawing a retaliatory fleet from Pearl Harbor temporarily in that direction. The following day, and hundreds of miles southward, Vice Admiral Chuichi Nagumo's First Carrier Striking Force, centered around the carriers *Akagi, Kaga, Soryu,* and *Hiryu,* was to approach Midway from the northwest and neutralize its defenses through air attacks. On 5 June, an Invasion Force, approaching Midway from the southwest, was to invade and occupy Midway. By 6 June, Admiral Yamamoto's Main Force of large battleships and heavy cruisers was to arrive in the Midway vicinity. Yamamoto speculated that the American fleet, now having recovered from the Dutch Harbor deception, would make a belated attempt to oppose the invasion, only to be surrounded by the various Japanese forces and be utterly destroyed.

Late in May 1942, the four major Japanese components got underway. The 3 June feint at Dutch Harbor was conducted on schedule and, by early 4 June, Nagumo's carrier force arrived at its appointed position, 240 miles northwest of Midway. Although Nagumo was certain that the element of surprise was in his favor, it was not. Admiral Chester W. Nimitz, Commander-in-Chief of the U.S. Pacific Fleet at Pearl Harbor, had known of the approximate date and location of the invasion since May. U.S. Army and Navy crypto-analysts, having broken the Japanese diplomatic and naval codes in a project appropriately named "Magic," had been supplying an abundance of information about Japanese plans from intercepted messages in code.

Foreknowledge of the invasion did not lessen Nimitz's mammoth task of providing the necessary fleet and island defenses to oppose the powerful naval force which would challenge Midway. Midway got its additional men, planes, and armament, but unfortunately, of the 141 aircraft which eventually filled the airstrips on Eastern Island, many were obsolete models. The F2A-3 Buffalo, a fighter of 1939 vintage, was sardonically dubbed the "flying coffin," while the no more modern SB2U-3 Vindicator, a dive bomber, was tagged the "vibrator" and "wind indicator." These older aircraft were augmented by 16 Dauntless SBD-2 dive bombers, seven F4F-3 Wildcat fighters, six TBF Avenger torpedo planes, four B-26 Marauder medium bombers, and about 27 PBY Catalinas and Boeing B-17 Flying Fortresses.

Fleet opposition of the Japanese invasion fell to the carriers *Enterprise, Hornet,* and *Yorktown*—the only available "flattops" in the Pacific at that time—eight

The *Yorktown* burning after being struck early on the afternoon of 4 June by three bombs from Type 99 dive-bombers (Vals) launched earlier from the *Hiryu*. It was this heavy smoke that convinced surviving Japanese pilots that they had left their target sinking. The smoke, and the damage to the *Yorktown*'s radar and communications gear, forced Admiral Fletcher to shift his flag to the heavy cruiser *Astoria*. Though at first stopped dead in the water by the Japanese bombs, the *Yorktown*'s crew was able to get her speed back to eighteen knots, extinguish the fires that had caused the heavy smoke, and repair her flight deck in time to launch the ship's CAP in the face of the second Japanese aerial attack later that day. Just visible behind the smoke is one of the *Yorktown*'s escorts, probably the destroyer *Morris*.

Navy Department, National Archives

cruisers, and 17 destroyers. Only the *Enterprise* and the *Hornet* were ready for battle. The *Yorktown*, suffering from damage and losses sustained in the Battle of the Coral Sea, would fight at Midway with only temporary repairs and minimal personnel replacements.

The American fleet was divided into two task forces. Task Force 17, centered around the *Yorktown*, was under the command of Rear Admiral Frank Jack Fletcher, a veteran of the Coral Sea engagement, while Task Force 16, centered around *Hornet* and *Enterprise*, was under the command of Rear Admiral Raymond A. Spruance. The latter was the personal choice of Admiral William F. Halsey when an acute skin infection prevented his own participation. Fletcher, the senior of the two flag officers, was appointed Officer in Tactical Command of the composite force. Task Forces 16 and 17 left Pearl Harbor on different days toward the end of May, but by the evening of 3 June, they were steaming together some 300 miles northeast of Midway. Admiral Nagumo's Striking Force was then only 400 miles west of Fletcher and Spruance.

On board his flagship the *Akagi,* Admiral Nagumo pondered the task before him. Anxiety ran high as the hour of battle drew near. A sailor on the 4 June mid-watch thought he sighted planes weaving in and out of the clouds, and the *Akagi* crew was ordered to battle stations. But the report proved false, and the lookouts were admonished not to mistake " . . . stars for moving lights due to the motion of the ship."

In retrospect, this innocuous incident aboard *Akagi* would, to some, be an omen of the crises then in the making. The Dutch Harbor feint had failed to produce the expected reaction; instead, the Pacific Fleet lurked nearby. And Admiral Nagumo was unaware of either the failure of the diversion or the closeness of the enemy fleet.

Still another thread of the delicately fashioned Japanese fabric had been snagged by unforeseeable circumstances. Overhaul repairs had delayed the departure of 15 submarines which were to patrol the most likely routes the American fleet would take out of Pearl Harbor to oppose the Dutch Harbor attack. Consequently, they reached their appointed stations two days late. A more punctual arrival might have resulted in their intercepting part of the U.S. fleet. Instead, the Japanese submarines were to maintain a constant vigil throughout the battle for an enemy who had already passed them by.

At 2:45 a.m., 4 June, loudspeakers on board Nagumo's carriers barked the order which brought air crews scrambling from their bunks to prepare for the dawn air assaults against Midway. Two hours later, Lieutenant Joichi Tomonaga, the *Hiryu*'s air officer, was leading 108 aircraft on a southeastward course toward Midway, 240 miles away. Just before the launching, Admiral Nagumo estimated the situation: "The enemy is not yet aware of our plan, and he has not yet detected our task force. There is no evidence of an enemy task force in our vicinity."

Both the Striking Force and its attacking aircraft were sighted by Midway patrol planes shortly before 6 a.m. The reports of enemy contact produced instinctive reactions among the people on Midway. Soon 20 Buffaloes and six Wildcats were hurrying northwestward to intercept the Japanese planes, but the American fighters—especially the sluggish Buffaloes—were no match for the Zeroes which provided protection for the bombers. Just ten American fighters returned after the raid, and of these only two were fit for further combat.

Although widespread damage was inflicted upon installations on Sand and Eastern Islands, total destruction of Midway's defenses was not achieved in the raid. Consequently, at 7 a.m., Lieutenant Tomonaga radioed the following message to Nagumo: "There is need for a second attack wave."

This simple message would set off a chain of events which would prove disastrous for the Imperial Striking Force.

When the report of contact with the Striking Force reached Midway shortly before 6 a.m., not only the 26 fighters had taken off.

Soon six TBF torpedo planes and four B-26 medium bombers—each carrying a torpedo—and 27 dive bombers were on a course to the enemy ships. The dive bomber contingent consisted of 16 SBDs and 11 of the old Vindicators. Additionally, 14 B-17s which had departed at dawn to bomb the Invasion Force were diverted to the Striking Force.

Shortly before 7 a.m. and continuously for more than an hour, the Striking Force defended itself against four waves of attacking Midway aircraft. But the deadly Zeroes in Nagumo's combat air patrol and the intense shipboard fire proved too much for these aircraft, conspicuously naked of fighter protection. Only the high-flying B-17s escaped unscathed, while two B-26s, five TBFs, eight SBDs, and two Vindicators were destroyed. And, to compound the agony of the losses, none of the missiles released by any of the American planes found a Japanese target.

Meanwhile, Admiral Nagumo had been considering Tomonaga's 7 a.m. recommendation for a second Midway strike. Another 108 planes had been assembled on his flight decks for use in the event of the "unlikely" appearance of an American fleet. Nagumo wondered whether he should risk sending these reserve aircraft against Midway. As he reflected upon the problem, the first wave of Midway planes—the TBFs and B-26s carrying torpedoes—came skimming over the water toward the Japanese formation. Although successfully repelled, the foray convinced Nagumo that the destruction of Midway's air power had not been achieved. This was all the assurance he needed that a second attack against Midway was required.

Therefore, at 7:15 a.m., Nagumo issued the following order: "Planes in second attack wave stand by to carry out attack today. Reequip yourself with bombs." The order necessitated having those bombers armed with torpedoes—36 standing on the *Akagi* and the *Kaga*—rearmed with bombs. Accordingly, crews on the *Akagi* and the *Kaga* began pushing the bombers to the elevators, where they were lowered to the hangar deck once again for the arduous task of exchanging torpedoes for bombs.

Shortly before sunrise, Nagumo had sent patrol planes to search for a possible American fleet in an area northeast to south of the Striking Force. Although no American ships were expected, the launching of patrol planes was a routine precaution. All but one of these departed at 4:30 a.m. as scheduled. But, due to catapult problems on the heavy cruiser *Tone*, one of the cruiser's two seaplanes was not launched until 5 a.m.—a half-hour late.

At 7:20 a.m., the pilot of the tardy plane from the *Tone* sighted American ships near the outer perimeter of his search area. He immediately reported contact with "enemy surface ships," giving their course and bearing. The time of the message was 7:28 a.m.

Nagumo and his staff were stunned by the contact report. Were there any carriers in the enemy formation? The search plane's message was vague. At 7:47 a.m.

the order was flashed to the *Tone*'s plane: "Ascertain ship types, and maintain contact."

The rearming of the *Akagi*'s and *Kaga*'s planes with bombs, having proceeded undisturbed since 7:15 a.m., was about half completed. Realizing now that a second attack against Midway was of secondary importance to destroying the American fleet, Nagumo called a halt to the exchange of torpedoes for bombs and waited for further information from the *Tone*'s plane.

Subsequent reports from the seaplane suggested that the U.S. force contained at least one carrier; therefore, Nagumo calculated that the enemy fleet posed too great a threat to postpone its destruction until Midway's defenses were neutralized. Two considerations, however, prompted him to conclude that the most effective assault against the U.S. Fleet could not be conducted immediately. First, half of the *Akagi*'s and *Kaga*'s bombers were now rearmed with bombs—a weapon considered inferior to torpedoes against ships. Second, the fighters had been expending ammunition and fuel against Midway aircraft for over an hour, and were not ready to accompany the bombers.

Nagumo decided that he would first clear his flight decks in order to recover the planes returning from the Midway raid, and then retire temporarily northward

There are three aircraft in this photo. At least one is a torpedo plane from the *Hiryu*, flying low after releasing its torpedo at the *Yorktown* on the afternoon of 4 June. One of the others may be an F4F-4 fighter trying to defend the *Yorktown*, though it also might be one of the *Hiryu*'s torpedo planes. The dark bursts in the air, and the spouts in the water, are from antiaircraft guns. Japanese and American aircraft fought one another within the barrage thrown up by the *Yorktown*'s escorts.

U.S. Naval Institute Photo Archive

to prepare for a mass attack against the American fleet. In conjunction with this plan, Nagumo ordered that those bombers formerly containing torpedoes, but now carrying bombs, be armed again with torpedoes.

As Admiral Nagumo reflected upon the events which had thus far occurred that morning, he must have been angry. If there had been no catapult problems on the *Tone,* her search plane would probably have sighted the American fleet a half-hour earlier. The report of contact would have preceded Tomonaga's 7 a.m. message and therefore the muddled exchange of aircraft ordnance would have been avoided. Accordingly, all of Nagumo's bombers, sitting in their original flight deck positions, could have been launched at once against Fletcher and Spruance.

Instead, shortly before 9 a.m., after all aircraft had been recovered, the Striking Force turned northward to prepare for an engagement which by then might have been over. In the hangar deck areas of the *Akagi* and the *Kaga,* crews working feverishly to arm the bombers again with torpedoes did not have time to lower the dislodged bombs to the magazines. They were simply stacking the bombs in the open.

Dawn had begun to break about 4 a.m. on 4 June. Shortly before 5 a.m., the first rays of the sun stretched forward from the eastern horizon and danced off the steel hulls of the ships in Task Forces 16 and 17. Ten *Yorktown* scout planes, launched just before sunrise to locate the Japanese Striking Force, disappeared in the distance. Nagumo was then 215 miles west of the American fleet.

Fletcher and Spruance intercepted the message from the Midway patrol plane which just before 6 a.m. announced contact with the Striking Force. Having to recover his own search planes, Fletcher was not then ready to alter course toward the enemy. He freed Spruance to engage the Japanese independently, promising to follow once his aircraft were again safely aboard. Speeding southward with Task Force 16, Spruance surmised that he must conduct an air strike against the enemy before Nagumo had an opportunity to bomb Midway a second time.

Shortly before 8 a.m., torpedo planes, dive bombers, and fighters from the *Hornet* and the *Enterprise*—six squadrons in all—were winging toward Nagumo's estimated position. But the Striking Force had altered its course northward shortly before 9 a.m., and an open sea taunted each squadron as it arrived at the point of anticipated contact with the enemy.

The *Hornet*'s dive bombers and fighter squadrons gambled that the Japanese had turned southward and the subsequent search in that direction resulted in their missing the enemy entirely.

The 15 TBD Devastators of the *Hornet*'s Torpedo Squadron 8 were successful in locating the Striking Force but that was to be the extent of their success on this terrible day. Torpedo 8 sighted Nagumo's ships about 9:25 a.m. and immediately took aim on the primary target, the carriers in the center of the formation of battleships, cruisers, and destroyers. Lumbering over the water's edge in the level and even flight required for an efficient torpedo launch, the Devastators were easy prey for the swarm of Zeroes that intercepted their approach. Those few planes which escaped the deadly enemy fighters quickly fell victim to Nagumo's fierce shipboard fire. Plane after plane spouted fire and smoke, crashed hard on the water, and disappeared. All 15 planes were destroyed and not a single torpedo hit was obtained.

No sooner had the Torpedo 8 attack been repelled when, just after 9:30 a.m., the 14 Devastators of the *Enterprise*'s Torpedo Squadron 6 arrived on the scene. Although the pilots bore in determinedly toward the Striking Force, the hopelessly vulnerable Devastators were quickly reduced to four, and the few torpedoes released never found their target.

A regrettable quirk of fate may have contributed to the appalling toll exacted from Torpedo Squadrons 6 and 8. The *Enterprise*'s Fighting Squadron 6 was to have accompanied Torpedo 6 to battle. Upon contact with enemy fighters, Torpedo 6 was to have radioed a prearranged signal which would bring the ten Wildcats of Fighting 6 sweeping down on any intercepting Zeroes. Unfortunately, on take-off, Fighting 6 had mistakenly attached itself to Torpedo 8—a plausible error since the aircraft of Torpedo 6 and Torpedo 8 were identical in type and very similar in number.

About the time Torpedo 8 was nearing the Striking Force, clouds began to obliterate the visual contact of Fighting 6 with the *Hornet* aircraft. But the Wildcats continued to circle overhead waiting for the signal which, of course, never came. As a result, Fighting 6 orbited uselessly for 30 minutes, and when gas finally ran low, returned to the *Enterprise* without having fired a shot.

Admiral Fletcher, having finally recovered his search planes, and now possessing more exact information about the Striking Force's whereabouts, at last launched part of the *Yorktown* air group of torpedo planes, dive bombers, and fighters. Twelve Devastators of the *Yorktown*'s Torpedo 3 reached the Striking Force about 10 a.m., just as the remnants of Torpedo 6 were scurrying off into the distance. Torpedo 3 pressed its attack while Fighting 3 struggled to overcome three-to-one odds against Nagumo's Zeroes. Seven Devastators were shot down during their approach to the target, and, although five planes succeeded in launching torpedoes, only two managed to pull away safely. Ten Devastators were eliminated, but, once again, there had been no hits.

The last of the carrier plane torpedo attacks ended at 10:15 a.m. Exultant Japanese crews had cheered wildly while witnessing the one-sided spectacle of the previous 50 minutes. They had good reason to be jubilant, for the performance of the Striking Force that morning against both Midway and carrier aircraft had been nothing short of sensational. Now Nagumo was prepared to strike back. The flight decks of his unscathed carriers were filled with fully armed and fueled aircraft for an immediate attack against Fletcher and Spruance.

Earlier that morning, while Midway-based aircraft were still providing Nagumo with some uneasy moments, the U.S. submarine *Nautilus*—one of 12 boats assigned to patrol Midway's approaches—came to periscope depth right in the center of the Striking Force. She hurried off one ineffectual torpedo shot before plunging to deeper waters. The inevitable depth charge attack followed. When Nagumo turned northward after 9 a.m. a lone destroyer, the *Arashi,* was left behind to keep up the attack on the U.S. submarine. After about 30 minutes the *Arashi* gave up the futile chase and hurried northward to overtake the Striking Force.

Meanwhile, the *Enterprise*'s dive bomber squadron, the only one of the six squadrons launched by Spruance against Nagumo which was not yet accounted for, had been conducting a widespread search for Nagumo's ships. After having searched an extended area around Nagumo's position as reported at 6 a.m., the 37 SBDs of Bombing 6 were attracted suddenly by what appeared to be a tiny vessel far off to their right. Closer inspection identified the solitary ship as a Japanese destroyer—she was the *Arashi* hurrying to rejoin the Striking Force. With directions so obligingly provided, the mystery of the Striking Force's whereabouts was soon solved. At 10:05 a.m., Bombing 6 finally sighted the Japanese ships. At that very moment, Bombing 3's 17 SBDs, which accompanied Fighting 3 and the luckless Torpedo 3 from the *Yorktown,* were approaching the enemy formation from another direction.

Several factors aided an undetected approach by the dive bombers. At 20,000 feet, they were barely visible above a scattered cloud formation. But equally relevant was the fact that Nagumo's lookouts were distracted by the spectacular defense being put up against the American torpedo planes. Additionally, with the Zeroes drawn to the water's edge to repel the torpedo plane attacks, the SBDs encountered no fighter opposition at their high altitude.

If the dive bombers were imperceptible to the Japanese lookouts, quite the opposite was true of Nagumo's ships as viewed by the pilots from overhead. The flight deck of each carrier, painted yellow, stood out sharply against the dark blue sea water. The bow or the stern of each flight deck contained the orange circular symbol of the rising sun. The disc, about 50 feet in diameter, was enclosed in a five-foot band of white. One pilot, convinced that the colorful spectacle sharpened his perception, later stated: "I saw the huge orange disc of the rising sun painted on the vessel's clean, yellow flight deck. . . . It seemed as though they'd painted a bull's eye there for me to aim at . . . I screamed down from several thousand feet, hypnotized by that big orange blob."

Nagumo's flight decks were packed with fully armed and fueled aircraft. At 10:20 a.m., the Admiral gave the order to commence launching when ready. Four minutes later the first of the *Akagi*'s planes roared down the flight deck. At that very moment, one of the *Akagi*'s crew screamed: "Hell-divers!" But it was too late. Bombs from American Dauntless dive bombers were already falling on three carriers.

Bombing 6 selected the *Akagi* and the *Kaga* for attack, while by a stroke of luck, Bombing 3 picked out a third carrier, the *Soryu*. The *Enterprise* aircraft carrying 1,000-pound bombs were directed to the *Akagi* and those carrying one 500-pounder and two 100-pounders, to the *Kaga*. Fate intervened as a few SBDs carrying the heavier missiles fortuitously took aim on the *Kaga*. Consequently, both Japanese carriers received a fairly equal share of the half-ton bombs.

Two bombs found their mark on the *Akagi*. According to Nagumo, neither hit was fatal in itself. But as the fire spread among the aircraft crammed together on the flight deck, their torpedoes began to explode, making firefighting virtually impossible. The inferno spread rapidly to parts of the hangar deck and detonated the bombs which had been carelessly stacked in the open a few hours before. By evening, it was obvious the ship could not be saved. She was therefore abandoned and early the next morning scuttled with torpedoes.

The *Kaga* was no more fortunate. Of the four bombs which hit her, one exploded in the vicinity of the bridge, killing all of its occupants. Induced explosions seemed to occur everywhere until fires extended almost the entire length of the carrier. Early that evening the conflagration reached both the forward and after fuel tanks, causing two tremendous explosions which completely destroyed the ship. The *Kaga* sank immediately.

The *Yorktown* pilots planted three bombs on the *Soryu*, two of which fell among the parked planes on the flight deck causing a chain of induced detonations. Further induced explosions occurred in the bomb and torpedo magazines and in the antiaircraft and machine gun ammunition rooms. Fires ultimately engulfed the entire carrier. That evening, only minutes before the *Kaga*, in a crescendo of explosive claps, the *Soryu* slid beneath the sea.

The SBD pilots had turned the tide of battle, but the reversal of tactical advantage, unrecognized at first, did not bring an immediate halt to the fighting. Eighteen bombers from the unscathed *Hiryu* took up the trail of the withdrawing SBDs, followed them to the U.S. fleet, and made three direct hits on the *Yorktown*. Although the resultant fires were quickly extinguished, two torpedo hits by planes launched from the *Hiryu* about three hours later caused the *Yorktown* to take a precarious list to port, and the carrier was abandoned.

The *Yorktown*, however, refused to sink. The following day she was taken in tow and provided with a destroyer escort. By 6 June, with the destroyer *Hammann* tied alongside to furnish water to fight fires, pumps for counterflooding, and electricity, it appeared that the *Yorktown* would surely be saved. Yet, this was not to be. The Japanese submarine *I-168*, which had been stalking the crippled *Yorktown* for hours from the waters beyond the destroyer screen, at last found an opportunity to strike. Four torpedoes were fired; one missed, two passed under the *Hammann* and exploded on the *Yorktown,* and the fourth struck the *Hammann.* The helpless destroyer broke in two and sank in three minutes with staggering personnel losses. The *Yorktown*'s new injuries proved fatal. At 6 a.m., 7 June, she finally slid over and sank stern first.

About the time the *Yorktown* was first being evacuated, in the afternoon of 4 June, 24 SBDs departed for a second attack on the Striking Force. On the flight deck of Nagumo's only undamaged carrier, the *Hiryu,* the remnants of her air group sat fully armed and fueled for a planned twilight attack on Fletcher and Spruance. Incredibly, it was the early morning scene repeating itself.

The SBDs descended on the *Hiryu* shortly after 5 p.m. Four direct hits soon turned the *Hiryu* into an inferno as induced explosions among the parked planes caused fires to spread eventually over two-thirds of her length. The *Hiryu* lingered between life and death for many hours as every effort was made to save her. But further induced explosions were critical. The *Hiryu* was finally abandoned and early the next morning was scuttled with torpedoes.

Fighting between the Striking Force and the American fleet ended on 4 June. Although Midway and carrier aircraft conducted widespread searches for Nagumo on 5 June, he had by that time withdrawn beyond the search area. Admiral Yamamoto, who was 600 miles west of Nagumo when the *Akagi,* the *Kaga,* and the *Soryu* were hit, at first ordered a general rendezvous of all forces participating in the Midway-Aleutians campaign for the purpose of making a combined thrust against Midway and the American fleet. Then, for some mysterious reason, at 2:55 a.m., 5 June, he called off the Midway operations with the following order: "Occupation of AF (Midway) is cancelled." The cancellation by Yamamoto when he still enjoyed overwhelming superiority in surface ships, including four light carriers from the Invasion and Northern forces, is difficult to justify, and his reasons have never been adequately explained.

As if the events of 4 June had not been sufficiently humiliating to the Japanese, insult was added to injury in one final unhappy incident. Four cruisers from the Invasion Force sent to make a night bombardment of Midway were recalled shortly after midnight when still 90 miles short of the objective. While hurrying away from Midway, the Japanese sighted the American submarine *Tambor* following them on the surface. An emergency turn was ordered, but the *Mogami,* the last cruiser in the column, failed to get the signal in time and crashed into the port quarter of the *Mikuma,* the ship directly in front of her. The *Mogami* lost 40 feet of her bow and thereafter could make no more than 12 knots speed.

Limping along so close to Midway, the *Mogami* was practically defenseless against the air attacks that were sure to come with the daylight. Curiously, however, assaults by Midway and carrier aircraft on 5 and 6 June did not succeed in sinking the *Mogami.* By a strange twist of fate, it was the innocent *Mikuma,* while magnanimously serving as escort to the injured *Mogami,* that succumbed to these bombing raids. Ironically enough, the entire mishap occurred because an attempt had been made to evade a submarine that failed to make an attack either before or after the collision.

To say that the Americans were luckier than the Japanese at Midway would indeed be a gross understatement. Yet, fate alone did not determine the results of the engagement. The Pacific Fleet could not have sprung the trap on the Striking Force if the Japanese code had not been broken. There was nothing lucky about "Magic"; it was the end product of superb ingenuity and a great deal of frustrating work. Both German and British cryptanalysts had tried to break the same code, only to be baffled.

Furthermore, the "miracle" of the *Yorktown* was a tribute to American resoluteness and stands as a salient example of the unwavering determination to win which typified the American attitude both before and during the battle. Although it was estimated that it would take 90 days to repair the damages sustained by the *Yorktown* at Coral Sea, workmen operating around the clock completed temporary mending in less than 48 hours. Nimitz could easily have excused the injured *Yorktown* from the forthcoming operation, but he was determined to scrape together everything he had to throw at the Japanese. Since the *Yorktown* airmen sank the *Soryu* and assisted in the *Hiryu*'s sinking, who can say what the outcome at Midway might have been without her participation?

In striking contrast to the frantic urgency in the preparation of the *Yorktown* for battle was the evident confidence shown by the Japanese regarding use of one of their Coral Sea ships, the carrier *Zuikaku*. Minus any physical damage, the *Zuikaku* was excused from the Midway campaign simply because of the heavy losses in airmen suffered at Coral Sea. The *Yorktown* was faced with the identical problem, to say nothing of her damages, but Admiral Nimitz met the situation squarely by augmenting her ragged air group with replacements from two other carriers. The failure to include the *Zuikaku* in what was defined as a showdown engagement suggests that a certain amount of overconfidence contaminated Japanese planning for the approaching campaign.

The alleged overconfidence is supported by several incidents in the battle itself. "Spirits were high—and why not?" exulted a Japanese aviator, "Every man was convinced that he was about to participate in yet another brilliant victory." A Japanese pilot participating in the Midway air raid rolled his Zero over on its back and flew 50 feet above the ground thumbing his nose at Marine gunners—a spectacular exhibition perhaps, but of dubious value to the raid itself. When Midway Vindicators were attacking the Striking Force, intercepting Zeroes with guns silent did graceful rolls through the Marine formation. One American pilot stated that " . . . more attention to business might easily have wiped out 11 of the slowest and most obsolete planes ever to be used in war." These examples of glaring exhibitionism are indicative of a carefree mental attitude which was not at all consistent with the seriousness of the task at hand.

The attention to duty and great courage shown by the American airmen played a major part in the victory. If inexperience sometimes detracted from flawless performance, the void was more than filled by unyielding aggressiveness. The heroic manner in which the luckless carrier torpedo pilots pressed their attacks, despite overwhelming opposition, kept Nagumo's defenses so completely occupied that the destructive SBDs were not observed until it was too late.

Marine Captain Richard E. Fleming sacrificed his life by crashing his burning Vindicator on the turret of the *Mikuma* during a 5 June attack on the cruiser. His heroic act brought the *Mikuma* her first damage and was instrumental in the eventual destruction of the ship. Fleming became the first Marine aviator of the war to be awarded the Congressional Medal of Honor.

As the giant Japanese armada, bereft of the *Akagi,* the *Kaga,* the *Soryu,* and the *Hiryu,* steamed away from Midway, a feeling of emptiness prevailed among the men. An officer in the Invasion Force stated: "We are retreating. . . . It is utterly discouraging. . . . The Marines, who were showing off, have not even the courage to drink beer."

"I went to my station and was trying to refresh myself from sleepiness," a Japanese sailor asserted, "but I was rather shocked when I entered the engine room and saw the compass. . . . I knew then that we were heading for Yokosuka. It was the end of the campaign."

— *AUTHOR* —

A graduate of Loyola University in 1953, Lieutenant Commander Powers was an instructor at Pre-flight School, Pensacola, from 1953 to 1956, and at the Naval Reserve Officer School, Forest Park, Illinois, from 1959 to 1963. He was officer in charge, Instructor Training and Leadership School, Service School Command, Great Lakes, from 1964 to 1966. He received his master of arts from De Paul University in 1959, and his doctor of philosophy from the University of Chicago in 1966. He is now assigned to the Department of English, History, and Government, U.S. Naval Academy.

CHAPTER

27

Comment and Discussion: "Incredible Midway"

By J. D. Harrington, JOC, USN, and LTCOL R. E. Barde, USMC

Proceedings, September 1967: pp. 106–107 (originally published as "Incredible Midway," *Proceedings,* June 1967: [pp. 64–73])

J. D. Harrington, JOC, U.S. Navy (Ret.)

Oahu yard workers did not complete 90 days' work in less than 48 hours. The 90-day figure was the leisurely, peacetime estimate for putting the *Yorktown* into first-class condition. The 1,000-plus yard workers chiefly loaded provisions into the ship. Some bulkheads were braced, and some plates welded to her port side. Her superheater boilers, damaged at Coral Sea, were left untouched.

Bombing Three did not pick out a third carrier "by a lucky break," and that carrier was not the *Soryu.* Given astute advice about winds aloft and observing the sea's surface, all the *Yorktown* aircraft flew almost directly to the Japanese carriers, with only a slight course change to right for a direct approach once within sight of the enemy. This put Torpedo Three in position to attack the *Hiryu,* at the northeast "corner" of an aircraft carrier box formation. Bombing Three went after the *Kaga,* not the *Soryu,* making four direct hits and five near-misses. Later, on 4 June, Bombing Three made four direct hits on the *Hiryu,* plus near-misses on a battleship and a cruiser, and this after an *Enterprise* contingent missed.

Japanese bombers did not "follow" the American SBDs (Dauntless dive bombers) to the U.S. Fleet. They accomplished this by homing on a radio signal emitted by a Japanese scout which hovered around the *Yorktown* and her escort.

The Japanese were not "overconfident" in that they did not use the carrier *Zuikaku* at Midway. They simply could not furnish aircraft to the ship, because they were so committed in other areas, and production was not what had been hoped.

LTCOL R. E. Barde, U.S. Marine Corps

In the article, the ships, and in particular the carriers that launched the planes, are all positioned as they were on that bright and suspenseful day 25 years ago on 4 June 1942. On 4 June, the *Enterprise* launched a mix of aircraft, including fighters, dive-bombers, and torpedo planes. The 33 SBDs, not 37, were under the direct command of Lieutenant Commander C. W. McClusky, the air group commander. Unfortunately, all the Dauntlesses are shown belonging to Bombing Six. In fact, 16 were from Bombing Six, one belonged to the air group commander, and the remainder were from Lieutenant Wilmer E. Gallaher's Scouting Six. The 16 planes that flew with Gallaher contributed materially to the Japanese defeat at Midway.

The planes of VS-6 concentrated on the *Akagi*, following the dive of the air group commander. While few planes of VS-6 received damage during the dive, the extended range and the requirement for formation flying, combined with the failure of the carrier to make its projected Point Option, caused several planes to land in the water for the want of fuel. Eight of the 16 planes failed to return to the *Enterprise*. Both Lieutenant C. E. Dickinson and Ensign J. R. McCarthy ditched and were subsequently rescued, the former by the destroyer *Phelps*, in which he had served before going to flight training. Six pilots were never seen again.

Six of the eight returning VS-6 pilots flew again in the afternoon strike against the remaining operational carrier, the *Hiryu*. The squadron also participated in the search of 5 June and in the attack the following day on the damaged *Mikuma* and *Mogami*. Finally, it was Scouting Six which provided the plane that Lieutenant Cleo J. Dobson flew on the last mission of the battle, the one that produced the famous still photo of the heavily damaged and sinking *Mikuma*.

The submarines of Task Force Seven totaled 19 craft rather than 12. (Submarines were: TG 7.1: *Cachalot, Flying Fish, Tambor, Trout, Grayling, Nautilus, Grouper, Dolphin, Gato, Cuttlefish, Gudgeon, Grenadier*; TG 7.2: *Narwhal, Plunger, Trigger*; TG 7.3: *Tarpon, Pike, Finback, Growler*.) From Lieutenant Commander Lindsey's Torpedo Six, five rather than four retired from attacking the Japanese Mobile Force. One of these, piloted by Machinist A. W. Winchell, made a water landing before sighting the *Enterprise*. The experiences and the ordeal of Winchell and his gunner, Cossitt, surviving 17 days on the open seas in a rubber boat is a story in itself.

CHAPTER

28

Sweating Out the Strike

By John B. Lundstrom

Black Shoe Carrier Admiral (Annapolis, MD: Naval Institute Press, 2006): chap. 17 The Battle of Midway I: 'Give Them the Works', p. 256

Fletcher's wait after 0920 [on 4 June] in the *Yorktown*'s flag plot recalled two recent interludes of intense inaction. He could do little else than sit on the transom, pace the flag bridge, or lean over the chart table to ponder yet again the meager enemy data entered on the plot. All ears were attuned to the bulkhead speaker for additional sighting reports and to the phone circuits for alerts from the radar shack (Fletcher's great advantage over Nagumo) and ship lookouts.

Hovering unobtrusively, Commander [Michael] Laing, the British naval liaison officer, jotted in his little black notebook. He disapproved of the physical layout of the flag bridge and the procedures the fleet used to keep track of contacts. The first was "inadequate," and the other "rudimentary." Later at Pearl [Laing had been fished out of the water after abandoning *Yorktown* along with other survivors] he stressed the need for a grid system to facilitate secure reporting of positions and recommended the British lettered coordinate system. He swiftly acquired a copy via the attaché in Washington and presented it to Nimitz, who was very grateful and soon had the Pacific Fleet adopt the grid concept. . . .

There is some disagreement about this photograph of the *Yorktown* on 4 June. The official caption says that it shows a bomb landing close alongside the *Yorktown*, but historian Robert Cressman has argued that the photo shows a torpedo striking the carrier on her port side. The destroyer *Morris* is to the left of the carrier. The heavy cruiser *Astoria* is mostly hidden behind smoke to the carrier's right.

U.S. Naval Institute Photo Archive

Severely damaged by three bombs and two torpedoes, the *Yorktown* lists to port on 4 June. Near her is the destroyer *Balch*, sent to her aid by TF-16's commander, Rear Admiral Spruance. With the destroyers *Benham, Russell, Morris, Anderson, Hughes*, and *Hammann*, the *Balch* rescued almost 2,300 *Yorktown* sailors.

U.S. Naval Institute Photo Archive

CHAPTER

29

Lost Letter of Midway

By CAPT Bruce R. Linder, USN (Ret.)

Proceedings, August 1999: pp. 29–35

A lost manuscript, found literally in a closet sea chest, adds the final missing puzzle piece to the most climactic moments of the World War II Battle of Midway.

Over the past 57 years, in venues stretching from Naval War College gaming floors to screens of interactive Internet simulations, historians have scrutinized the strategies and fought and refought the Battle of Midway. This was the turning point of World War II in the Pacific and arguably one of the most important sea battles in the history of warfare. Yet elements of the battle, many of which remain doggedly wrapped in wisps of mist, still surprise strategists of all stripes.

One of those hidden stories is that of Commander Stanhope C. Ring, commander of the USS *Hornet* (CV-8) Air Group. On the morning of 4 June 1942, when U.S. and Japanese air fleets first opposed each other full-strength at the onset of the battle, Commander Ring held the responsibility for coordinating the attack of the *Hornet*'s fighters, dive-bombers, and torpedo bombers—a full one-third of U.S. naval striking power that day.

The *Yorktown* bow-on, dead in the water and listing heavily after being torpedoed twice on the afternoon of 4 June by the *Hiryu*'s torpedo planes. The carrier has been approached by five destroyers, including the *Hammann,* which is just visible beyond the *Yorktown*'s flight deck.

U.S. Naval Institute Photo Archive

But the *Hornet*'s dive-bombers and fighters never found the Japanese carriers that morning. Her torpedo bombers, led by Lieutenant Commander John Waldron, became separated from Ring, chanced upon the Japanese formation, and were repulsed by Japanese defenders in a brave but uncoordinated attack that failed to score a single hit. More than half of the *Hornet* Air Group failed to return to the ship, many of them crash-landing in the water, out of fuel, others landing on Midway Island. After only four hours, in the U.S. Navy's most important battle of the 20th century, the *Hornet* was stripped of the majority of her striking power, with nothing to show for that loss.

Under Ring's direction, the *Hornet* could fling more than 50 aircraft simultaneously at the enemy, but her air group had the least combat experience of any of the carriers, U.S. or Japanese, that morning. Ring had orchestrated an aggressive training regimen for his aviators since the *Hornet*'s commissioning just seven months before, but important training time had been lost, because her naval aircraft had been secured below decks when she was selected to carry Lieutenant Colonel James H. "Jimmy" Doolittle's raiders for their April raid on Tokyo.

At this early stage of the war, the U.S. Navy still was perfecting its carrier strike tactics. In a coordinated attack against an enemy fleet, air-group doctrine called for TBD Devastator torpedo bombers to sweep in low with their ship-killing heavy torpedoes. Dauntless dive bombers would scream down from 15,000 to 20,000 feet

Crew members descend on ropes from the *Yorktown*'s starboard side after her commander gave the order to abandon ship. CAPT Elliott Buckmaster feared that the bombed and torpedoed ship might capsize and carry many of her crew with her. The *Yorktown*, however, was well designed and strongly built. Struck by three bombs and two torpedoes on 4 June, she did not sink until torpedoed two more times by the submarine *I-168* on 6 June.

U.S. Naval Institute Photo Archive

in attack sections timed simultaneously to hit the port, starboard, and bow of their targets. And swift Wildcat fighters would blunt the attack of Japanese Zeroes. When Rear Admiral Raymond Spruance issued his strike orders at 0700 on 4 June, the *Hornet* launched her entire air group to execute this coordinated attack. Ring flew in a special command section of aircraft to lead the overall attack.

The *Hornet*'s actions on the critical morning of 4 June long have been the subject of conjecture and Monday-morning-quarterbacking, with a dichotomy of opinion rising over the years that has added to the drama of the controversy.

Gordon W. Prange, author of the comprehensive *Miracle at Midway*, was critical of the *Hornet*'s tactics. He cited Spruance's battle report to Admiral Chester Nimitz and interviews with two surviving squadron officers as the basis for his criticism.[1] Lisle Rose, in *The Ship That Held the Line*, also was critical of the air group for its performance on the first day of the battle.[2] But Prange and Rose never spoke with Ring, and their reconstructions of events reach conclusions based, in part, on a flawed "*Hornet* Action Report" or memories dulled with age.

Closer to the truth may be the fact that Admiral Marc Mitscher, an icon of naval aviation and skipper of the *Hornet* at the time, rose consistently in support of Ring's actions during the battle. He requested Ring specifically as his chief of staff in Patrol Wing Two following Midway and for his battle staff in the Solomons. He held Ring in such high esteem that he presented Ring his captain's shoulder boards when Ring was selected later for promotion. Mitscher's closeness with Ring emphasized another facet of Ring's personality. Mitscher's biographer wrote that "Mitscher disliked yes-men, shrinking violets and garrulousness. He wanted positive people on his staff, and usually eliminated officers who had to qualify their every statement. He preferred idea men, especially those who would contest him when they thought their ideas were better than his own."[3]

Formal Navy reaction to Ring's actions during the battle also supported the actions of the *Hornet* Air Group commander consistently. Ring received the Navy Cross personally from Nimitz for leading successful attacks on Japanese Vice Admiral Chuichi Nagumo's forces during the remaining days of the Battle of Midway, was selected ultimately for the command of three carriers and a carrier division, and climbed the ranks steadily to vice admiral.

Numerous theories have been advanced to explain the *Hornet*'s inability to engage during the critical 4 June attack: Errors in navigation must have been made, say some; the tactical attack plan designed by Captain Mitscher of the *Hornet* and Ring was faulty; U.S. multi-carrier coordination doctrine had fundamental weaknesses; or just that Ring's luck was unusually bad. Here, Ring's "lost letter" cites none of these explanations. Instead, he attributes the debacle to poor communications, an inexperienced air group, and his flawed estimate of the situation. In other words, Ring was the victim of the classic ingredients of the "fog of war."

Ring's family found his "Lost Letter of Midway," and it came to light only recently. It is dated March 1946, a time far enough removed from the battle to guarantee reflection and proper perspective, yet not too distant to hazard the possibility of errors in memory. The original manuscript is written in a bold, confident longhand. The text is nearly flawless, with but five editorial corrections across 22 pages of handwritten recollections. Ring's syntax draws heavily on a naval officer's proclivity for short, direct thoughts, its sentences purposely uncluttered with adjectives and modifiers. It is an intriguing mix of historical record and personal reflection, including specific reference to individual pilots and broad observations, such as the sighting of large groups of Japanese survivors still adrift two days after the battle.

None of the principal historians of the battle ever interviewed Ring.[4] In the most recent analysis of the battle (see *The Ship That Held the Line*), Lisle Rose had difficulty tracking Ring's perspective, concluding: "Group Commander Stanhope Cotton Ring . . . remains a cloudy figure more than half a century later."[5] In *Miracle at Midway*, Gordon Prange stated: "No doubt Ring had good reasons for his course of action, although to the best of our knowledge he never made a public explanation."

Now, after more than 50 years, the "Lost Letter of Midway"—faithfully reproduced here uncorrected and unedited—is effectively Stanhope Ring's "public explanation," serving to correct, or at least explain, the historical record of that epic sea battle. (Vice Admiral Ring's words appear in bold italic.)

28 March 1946

There has been much written about the Battle of Midway and in many respects there has been a startling lack of accuracy. This is an attempt, almost four years after the action, to set down in black and white my best recollections of what occurred.

Hornet *and* Enterprise *[CV-6] had been operating together during May 1942. The Battle of Coral Sea had been fought without our participation. We were guarding against a Japanese advance toward Australia or the Solomon Islands. Extensive daylight searches were run but it appeared to me that we were making no great effort to deny to the enemy knowledge of our presence in those waters. As a matter of fact, Japanese reconnaissance planes were known to have made contact with our force.*

The *Enterprise* and the *Hornet* had returned to Pearl Harbor on 25 April after Doolittle's Raid. After five days they were under way again, streaking south to reinforce the *Lexington* (CV-2) and the *Yorktown* (CV-5) in the Coral Sea but arrived too late to participate in the battle. The two carriers covered the withdrawal of the damaged *Yorktown* back to Hawaii and then were ordered there themselves on 16 May, as Nimitz began to gather his forces for Midway.

Probably as a result of interception of Japanese "high command" traffic, both* Hornet *and* Enterprise *were suddenly ordered to return to Pearl Harbor. We proceeded at high speed maintaining air searches enroute.

We remained in the Pearl area for a very short period—about twenty-four hours as I recall—and then sailed for the vicinity of Midway.

The *Enterprise* and the *Hornet* reentered Pearl Harbor on 26 May, mooring to berths at Ford Island by midday. After refueling and replenishing furiously, the *Enterprise* cast off lines at 1110 on 28 May and made her way slowly out the narrow channel. The *Hornet* followed in her wake 20 minutes later. Together the two carriers formed Task Group 16 under the command of Rear Admiral Spruance. By early evening they had recovered their air groups and had passed through the Kauai Channel, fashioning a course toward a rendezvous position north-northeast of Midway Island, some 1,100 miles distant from Oahu.

Early on the morning of 4 June we received word that the Japanese attacking force had been located and that initial attack on Midway had been made. Course from Hornet's position to the enemy was plotted and immediate preparations made to launch the Air Group.

It was decided to launch the entire group as a striking force and to adhere strictly to the doctrine of radio silence. VT Squadron 8 was to proceed at low level. VB-8, VS-8, accompanying fighters of VF-8 and the Group Commander were to proceed at high level (20,000 ft). Nearly one and a half hours were consumed in Group rendezvous after launching. All airplanes maintained moderate altitude (below 5,000 ft) until after rendezvous of the Group was effected.

Naval squadron nomenclature of the period emphasized the relationship between squadron and carrier. Thus, squadrons assigned to the *Hornet* (CV-8) were numbered with an 8. VF indicated a fighter squadron, VB a dive-bombing squadron, VT a torpedo bombing squadron, and VS a scouting squadron. During the battle, VF-8 consisted of 27 F4F-4 Wildcat fighters commanded by Lieutenant Commander Samuel G. Mitchell; VB-8 had 19 SBD-2 and -3 Dauntless bombers commanded by Lieutenant Commander Robert R. Johnson; VS-8 had 18 SBD-1, -2 and -3 Dauntlesses commanded by Lieutenant Commander Walter R. Rodee; and VT-8 had 15 TBD-1 Devastator torpedo bombers commanded by Waldron.[6]

On the morning of 4 June, Spruance boldly ordered the launch of a "full load" by the *Hornet* and the *Enterprise* air groups against the Japanese carriers that already had launched an attack against Midway at first light. Strategically, this proved to be the correct decision, as it struck the Japanese at the most critical moment with the maximum number of aircraft, but it took more than an hour to complete the launching (about half the planes had to be brought up from the hangar deck). The *Hornet* commenced launching at 0702 and completed at 0806.[7]

The projected intercept position of the enemy was based on a 0603 contact report from a U.S. patrol bomber (PBY) and a belief that the Japanese formation would continue on a southeast heading toward Midway Island and into the wind to recover its returning strike group. This proved to be an accurate assessment by Spruance's staff, however the efficient Japanese completed recovery of their aircraft earlier than projected and turned 90° left toward the northeast to close the reported position of the U.S. carrier task force. No scout had reported this major change in the enemy's movement, but even if it had, U.S. forces were operating in radio silence and word probably would not have been passed to the already airborne strike groups. The *Hornet*'s and the *Enterprise*'s strike aircraft were heading to an intercept position in the open ocean predicated on the Japanese course and speed detected at 0603—a position the Japanese never would occupy after their course had been changed toward the U.S. carriers.

Departure from* Hornet *was taken on pre-estimated interception course, Group Commander leading. High altitude elements commenced their climb.

Within thirty minutes after departure from* Hornet, *scattered cumulous clouds intervened between high and low elements. Speed of high elements was regulated in an attempt to remain above the invisible VT-8.

"Regulating" the formation's speed in this manner undoubtedly was not as fuel-efficient as other tactics would have allowed and opened Ring to criticism, especially in light of the subsequent loss of aircraft, some because of fuel exhaustion. Prange analyzed this action by Ring, concluding that Ring had ordered the formation to stretch his aircraft into a scouting line, better to detect the enemy. Historian Walter Lord commented that Captain Mitscher—undoubtedly with Ring's knowledge and concurrence—had ordered a coordination plan that sent his slower-flying torpedo planes ahead of the rest of the group. The faster bombers and fighters would climb to rendezvous over the *Hornet*, while the torpedo planes headed directly to the enemy. All aircraft then would attack together. Rose makes a compelling case that VT-8 was the last squadron launched that morning from the *Hornet*, underlining the requirement for careful group coordination by the air group commander. Ring makes clear that he based his decision to regulate speed primarily on a desire to stay in contact with his torpedo planes to make a coordinated attack on the enemy formation.[8]

Upon arrival at the line between the last reported position of the enemy and Midway Island, since the high group had made no contact, I decided that I should proceed on the assumption that the enemy was closing Midway and directed the course of the high element accordingly.

It is appropriate at this time to interject my understanding that* Enterprise *Group was favored with later information of the whereabouts of the enemy than was* Hornet *Group. Although communications in 1942 were most unreliable between air and surface craft, even though* Hornet *might have broken radio silence to keep the Group informed of the latest developments, there was no assurance that such information would have been received by the Group. As a matter of fact, I do not believe that* Hornet *received the reported new position of the enemy. Therefore my change of Air Group course to the south was based entirely on my estimate of the situation (which proved faulty) and not on definite information of the enemy movements.

Clearly, Ring's decision was wrong. He had reached the expected point of interception, which had been calculated based on enemy position information, course and speed nearly three hours old. As the *Hornet*'s group was approaching on a nearly perpendicular course to the Japanese position of intended movement (PIM), Ring was faced with the classic dilemma of turning either right (in the event that the enemy's speed was less than that reported or in the event that the Japanese had turned away from their objective of Midway Island) or left (with the assumption that the Japanese would be pressing their attack vigorously on the island). With no updated tactical data from the *Hornet* or Spruance, Ring was forced to make a decision that many would characterize as 50/50, made worse by the perpendicular relationship of Ring's approach to the Japanese advance. If Ring chose wrong (as he did), he would have no chance to reorient a new search with his limited remaining fuel.

> *VT-8 and* Enterprise *Group made contact with the enemy, north of the point at which I turned south. Again, reliable communications should have permitted direction of the high elements of the* Hornet *Air Group to the point of contact.*
>
> Hornet *Group proceeded south until smoke from Midway was sighted. At that time it was apparent that immediate return to the carrier was necessary if landings aboard were to be effected, since fuel supply was running low.*

Walter Lord made an interesting observation in quoting Waldron's last ready-room briefing to VT-8 shortly before the strike: "Commander Waldron gave them a few final words. He said he thought the Japanese ships would swing around once they discovered U.S. carriers present; they would not go on to Midway as everyone seemed to think. So don't worry about navigation; he knew where he was going. 'Just follow me. I'll take you to 'em.'"[9]

As a squadron commander, Waldron undoubtedly was aware of Mitscher's and Ring's plans to intercept the Japanese carriers that morning. Waldron's allusion to favoring a course of action different from what "everyone seemed to think" (meaning probably Mitscher and Ring) is an insight into Ring's apparent mindset before takeoff.

> *Great reliance was placed on the YE homing beacon. I switched radio at the time to the homing frequency but* Enterprise *was all that could be heard. The letter signal received, compared to the YE letter chart furnished us by* Hornet *prior to takeoff, convinced me that something was wrong. It later developed that* Enterprise *and* Hornet *were on different YE homing codes and that the change in code prescribed by CTF in* Enterprise *had not been received by* Hornet. *Because of the obvious discrepancy in* Enterprise *YE signal received as applied to the YE homing chart of* Hornet, *I disregarded the YE signal and attempted to change course of the group toward the dead reckoning position of* Hornet. *VS-8 under Lt Cdr. Rodee followed me in my change. VB-8 under Lt Cdr. Johnson appeared to follow the false course indicated by YE signal and was followed by VF-8, Lt Cdr. Mitchell. I left VS-8 and attempted to rally the departing aircraft of VB-8 and VF-8 in order to lead them back to* Hornet, *but I could not catch them. When I finally gave up the chase VS-8 had disappeared from sight and VB-8 was apparently headed for Midway. I then resumed my dead reckoning course to intercept* Hornet, *proceeding singly at 20,000 ft. Since oxygen supply was failing and I began to notice the effects of lack of oxygen, I dropped gradually to 10,000 ft.*

Eventually, I sighted aircraft below me and noticed water landings of at least two airplanes.

After about 4.5 hours in the air (and having assured Parker, my radioman, that a water landing could be easily effected), I sighted the white wakes of a Task Force at high speed. Further investigation revealed it to be our own force. I made a wide approach to arrive within the "recognition sector"; Hornet *turned into the wind and received me aboard. VS-8 had landed; VB-8, VT-8 and VF-8 were missing. It later developed that VT-8 had, with the exception of Ens. [George H.] Gay been lost in an attack on the Japanese carriers. Lt Cdr Waldron leading the squadron had courageously and in the face of certain destruction led his command in a torpedo attack against the enemy. VB-8 had (with the loss of two planes) landed at Midway. VF-8 had apparently landed at sea, out of fuel.*

I was shaken at the realization of such losses and will admit that I was in poor condition to take the air in a renewed attack on the Japanese carriers which had, by then, been located. About one hour after my landing the remaining aircraft of the Group were ordered launched for the next attack.

Both Rodee and I were spotted on the hangar deck so, when launchings were suddenly terminated after the aircraft on the flight deck had taken off, the "Group" command devolved upon Lt. Stebbins of VS-8. He did a magnificent job of locating and attacking the enemy forces and is wholly deserving of all the credit for the success of the operation as far as Hornet *Group was concerned.*

According to Morison, the *Hornet* launched an attack group of 16 dive-bombers at 1603, but they arrived too late to help the *Enterprise* dive-bombers dispatch the last surviving Japanese carrier, the *Hiryu*. They dove on two of the escorting cruisers, scoring near misses. Lieutenant Edgar E. Stebbins amassed an excellent combat record during the war, advancing to command Air Group Five on the *Yorktown* (CV-10).[10] Lisle Rose reported Ring's presence in this attack erroneously in *The Ship That Held the Line*, then compounded his error by alluding to a story that Ring had returned early with "his bomb still snugly secured aboard his aircraft."[11] Ring's "lost letter" does not appear to support this.

It is my recollection that launching was stopped after the planes on the flight deck had taken off because of the reported approach of enemy aircraft. At any rate, it was at about this time that Yorktown *was attacked. Damage to that carrier required landing part of* Yorktown *air group aboard* Hornet. *One of the planes of that group, the pilot having been wounded in the foot, made a bad landing, his right wheel collapsed and the airplane slewed toward the island. The pilot had failed to turn off his gun firing switch and as the deck crash occurred the 50 cal guns cut loose, firing into the island. Several of our personnel, including Lt. Royal Ingersoll were killed and several were wounded. Later in the afternoon, a second* Yorktown *pilot landed with firing switch on, but the plane made a normal landing the resultant firing passed safely along the flight deck and not into the ship. It was at the start of this second firing that Capt Mason (makee-learn Captain and prospective relief for Capt Mitscher) knocked me flat on the deck of the port wing of the bridge to escape the possible line of fire. I don't know whether his thoughtful but rough treatment was more of a shock than the actual firing or not.*

Our attack group returned before dark and gave glowing accounts of the damage done to the enemy.

The Task Force retired during the night, in an easterly direction. I believe that it was during the forenoon of the 5th of June that we received flyable airplanes of VB-8 that had landed the day before at Midway. Airplanes of VF-8 that accompanied the initial attack group were unaccounted for, but several days later all but two of the pilots were recovered by PBYs.

Reports concerning the enemy were meager on 5 June, but in mid-afternoon contact report was received on an enemy carrier "disappearing to the westward into a front." Hornet *and* Enterprise *Air Groups were launched to search and attack. We searched to the extreme range of 325 miles from* Hornet *but discovered nothing except one light cruiser. On the way out on the search we flew over the scene of 4 June attack on Japanese CVs and observed many survivors in the water.*

Since the search for the carrier proved negative we returned to attack the CL which was about 275 miles from our task force. Although AA fire was neither excessive nor uncomfortably accurate, the dive bombing attack was a fizzle. I never saw a ship go through such radical maneuvers at such high speed as did that Jap. We completed our attack shortly after sunset and started the long trip home.

Their target was the destroyer *Tanikaze*, which had been dispatched by Nagumo to guarantee the scuttling of the *Hiryu* and to save survivors. Lord wrote: "Commander Motomi Katsumi (commanding officer of the *Tanikaze*) was one of the best in the business; he maneuvered the destroyer *Tanikaze* with enviable skill as the American bombs rained down from above. All those bombs on one destroyer. Yet Katsumi managed to dodge everything. The only damage came from a fragment of a near-miss that slashed through his No. 3 turret; it set off an explosion that killed all six men inside."[12]

Group doctrine had called for individual return rather than complete rendezvous. This was a mistake, perhaps, in the absence of air opposition, but under the circumstances was essential since diminishing fuel supply precluded wasting time and fuel to get the group together, Ens. White of VS-8 joined me on the return trip.

Hornet *Group had never qualified in night landings aboard, which fact would be expected to cause some concern under the circumstances. Actually, the night landings were themselves made without incident or difficulty. One plane of VS-8, Lt. Davis pilot, ran out of gasoline in the groove and made a water landing, but personnel were picked up by plane guard destroyer.*

It proved fortunate for me that Ens. White had joined company because when I lowered my wheels preparatory to landing, he by frantic signaling to me got across the idea that only one wheel was extended. My first thought was that a fragment of shell from the AA fire of the cruiser had damaged a hydraulic line but after a bit of violent maneuvering both wheels extended properly.

There was a general mix-up of pilots that night. Some Enterprise *crews landed aboard* Hornet *and some of our people landed aboard* Enterprise*. Despite the possible presence of Japanese submarines, Captain Mitscher had illuminated the ship in order to get us all back. There was no one lost in the operation nor were any injuries incurred. Duration of flight: 4.3 hours.*

In large measure, U.S. carrier pilots were untrained in night carrier landings. Morison called the return landings that night "one of the first successful night landings in our carrier combat history." Both Captain George Murray of the *Enterprise* and Captain Mitscher of the *Hornet* had illuminated their ships with running lights and searchlights, despite the danger of nearby Japanese submarines.[13]

During the forenoon of 6 June we received a contact report on an enemy force, distant about 150 miles, retiring to the westward. Hornet *Air Group was launched to search and attack.*

On the way out toward the enemy, I received a CW message from Hornet *stating that enemy force might consist of cruisers rather than carriers as first reported. In as much as we believed that all enemy carriers had been sunk on 4 June this made sense and since we did not expect air opposition to our attack we cruised at medium rather than high altitude (approximately 14,000 feet).*

During these operations "first name" calls were used, so that when VB-8 which was on the left flank of our scouting line, sighted the enemy, Lt. Cdr Johnson called on the voice radio: "Stanhope from Robert, enemy below on port bow." As an indication of how alert the Japanese were, in a very short time the following message in very oriental tone came over the air: "Stanhope from Robert, Return to base."

In executing our dive bombing attack, everyone did much better than he had the day before, when buck fever probably had us. Hits were registered on each of the two large cruisers (Mogami class) and the escorting destroyers were bombed and strafed. On the way back to Hornet*, I detoured about 25 miles to the southward to see if any other enemy were in the area. None was sighted.*

Both targets were heavy cruisers, the *Mogami* and the *Mikuma*, but they had no air cover and operated with reduced maneuverability. The day before, the *Mogami* had collided with the *Mikuma*, smashing her own bow, restricting her speed to 12 knots, and causing both she, the *Mikuma*, and two destroyers to lag behind the general Japanese retirement to the west. At least two hits were recorded in the first attack, one penetrating the *Mogami*'s Number 5 turret, killing the entire turret crew.

> *When I returned aboard after about 3 hours flying it developed that the radio in my plane was not functioning properly.* Hornet *had not received my report of attacking the enemy nor had I received their dispatches requesting information as to the latitude and longitude of the Group attacked. Capt. Mitscher decided, therefore, that I should not accompany the final attack group which was being readied for takeoff. Unfortunately, Ens. Griswold, a very promising pilot of VB-8 had been lost during the morning attack, probably the victim of AA fire. Other aircraft of the Group were slightly damaged by AA fire.*
>
> *While* Hornet *Group was preparing for the second launch,* Enterprise *Group attacked a cruiser task force. It is not definitely known whether it was the same force* Hornet *had attacked or not.*
>
> Hornet*'s second attack was even more successful than the first and the group had the satisfaction of witnessing a terrific explosion aboard one of the cruisers. Later intelligence indicated that* Mikuma *was sunk as a result of this attack.*

The second attack scored hits on the *Mikuma* and the destroyer *Arashio*. The *Mikuma* sank that night, and the *Mogami* limped to Truk for temporary repairs. Prange wrote mistakenly in *Miracle at Midway* that the second strike was under Ring's command.[14]

> *At this point, fuel in escorting destroyers was running dangerously low, darkness was approaching, and CTF [Commander Task Force] decided to break off the engagement. We had lost* Yorktown, Hammann *[DD-412], VT-8, and many other pilots but the Japanese had suffered heavily. Undoubtedly the cream of their naval aviation was destroyed in the sinking of their four carriers. We felt then (as was later proved) that we had dealt the Japanese a decisive defeat.*

— AUTHOR —

Captain Linder commanded a guided-missile frigate and two major shore bases while in active service. He has written a history of the Navy in San Diego for the Naval Institute Press.

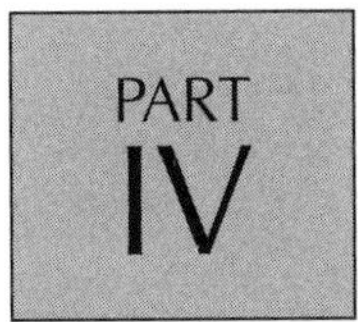

PART IV

The End of the Battle

Most people mistakenly believe that the Battle of Midway was over by 6 June, with the remnants of the *kidō butai* and the other Japanese forces withdrawing from the Midway area. But there were still the Aleutians. The Japanese had attacked U.S. installations there with carrier aircraft, and Admiral Nimitz was not sure how many carriers the Japanese had near the Aleutians or whether Japanese forces were ashore in U.S. territory. Given that uncertainty, Nimitz wanted to send at least the *Enterprise* and *Hornet* north after they had received aircraft reinforcements from the newly arrived *Saratoga*.

Moreover, Nimitz still did not know for sure just what had transpired in the Midway battle. Midway itself was secure, but U.S. forces had lost a large number of planes plus the carrier *Yorktown* and the destroyer *Hammann.* Could the *Yorktown* have been saved? Remember that the number of U.S. carriers was limited. The *Lexington* had been lost at the Battle of Coral Sea. Now the *Yorktown* at Midway was also lost. Only the *Saratoga, Enterprise, Hornet,* and the smaller and less-well-protected *Wasp* remained for Pacific duty. Nimitz was constrained in his planning by the limited number of carriers and by the limited number of escorts he could provide them. He was short of ships in other categories, too, especially in tankers. His forces had won a major victory, but it had not been decisive. He was sure of that while being much less certain what the still-strong Japanese would do next.

After Midway, there was concern among officers serving under Admiral Nimitz and Admiral King about the Pacific Fleet's carrier loss rate. If one or two were lost in each battle, the Pacific Fleet would run out of carriers before new ones arrived from the United States. Was Rear Admiral Fletcher, who had been in overall tactical command at both Coral Sea and Midway, responsible for possibly "excessive" losses? Nimitz needed to know. If he needed to replace Fletcher, then he had to do so quickly so the new carrier task force commander and his staff could get up to speed quickly. In Washington, RADM John H. Towers, head of the Navy's Bureau of Aeronautics and a pioneer aviator, suspected that carrier task force commanders who were not aviators—like Fletcher and Spruance—lacked the necessary perspective to handle their units with the flair required to defeat their aggressive and sophisticated Japanese opponents.[1] Towers had the ear of Secretary of the Navy Frank Knox and was pressing to have aviators command carrier task forces.

Should Spruance have been more aggressive in pursuing the Japanese the night of 4 June? As you will see, this question—and his fear that his decision to withdraw to the east had been a mistake—dogged Spruance until it was clear that the Japanese had sent the surface escorts of the *kidō butai* after the *Enterprise* and *Hornet*. But Spruance's decision echoed the Navy's own *War Instructions* (Fleet Tactical Publication 143), which stressed that carriers needed to use "every means" to avoid fighting surface combatants at night. Spruance simply followed doctrine and his own reasoned judgment.

But what about the surface units of TF-16 and TF-17? In a 1973 interview conducted by the Naval Institute, VADM Lloyd M. Mustin, who was an assistant gunnery officer on light cruiser *Atlanta* at Midway, criticized the performance of the ships escorting the U.S. carriers. TF-17's cruisers, the *Astoria* and *Portland,* were busy protecting the *Yorktown* and then taking on her many survivors, but the cruisers of TF-16, the *Northampton, Pensacola,* and the new *Atlanta,* were not subject to attack by Japanese aircraft at any time.

The U.S. submarine *Tambor* had trailed the damaged *Mogami* and her escort, the *Mikuma,* through the early morning of 5 June, and had alerted Nimitz's headquarters of their presence just over one hundred miles west of Midway. But Nimitz was not sure on 5 June if the Japanese had called off the amphibious assault against Midway; he had no forces that he could send after the two enemy ships. On 6 June a scout from the *Hornet* located the two Japanese cruisers and two destroyers 133 miles southwest of TF-16.[2] According to Mustin, that sighting should have triggered an attack by the cruisers of TF-16. As he told the Naval Institute, "One or two cruisers dispatched to go on over there could have polished [the *Mogami*] off, and that would have been the end of it there and then, once and for all, but we didn't think that way."[3]

But what the young Mustin did not appreciate at the time was what the older Admiral Nimitz knew all too well—that the Pacific Fleet was short of ships. There were not enough carriers, cruisers, and destroyers—and no fast battleships at all—in the Pacific, and therefore Nimitz was reluctant to risk the carrier escorts, even on the chance that they might sink one or two Japanese cruisers.

CHAPTER
30

Finale

By John B. Lundstrom

Black Shoe Carrier Admiral (Annapolis, MD: Naval Institute Press, 2006): chap. 18 The Battle of Midway II, chap. 19 The Battle of Midway III

To Save the *Yorktown* (pp. 280–281)

Fletcher's decision to leave the *Yorktown* on the night of 4 June without attempting salvage drew bitter criticism. The February 1943 Cominch Secret Information Bulletin No. 1 declared that the *Yorktown* "might have been saved if she had not been completely abandoned during the night but salvage work carried on." The same bulletin also categorically disapproved of Spruance's decision to withdraw that night. "Task Force 16 would have done better if it had headed westward and not eastward after attacking the *Hiryu* in order to follow up the success of 4 June." Late in 1942, however, Japanese messages found on Guadalcanal sketched the menace of superior surface forces to TF-16 had it continued westward. When told of them, Spruance felt, "The weight of a score of years has been lifted from my shoulders." . . . If one accepted the logic of Spruance's decision, how could Fletcher, with only four cruisers and whose destroyers were far less combat ready, be criticized for leaving the stricken, stationary *Yorktown?* She was even closer to the enemy than TF-16, and moreover Fletcher was aware the Japanese knew her position. If they were hell-bent on a night surface battle north of Midway, they would have hardly neglected to finish off the crippled carrier and deal with the ships left behind to protect her.

The destroyer *Ralph Talbot* approaches the *Enterprise* in May 1942 prior to taking on fuel. The carriers could and did refuel their escorting destroyers, but they could not do that if air or submarine attacks were likely. Accordingly, task force commanders kept careful track of the fuel levels in their destroyers. Elements of the *Enterprise*'s antiaircraft battery are visible: a 1.1-inch gun, 20-mm guns, and 5-inch dual-purpose guns. Atop the destroyer's bridge is her director for her dual-purpose 5-inch guns.

Navy Department, National Archives

According to Poco [RADM William W.] Smith, "The unfortunate aspect of the situation was that the crew of *Yorktown* had been pulled at random, not by selection, from the sea." Under the circumstances that pertained on the night of 4 June, he thought TF-17 "could not hover on the scene while sorting them out and selecting those whose experience best qualified them for the salvage job at hand."

The "One Blot" (p. 293)

In retrospect it appears the *Yorktown*'s sudden complete loss of power, her dire condition, and the nearness of the enemy combined to delay effective salvage. Had any one of these factors not been present, Fletcher and [CAPT Elliott C.] Buckmaster would have had an easier time saving her. In hindsight probably the only way to have avoided the *I-168* was if a cruiser commenced towing her either the night of 4/5 June or early the next morning. That did not appear feasible under the circumstances prevailing at the time. [Historian S. E.] Morison called the "abandonment and subsequent loss" of the *Yorktown* "the one blot on an otherwise golden scroll of victory" at Midway. It certainly harmed the reputations of both Fletcher and Buckmaster. Perhaps all of that was not too high a cost for such a tremendous triumph.

New Flagship, New Mission (pp. 293–295)

Early on 6 June Fletcher detached [CAPT Laurance T.] DuBose's group (*Portland*, *Morris*, and *Russell*) crammed with *Yorktown* survivors to meet the oncoming *Fulton*. He himself pressed eastward with the *Astoria* and *Anderson* to fuel from the *Platte*. That afternoon Nimitz had to delay the departure of the *Saratoga* group (TG-11.1) until the next morning (it had only arrived on 6 June) and postponed the rendezvous until 8 June two hundred miles closer to Pearl. Fletcher had time to fuel, reunite his force, and be there on schedule. Late that afternoon came the sad news of the torpedoing of the *Yorktown*. Fletcher could only hope Buckmaster's optimism of saving her was warranted. Near to sundown he completed fueling. Not until well after dark did the last of the nearly twenty-two hundred survivors cross over to the *Fulton* and her two escorts. DuBose returned as expected early on 7 June and took his turn alongside the *Platte*. Later that morning Fletcher released the oiler to Pearl, while TF-17 shaped course southeast to meet the *Saratoga* task group the next day. Even the terrible word of the sinking of the *Yorktown* could not erase the great relief on the U.S. ships as the staggering scope of the Midway victory became apparent.

Inasmuch as overall enemy intentions remained unclear despite the debacle off Midway, the top brass reassessed their options. [Admiral] King speculated whether the second enemy carrier group had already left the Aleutians. "Consider strong possibility that part or all of this force departed that area night of 4/5 June for rendezvous to the southwest with retreating Midway forces and possibly with the remainder of the Combined Fleet." The Alaskan command begged to differ. Rear Adm. Charles S. Freeman (Commander, Northwest Sea Frontier) warned that the situation there was "rapidly deteriorating." The enemy's puzzling "cat and mouse tactics" were "wearing us down preliminary to delivering all out attack." Now that Midway was secure, Freeman recommended "quick reinforcement" of Alaska, where the "need approaches desperation." King swiftly changed his mind. Citing Freeman's message with its "indications of continued presence of Orange force in the Aleutians," he told Nimitz to consider sending *Saratoga* there with a strong force and offered land-based air reinforcements as well.

Nimitz already inclined in that direction and chose Spruance to go north. That afternoon he set the rendezvous for the morning of 10 June 650 miles northeast of Midway. Fletcher would provide the planes and personnel to restore the *Enterprise* and *Hornet* to "best practicable strength," and return to Pearl. TF-16 was to voyage north to the aptly named Point Blow, only 425 miles southwest of Dutch Harbor. There on the afternoon of 12 June he would come under the command of CTF-8, his classmate [RADM Robert A.] "Fuzzy" Theobald, whose mission was to "destroy or drive out enemy forces in the Aleutian-Alaskan area." Nimitz explained to King why he did not commit Fletcher and the *Saratoga* instead. Not only did the job properly require two carriers, but also the ragtag *Saratoga* Air Group itself was not ready for combat.

On the afternoon of 8 June Fletcher transferred his flag and incorporated the *Saratoga* group into TF-17. The giant old carrier was in excellent shape, much enhanced after the repair of the torpedo damage and a major refit. Capt. Dewitt Clinton "Duke" Ramsey, who took command in May, was a 1912 Annapolis graduate from New York who qualified as naval aviator number forty-five in 1917. Sharp-witted, level headed, and personable, he prospered in a wide variety of operational and staff posts as well as at the Naval War College. In 1937–38 he served as the fleet aviation officer for Cincus, then as executive officer of the *Sara* [*sic*], before reporting in 1939 to Buaer [the Bureau of Aeronautics]. As [RADM] Jack Towers's protégé, he rose to assistant chief in 1941. The *Saratoga* improved dramatically under Ramsey's firm hand. Fletcher found him a highly capable and congenial shipmate. Ramsey only reached Pearl on 6 June and immediately refueled. The *Saratoga* now carried 107 planes (forty-seven fighters, forty-five dive bombers, and fifteen torpedo planes, including ten new TBFs) from all or parts of seven squadrons, most of which never served together. Ramsey sailed the next morning with the *Saratoga, San Diego,* oiler *Kaskaskia,* and five destroyers. . . .

Fletcher's reconstituted TF-17 set off at fifteen knots to meet TF-16 some seven hundred miles northwest. Likewise that day Spruance reassembled his force and saw to its logistical needs. At dawn he met the *Cimarron* 235 miles north of Midway and fueled his destroyers, all of which were nearly out of oil. The

Balch and *Monaghan*, accompanied by the orphaned *Hughes*, rejoined after their grim sojourn with the *Yorktown*. Later that day the oiler *Guadalupe* arrived from Midway with a welcome load of aviation gasoline and more black oil. Spruance fueled during the day, ran northeast at night, and resumed fueling on the ninth. Another overnight dash at twenty knots saw him to the rendezvous with Fletcher. Then it was the stormy Aleutians and perhaps another carrier battle.

Early on 9 June occurred the last gasp of the MI operation. Cincpac intercepted plain language messages, complete with position, course, and speed, purportedly from a disabled enemy fleet unit fumbling about northeast of Wake. Nimitz, who knew Spruance was in no position to intercept anyway, correctly warned him, "This may be a deception." Yamamoto detailed Admiral Takagi's 5th Cruiser Division to simulate the calls of a battleship in distress and hopefully draw overconfident pursuers into a trap. He had no takers. Equally symbolic of the vast reversal of fortune, the *Nagara* drew alongside flagship *Yamato* that day and delivered chief of staff Kusaka, air staff officer Genda, and a few others (but not Nagumo) to report to Yamamoto. Kusaka prefaced his statement, "I don't know what to say except to offer utmost apologies."

During 9 June the odds of Spruance having to sail north dramatically lessened. Theobald's searchers found no trace of the Japanese in the Aleutians. Consequently King reinstated his assessment that the Midway and Aleutian attack forces, now three carriers including the *Zuikaku*, gathered somewhere in the northwest Pacific and predicted they would race down to the South or southwest Pacific before the United States could react. Therefore deploying Spruance to the Aleutians was "questionable." Nimitz replied that if nothing major turned up in the Aleutians that day or the next, he would return Spruance to Pearl Harbor. The enemy might have landed troops somewhere in the Aleutians, but he had no proof. In fact the Japanese occupied both Kiska and Attu in the western Aleutians on 7 June without resistance.

By dawn on 10 June a thick overcast shrouded the two carrier task forces. Scheduled to reach far-off Point Blow on 12 June, Spruance was in a bind, because no aircraft could fly. After 0800 he received a welcome reprieve. Nimitz told him not to start north until he received new orders. Meanwhile, he told Fletcher to arrive at Pearl during forenoon on 13 June. Nimitz explained to King that TG-16 would stay where it was until he knew more of what transpired in the Aleutians. Having located each other by radar, the two task forces moved south in hopes the weather might cooperate later that afternoon. In less than an hour heavy fog closed in. By dawn on 11 June, about two hundred miles south of the original rendezvous, the weather cleared sufficiently for flight operations. The *Saratoga* promptly ferried ten SBDs and five TBDs to the *Enterprise* and nine SBDs and ten TBFs to the *Hornet*. Immediately thereafter Fletcher set course for Pearl eight hundred miles southeast, while TF-16 started north toward Point Blow, now twelve hundred miles away.

Spruance did not get far. Shortly after 0900 Nimitz ordered TF-16 to return to Pearl. The previous day he learned of enemy troops on Kiska and Attu and conceded a "strong screening force" would contest any U.S. reaction to the loss of the two islands. Instead, he proposed to recall TF-16 and the "fleet units" of Theobald's TF-8 to Pearl and later commit them against a "greater threat to our interests," namely Port Moresby and the South Pacific bases. King approved.

Welcome Home (pp. 296–297)

The victory at Midway sublimely vindicated Nimitz's aggressive but perilous strategy of confronting the Japanese carriers while they were exposed assaulting an important base. He asserted that the battle had "frustrated the enemy's powerful move against Midway that was undoubtedly the keystone of larger plans," and certainly did not exaggerate. Yamamoto's "larger plans" sought no less than the destruction of the Pacific Fleet. By late June, from more recent information derived from radio intelligence and the interrogation of prisoners, Nimitz concluded that four large carriers and a heavy cruiser went down, plus possibly another heavy cruiser and a destroyer. The cost of victory was high: the *Yorktown, Hammann,* 144 aircraft, and 362 dead sailors, marines, and airmen, including 104 carrier pilots and aircrew. Actual Japanese losses comprised the *Akagi, Kaga, Soryu* and *Hiryu,* the *Mikuma,* more than 250 aircraft, and more than 3,057 dead. Contrary to legend, Japanese casualties did not include the majority of their carrier aviators. Instead only 110 pilots and aircrew, mainly from the valiant *Hiryu* Air Group, were lost.

Immensely relieved by the scope of the victory, Nimitz was humble in the face of the effusive praise. "All participating personnel, without exception, displayed unhesitating devotion to duty, loyalty and courage." The what-ifs would come soon enough. Not content with congratulatory messages, Nimitz made a point of greeting every group returning to Pearl, beginning the evening of 8 June with the *Fulton* loaded with *Yorktown* survivors. Cheerful and sincere, Cincpac shook hands with numerous men, commiserated with their loss, and told them how proud he was of what they did. [CDR Walter G.] Schindler briefed him on Fletcher's perception of the battle and the crippling of the *Yorktown.* On the ninth when the *Gwin* and *Benham* reached port, Nimitz likewise sounded out Buckmaster for details as to her loss. What he learned dispelled his concern that errors by Fletcher might have cost a second carrier within a month [*Lexington* at Coral Sea being the first].

On the evening of 12 June with the arrival of the Fueling Group directly from TF-16, Nimitz received the clearest statement yet of what transpired. Spruance wrote a letter on the eighth when it looked as if a side trip to the Aleutians might substantially delay his return. His straightforward description of his decisions and actions cemented his reputation as one of the navy's finest leaders. Spruance expressed his "admiration for the part that Fletcher in the *Yorktown* played in this campaign." There was "a fine and smoothly working co-ordination between the two Task Forces before the fighting commenced." During the battle "the *Yorktown*'s attack and the information her planes furnished were of vital importance to our success, which for some time," Spruance noted with characteristic understatement, "was hanging in the balance." Because the *Yorktown* happened to be between TF-16 and "the enemy's fourth and still functioning carrier," she "took his blows." Another personal letter Spruance wrote on 8 June thanked Fletcher. "You were certainly fine to me all during the time the two task forces were operating together under your command, and I can't tell you how much I appreciate it." Fletcher reciprocated the good feeling, describing Spruance as "a splendid officer and a wonderful person," whose "two outstanding qualities were excellent judgment and courage."

The biggest welcome took place on 13 June, when both carrier task forces entered Pearl to cheers and triumphal celebrations. A reception of a different sort occurred eight hours later when Nagumo reported to Yamamoto in Hiroshima bay. He had to answer for why the heart of Japan's magnificent carrier force now lay on the bottom of the Pacific. . . .

Nimitz was generous with praise for his two task force commanders. On 13 June he included in a letter to King: "Inasmuch as Fletcher was the Senior Task Force Commander in the Battle of Midway and did an excellent job, despite the fact that the *Yorktown* was lost, I desire to reiterate the recommendation which I recently made by dispatch and amplified to you in a personal letter, that Fletcher be designated a Task Force Commander with the rank of Vice Admiral and that he be awarded the Distinguished Service Medal." The next day Nimitz recommended to King that Spruance also receive the DSM "for exceptionally meritorious service involving highest qualities seamanship endurance and tenacity in handling of his task force [in the] Midway engagement which resulted in defeat and heavy losses to enemy fleet." King let the matter of Fletcher's promotion rest, then on 19 June asked Nimitz whether "upon review of handling of Task Force 17 during Midway operations," his views had changed. Nimitz replied: "During Midway operations Fletcher was senior task force commander in area and responsible for activities Task Forces 16 and 17. For his services Midway and prior services Coral Sea I reiterate with added emphasis my recommendations in my 092219 of May that Fletcher be designated Task Force Commander with rank Vice Admiral and awarded Distinguished Service Medal." He again urged Spruance be decorated "for distinguished service as Commander Task Force 16 in Battle of Midway." King gracefully acceded. "All being done as recommended."

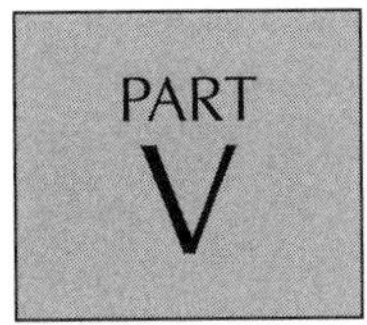

PART V

The Official Report of the Battle

Part V includes the report Admiral Nimitz sent to Admiral King and an excerpt from the oral history of RADM Ernest M. Eller, who served on Admiral Nimitz's staff during the Battle of Midway. Eller interviewed many of the American participants in the battle and worked with Admiral Nimitz to craft Nimitz's formal report to King.

The headquarters of the CominCh, U.S. Fleet, issued a number of classified combat reports during World War II. In each case, the report sent to the headquarters was annotated by the staff of the CominCh and bound with similar reports of battles that took place at about the same time. The first "Battle Experience" report covered operations from the attack on Pearl Harbor to the Battle of Midway; it was promulgated on 15 February 1943.

The report on the Battle of Midway captures the inferences drawn by the staff of Admiral Nimitz from the information that was available to Nimitz soon after the engagement. The report is a best estimate of what happened and shows how Admiral Nimitz presented the results of the battle to his superior, Admiral King. The comments of King's staff have been removed so the reader can see the report as it was communicated to Admiral King.

The report used standard U.S. Navy abbreviations and terminology, even for the Japanese. Cardiv is carrier division, and Desron is destroyer squadron. Airon is an aviation (or air) squadron, and a Transdiv is a transport division. BB stands for battleship, CA and CL stand respectively for heavy and light cruiser, carriers are CVs, destroyers are DDs, submarines are SSs. AP and AK (or Ak) are auxiliaries used for transporting troops and supplies. Navy aircraft designators are VSB for bombing aircraft and VTB for torpedo bombers; the Marine Corps designator for its bombers is VMB.

This report was carefully crafted and bears close reading. The full story of Midway was by no means complete when the report was sent to Admiral King. Admiral

Nimitz avoided dramatic claims for U.S. forces, preferring to let the known facts speak for themselves. At the same time, Nimitz's report shows the discerning reader what was clear to Admiral King's staff—for example, the failure of the B-17 high-level bombing attacks to destroy maneuvering warships, and the inability of U.S. air forces in June 1942 to conduct coordinated mass attacks on Japanese task forces.

This excerpt covers only events from 3–5 June. Though classified as Secret, the report deliberately avoids a discussion of the vital importance of code-breaking, which was a well-concealed operation. Note that it reveals there was no U.S. carrier available for the defense of the Aleutians, and that the air units based on Midway were nearly wiped out during their attacks against the *kidō butai* on 4 June. The report also carefully reminds Admiral King of his directives to Admiral Nimitz, and explains at some length why Nimitz's commanders at Midway believed there was a fifth Japanese carrier involved in the battle. Finally, the report notes that the *Hornet*'s torpedo plane squadron courageously attacked the Japanese carrier formation on 4 June, while *Hornet*'s dive-bombers and fighters went in the opposite direction. The report does not explain *why* this occurred, however.

CHAPTER

31

Battle Experience from Pearl Harbor to Midway, December 1941 to June 1942

United States Fleet, Headquarters of the Commander in Chief

Navy Department Library, Washington Navy Yard, Washington, DC

The Commander in Chief, Pacific Fleet, summed up the Battle of Midway as follows:

(Slight changes have been made in the text where later information indicated the necessity therefor.)

PRELIMINARY OPERATIONS

After the Battle of the Coral Sea it became evident that Japan was concentrating her fleet for movements of major importance against the Aleutians and Midway. Later indications were that the Midway expedition was a powerful fleet composed of a STRIKING FORCE, SUPPORT FORCE, and OCCUPATION FORCE. An estimate of the composition of this fleet, since largely verified by reports of the battle, was:

STRIKING FORCE	SUPPORT FORCE	OCCUPATION FORCE
CinC 1st Air Fleet (F)	Crudiv 7	1 *TAKAO* Class CA
Cardiv 1	MOGAMI (F)	1-2 MYOKO Class CA (?)
AKAGI (F)	*MIKUMA*	
KAGA	*SUZUYA*	Airon 7
	KUMANO	*CHITOSE*
Cardiv 2		*CHIYODA*
SORYU (F)	Cardiv —	
HIRUY	1 CV or XCV	Airon 11(?)
Desron 10	Batdiv 3, 2nd Sect.	
NAGARA (F)	*HIYEI*	Transdivs ?
12 DD	*KONGO*	8–12 AP
Batdiv 3	Crudiv 4 Part	Transdivs
HARUNA (F)	1 *ATAGO* Class CA	4–6 AK
KIRISHUMA		
	Desron 2 Part	Desron 4
Crudiv 8	*JINTSU* (F)	12 DDs
TONE (F)	10 DD	
CHIKUMA		

In addition, the plan was believed to provide for approximately 16 SS to be on reconnaissance and scouting mission in the Mid-Pacific–Hawaiian Islands Area.

The status of the important Pacific Fleet forces at the time the afore-mentioned threats developed was as follows:

(a) Task Force 17 had fought the battle of the Coral Sea from 4 to 8 May and was still in the South Pacific. The *LEXINGTON* had been sunk and the *YORKTOWN* damaged to an extent which might require a considerable period of repair—possibly even a trip to a West Coast Navy Yard. The remainders of the air groups of these two carriers were on the *YORKTOWN* urgently requesting reorganization and rest. This force had been continuously at sea since February 16.

(b) Task Force 16 (*ENTERPRISE* and *HORNET* with supporting cruisers and destroyers) was in the South Pacific, having arrived just too late for the Coral Sea action. It had been sighted recently, however, by an enemy reconnaissance plane and thus probably prevented an enemy occupation of Ocean and Nauru Islands.

(c) Task Force 1 (containing battleships and a small destroyer screen) was on the West Coast.

It was evident, if estimates of the enemy's strength and intentions were true, that the situation was most serious. Midway itself could support an air force only about the size of a carrier group; our carriers were far away; and perhaps only two would be fit to fight. Task Force 17 had already been recalled for repair and replenishment. Task Force 16 was immediately ordered north. At the same time a new force, Eight, was formed out of all cruisers within reach (five), and all destroyers available (four), and sent to Alaskan waters to assist the Sea Frontier Forces which were being assembled in that Area.

Midway was meanwhile given all the strengthening that it could take. Long range Navy and Army aircraft, though necessarily difficult to protect on the ground and water, were moved in. It was considered most important that the enemy be discovered at a distance and promptly attacked. To provide essential close-in air striking power, the Marine Air Group was increased to approximately 30 fighters and 30 dive bombers supported by six Navy new TBF torpedo planes and four Army B-26's fitted for dropping torpedoes. Many of these planes arrived just before the engagement. Despite a heavy inflow of planes from the mainland to Oahu and from there to Midway, the available numbers were never large enough to give a comfortable margin for losses. So critical, in fact, was this condition that after the first morning attacks at and off Midway the dive bombers, fighters and torpedo planes stationed there were nearly wiped out. Replacements of these types on Oahu were scanty and could not be got to Midway for the remainder of the battle.

Midway's ground defenses were strengthened by the emplacement of new batteries, completion of underwater obstacles, laying of mines, etc. Additional Marine forces were moved in, including a part of the 2nd Raider Battalion with special equipment for meeting a mechanized landing assault. Other reinforcement included motor torpedo boats and YP's.

Beginning at 0645 on 4 June, attacking Japanese aircraft bombed fuel tanks and the seaplane hangar on Sand Island and the Marine mess hall, galley, command post, and powerhouse on Eastern Island. By 0715 the first and only air attack on Midway during the battle was over, but the bombing had broken the aircraft fuel supply lines on Eastern Island and the Marines there had to refuel aircraft by hand from fuel drums. Most Marine Corps casualties were suffered by Marine pilots and aircrew: sixty-seven killed, missing, or wounded. Only seven Marines were killed and twenty-eight wounded during the Japanese air attack on the atoll.

U.S. Naval Institute Photo Archive

Thirteen submarines were stationed on the 200 and 150 mile circles covering the western and northern approaches to Midway. A few submarines were placed in support on the 800 mile circle northwest of Oahu, and the last ones to become available on the 100 mile circle from that place. All submarines which could reach the Oahu-Midway area were employed and the consequent cessation of their offensive patrols accepted.

Daily searches from Midway to distance of 700 miles generally through bearings 200° to 020° to westward were made as sufficient planes become available to accomplish this. From May 30th this coverage was maintained except in [*sic*] generally northwesterly direction where low visibility prevented search to maximum distance.

Full consideration was given to employment of Task Force One in the defense of Midway. It was not moved out because of the undesirability of diverting to its screen any units which could add to our long range striking power against the enemy carriers. Events proved that every air unit which was employed could have ill been spared from the purpose for which it was used, even though the results were far beyond the expectations of most.

As our air forces increase in strength relative to the enemy, and surface screening forces become available to permit a balanced force, the application of battleships' striking power will become practicable.

The Commander in Chief, United States Fleet estimated that the enemy's plans included an attempt to trap a large part of our Fleet. He directed that strong attrition tactics, only, be employed and that our carriers and cruisers not be unduly risked. The whole situation was a most difficult one requiring the most delicate timing on the part of our carriers if they could reach supporting stations in time. It so happened that they did. Task Force 16 arrived at Pearl Harbor on 26 May and departed on the 28th under command of Rear Admiral R. A. Spruance, U.S.N., as Task Force Commander, with Rear Admiral T. C. Kinkaid in Command of Cruiser Group, and Captain A. R. Early in command of the destroyers. Task Force 17 reached here on the 27th and sailed on the 30th, under Command of Rear Admiral F. J. Fletcher as Task Force Commander with Rear Admiral W. W. Smith in command of the Cruiser Group, and Captain G. C. Hoover in command of the destroyers. It was found, most fortunately, that the *YORKTOWN* and her aircraft could be placed in reasonable fighting condition in three days. Excellent work by the Navy Yard, the Service Force and all supporting services at Pearl Harbor made possible these prompt sailings.

Task Forces 16 and 17 joined at assigned rendezvous northeast of Midway on 2 June, having previously refueled at sea. In compliance with his directive, Rear Admiral Fletcher, Commander Task Force 17, then moved the combined forces to an area of operations north of Midway.

Albatross chicks with a burning oil tank on Sand Island on 4 June. The Navy deliberately chose to let several species of sea birds continue to mate and nest on the atoll, despite the problems they created for aircraft. In his award-winning documentary film of the battle, John Ford noted that the birds were the original inhabitants of Midway and that "Tojo" (Japanese Premier Tojo Hideki) had "sworn to liberate them."

U.S. Naval Institute Photo Archive

Broad tactical direction of all the forces in the Midway Area was retained by the Commander in Chief Pacific Fleet.

THE BATTLE
3 JUNE

The enemy Occupation Force and perhaps part of the Support Force was picked up in several contacts west of Midway on the 3rd. . . . The first contact was at about 0900 when a large number of ships (later reported at 11) were sighted by a Navy patrol plane, bearings 261° distant 700 miles from Midway, reported course 090, speed 10.

There were several smaller groups of ships, indicating that the escort group for the occupation force and the various ships of this force were converging on a rendezvous for the final advance on Midway.

About 1623, striking unit of 9 B-17's with four 600 lb. demolition bombs each, contacted and attacked the large group. They reported the force now consisted of

5 BB or CA and about 40 other ships—DD, AP, AK, etc. The course made good since the morning contact was about 081°, the bearing of Midway. Distance was then about 570 miles from Midway. Two ships, a CA or BB and an AP or AK were reported hit and injured severely so that they fell out of column and sent up "huge clouds of black smoke which mushroomed above them."

This was the only attack of the day, though at its close 4 PBY's armed with torpedoes were en route to attack. Estimated results are:

No damage to enemy.

4 JUNE

Attacks on the Japanese fleet began early this day and continued in force until nearly noon, with other attacks before sunset. Between 0130 and 0200 the 4 PBY's found and 3 attacked probably the same force as the B-17's had sighted; 10 or more big ships in 2 columns with 6 DD were observed. There were indications of another large group nearby. Bearing was still about 261° from Midway, distance reported about 500 miles, though part of the enemy force was closer. Two of the planes were able to press home attacks unobserved. One plane machine gunned a transport with good result. This night attack by Catalinas was a daring and historical feat, even though the exact damage is unknown.

The Japanese Main Striking Force assumed to have 4 carriers was not sighted on the third. These ships were apparently riding a weather front bearing down on

The burned-out large seaplane hangar on Sand Island the morning of 4 June. The hangar had been hit first on 7 December 1941 when two Japanese destroyers shelled Midway Atoll. It was repaired, only to be bombed by Japanese planes of the *kidō butai*.

U.S. Naval Institute Photo Archive

Midway from the northwest. One carrier had been reported among of Midway, but this contact was not verified. It is possible that the [illegible] five carriers off Midway and that the fifth one moved from the west t [illegible] west for the engagements of the fourth of June, but there is no clear evidence yet to bear to this.

Before dawn on 4 June PBY's took off from Midway continuing their invaluable scouting that contributed so greatly to the success of the action. Sixteen B-17's were dispatched by Commanding Officer, Midway, to attack the enemy transport force to the westward. At 0545 the most important contact of the battle was made. A PBY reported many planes heading for Midway 150 miles distant on bearing 320; 7 minutes later another PBY sighted 2 of the enemy carriers and many other ships on the bearing, distant 180 miles, coming in at 25 knots on course 135.

All serviceable planes at Midway were in the air before 0600 (except for 3 SB2U spares); 6 Navy TBF and 4 Army B-26 armed with torpedoes, and 27 Marine dive bombers were dispatched to strike the enemy carriers. The B-17's proceeding westward were also diverted to the carriers. Midway radar picked up the enemy planes and, at 0615, 14 of the 27 fighter planes available made contact 30 miles distant with 60 to 80 dive bombers (possibly a few of these were twin-engined horizontal bombers) and about 50 fighters. Severe fighting continued as long as our fighters were in the air, which was not long for most of them against these odds, accentuated by the poor maneuverability of these planes. Of the 27 fighters available, 15 were lost and 7 severely damaged. Statements from 9 of the 11 surviving pilots show that they shot town a total of 3 Japanese Zero fighters and 8 Aichi Type 99 dive bombers. Survivors believe the total number destroyed by all the fighter planes was probably 8 zero fighters and 25 dive bombers.

The first bomb hit Midway at about 0633 from horizontal bombers. Dive bombing and strafing continued for about 17 minutes. Considerable damage was done to nearly all structures above ground, the most serious at the time being the destruction of the power plant on Eastern Island. Little damage was done to the runways, the Japanese apparently leaving these intact for their own anticipated use. The anti-aircraft batteries shot well, downing 10 planes and, with the fighters, damaging many more, so that our returning airplanes reported "large numbers of enemy planes down on the water and falling out of formation."

The B-26's found their targets, 2 CV, about 0710 and made a most gallant attack. This is likewise another historical event, and, it is hoped, one soon to be repeated under better conditions—our Army's first attack with torpedo planes. Heavy fighter concentrations were encountered; 2 of the 4 planes did not return; one was shot down before launching his torpedo, and possibly the other, though it is said to have attacked and in pulling out touched the flight deck of the target before crashing into the sea. Both of the 2 planes that did return were so badly shot up by the terrific fighter and AA fire encountered that they were unserviceable. Survivors had no time to observe results but approaches were such that it is believed probable that one torpedo hit.

The TBF's made a similarly gallant attack almost simultaneously with the B-26's and against an equally determined and overwhelming number of fighters. At least 2 of them were shot down before they could launch torpedoes. Only one badly shot-up plane returned. The pilot could not tell what happened to the remainder of his unit or how the attack fared. A B-17, on reconnaissance, reports seeing one of the planes make a hit. Although the TBF is a well armed plane, it is obvious that it cannot go through fighter opposition without fighter protection.

At 0755 a group of 16 Marine dive bombers, under Major L. R. Henderson, U.S.M.C., made a gallant glide bombing attack on one of the carriers in the Striking Force. The planes had been received too recently for training in dive bombing, so the Commander chose this less effective and more hazardous method of attack because it permitted lower pullouts. His and 7 other planes were shot down by overwhelming fighter opposition. The 8 planes that did return were badly shot-up, one having 210 holes. The target, probably the *SORYU,* was hit 3 times and left afire.

Soon afterward, at about 0820, the 11 SB2U Marine bombers from Midway made a glide bombing attack on a battleship, likewise against heavy fighter attack. Two hits are reported. When last seen the battleship was smoking and listed.

The B-17 unit of 16 planes, under the Commanding Officer of the 431st Bombardment Squadron, Lt. Col. W. C. Sweeney, U.S.A., who led each flight he made in an outstanding manner, was directed to change its objective from the Transport Force to the carriers. Promptly and with skillful navigation the planes proceeded, picked up the enemy fleet on bearing 320° about 145 miles from Midway, and at 0814 began attacking from 20,000 feet, each plane carrying 8 500-pound demolition bombs. Results were reported as a total of 3 hits on the carriers present, possibly 2 carriers hit with heavy smoke from one; carriers still maneuvering and operating normally. Since only one carrier was reported smoking, this was probably the same one, *SORYU,* the Marine dive bombers had set afire a few minutes earlier with 3 hits.

The Midway Forces had struck with full strength, but the Japanese were not as yet checked. About 10 ships had been reported damaged, of which 1 or 2 AP or Ak [*sic*] may have sunk. But this was hardly an impression on the great force of about 80 ships converging on Midway. Most of Midway's fighters, torpedo planes and dive bombers—the only types capable of making a high percentage of hits on ships—were gone, and 3 of the Japanese carriers were still either undamaged or insufficiently so to hamper operations.

This was the situation when our carrier attack began. Task Force 16 and 17, ready about 200 miles to the northeast of the Japanese carriers, had intercepted the first contact reports by the Midway scouts. At about 0700 launching commenced of the following attack groups, *YORKTOWN*'s being temporarily held in reserve until her scouts returned (majority of fighters retained for combat patrol):

HORNET—35 VSB, 15 VTB, 10 VF
ENTERPRISE—35 VSB, 14 VTB, 10 VF

(Bombers carrying one 1,000-lb., or one 500-lb., or one 500- and two 100-lb. bombs.)

These two groups proceeded independently to attack.

Dive bombers proceeded at a high altitude with the torpedo planes at about 1,500 feet below the cloud base. Fighters failed to accompany the torpedo planes. *HORNET*'s accompanied dive bombers expecting to provide protection for the bombers and torpedo planes over enemy fleet. Torpedo planes proceeded separately and contact was lost with them. *ENTERPRISE*'s fighters likewise operated at a high altitude expecting fighters there and were not able to reach torpedo planes in time to assist. Lack of fighter support, visibility conditions, distance of attack, delay in locating the Japanese force, and Japanese tactics of concentrating fighters on torpedo planes all combined to prevent coordination of bombing and torpedo attacks, with resultant heavy loss of torpedo planes.

Sometime after 0830, when the last attack that morning by Midway planes was completed, the Japanese Striking Force commenced retirement to the north or northwest. Consequently it was not found in the estimated position by our carrier attack groups. *HORNET* Group Commander made the decision to turn south,

An image of defiance: raising the flag on Sand Island in the aftermath of the 4 June bombing by Japanese aircraft. Sand and Eastern Islands were actually tough nuts to crack. The Marines had planted antiboat mines and obstacles off the likely landing beaches, sowed antipersonnel and antitank mines on the beaches themselves, and surrounded every installation on both islands with bands of barbed wire. As many aircraft as possible were protected by revetments, and dynamite was set next to the underground fuel storage on Sand Island to blow the tanks sky high in the event the Japanese got on to the beaches.

U.S. Naval Institute Photo Archive

to search along the enemy's reported track, and failed to make contact. All 10 of the fighters were forced down for lack of gas and lost at sea, though 8 of the pilots have been recovered. All but two of the dive bombers eventually got back to the *HORNET* (11 via Midway) without attacking.

The *ENTERPRISE* Group Commander, proceeding separately decided to turn north to search, estimating that enemy must have reversed course. This was one of the most important decisions of the battle and one that had decisive results. Soon after 1000 he made contact and prepared to attack.

Meanwhile the *HORNET*'s torpedo squadron led by Lt. Comdr. J. C. Waldron had found the enemy and without hesitation at about 0920 conducted a most gallant and heroic attack entirely unsupported. They were met by overwhelming fighter opposition about 8 miles from the 3 carriers when attacked, and followed all the way in, being shot down one by one. The remnant drove in their attack to close range. Voice intercepts indicate that they shot down some Japanese fighters and made some hits.

Not a plane survived this magnificent devotion to purpose. One pilot, after attacking and probably hitting the *KAGA* at close range, with his gunner already killed, crashed near the *AKAGI*, ducked under his seat cushion to prevent being machine-gunned, and from this reserved position observed the fierce attacks that followed.

YORKTOWN and *ENTERPRISE* torpedo squadrons led respectively by Lt. Comdr. L. E. Massey, U.S.N. and Lt. Comdr. E. E. Lindsey, U.S.N. attacked later with equal courage and determination, and similar crushing losses. Both are believed to have made hits, but both were almost completely destroyed, *ENTERPRISE* losing 10 out of 14 planes and *YORKTOWN* 10 out of 12. Despite the many difficulties, exact coordination with dive bombers was almost achieved, the torpedo planes launching their attack only a few minutes before the bombers. Even had they attacked later, in perfect coordination, without adequate fighter protection their losses would have been probably as great. Recognizing the torpedo plane for the menace it is, the Japanese concentrated most of their fighters and anti-aircraft fire on it. The result was that the VT squadrons were a sacrifice that enabled the dive bombers to make their attack almost unopposed, with disastrous results for the enemy.

At 0830 *YORKTOWN* commenced launching the following attack group, dive bombers being armed with 1,000-lb. bombs:

C17 VSB 12 VT 6F

These proceeded with VT's at 15,000 feet, 2 VF at 2,500 feet, 4 VF at 5,000–6,000 feet and bombers at 16,000 feet. Contact was made at about the same time as by the *ENTERPRISE* planes and attack delivered almost simultaneously.

When the *HORNET* torpedo squadron attacked, there were 4 carriers dispersed in a wide roughly circular formation. *AKAGI, KAGA* and *SORYU* were in the same general vicinity, probably having just landed planes. *SORYU* was smoking, showing signs of heavy damage, as was also a ship some distance away that resembled a battleship. The surviving *HORNET* VT pilot, Ensign Gay, U.S.N.R., had been in the water only a few minutes when the *ENTERPRISE* and *YORKTOWN* dive bombers struck hard and most effectively. Both *KAGA* and *AKAGI*, between which he lay, were hit repeatedly, the planes on deck that they sought to launch being ignited until the two ships burned fiercely from stem to stern. *SORYU* was also hit again and continued to burn.

The dive bombing attacks by both *ENTERPRISE* and *YORKTOWN* squadrons began at about the same time, between 1020 and 1025. Many hits were made on each carrier. Some pilots considering them destroyed attacked other ships. The following damage was inflicted:

3 carriers—*AKAGI, KAGA, SORYU* set afire and ultimately destroyed.
2 battleships—one 1,000-lb. hit each, one a mass of flames.
1 CL or DD—one 1,000-lb. hit, believed DD sunk.

All submarines were ordered to close on the enemy Striking Force but the only submarine attack of the day was by *NAUTILUS* which at 0710 sighted smoke from torpedo hits and anti-aircraft fire on bearing 331° True. As she approached a formation consisting of one battleship of the *ISE* class and one *JINTSU* class cruiser she was twice attacked by aircraft, once by strafing, once by bombs, and depth-charged by the *JINTSU* class cruiser. On again coming to the surface she found herself in contact with a large number of ships. An unsuccessful long range torpedo attack was made on the battleship which headed away. After repeated depth charge attacks on her she eventually reached position to fire torpedoes at a burning carrier of the *SORYU* class, obtaining three hits on the carrier which burst into flames throughout its length. The carrier soon after was abandoned by the cruisers that had been attempting to take it in tow when attacked by *NAUTILUS*. About 1840 *NAUTILUS* on hearing heavy explosions, came to periscope depth and saw nothing but heavy smoke from burning oil. On surfacing at 1941, no ships, smoke or flames were to be seen. The *GROUPER* in a similar situation was unable to get in to attack because of the enemy's intensive anti-submarine measures.

At 0815 Task Force 16 radar had picked up a twin float seaplane, 36 miles to the south, which probably reported our formation's position. During *YORKTOWN* and *ENTERPRISE* Group dive bombing attacks on the Japanese carriers, the *KAGA* and *AKAGI* tried to launch planes. They were probably at the time preparing to attack our carriers. The carrier *HIRYU*, according to survivors picked up on 18 June (4 officers and 31 men), at this time drew off to the northward undamaged. Soon afterwards a Japanese message was intercepted "inform us position enemy carriers."

Lacking complete information on the number and location of enemy carriers, at 1150 *YORKTOWN* launched scouts to search sectors 280°–030° to 200 miles. Immediately thereafter at 1152 *YORKTOWN*'s radar picked up many planes approaching from westward, distant 32 miles. These were later determined to be 18 dive bombers and 18 fighters. As one fire precaution *YORKTOWN* drained the gas system and introduced CO2.

The Combat Air Patrol of 12 fighters located the enemy planes at about 9,000 feet altitude and attacked, shooting down 11 of the bombers. Out of the melee from time to time seven planes broke out and dived through heavy anti-aircraft fire. Of the first 3, one was caught by a 5" burst and disintegrated; the second dropped its bomb, which was a miss and plunged into the sea; the third was cut into fragments by automatic gun fire, but the bomb tumbling down exploded on the flight deck aft of the island and wiped out two 1.1 mount crews. At 1214 a hit in the uptake forced the *YORKTOWN* to stop, largely because boiler gases were drawn into firerooms making them uninhabitable. A third hit landed in the forward elevator well starting fires adjacent to the forward tanks of gasoline without igniting it [*sic*].

At 1402 with all fires extinguished and temporary repairs to the uptake completed, *YORKTOWN* was able to go ahead. Her position then was Latitude 33° 51' N, Longitude 176° W., course 090°. Speed was gradually increased to 19 knots by the time of the next attack. *PENSACOLA, VINCENNES, BALCH,* and *BENHAM* had meanwhile joined from Task force [*sic*] 16.

Approaching aircraft were again picked up on various bearings, the largest group being on 340°, distant 25 miles at 1433. The total attacking force was 12 to 15 torpedo planes and 10 to 18 fighters. The fighter combat patrol shot down 4 to 7 of the planes. About eight of the torpedo planes came on into the fire of *YORKTOWN*'s screen which was so heavy that observers thought it incredible that any got through. Three were shot down. Fighters just launched by *YORKTOWN* went into heavy anti-aircraft fire to attack the remaining five, which succeeded nevertheless in launching torpedoes. The last two, released at about 800 yards, at 1445 hit *YORKTOWN* amidships on the port side. All the torpedo planes were shot down. Three by fighter and ship fire before or as they passed *YORKTOWN,* two as they attempted to pass through the heavy fire of the screen.

Within ten minutes after being hit, *YORKTOWN* was listed 20° to 25° to port. In another ten minutes personnel began abandoning ship. It seemed that the *YORKTOWN* might capsize, and that she certainly would should she be hit again. Another attack seemed imminent throughout the afternoon. Radar contacts of unidentified planes were frequent, three of which at different times turned out to be Japanese seaplanes. The ship, however, continued to float through the night, list remaining about constant.

Both attacks on *YORKTOWN* were made by *HIRYU* planes. At 1430, just as the *HIRYU* torpedo planes were coming in radar range of *YORKTOWN*, one of the *YORKTOWN*'s scouts contacted the *HIRYU* with 2 BB, 3 CA and 4 DD in 31° 15' N., 179° 05' W., course north, speed 20. Task Force 16 launched an attack group of 16 dive bombers from *HORNET* and 24 from *ENTERPRISE* (14 of these being *YORKTOWN* planes) which beginning at 1705 for half an hour dived on the Japanese formation. Only 6–12 fighters were encountered, good evidence that Japanese plane losses had been very heavy in the day's fighting. Results of attack were:

CV *HIRYU*	Hit many times and aflame from bow to stern.
1 BB	Two 500- or 1,000-lb. bomb hits.
1 BB	Two 1,000- and one 500-lb. bomb hits.
1 CA	Two 500-lb. hits

With the destruction of the *HIRYU* our forces had won mastery of the air, although at the time it was not clear whether all carriers had been accounted for and whether or not more than four carriers were in the area.

Between 1810 and 1830 twelve B-17's in several flights struck the last blow of 4 June. Of these, 6 planes, attacking directly out of Oahu, in order to conserve gas did not climb to the usual attack level but made runs at 3,600 feet. Each group was attacked by zero fighters. These may have come from the *HIRYU*. Since these attacks occurred about an hour after *HORNET* attack and four hours after the first attack on *YORKTOWN* by *HIRYU* planes was picked up by radar and since *HIRYU* was impossible as a reservicing base, these attacks on B-17's may have been made by *HIRYU* fighter protection launched prior to attack on *HIRYU* or by planes from a fifth carrier not yet located. Some of the flights report a large CV burning and 1 or 2 small CV; but the unit most experienced in operations over the sea reported only one carrier which was burning, and a burning BB or CA accompanied by a number of other ships. Three 500-lb. bomb hits are reported on the damaged CV, one on a BB (probably CA), one on a CA (smoking badly), and one on a DD (probably sunk). A patrol plane, in this vicinity until about 1800, from a distance reported that a ship sank when hit by a salvo of bombs.

Summary of Losses Reported Inflicted on the Enemy on 4 June. Midway Forces

TIME	ATTACKING UNIT	TYPE ATTACK	SHIP SUNK	SHIP DAMAGED
0130	4 PBY	Torpedo	[None]	1 AP or Ak hit by machine gun fire
0710	4 B26 & 6 TBF	Torpedo	[None]	2 CV (estimate 2 hits)
0755	16 VMB	Glide Bombing	[None]	SORYU (CV) 3 hits
0820	11 VMB	Glide Bombing	[None]	BB 2 hits
0814	16 B17	Horizontal High Altitude	[None]	1 CV 1 hit *SORYU* (CV) 2 hits

Only 1 Carrier, *SORYU*, damaged enough to limit operations at this time.

Carrier Forces

TIME	ATTACKING UNIT	TYPE ATTACK	SHIP SUNK	SHIP DAMAGED
0920	15 VTB (*HORNET*)	Torpedo	[None]	*KAGA* (CV) 1 hit 1 CV hit (est.)
1020	26 VTB (*ENTERPRISE*) (*YORKTOWN*)	Torpedo	[None]	1 CV 2 hits (est.) 1 CV 1 hit (est.)
1022	50 VSB (*ENTERPRISE*) (*YORKTOWN*)	Dive Bombing	*AKAGI* *KAGA*— [Both] hit many times, burning fiercely.	*Soryu*—several hits. 1 BB 1,000-lb. hit, severe damage, mass of flames. 1 BB 1–1,000 lb. hit 1 CL or DD 1–1,000 lb. hit; believed sunk.

After these attacks 3 carriers out of action and later sank.

Submarine

TIME	ATTACKING UNIT	TYPE ATTACK	SHIP SUNK
01359	*NAUTILUS*	Torpedo	*SORYU*— 3 hits, this ship sunk by Aircraft and Submarine

After this attack 4 Japanese carriers were out of action.

Carrier Forces

TIME	ATTACKING UNIT	TYPE ATTACK	SHIP SUNK	SHIP DAMAGED
1750	40 VSB *(HORNET ENTERPRISE & YORKTOWN)*	Dive Bombing	*HIRYU*— Many hits, sank next morning.	1 BB—2 hits 1 BB—3 hits 1 CA–2 hits

Midway Forces

TIME	ATTACKING UNIT	TYPE ATTACK	SHIP SUNK	SHIP DAMAGED
1810	12 B17	Horizontal bombing	1DD	*AKAGI* (CV) 3 hits 1 CA—1 hit 1 CA—1 hit, smoking

5 JUNE

After attacking the *HIRYU*, Task Force 16 stood to the eastward and back to the westward during the night. Fighter attacks on B-17's before sunset indicated possibly a fifth Japanese carrier northwest of Midway and there was every indication that the enemy was continuing to close. The first information on the 5th was *TAMBOR*'s report of many ships 90 miles west of Midway. This looked like a landing attempt, so Task Force 16 changed course to a point north of Midway and increased speed to 25 knots. When reports after daylight made it clear that the Japanese had reversed course, the Task Force headed west and then northwest in a stern chase to try to reach a position from which attacks could be made on the retiring forces. Contacts were made by patrol planes with the remnant of the striking force in the early morning and again during the late afternoon on westerly courses, as well as with a carrier sighted at 0855 well to the north on a southwesterly course apparently to join the striking force. A burning carrier, *HIRYU*, still was reported with the retiring force at the time of the morning contacts. On the afternoon of the 5th, Task Force 16 reached a position from which attacks could be launched against the striking force, based on forenoon contact reports. Search and attack groups from *ENTERPRISE* and *HORNET* were launched between 1500 and 1528 to the northwestward but both groups failed to locate the enemy force, passing astern of that force both on the flight out and on the return flight. Each group contacted and attacked a single destroyer or small cruiser, both groups failing to hit their targets. Task Force 16 engaged in no other operations on the 5th.

Because of the night contact indicating that the enemy was persisting in his plans for a landing attack, all submarines were directed to close Midway in order to take advantage of the opportunity to attack transports and supporting ships when they were most vulnerable. After the retirement of the enemy became apparent, the fastest submarines were sent in chase and others returning from western patrols were directed to the expected lines of retirement of the enemy.

There were several contacts on the 5th by scouting planes, the two major ones being:

(a) A transport group west of Midway trailed by 2 damaged CA (reported as BB);

(b) The already mentioned retiring striking force of 2 BB (1 damaged), 3 CA, 4 DD trailed by a burning carrier to the northwest.

About 0430 12 B-17's departed in search of the western group but because of unfavorable weather could not locate them. Later, as more patrol plane reports came in, they found the target and attacked just after a group of 12 marine dive bombers. These leaving Midway at 0700 had struck a wide oil slick about 40 miles from the CA's and followed it in to attack position. Dives began at 0808. Results were:

1 CA (already damaged)	1 hit forward
	1 close miss astern

When the planes left between 0820 and 0830 the CA was listed "badly" to starboard and turning in sharp circles to starboard.

Eight B-17's attacked both the damaged CA's about 0830 with four to eight 500-pound bombs per plane, altitude 19,000–20,000 feet. They report one certain hit on stern on 1 CA.

At 1320 in the afternoon, 7 B-17's armed with eight 500-pound bombs each set out to the northwest to attack the remnants of the Japanese striking force; and at 1545 another group of 5 departed. En route, the first group sighted 1 CA but found nothing beyond. On the return journey, bombing from 9,000 to 16,000 feet, they report making 3 hits on the CA, bearing 300°, distant 300 miles from Midway. The second group likewise found and attacked only 1 CA, bearing 320°, 425 miles from Midway, no hits. On this attack one pilot dropped his bomb-bay gasoline tank with the bombs and did not return. One other plane ran out of gas and landed in the sea 15 miles from Midway, plane and 1 of the crew lost. These were the only losses of B-17's attack on the Japanese fleet.

Summary of Losses Reported Inflicted on the Enemy 5 June.

1 CA (already damaged)	1 hit (Both hits may have been on same CA)
1 CA (already damaged)	1 hit
1 CA	3 hits

COMMENT

During the night of the 4th and day of the 5th the retiring striking force apparently maintained a course about 280°, accompanied by the burning *HIRYU,* and making good a speed of but five and one half knots from time of attack on *HIRYU* the evening of the 4th to late afternoon of the 5th. From the attacks by fighters on B-17's during their attacks on *HIRYU* the evening of the 4th, and from the sighting by a Midway patrol plane of a carrier to the northward the morning of the 5th as well as subsequent contacts the afternoon of the 5th, it would appear that a fifth carrier to the northward joined up with the striking force the forenoon of the 5th, possibly to salvage personnel and material from burning *HIRYU.* At 1612 on the 5th a Midway patrol plane reported a force of one carrier, two battleships, three cruisers and five destroyers bearing 325° from Midway on course 280°, speed 10 knots. The report contained no mention of a burning carrier and it is probable that this carrier was the fifth carrier that had joined up during the day and that *HIRYU* had sunk or been sunk shortly prior to this contact.

At 1852 [on] the 5th a Midway patrol reported a carrier disappearing into a front to the northwest on course 315° and that a formation of nine planes was overhead and followed a few minutes later with a report that he was being attacked by planes.

It is probable that the contact made by the patrol plane with the striking force at 1612 was known to that force and that that force shortly after made its usual radical change of course, to about 240°.

The carrier departed to the northwest not to be sighted again. It is not entirely clear what course was pursued by the battleships of the force. Two were still reported present at the last contact. One was reported in a contact the following morning although its presence in the force at that time appears to be controversial. One of the two battleships formerly with this force almost certainly had been heavily damaged. Whether one of the two battleships parted company with the rest of the force during the night, or possibly sank, while the other continued to the southwestward with the striking force remnant, to be attacked and possibly sunk the following morning, or whether both battleships parted company from the rest of the force during the night is not clear. However, it is probable that part of the former striking force, cruisers and destroyers with possibly one battleship, maintained a generally southwesterly course during the night of the 5th while Task Force 16 maintained a generally westerly course. The occupation and support force presumably continued their retirement to the westward unmolested.

Submarines that had been drawn in close around Midway the night of the 4th to assist in repelling the prospective attack, were directed to the westward to attack the retiring forces on the 5th when the retirement was ascertained but apparently never again made contact with any of those forces.

CHAPTER
32

"This Was All Happening So Fast": Oral History of RADM Ernest M. Eller

Interviewed by John T. Mason Jr.

"Reminiscences of Admiral Ernest M. Eller" (Annapolis, MD: U.S. Naval Institute, 1986): pp. 540, 542, 544–546

LCDR Ernest M. Eller was assistant gunnery and anti-submarine training officer on the staff of Admiral Nimitz. After the Battle of Midway, Lieutenant Commander Eller was responsible for drafting the report Admiral Nimitz sent to Admiral King in Washington.

During the intense fighting on 4 June, then-Lt. Cdr. Eller recalled that Nimitz's staff in Hawaii was "enveloped in a maze of information." As Eller told his interviewer in 1986, the staff wasn't "sure, really, of the full outcome of the battle . . . for several days." To obtain as clear an understanding of what had happened as possible, Admiral Nimitz put Eller—who had taught writing at the Naval Academy—to work.

After the battle, I started on the report, and I interviewed everyone I could get in touch with. I interviewed all the flag officers, captains of ships, gunnery officers, squadron commanders of planes, and others, and I asked them to all send in full reports. So I guess that for Midway, I got the fullest picture

> of any battle that I wrote action reports on, because they were all there. They all came into Pearl, and I talked to them right away when their recollections were fresh and not colored by what they wanted to remember. . . .
>
> I collected these reports and all the recollections of people, wrote the first draft of the report, and took it in to Admiral Nimitz. He worked on it. He was very much interested in it, of course, because it was a great victory. Then I worked on it and worked on it, changing words, making revisions he desired. Meanwhile, I think about the sixth, Army Air Forces flashed back the news, or else they let newspapermen flash it back to the States, that the high-level bombers had defeated the Japanese fleet. . . .

So this misinformation was widespread while we kept working on our report. At this time [Under Secretary of the Navy] Forrestal came out for a visit and lived with Admiral Nimitz for a couple of days. The first evening I took the report to [his] quarters and he looked it over. He was very much interested and thought we ought to rush it back, but we worked on it still. Admiral Nimitz wanted it just right and I did too. In a few more days we did send it, and it was finally published, but the first news had filled most men's minds. It took years for the truth to really sink in.

— *AUTHOR* —

RADM Ernest M. Eller served as gunnery officer on aircraft carrier *Saratoga* in 1942 and then moved to the staff of ADM Chester Nimitz, where he wrote CINCPAC's war reports. During the Korean War, he was Commander, Middle East Force. From 1956 to 1970, he was the Director of Naval History in Washington.

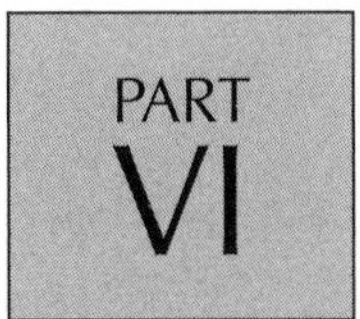

PART VI

The Commanders

This part of the anthology focuses on the senior commanders, though the reader must remember that there were numbers of mid-grade commanders in both navies who performed their duties responsibly and at times with great dash and courage. Three of the selections ("Admiral Nimitz and the Battle of Midway," by E. B. Potter [chapter 33]; "Excerpt from *Nimitz,*" also by E. B. Potter [chapter 34]; and "Chester W. Nimitz: Victory in the Pacific," by John Lundstrom [chapter 35]) concern ADM Chester Nimitz. Admirals Fletcher ("Harsh Lessons," from *Black Shoe Carrier Admiral* by John Lundstrom [chapter 37]) and Spruance ("Commentary on RADM Raymond A. Spruance," by this anthology's editor [chapter 36]) merit one selection each. Historian John Lundstrom offers his assessment of Admiral Nagumo and of Nagumo's command dilemma on the morning of 4 June 1942 ("Enemy Carriers," also from *Black Shoe Carrier Admiral* [chapter 38]).

No two of these four admirals were alike. All became young officers before it was clear that aviation and submarines would profoundly change naval warfare. Not one of the four was an aviator or even had aviation training late in his career. Of the three Americans, only then–Rear Admiral Fletcher was considered one of the "most capable" serving admirals by a board of nine active and retired admirals that advised Navy secretary Frank Knox in March 1942. Fletcher certainly lived up to expectations, but he, Nimitz, and Spruance were under great pressure in May and June 1942—from Admiral King in Washington and from the Japanese, who had shown what their navy could do with carriers and carrier aircraft.

Admiral Nagumo lacked the charisma of his superior, Admiral Yamamoto, but he had had to make his own difficult decisions, starting with his choice to withdraw after the initial successful surprise attack on Pearl Harbor on 7 December 1941. Japanese aviators who had criticized Nagumo for not being aggressive enough then were too quick to remember what the admiral never forgot that first day of the war, which was that he did not know where the U.S. carriers were, and the three that he suspected might be at sea could ambush his *kidō butai* and catch him by surprise as he had caught the Pacific Fleet by surprise. Admiral Nagumo also had to bear great command responsibility as his carrier force rampaged across the South Pacific after Pearl Harbor. As Walton L. Robinson noted in his "*Akagi*, Famous Japanese Carrier," Nagumo's *kidō butai* was in action or preparing for it from the beginning of December 1941 through April 1942—five months of intense planning and focused decision making by Admiral Nagumo and his staff.[1] We should not be surprised that such a pace of operations had taken its toll on Nagumo's spirit and strength.

CHAPTER

33

Admiral Nimitz and the Battle of Midway

By E. B. Potter

Proceedings, July 1976: pp. 60–68; adapted from *Nimitz* (Annapolis, MD: Naval Institute Press, 1976)

It is now generally accepted that the American victory over potentially overwhelming odds in the Battle of Midway (3–6 June 1942) was made possible mainly through cryptanalysis of radio transmissions the Japanese sent in their naval operational code. Information from this source reached Admiral Chester W. Nimitz, Commander-in-Chief, Pacific Fleet (CinCPac), via the Pearl Harbor radio intelligence unit (Station Hypo). The unit was headed by Lieutenant Commander Joseph J. Rochefort, who generally made contact with CinCPac headquarters by scrambler ("hotline") telephone to Lieutenant Commander Edwin T. Layton, Nimitz' intelligence officer.

To save Port Moresby, Nimitz rushed Rear Admiral Frank Jack Fletcher to the Coral Sea with a force including the carriers *Lexington* (CV-2) and *Yorktown* (CV-5). Vice Admiral William F. Halsey, with the carriers *Enterprise* (CV-6) and *Hornet* (CV-8), also headed for the South Pacific. Halsey was delayed, however, by having launched a carrier raid on Tokyo and did not reach the combat area in time. In the Battle of the Coral Sea (4–8 May 1942), the force under Fletcher turned back the seaborne Port Moresby invasion force and sank the light carrier *Shoho.* In the climactic action of 8 May, the Americans lost the *Lexington* and suffered damages to the *Yorktown.*

Admiral Nimitz now ordered Halsey and Fletcher to return to Pearl Harbor on the double. By this time Nimitz had fairly complete information on the Japanese operational plan for Midway. The Second Carrier Striking Force, including two carriers, was to make a diversionary air raid on the American base at Dutch Harbor in the Aleutians. Transports would then land Japanese troops on the far-western Aleutian Islands. On the morning following the Dutch Harbor raid, the First Carrier Striking Force, coming down from the northwest, was to launch the main attack by raiding Midway. Meanwhile, an invasion force would be approaching Midway from the southwest. Admiral Isoroku Yamamoto, Commander-in-Chief of Japan's Combined Fleet, planned to be at sea, backing up the whole operation with a powerful battleship force, but this fact was unknown to CinCPac.

To Admiral Nimitz the wide dispersion of the Japanese fleet spelled opportunity. He sent Rear Admiral Robert A. Theobald north with a surface force to do what he could to derail the enemy invasion of the far Aleutians. It was clear to the CinCPac staff, however, that the crucial element of the enemy disposition was the First Carrier Striking Force, commanded by Vice Admiral Chuichi Nagumo, who six months previously had led the attack on Pearl Harbor. In Nagumo's force were the carriers *Akagi* (flagship), *Kaga, Hiryu,* and *Soryu,* all veterans of the Pearl Harbor attack, with a screen of two battleships, three cruisers, and 11 destroyers. Only this force could provide the punch needed to knock out Midway's ground and air defenses, and it alone could provide a concentration of air power great enough to cover the other components of the Japanese fleet. Thus, it alone was essential to the attack. Therefore, Nimitz laid plans to eliminate Nagumo's carriers. He would place his own carriers northeast of Midway, on the flank of Nagumo's oncoming force. With the advantage of surprise, his three carriers might knock out Nagumo's four.

For this plan to succeed, Nimitz had to know when and where to find Nagumo. He assigned the problem to Layton, who reviewed the intelligence findings of the previous three weeks, brooded over charts, and studied Pacific Ocean winds, weather, and currents. He repeatedly telephoned Rochefort to compare notes. At last he felt safe in reporting his estimates to Nimitz.

Layton predicted that the enemy carriers would attack Midway on the morning of 4 June. "They'll come in from the northwest on bearing 325 degrees," he said, "and they will be sighted at about 175 miles from Midway, and the time will be about 0600 Midway time."

The apparent completeness and the detail with which the Japanese plan had been made known through cryptanalysis aroused the suspicions of some officers stationed at Pearl Harbor. Why, they asked, should practically the whole Combined Fleet be assigned to the capture of one tiny Central Pacific atoll and a couple of useless islands in the Aleutians? Might not the messages be fakes, deliberately planted to mislead the Americans? Such top secret information is not usually transmitted by radio, even in the securest codes, for all the world to record, scrutinize, and perhaps cryptanalyze.

Nimitz pointed out that the Japanese could be operating in strength in order to meet American opposition. Their main objective might even be to draw out the inferior U.S. Pacific Fleet so that it could be destroyed. The transmission of the plans by radio could mean that Yamamoto was operating on so tight a schedule that he could get them distributed in time by no other means. Nimitz, for want of anything better, decided to base his strategy on the assumption that the intelligence estimates were correct.

He had expected Admiral Halsey, his senior carrier commander, to command the U.S. forces off Midway, but Halsey fell ill with a severe attack of dermatitis. Therefore, Fletcher assumed the tactical command, as he had in the Coral Sea. Rear Admiral Raymond A. Spruance. Halsey's cruiser commander, took temporary command of the *Enterprise–Hornet* force (Task Force 16). On the morning of 28 May, this force steamed out of Pearl Harbor and headed for the Midway area. Two days later, Fletcher followed with a hastily patched-up *Yorktown*, escorted by two heavy cruisers and five destroyers (Task Force 17).

U.S. radio traffic analysis indicated that all segments of the Japanese fleet were under way. Intercepts revealed that seaplanes were en route from the Marshall Islands to scout Pearl Harbor. They never arrived because they could not complete the long flight from the Marshalls and back without refueling. For that purpose they were supposed to meet tanker-submarines in the lagoon of French Frigate Shoals, but Admiral Nimitz had forehandedly stationed a vessel there.

Meanwhile Sand and Eastern islands in Midway Atoll had been converted into the most strongly fortified two square miles in the Pacific. The 3,000 defenders, protected by ground mines, underground shelters, guns in concealed emplacements, and a wilderness of barbed wire, were prepared to hurl back any force that was likely to try a landing. However, Nimitz was dubious about what Midway's planes could do against enemy carriers. Tiny Eastern Island, where the airfield was, could handle only so many aircraft, and those available were ill adapted for attacking ships. Not a flier on Midway had had any combat experience. About the most that could be expected of them was that, by breaking up the formation of the enemy fleet and drawing off its fighters, they might set it up for the better-trained U.S. carrier aviators.

CinCPac and his staff had shot their bolt. They had deployed their available forces to the best of their ability to meet what looked like impossible odds. There was little more they could do until the enemy appeared. Then they would have their hands full, for Admiral Nimitz, acting as coordinator, was retaining overall command—land, sea, and air.

At dawn on 3 June, key members of the CinCPac staff were at their stations. A little after 0400, U.S. radio-intercept stations began to pick up bits of radio traffic suggesting unusual, possibly enemy, air activity in the eastern Aleutians. Dutch Harbor had in fact been raided from the air, but a report from that base seems to have got no farther than Admiral Theobald, who was at sea under radio silence. Analysis of the intercepts, however, at length convinced CinCPac staff that there had indeed been enemy planes over Dutch Harbor.

Admiral Nimitz conservatively assessed the overflights as enemy reconnaissance, possibly by cruiser planes, rather than as part of the Japanese operation plan, unfolding right on schedule. Even if he could be sure that the planes were from the Japanese Second Carrier Striking Force, he would still not be certain that Midway was the enemy's main target or that Nagumo's First Carrier Striking Force was speeding down from the northwest in the fog to attack Midway. The best evidence of that would be a sighting of the slower invasion force from Saipan heading for the atoll.

Several hours passed without any further word from the north and none at all from the west. At last, a little after 1100 (1230 at Pearl Harbor), the cable from Midway came to life. It was relaying a report, sent in segments from a Catalina patrolling 700 miles to westward: "Main Body . . . bearing 262, distance 700 . . . eleven ships, course 090, speed 19." Nine B-17s, held in readiness at Midway for just such a contact, had promptly taken off and headed west to attack the oncoming enemy force with bombs. At Pearl Harbor, Commander Maurice E. Curts, the CinCPac communication officer, rushed the contact report to Nimitz' office, where the admiral was consulting with Commander Layton. Nimitz glanced at the dispatch, then sat suddenly erect.

"Layton," he said excitedly, "have you seen this?"

"What is it, sir?"

"The sighting of the Japanese forces!"

Nimitz was smiling. That in itself was nothing unusual, for he smiled often. His expression now, however, was nothing less than radiant, what Layton called "that brilliant white smile."

"It just lights up," said Layton, as though "somebody let in the sun by raising a window shade. His smile and his blue eyes would go right through you." Nimitz had successfully concealed his anxiety, but now he made not the slightest attempt to hide his relief. He handed the dispatch to Layton.

"This ought to make your heart warm," he said, chuckling. "This will clear up all the doubters now. They just have to see this to know that what I told them is correct."

Though the U.S. task forces would almost certainly have picked up the radioed contact report directly from the Catalina, CinCPac communications took the elementary precaution of relaying the report to Admiral Fletcher. In view of the report's misleading phrase "Main Body," Nimitz warned: "That is not, repeat not, the enemy striking force." Thus far, only the invasion force had been sighted, he added, and he reminded Fletcher that the Japanese carriers were due to strike from the northwest the following morning. The chances of sighting them on 3 June were slight because, from a foggy area almost all the way to Midway, dense clouds obscured the ocean.

Before sunset on the 3rd, Admiral Nimitz knew that Dutch Harbor had been bombed that morning and that four Japanese carrier planes had been shot down over the Aleutians. From Midway he learned that the B-17s sent against the invasion force found and attacked it 570 miles out. They reported having hit two battleships or heavy cruisers and two transports—news that the CinCPac staff received with a certain amount of skepticism. In the early evening, four Catalina amphibians took off from Midway for a moonlight torpedo attack on the invasion force. CinCPac relayed all this information to the appropriate commands. Then to Midway and to his task force commanders Nimitz sent a special message: "The situation is developing as expected. Carriers, our most important objective, should soon be located. Tomorrow may be the day you can give them the works." The concluding words of the entry in the CinCPac Command Summary for 3 June were prophetic: "The whole course of the war in the Pacific may hinge on the developments of the next two or three days."

Though few persons on Oahu knew exactly what was going on or what to expect, all felt the tension that spread throughout the area like a tangible presence. At nightfall CinCPac headquarters, not aware that the scheduled Japanese seaplane reconnaissance had been canceled, passed an air-raid warning to 14th Naval District, which sounded an all-out "red" alert. Pearl Harbor Navy Yard was promptly blacked out. Machinery in the repair shops was shut down. Workmen and Marines manned machine guns. Trucks blocked the gates. On the ships in the harbor, gun crews hurried to their stations. At Schofield Army Barracks, many patients were discharged from the hospital to make way for anticipated casualties. In Honolulu civilian defense workers were summoned to duty.

Few CinCPac staff officers slept that night. One of them recalled that Admiral Nimitz dozed on a cot in his office—storing up rest against the coming 48 or more hectic hours, yet ready for any eventuality. Around 0200, the staff communication office, which operated 24 hours a day, received and passed on to Nimitz a report, relayed via Midway, from the Catalina amphibians. It stated that they had torpedoed two of the oncoming invasion force's ships.

At dawn, 4 June, all the CinCPac staff were at their stations. They knew that when first light came to Midway, where the sun rose one and a half hours later than it did at Pearl, Catalinas would be out to the northwest, patrolling at the edge of the overcast. They were aware also that the report they were awaiting might well be the pivotal communication of the war. Shortly after 0600 it came, an urgent message in plain language, sent via the cable from Midway: "Plane reports two carriers and Main Body ships bearing 320, course 135, speed 25, distance 180."

Though the Catalina pilot had reported seeing only two carriers, Nimitz was sure that there were four, perhaps five. He glanced at the date-time group on the dispatch. He then went into operations plot and pinpointed the enemy's position. Afterward he remarked to Layton, "Well, you were only five miles, five degrees, and five minutes off." At least half the credit for the remarkable accuracy of Layton's prediction is due to Admiral Nagumo's navigator, who, through three days of fog and overcast had guided his force unerringly toward its objective.

Here at last was the target the Americans had been waiting for—Nagumo's First Carrier Striking Force, the force that had opened the war six months before with its raid on Pearl Harbor, the force that now had to be defeated. The brief contact report made clear to Nimitz and his staff that Nagumo had already launched an air attack on Midway. He must have launched his planes much farther out than a mere 180 miles, and he would have done so while his ships were still hidden by the overcast. He had remained on course 135°, toward Midway, so that his returning aircraft could find their carrier decks and in order to shorten their return flight. Nagumo could not have known at the time of launching that the American carriers were on his flank, or he would have launched his planes and shaped course in their direction.

CinCPac staff took for granted that, on receiving the contact report, Midway had launched all its planes so that none could be caught on the ground. The Midway-based bombers and torpedo planes would be heading to attack Nagumo's carriers, the 28 Marine fighters to tackle his oncoming planes. Off to the northeast, Fletcher had undoubtedly heard the contact report and was acting upon it. Nevertheless, CinCPac communications faithfully relayed the report to him—just in case.

The CinCPac Staff was sure that, despite resistance from the 28 fighter planes, some, perhaps most, of the Japanese bombers would get through to Midway. An attack on the atoll was inevitable, and imminent. At 0625 the expected message came in via the cable, a three-word dispatch: "Air raid Midway."

Two hours of trying uncertainty ensued, with no messages at all reaching Pearl from U.S. forces at the battle front. Fletcher and Spruance would of course maintain radio silence until they had been located by the enemy. Then, at 0830 there came in from Midway a sad little message: "Only 3 undamaged fighting planes remain. No contact our dive-bombing planes."

Meanwhile Rochefort and Layton were in excited conversation on the scrambler telephone. Rochefort's radio intelligence unit had picked up a Japanese voice contact report, evidently from one of Nagumo's search planes. As interpreted by

Rochefort, it read: "Sighted 10 surface ships, apparently enemy, bearing 10°, 240 miles from Midway, course 150°, speed over 20 knots."

Layton took the sighting report immediately to Admiral Nimitz, who glanced at it.

"Are you sure the report didn't include our carriers being sighted?"

"Yes, sir."

Nimitz, report in hand, strode into operations plot and handed it to the watch officer, who entered it on the plot. If the reported ships were one of the American carrier groups—and they could hardly be anything else—then the opposing forces were about 150 miles apart, that is, just within effective attack radius, and the Japanese carrier force was about 150 miles from Midway.

The Midway-based aircraft must have been attacking Nagumo at about the same time that Nagumo's search plane was informing him of nearby U.S. forces afloat. Intense static in the area through which Nagumo was steaming had, however, blotted out all radio reports from the American aircraft. Only as they returned to Midway were the aircraft able to forward reports to CinCPac, thanks to the cable connection. Their reports were not particularly encouraging. The dive-bombers had apparently hit one enemy carrier, which they said was left smoking. The B-17s reported making three hits on two carriers. On the other hand, the American planes had encountered heavy opposition from Zero fighters and suffered severe losses.

Nagumo's myopic search pilot, transmitting outside the zone of intense static, continued to send in reports that were heard at Pearl. At 8:09 he identified the "10 surface ships, apparently enemy" as "five cruisers and five destroyers." Eleven minutes later, having taken another look, he reported, "The enemy is accompanied by what appears to be a carrier bringing up the rear."

This report brought the CinCPac staff crowding around the plot. They were sure that Nagumo now had information on which he was bound to act. He had to do something, and do it quickly, about that American carrier. CinCPac staff agreed that the Japanese admiral had two choices. He could launch an attack at once with his reserve aircraft. If he did that, the planes returning from Midway would have to remain in the air until the launching had been completed. There was a strong possibility that many of them, low in fuel after their long flight, would crash into the sea. Or Nagumo might first recover, refuel, and rearm the Midway planes before launching. He would thus be able to send out a much more powerful attack, but the attack would be delayed at least an hour. Meanwhile American planes would certainly be en route to strike Nagumo's force. Should they succeed in bombing the Japanese carriers while the latter were refueling and rearming aircraft, the carriers would explode like giant firecrackers.

Although Midway-based Catalinas were out patrolling, no new information about the position or course of the Japanese carriers came over the cable. Nimitz was equally uninformed about the operations of the American forces. Fletcher continued to maintain radio silence, even though the Japanese now knew where he was.

Thus, just as the crucial battle of the war was reaching a climax, CinCPac suffered an information blackout. Nimitz managed to look unruffled, but officers who knew him well could see that he was deeply worried. One officer said, "Admiral Nimitz was frantic; I mean, as frantic as I've ever seen him." The admiral sent for Commander Curts. "Why aren't we getting messages?" he demanded. "Why aren't we hearing something?" Curts replied somewhat lamely that he didn't know, but that he didn't want to send a message out there saying, "I'm having no reports. Report something." Nimitz agreed that that would not do at all.

The Japanese were not so reticent. Before 1000, two fairly long radio messages emanated from their carrier force. The Americans could not read the encoded messages, but Rochefort's men reported that they came from the carrier *Akagi*, Nagumo's flagship. One of them had recognized the touch on the key as that of one of the *Akagi*'s chief warrant officers, an operator whose "fist" was so bad that someone had remarked that he "hits the key like he's kicking it with his foot." If Station Hypo could not read the messages, it at least now had Nagumo's current call sign for future reference.

Nimitz' sole source of information concerning the U.S. carrier forces continued to be the Japanese search pilot. A little before 0900, the pilot had radioed to the Japanese force: "Ten enemy torpedo planes heading toward you." The planes could only be from the American carriers. CinCPac and his staff concluded that Nagumo was now either just completing the launching of his reserve aircraft or, as seemed more probable, he was recovering his planes from Midway, in which case he would not be able to launch until after 1000.

At 0926, the cable relayed to Pearl a Catalina report placing the oncoming invasion force 320 miles from Midway. Next over the cable came reports from Midway-based bombers and torpedo planes newly returned to the atoll. Apparently the Midway aircraft were continuing to take heavy losses while inflicting little or no damage on the enemy. Finally at 1008 the *Enterprise* broke silence in an unexpected manner. In CinCPac's communications center a voice on the carrier's audio frequency was heard to shout, "Attack immediately!" Someone identified the voice as that of Captain Miles Browning, the chief of staff whom Spruance had inherited from Halsey. Browning's cry must have been in response to a report from American aviators that they had found the enemy.

After another long period of silence, Nimitz sent out inquiries, and Layton asked Rochefort via the hot-line telephone whether the U.S. carriers had attacked Nagumo's force and, if so, what the Japanese reaction was. "Don't we have anything on this?" Layton inquired.

"Not a thing."

"Have we tried the other frequencies?"

"We've tried every frequency we know they've got." Admiral Nimitz and his staff concluded that in this instance no news might be good news. If the enemy carriers were not transmitting, it could be because they were no longer able to do so. At 1100 Rochefort's radio intelligence unit intercepted a transmission, or a fragment of a transmission, in plain-language Japanese: "Inform us position enemy carriers." This message, which obviously had been sent from the Nagumo force to one of its search planes, implied that at least one Japanese carrier was able and ready to counterattack. Fifty minutes later Nagumo himself radioed a long message in code to an unidentified addressee. The call sign was his, but the operator was not the heavy-handed warrant officer of the *Akagi*. One of Rochefort's people had made a study of identifying operators and recognized the fist as that of the chief radioman in the cruiser *Nagara*. Evidently the *Akagi* had been damaged too heavily to serve as flagship, and Nagumo had shifted to the cruiser.

Admiral Fletcher, informed of these intercepts, at last broke radio silence, but only to report that *Yorktown* planes had attacked two enemy carriers. He added: "Have no indication of location of additional carriers which have sighted this force." Shortly afterward, the Pearl Harbor radio intelligence unit intercepted the report of an airborne Japanese flight leader, "We are attacking the enemy carrier." The flight leader was then heard ordering the aircraft under his command, "Attack! Attack! Attack!"

Then into CinCPac communications center came a message in plain English, "Am being attacked by large number of enemy bombers." It was sent by ship's radio to CinCPac, but no originator was shown, and attempts to authenticate it were fruitless. The explanation came twenty minutes later, when Fletcher sent a correctly identified coded message, "Have been attacked by air 150 miles north of Midway."

CinCPac was kept informed, if somewhat belatedly, of what was happening to the *Yorktown*. Three bomb-hits having left her dead in the water, Admiral Fletcher and his Staff had transferred to the cruiser *Astoria* (CA-34). Shortly after 1500, when the damaged carrier was again under way, she was the target of a second attack, this time by torpedo planes, which hit her at least twice. Because the *Yorktown* began to list badly and was apparently about to capsize, Captain Elliott Buckmaster gave the order to abandon ship. Hours later, after the last of her crew had been fished out of the water, the carrier was still afloat and had undergone no appreciable change in trim. Fletcher therefore requested CinCPac to send tugs and told him that, unless otherwise directed, he and his Task Force 17 would protect and attempt to salvage the *Yorktown,* while Spruance's Task Force 16 continued to engage the enemy. Admiral Nimitz raised no objections; he wanted no effort spared to save the carrier, and in his opinion Spruance was entirely capable of taking over the tactical command.

The bad news about the *Yorktown* was somewhat offset by a dispatch from Spruance. He reported that between 0930 and 1100 that morning "air groups from Task Forces 16 and 17 attacked carriers of enemy force consisting of probably 4 carriers, 2 battleships, 4 heavy cruisers, and 6 destroyers. All 4 carriers believed badly damaged." He concluded his report: "Our plane losses heavy."

Aircraft from Midway and from the *Yorktown,* the latter launched before she was damaged, were frantically searching the ocean for the source of the attacking planes. A shore-based Catalina found three burning ships 170 miles northwest of Midway. Some 45 miles farther out on the same bearing, the *Yorktown* planes found an undamaged enemy carrier, identified as the *Hiryu.* She was accompanied by two battleships, three cruisers, and four destroyers. Against this target the *Enterprise* and the *Hornet* launched 40 dive-bombers, while Midway sent a dozen B-17s, six of which were just approaching Eastern Island, having been ordered from Hawaii to Midway.

By the early evening of 4 June, Admiral Nimitz and his staff were reviewing the events of the day with guarded optimism. If the information thus far received was to be taken literally, the Americans had defeated the Nagumo force. But most of the favorable reports were based on observations by Army aviators, and they were not trained in assessing battle damage at sea. Even the careful Spruance had reported "all 4" enemy carriers badly damaged that morning. Yet in the early afternoon planes from one of those carriers had knocked out the *Yorktown.*

Results of the attack launched against the *Hiryu* from Midway and by Task Force 16 were not transmitted to CinCPac until the bombers had returned from their mission, the crews had been debriefed, and repetitions had been removed from their reports. Midway's dispatch arrived at Pearl Harbor a little after 2200; Task Force 16's, some 20 minutes later.

Said Midway: "Fortresses en route from Pearl made 2 hits on smoking carrier bearing 320, distance 170. Reported 2 other ships in area burning and 2 additional on fire about 125 miles on same bearing."

Spruance reported: "At 1700 to 1800 air groups of Task Force 16 attacked enemy force consisting of 1 carrier, 2 battleships, 2 or more heavy cruisers, several destroyers. Carrier hit several times with 500- and 1000-pound bombs and when last seen burning fiercely. At least 4 hits on battleship, which was burning. One heavy cruiser also hit and burning. At 1750 enemy force in position lat. 30–41 north, long. 177–41 west, course west, speed 15 knots, with destroyers joining from southeast. Three ships believed carriers previously attacked were observed to southeastward still burning. . . . "

When Nimitz had read that far, he looked up. His countenance was glowing with "that brilliant white smile." If the *Hiryu* was burning fiercely and the *Akagi, Kaga,* and *Soryu,* hit that morning, were still burning, all four carriers were almost certainly beyond salvage. An American victory seemed assured unless Spruance were to blunder badly, and Nimitz believed Spruance was no blunderer. Nimitz immediately released a prepared message to all his forces: "You who participated in the Battle of Midway today have written a glorious page in our history. I am proud to be associated with you. I estimate that another day of all-out effort on your part will complete the defeat of the enemy." The CinCPac Command Summary, probably echoing Nimitz, called the day's operations "the start of what may be the greatest sea battle since Jutland. Its outcome, if as unfavorable to the Japs as seems indicated, will virtually end their expansion."

The battle did indeed end the Japanese expansion, but of that the Americans could not then be sure. On the other hand, the Americans did not suspect until the end of the war how perilously close their own forces had come to defeat. Admiral Nagumo had elected to land, refuel, and rearm his planes from the Midway strike before launching against the American ships. Meanwhile, Midway was counterattacking. Aircraft from Eastern Island struck at the Japanese force in five successive waves. They achieved no hits. Next came three separate attacks by torpedo planes from the *Hornet*, the *Enterprise*, and the *Yorktown*. Nearly all of these were shot down without inflicting any damage whatever.

At 1000, the four Japanese carriers had on their flight decks a strike force armed, fueled, and ready to take off, and a second strike force being readied below. Nagumo ordered his counterattack, and his carriers turned into the wind to launch. At that moment, bombers from the *Yorktown* and the *Enterprise*, undetected by the Japanese, dove from 15,000 feet and, in seconds, changed the whole course of the war. They released bombs that hit the *Soryu*, the *Kaga*, and the *Akagi*, setting off lethal fires and explosions in all three.

The *Hiryu*, escaping unscathed to the north with some of the Japanese surface vessels, first launched bombers, then torpedo planes that found and disabled the *Yorktown*. At 1700, dive-bombers from the *Enterprise* located the *Hiryu* just as she was about to launch an attack on the other American carriers. They scored four direct hits on the Japanese carrier, setting off explosions and uncontrollable fires.

Admiral Fletcher, having transferred from the heavily listing *Yorktown* to a cruiser, turned the command over to Admiral Spruance. That night, Admiral Yamamoto canceled his Midway operation and ordered a general retirement of his forces. Spruance pursued the enemy fleet through 5 June. On the 6th, his dive-bombers overtook two heavy cruisers, damaged and slowed down by having collided with each other. The bombers sank one of the cruisers and left the other a barely floating wreck.

Japanese troops landed without opposition on the Aleutian islands of Attu and Kiska. The *Yorktown*, en route for Pearl Harbor under tow, was torpedoed and sunk by a Japanese submarine. Despite these setbacks, the Battle of Midway was a clear-cut American victory. It was won by carrier planes. The land-based bombers, their crews untrained for hitting moving ships, dropped more than 300 bombs without achieving a single hit.

For the Americans the victory was not cheap: one carrier and one destroyer sunk, 307 men killed, 147 aircraft lost, extensive damage to installations at Midway, moderate damage to installations at Dutch Harbor, and Attu and Kiska lost. Japanese losses were not so severe as wartime estimates indicated, but they were severe enough to reverse the course of the Pacific war [*sic*]: four carriers and one heavy cruiser sunk, another heavy cruiser wrecked, one battleship, one oiler, and three destroyers damaged, 322 aircraft lost, and 2,500 men killed, including many experienced pilots.

In the first euphoria of victory, before the cost in lives had been totted up, Admiral Nimitz could not resist making a pun in his famous communiqué of 6 June: "Pearl Harbor has now been partially avenged. Vengeance will not be complete until Japanese sea power is reduced to impotence. We have made substantial progress in that direction. Perhaps we will be forgiven if we claim that we are about midway to that objective."

— AUTHOR —

Professor Potter first joined the faculty of the U.S. Naval Academy in 1941. During World War II he served as an officer in the Naval Reserve and was stationed at Pearl Harbor while Admiral Nimitz had his headquarters there. He was coauthor and editor (with Admiral Nimitz) of *Sea Power: A Naval History,* long used as a textbook at the Naval Academy. His most recent published book is *The Naval Academy Illustrated History of the United States Navy.*

CHAPTER
34

Excerpt from *Nimitz*

By E. B. Potter

Nimitz (Annapolis, MD: Naval Institute Press, 1976):
chap. 7 The Battle of Midway, pp. 103–105

For his Midway victory, Admiral Nimitz received congratulations from all over the world, except the Axis countries. Army and navy officers and other students of warfare recognized the Battle of Midway as decisive in that it erased Japan's military advantage in the Pacific, bringing the antagonists to something approaching equality. Those who best knew the facts recognized that Japan's severest loss was not in carriers or planes but in trained aviators. Military analysts predicted that the United States would soon shift to the offensive.

Admiral Nimitz did his best to share the praise and give credit to those who deserved it. He was not always successful. For example, Admiral King rejected his recommendation that Joseph Rochefort be awarded the Distinguished Service Medal. CominCh recognized the vital part that cryptanalysis had played in recent American successes, but he considered it the work of too many people in Washington, at Pearl Harbor, and at Melbourne, for any one man to be singled out. With that example, Nimitz must have been thankful that he had secured promotions for Colonel Shannon and Captain Simard in advance. When Simard, on his way from Midway to a new duty post, called on Nimitz, the admiral praised him for his gallant fight and, pointing to his new silver eagles, remarked, in dubious metaphor, "I sent you the flowers before the funeral."

From Midway the army [*sic*] bombers, the few B-26s and the many B-17s, came back in small groups. Admiral Nimitz could not meet them all, but he saw to it that he was at least represented and that each squadron leader received his personal thanks to pass down to the individual aviators. On June 13 Admiral Fletcher with part of Task Force 17 entered Pearl Harbor, followed a few hours later by Admiral Spruance with Task Force 16. Ships in the harbor dipped their flags in salute. Admiral Nimitz and members of his staff, standing on the wharf, awaited each task force. They went aboard the flagships and shook hands with the commanders and as many of the officers and enlisted men as possible, thanking all, in the name of the nation, for a splendid performance.

Distributing proper credit now became something of a problem. The army [*sic*] flyers were the first to return to Pearl and had given representatives of the press their version of the Battle of Midway. The aviators knew that they had dropped bombs and that enemy ships had been damaged and sunk, but the B-17s had bombed from such a height that it was impossible for their crews to recognize ship types or to tell a hit from a near miss. Quite honestly they took the credit. None of them recognized that the "cruiser" they had reported sinking in fifteen seconds on June 6 was, in fact, the U.S. submarine *Grayling* indignantly crash diving. None of these flyers was more than dimly aware that the Navy had been involved in the battle. On June 12, the day before Task Forces 16 and 17 returned to Pearl Harbor, *The New York Times* ran an article with the interesting headline: Army Fliers Blasted Two Fleets Off Midway.

Admiral Nimitz, recognizing that the aviators made up in gallantry what they lacked in aim and damage-assessment, declined to contradict the Army's extravagant pretensions. His spokesman merely claimed for the Navy a share in

A B-17E of the Seventh Army Air Forces takes off from Midway in search of the *kidō butai.* There was no joint air commander at Midway. CAPT Cyril T. Simard initially commanded the Navy and Marine air units on Midway, and the Army's B-26s and B-17s were responsible to Maj. Gen. Willis P. Hale, USAAF. As it turned out, the B-17s were less valuable as attack aircraft and potentially much more valuable as long-range reconnaissance planes because they were far less vulnerable to Japanese fighters than were the Navy's PBYs. But both the Navy and Army air commanders executed existing doctrine, which assigned the B-17s a major attack role and gave the scouting mission to the PBYs.

U.S. Naval Institute Photo Archive

the victory. Later, when the battle had been carefully analyzed, Nimitz issued a statement that went a little further: "The performance of officers and men was of the highest order, not only at Midway and afloat, but equally so among those at Oahu not privileged to be in the front line of battle. I am proud to report that the cooperative devotion to duty of all those involved was so marked that, despite the necessarily decisive part played by our three carriers, this defeat of the Japanese arms and ambitions was truly a victory of the United States' armed forces and not of the Navy alone."

Nevertheless the myth that the B-17s had won the Battle of Midway persisted until some time after the end of World War II, when extensive questioning of Japanese officers made it clear that all of the army [*sic*] bombs fell in the water. Not one of the 322 bombs dropped by the B-17s scored a hit.

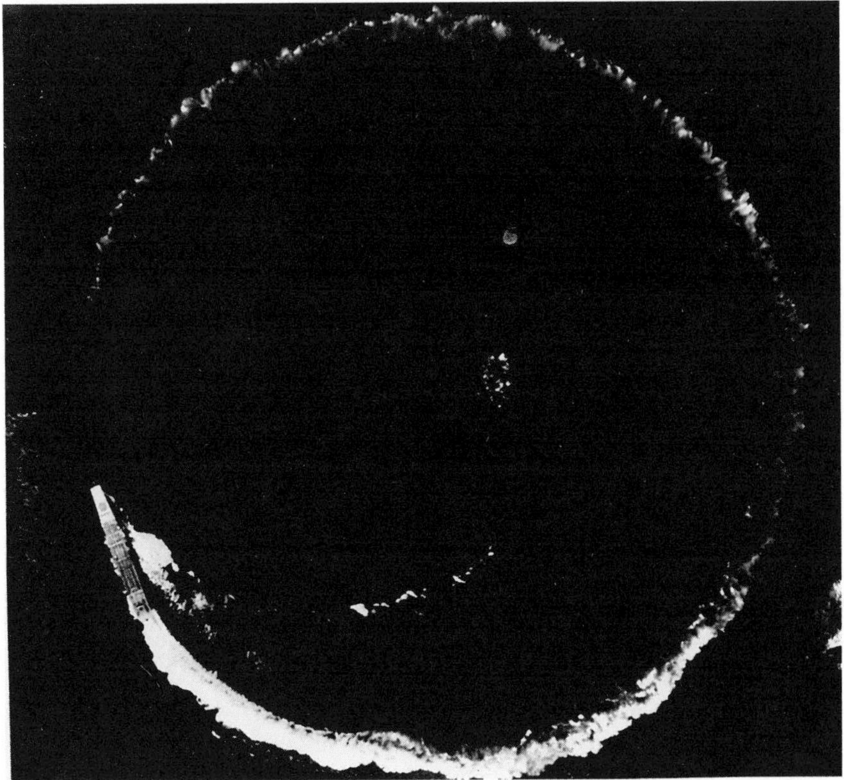

The Japanese carrier *Soryu* executes a high-speed turn in order to frustrate a high-level bombing attack. The B-17s that attacked the carriers of the *kidō butai* were less vulnerable to fighters and antiaircraft fire if they bombed from high altitude (20,000 feet), as they had been trained to do. But the ships they aimed at could—and did—avoid their "sticks" of bombs, which is why the B-17s did not sink any Japanese ship at Midway.

U.S. Naval Institute Photo Archive

CHAPTER
35

Chester W. Nimitz: Victory in the Pacific

By John B. Lundstrom

Quarterdeck and Bridge: Two Centuries of American Naval Leaders, ed. James C. Bradford (Annapolis, MD: Naval Institute Press, 1996): pp. 327–338

Tension manifested almost a physical presence in fleet headquarters at Pearl Harbor on Oahu in the Hawaiian Islands for the first two days of June 1942. During the past two weeks, Admiral Chester W. Nimitz, Commander-in-Chief, United States Pacific Fleet (CinCPac), had engineered a drastic redeployment of his striking force in outright defiance, at least initially, of the orders of his superior, Admiral Ernest J. King. Nimitz recalled his three aircraft carriers from the South Pacific, thousands of miles away, to the Central Pacific to battle a massive offensive that he believed the Japanese Combined Fleet was about to unleash against Midway and also the Aleutian Islands well to the north.

Nimitz acted solely on the basis of intelligence estimates derived from incomplete deciphering of Japanese fleet radio messages. They were served up by the very same analysts who, six months before, could not warn Nimitz's predecessor, Admiral Husband E. Kimmel, that Japanese carriers would strike the fleet at Pearl Harbor. The result then was the crippling of the battleship force. The stakes now were much higher.

Until 3 June, Nimitz had to rely on his professional judgment, moral courage, and a great deal of faith that his radio intelligence specialists had indeed predicted the place and time of the Japanese onslaught. Never did he reveal to his anxious staff a glimmer of doubt or worry over one of the more momentous decisions made by any commander during World War II. That morning, however, sighting reports radioed by American search planes confirmed that the enemy appeared to be coming as expected.

Present with the admiral was the fleet intelligence officer, Lieutenant Commander Edwin T. Layton, who, along with code-breaker Commander Joseph J. Rochefort, had championed the value of radio intelligence. Nimitz flashed to Layton "that brilliant white smile" that "just lights up."

"This ought to make your heart warm," Nimitz congratulated Layton. "This will clear up all the doubters now. They just have to see this to know that what I told them is correct."

The ensuing Battle of Midway (4–6 June 1942) was one step, albeit perhaps the most important, that led to ultimate total victory over Japan. Pounded by bombs and gutted by fire, four Japanese carriers and a heavy cruiser slipped beneath the waves at the cost of one American carrier, one destroyer, and many brave aviators. The courage, skill, and sacrifice of the Pacific Fleet's flyers and the Midway defenders, along with the good fortune that is absolutely essential in warfare, completely vindicated Chester Nimitz's decision to risk an early decisive battle with the Japanese Combined Fleet and regain the initiative in the Pacific.

What sort of man was this admiral who so swiftly reversed the Pacific balance of power? Within the Pacific Fleet and the U.S. Navy as a whole, Nimitz inspired not only great respect for his skill and insight but tremendous affection for his congenial and considerate personality. Lacking bluster and imperiousness, he was the master of consensus and cooperation. In a biographical sketch, one prominent naval historian referred to Nimitz as the "principal Allied naval *administrator*" in the Pacific, that is, more of a "manager" than a warrior. In fact, Nimitz made it look much too easy. His very success in nearly four years of bitter warfare obscured the obstacles that he had to surmount and his quick adaptation to new ways of naval warfare. His avuncular manner concealed a will of steel that he rarely needed to reveal except in times of extreme crisis, such as the spring of 1942 and in the Guadalcanal campaign later that year.

The grandson of German immigrants, Chester William Nimitz was born on 24 February 1885 in Fredericksburg, a small town in South Texas. He grew up in nearby Kerrville, where his parents, far from being well to do, ran a small hotel. Unable to gain an appointment to West Point, Chester successfully competed for a slot at the Naval Academy and, in the summer of 1901, enrolled as a member of the class of 1905.

Befitting the growing strength of the U.S. Navy, Nimitz's class, nearly twice as large as its predecessors, was the first to exceed 100 midshipmen. Even so, the number of nascent naval officers was small enough for everyone to get acquainted.

During Nimitz's time at Annapolis, he served with all of his future key subordinates in World War II: William F. Halsey (1904); John H. Towers, Robert Lee Ghormley, and Frank Jack Fletcher (1906); Raymond A. Spruance (1907); and Richmond Kelly Turner (1908). In January 1905, Nimitz graduated 7th in his class of 114.

After nearly two years on the battleship *Ohio*, Nimitz reported in 1907 to the Asiatic Squadron as commander of the small gunboat *Panay*. That summer, at the age of twenty-two, Ensign Nimitz became skipper of the destroyer *Decatur* and took her throughout the Philippines and to Southeast Asia. Only one untoward incident marred an otherwise spotless tour of duty. In July 1908, he ran the *Decatur* aground and survived a charge of "neglect of duty." Thereafter, Nimitz always gave young officers the benefit of the doubt for one mistake, provided they learned, as did he, from their error.

Nimitz returned home in January 1909 to serve, albeit reluctantly, in submarines. Only recently developed and certainly far from reliable, the small, rotund American "pigboats" were considered suitable mainly for harbor defense, and their gasoline engines made them dangerous to operate. Nimitz commanded three submarines in succession and, by September 1911, also led a division. A pioneer of diesel propulsion for submarines, Nimitz in early 1912 became skipper of the E-1 (*Skipjack*), the first American diesel-powered submarine, and took command of the Atlantic Submarine Flotilla that spring. In later life, he proudly wore the gold dolphin insignia subsequently adopted for officers who qualified in submarines.

Nimitz's expertise in diesel engines led to study in Germany and the job, as prospective executive officer and chief engineer, of helping to design and install diesels in the fleet oiler *Maumee*. In early 1917, the *Maumee* experimented with underway refueling and, in April, provided oil far out at sea for destroyers bound for the War in Europe. That summer, Lieutenant Commander Nimitz became an aide to Captain Samuel S. Robison, commander of the Atlantic Fleet submarines. Nimitz spent the balance of World War I on staff duty, but he made the important transition from engineering, which would limit his career opportunities, to command. As his eminent biographer E. B. Potter wrote, Nimitz became "concerned less with machinery than with people, less with construction and maintenance than with organization, and thus he found his true vocation."

In 1920, Commander Nimitz erected, virtually from scratch, a submarine base at Pearl Harbor, Hawaii, and took command. He attended the Naval War College in Newport, Rhode Island, in 1922 to study naval strategy, particularly the conduct of a naval war across the vast Pacific to defeat Japan (War Plan Orange). Nimitz also joined in tactical experiments on ship formations to devise something better than the cumbersome columns of ships used in 1916 by the British and German fleets at the Battle of Jutland. He helped to develop the circular formation with capital ships surrounded by concentric circles of screening vessels. In 1923, by a fortunate circumstance, Nimitz joined the staff of then Vice Admiral Robison, commander of the Battle Fleet, which enabled him to test the circular formation at sea. Two years later, Robison became Commander-in-Chief, United States Fleet, with Nimitz as his assistant chief of staff and tactical officer. Although the Navy did not take immediately to the circular formation, the fleet was aware of its potential, particularly in connection with carriers, and revived it just prior to World War II, when it really counted.

Captain Nimitz demonstrated his "people" skills when he turned the Naval Reserve Officer Training Corps program at the University of California-Berkeley into an unqualified success. After several administrative posts, he gratefully returned to sea in October 1933 as commanding officer of the heavy cruiser *Augusta* with the Asiatic Fleet. Her crew reckoned themselves fortunate to have such a competent, yet genial captain. On voyages throughout the Far East, the *Augusta* became known as one of the finest ships in the Navy.

In 1935, the Navy brass had the opportunity to take the measure of Captain Nimitz when he reported as assistant chief to the Bureau of Navigation (predecessor to the Bureau of Naval Personnel) in Washington, D.C. They liked what they saw and only let him escape that hotbed of politics and red tape for a short interval. In July 1938, newly promoted Rear Admiral Nimitz assumed command of a light cruiser division, but illness forced his immediate relief. That September, he took over Battleship Division One at San Pedro, California, with his flag on the *Arizona*. In January 1939, when most of the U.S. Fleet departed for the Caribbean and Fleet Problem XX, Nimitz was left as senior officer in the Pacific. He conducted gunnery and amphibious exercises, as well as more underway refueling tests, for the first time with heavy ships. In one of his few questionable calls, he recommended the stern-to-bow, rather than what became the standard beam-to-beam, refueling configuration, only to be overruled by Admiral William D. Leahy, Chief of Naval Operations (CNO).

Nimitz returned to Washington in June 1939 to run the Bureau of Navigation under the new CNO, Admiral Harold R. Stark. Thus, he became a key player in President Franklin D. Roosevelt's vast expansion of the Navy to prepare for the war that Roosevelt felt to be inevitable after Europe erupted in conflict. Nimitz's superb administrative ability and political skills were put sorely to the test as he oversaw programs to acquire and train the greatly increased numbers of personnel required by the Navy. The urgency became more apparent in May 1941 after the President declared an unlimited national emergency. Faced toward Europe, Washington focused on what became an undeclared war with Germany in the North Atlantic, while discounting the growing threat of Japan in the Far East.

When war finally came on 7 December 1941, the principal blow landed neither in the Atlantic nor in the Far East, but where it was least expected, against the Pacific Fleet at Pearl Harbor. His reputation permanently scarred by the devastation of his battle line, Admiral Kimmel could no longer effectively exercise command. On 15 December, he offered Stark the names of seven admirals that he recommended to replace him as CinCPac. Last on the list was Rear Admiral Chester Nimitz. Kimmel evidently was unaware that, in January 1941, the President had offered Nimitz the same post. Nimitz declined because he felt that he lacked seniority, and the job went to Kimmel. Now in the aftermath of disaster, Nimitz again stood first on the President's own list. On 16 December, Secretary of the Navy Frank Knox informed Nimitz of his promotion to admiral and his new command, then relayed Roosevelt's valedictory: "Tell Nimitz to get the hell out to Pearl and stay there till the war is won."

Kimmel was relieved of command on 17 December by Vice Admiral William S. Pye, the Battle Force commander whose only significant (and correct) decision as caretaker CinCPac was to recall the carriers attempting to reinforce besieged Wake Island, which fell on 23 December. On 31 December, Nimitz assumed command of the Pacific Fleet in a ceremony conducted at Pearl Harbor on the deck of the submarine *Grayling*. He liked to joke that a submarine was the only vessel that the Japanese left for him there.

Why Nimitz? Of all the senior admirals, he had probably accumulated the least sea duty as a flag officer and had never exercised command in any of the massive fleet problems that so dominated the pre-World War II Navy. Since his stints at the Naval War College and on Robison's staff during the early 1920s, he had not moved within the inner councils that formulated fleet strategy and doctrine. On the positive side, Nimitz had acquitted himself superbly in all of his duty assignments. The President knew personally from Nimitz's performance as a bureau chief that he was clear thinking and innovative, an excellent administrator, calm, resolute, and unflappable under pressure. His gracious, cheerful personality seemed just the thing to revive sagging morale in Hawaii. Another possible plus in the President's mind was that Nimitz, not wedded to any particular faction in the Navy, would approach his daunting task with an open mind.

Perhaps the only concern regarding the new CinCPac was whether he really was a fighter. Only battle would tell the tale. Just appointed Commander-in-Chief, United States Fleet (CominCh), imperious Admiral Ernest J. King (whose pugnacity nobody doubted), was evidently unsure of his new subordinate. Deeply distrusting those he thought were political admirals, the "fixers" who supposedly owed their advancement to their proximity to the President, King was not about to keep Nimitz on anything but a short leash. As to which of the two admirals was the more aggressive, however, the reader can judge. Throughout the war, their relations, while always correct, certainly were not cordial.

At Pearl Harbor, Nimitz discovered that his principal mobile fleet assets were the three carriers *Lexington*, *Saratoga*, and *Enterprise*, with a total of about 210 aircraft. Each flattop was the nucleus of a task force screened by two or three cruisers and about a half dozen destroyers. Nimitz also controlled half of the fifty-odd submarines in the Pacific, with the rest under the Asiatic Fleet. He realized, far sooner than most admirals, that battleships were no longer the cynosure of naval warfare. Japanese carrier airpower, an order of magnitude more powerful than any American had understood, rendered what was left of Kimmel's proud battle line virtually irrelevant. The old battleships were far too slow to operate with the swift carriers and too poorly protected to face enemy aircraft alone. In January 1942, Nimitz relegated them to escorting convoys between the West Coast and Pearl Harbor in order to free up his cruisers. Later at Coral Sea and Midway, he deliberately kept them far away from the battle.

Nimitz faced a frustrating situation during the first months of 1942 as he settled in as CinCPac. The disaster at Pearl Harbor and manifest Japanese naval strength prevented the Pacific Fleet from seizing the strategic initiative. Despite public expectations, there could be no dramatic rush westward to stem the tide of conquest in the Philippines and the Dutch East Indies. Equally unfeasible for the immediate time was the amphibious advance to the Marshall Islands long enshrined in the War Plan Orange studies. King harped on the need to divert enemy strength away from the collapsing Far East, but Nimitz felt that any significant target he could reach would prove too tough for the weak Pacific Fleet. Instead, he had to concentrate on holding Hawaii and Midway because the Japanese Combined Fleet appeared powerful enough to threaten America's strongholds in the Central Pacific. That left only swift, small-scale raids against outlying bases in the Central Pacific. Even so, they proved difficult to orchestrate. Finally, on 1 February 1942, Vice Admiral William F. Halsey's *Enterprise* and Rear Admiral Frank Jack Fletcher's newly arrived carrier *Yorktown* raided widely throughout the eastern Marshall and Gilbert Islands and provided a vital boost to American morale.

Within a month of taking command, Nimitz found himself in fundamental strategic disagreement with King, his difficult superior in Washington. In a 30 December 1941 directive, King had stated the obvious need to defend Hawaii and Midway but added that "only in small degree less important [is the] maintenance of communications [from the] West Coast to Australia." That foreshadowed his growing interest in the South and Southwest Pacific that would decisively affect fleet deployment.

Passionately committed to fighting Japan in the Pacific, King battled both his colleagues in Washington and the Allied Combined Chiefs of Staff (CCS) within the constraints of the basic strategic question of Germany first. He feared that the Allies would effectively shut down offensive operations in the Pacific by shifting badly needed resources to the European theater. In January, King arranged with the CCS to set up, under his direct command and not Nimitz's, the so-called ANZAC Area to control U.S. and Allied naval forces in Australia and New Zealand and waters north of there. He matured plans to build up strength and create new bases in the distant South and Southwest Pacific to halt the enemy advance. That became crucial after 23 January when the Japanese invaded Rabaul on New Britain in the Bismarck Archipelago. From there, they threatened not only eastern New Guinea (and ultimately Australia itself) but also key South Pacific islands on the sea route between the United States, New Zealand, and Australia. Once the Allies could regain the initiative, King intended to launch his first counteroffensive in the South Pacific, rather than the Central Pacific.

Because the Allies lacked the strength to defend the South Pacific, King informed Nimitz that he must provide the requisite forces. Worry about the havoc the Japanese could wreak if they returned in strength to the Central Pacific precipitated vigorous debate at Pearl Harbor: "Are we going to gamble all upon securing Australia as a base of future operations against the enemy and leave our Pacific Area open to attack?" In early February, King removed the *Lexington*, one third of CinCPac's striking force, from Nimitz's command and sent her south. Vice Admiral Wilson Brown, the task force commander, noted the lack of suitable friendly harbors in the remote South Pacific. He likened his mission to "jumping off into space." The staff at Pearl Harbor agreed. Nimitz felt reluctant to disperse his meager forces in the South Pacific but slowly recognized its inevitability. On 21 February, the War Plans Section opined that the South Pacific region was "one in which our forces will meet advancing enemy forces, and we may be forced to make the move due to political or 'desperation strategical' consideration."

King showed he meant business on 24 February when he also detached the *Yorktown* for the Southwest Pacific. That left Nimitz only the *Enterprise*, which he had committed to raids on Wake and Marcus Islands in the Central Pacific. (A submarine had torpedoed the *Saratoga* on 11 January, and Nimitz sent her limping back to the West Coast for repairs). On 19 March, Nimitz learned that King had again appropriated his carriers. In a grandstand play designed to appeal to President Roosevelt, CominCh decreed that, in April, the *Enterprise* and the new *Hornet* were to bomb Japan.

For Nimitz, the first three months as CinCPac proved disappointing, relieved only by brief triumph when the carriers fought. To those around him, the ever imperturbable, intensely private admiral managed to conceal his growing frustration, but, on 22 March, he confided to his wife, Catherine:

"Ever so many people were enthusiastic for me at the start but when things do not move fast enough—they sour on me. I will be lucky to last six months. The public may demand action and results faster than I can produce."

For most of this period Nimitz exercised little control over his carriers. Quite likely, he felt that King might never give him the latitude to lead his fleet and fight the enemy his own way. He could not know that the next three months would bring him glory.

King's strategy of projecting American naval power into the South Pacific was brilliant. On 10 March, the *Lexington* and *Yorktown* combined at Lae and Salamaua in northern Papua to deal the Imperial Navy its heaviest losses to date. That compelled the Japanese to divert significant forces to further their own rather modest offensive plans in that region. Envisioning an enlarged ANZAC Area under his own and not Nimitz's command, King looked forward to directing his offensive through the South Pacific island chains straight to Rabaul; however, a great obstacle to his grand design appeared in the form of General Douglas MacArthur, just recalled from the Philippines and eager to lead the way back. Suddenly, Nimitz was back in the picture as a counterweight to MacArthur, whom King distrusted intensely. On 4 April, Nimitz learned that the entire Pacific command would soon be reorganized and the ANZAC Area abolished. As Commander-in-Chief, Pacific Ocean Areas, he would exercise direct control of the North and Central Pacific Areas and run the South Pacific Area (SoPac) through a subordinate. (Nimitz later nominated and King approved Vice Admiral Robert Lee Ghormley.) MacArthur became Supreme Commander, Southwest Pacific Area (SWPA). King saw to it that the boundary between SoPac and SWPA was blurred so that the Navy could control at least the opening stages of the assault on Rabaul.

Finally, Nimitz could fight his fleet. Quite providentially, the increasingly efficient radio intelligence in April detected hints of major enemy moves in the Southwest and South Pacific set to begin in late April or early May. Actually, the code breakers had uncovered elements of Japanese plans for an offensive (the MO Operation) using three carriers to capture Port Moresby in Papua and the Solomon Islands. Yet, Nimitz's analysts thought that Port Moresby would be only the first stage of a wider rampage by as many as six or more enemy flattops against northeastern Australia, New Caledonia, Fiji, and Samoa. That would seriously threaten communications with Australia and delay any Allied offensive in the region.

Nimitz boldly proposed to counter the Japanese South Pacific onslaught by committing all four of his carriers and their three hundred aircraft to battle. Fletcher, with the *Yorktown* and *Lexington*, would tackle the first blow in early May against Port Moresby. About two weeks later, Halsey, back from the Tokyo raid with the *Enterprise* and *Hornet*, would join Fletcher and take command. Nimitz quickly recognized that, although the bombing of Japan, which went off spectacularly on 18 April, provided good propaganda, it ultimately harmed his strategy because it deprived him of half his carriers when he especially needed them.

The traditional view is that Nimitz, cued by his superb radio intelligence, simply reacted to the enemy's moves and, in desperation, threw his forces into the path of the Japanese in the hope of an "incredible victory." Actually, Nimitz saw the defense of the South Pacific bases as a great opportunity to accomplish what he felt to be his primary mission—the destruction of the Japanese carriers. Since January 1942, the enemy had employed its flattops in the Dutch East Indies or the Indian Ocean, where the Pacific Fleet could not get at them. To Nimitz, the tremendous advantage of reading the enemy's naval ciphers went far to negate the fact that the Japanese enjoyed interior lines and held the initiative. Mobility and the concentration of forces became the keys to defeating them. Cautiously confident, Nimitz felt: "Because of our superior personnel in resourcefulness and initiative, and the undoubted superiority of much of our equipment, we should be able to accept odds in battle if necessary." King approved the plan to use all four carriers in the South Pacific. Concerned as always with protecting his vital foothold, however, he ordered Nimitz to keep at least two carriers in the South Pacific until further notice.

In the Battle of the Coral Sea (4–8 May 1942), Fletcher fought the first carrier-versus-carrier duel in history. It cost the Japanese the light carrier *Shoho*, damage to the big carrier *Shokaku*, and such severe aircraft losses that they called off the Port Moresby invasion. Coral Sea became the first Allied strategic victory in the Pacific. Unfortunately, the gallant *Lexington* succumbed to fires, while the *Yorktown* ran southward with bomb damage deep in her vitals. Racing down from Pearl Harbor, Halsey's two flattops reached the South Pacific too late to fight in the first battle.

Nobody expected the Japanese to give up after just one try for Port Moresby. Yet, by 10 May, Rochefort and Layton, Nimitz's radio intelligence analysts at Pearl Harbor, could find no evidence that strong enemy forces were indeed concentrating in the south. Instead, indications pointed to the Central Pacific as the next Japanese target. That was always the gravest danger to the Pacific Fleet. Rochefort's code breakers had detected elements of the plan by Admiral Isoroku Yamamoto, commander of the Combined Fleet, to capture Midway in early June and entice the Pacific Fleet into decisive battle.

In contrast to their colleagues at Pearl Harbor, King's own intelligence specialists forecast another major enemy South Pacific assault and failed to see the growing danger to Midway and Hawaii. Deeply worried about the threat to his bases and shaken by the loss of the *Lexington*, King suggested to Nimitz on 12 May that the damaged *Yorktown* leave her planes (and the *Lexington*'s) to help defend the South Pacific. His thoughts regarding the *Enterprise* and *Hornet* betrayed his fears over the next battle: "In order to preserve our carriers during such an attack on islands it may be better to operate one or more carrier air groups from shore."

Restricting the mobility of his carrier striking force was the last thing Nimitz desired, especially now. He needed all of them back in the Central Pacific as soon as possible. Forcefully but tactfully, he tried to warn King that the Japanese were about to descend on Midway and possibly Hawaii. Even so, he took the extraordinary step of using a ruse to contravene King's direct orders to retain two carriers in the South Pacific until further notice. On 13 May, Nimitz sent an "eyes-only" order telling Halsey to let his carriers be sighted by the Japanese, both to deter the enemy and to give Nimitz the excuse to pull them back. Not waiting for CominCh's concurrence, Nimitz followed on 15 May with orders for Halsey and Fletcher to return immediately to Pearl Harbor. To King, he explained, "Will watch situation closely and return Halsey to Southward if imminent [enemy] concentration [in] that area is indicated." CinCPac's faith in the validity of his radio intelligence gave him the courage to shift his carriers three thousand miles to the northeast.

On 17 May, King informed Nimitz of his general agreement with CinCPac's estimate of Japanese intentions. If he ever knew of Nimitz's subterfuge regarding Halsey, he never admitted it. Fully realizing the vital necessity of fighting for Midway, King nevertheless feared the possible cost. . . . CominCh much preferred a "fleet-in-being" strategy to risking all his forces in one battle. King urged Nimitz to: "Chiefly employ strong attrition tactics and not repeat NOT allow our forces to accept such decisive action as would likely to incur heavy losses in our carriers and cruisers."

The Pacific Fleet staff situation estimate outlined the problem and suggested the tactics to be followed:

Not only our directive from Commander-in-Chief, U.S. Fleet, but common sense dictates that we cannot now afford to slug it out with the probably superior approaching Japanese forces. We must endeavor to reduce his forces by attrition—submarine attacks, air bombing, attack on isolated units. . . . If attrition is successful the enemy must accept the failure of his venture or risk battle on disadvantageous terms.

Despite all the pious talk about standing off and inflicting attrition, however, Nimitz knew full well that defending Midway still meant meeting the Combined Fleet in battle, where anything could happen. Expecting to do that without risking significant loss was like jumping into the water and hoping not to get wet. With typical sangfroid, Nimitz summed up his feelings in a 29 May 1942 letter to King: "We are very actively preparing to greet our expected visitors with the kind of reception they deserve, and we will do the best we can with what we have."

By 2 June, Nimitz had deployed off Midway all three carriers, including, remarkably, the damaged *Yorktown*, as well as fifteen submarines. More than 120 aircraft crowded the tiny atoll. This time, the Pacific Fleet enjoyed superior reconnaissance and, because of superb radio intelligence, the priceless advantage of surprise. During the battle on 4 June, both Midway's airpower and the submarines proved much less effective than anticipated, but the carriers under Fletcher and Rear Admiral Raymond A. Spruance came through splendidly. Himself counting on surprise, Admiral Yamamoto had so contrived his plans that his four carriers, the *Akagi*, *Kaga*, *Soryu*, and *Hiryu*, led the Midway assault, but, in traditional fashion, his battleships were to deliver the coup de grace to the U.S. Pacific Fleet. After his carriers were ambushed and crushed, however, he could only meekly withdraw the rest of his vast armada.

Never again would Nimitz exercise such direct personal influence over the course of the Pacific War as he did during the period between 15 April and 15 June 1942. As was said of British Admiral Sir John Jellicoe during World War I, Nimitz literally could win or lose the war in an afternoon. Thereafter, he operated within the tight framework of policy and strategy formulated by the Joint Chiefs and CominCh. His overwhelming victory at Midway completely changed the complexion of the Pacific War. Japan's initial superiority dwindled to parity at best. Despite the benefits, one wonders if King ever quite forgave Nimitz for putting the fleet in jeopardy at Midway. He certainly allowed his communications bureaucrats, the Washington experts embarrassed when Rochefort and Layton were proved correct about enemy plans for Midway, to supplant their counterparts at Pearl Harbor. Rochefort was cast off, but Nimitz managed to save Layton. . . .

Probably Nimitz's biggest row within the Pacific Fleet was with his naval aviators, personified by Vice Admiral John H. Towers (Naval Aviator No.3), who became Commander, Air Force, Pacific Fleet, in October 1942. Obviously, carrier airpower had become central to the offensive mission of the Pacific Fleet; with full justification, the air admirals felt that they and not non-aviators should lead carrier task forces. They also campaigned to exclude non-aviators automatically from the top echelons of naval command, however, something that Nimitz would not tolerate. He brokered a series of compromises to see that the aviation viewpoint always would be represented. In 1944, Towers, a superb administrator who hankered for combat command, became Deputy CinCPac. Despite Nimitz's personal dislike of the ambitious Towers, the two worked together effectively.

Unlike his overbearing and devious neighbor MacArthur, Nimitz did not consider himself a prime initiator of strategy in the Pacific. That role he left to his irascible but astute superior, Admiral King, who hammered out policy with his colleagues on the Joint Chiefs of Staff. Once a plan was proposed, however, Nimitz gave it the closest scrutiny and did not hesitate to offer his informed opinion. He encouraged his subordinates to come forward with their ideas and particularly valued the keen insights of Raymond Spruance, one of the victors of Midway and his chief of staff in 1942–43; Captain Forrest P. Sherman, his war plans officer; and Rear Admiral Charles H. McMorris, Spruance's successor as chief of staff. . . .

Further Reading

The papers of Fleet Admiral Nimitz are in the Naval Historical Center in Washington, D.C., which also holds, among many other vital documents such as action reports and the "CINCPAC Greybook," a war diary kept by the War Plans Section on the CinCPac staff. The CinCPac Secret and Confidential Message File 1941–45 is on microfilm in Record Group 38 of the National Archives. Throughout his life, Nimitz hoped to avoid controversy and kept his personal opinions to himself. During World War II, he wrote daily to his wife Catherine, but only a few of these letters have been preserved. He was adamantly opposed to writing a memoir, but did act as an associate editor to a naval history textbook, E. B. Potter, *Sea Power* (Englewood Cliffs, N.J., 1960), a role that he took seriously and in which he offered suggestions to ensure proper assessment of the roles played by naval officers in the Pacific. The chapters dealing with World War II were also separately published as *The Great Sea War: Story of Naval Action in World War II* (Englewood Cliffs, N.J., 1960).

The best biography of Nimitz and an indispensable source on his life is E. B. Potter's *Nimitz* (Annapolis, Md., 1976). Memoirs by close associates of Nimitz include: Fleet Admiral Ernest J. King and Commander Walter Muir Whitehill, *Fleet Admiral King: A Naval Record* (New York, 1952); Fleet Admiral William F. Halsey and J. Bryan III, *Admiral Halsey's Story* (New York, 1947); Rear Admiral Edwin T. Layton, with Roger Pineau and John Costello, *"And I Was There"* (New York, 1985); Admiral James O. Richardson, *On the Treadmill to Pearl Harbor: Memoirs of Admiral J. O. Richardson* (Washington, D.C., 1973); and Vice Admiral George C. Dyer, *The Amphibians Came to Conquer: The Story of Admiral Richmond Kelly Turner*, 2 vols. (Washington, D.C., 1971). Also extremely useful are four biographies of naval officers: Thomas B. Buell, *The Quiet Warrior: A Biography of Admiral Raymond A. Spruance* (Boston, 1974), and *Master of Sea Power: A Biography of Fleet Admiral Ernest J. King* (Boston, 1980); E. B. Potter, *Bull Halsey* (Annapolis, Md., 1985); and Clark G. Reynolds, *Admiral John H. Towers: The Struggle for Naval Air Supremacy* (Annapolis, Md., 1991). Robert W. Love Jr., *Chiefs of Naval Operations* (Annapolis, Md., 1980) offers biographical sketches of the CNOs, including Nimitz.

Literature on World War II in the Pacific is vast, but the starting point is Samuel Eliot Morison, *History of United States Naval Operations in World War II*, 15 vols. (Boston, 1947–60). Two general histories are John Costello, *The Pacific War* (New York, 1981), and Ronald H. Spector, *Eagle against the Sun: The American War with Japan* (New York, 1985). Indispensable for understanding strategy is a once-classified study by Grace Person Hayes, *The History of the Joint Chiefs of Staff in World War II: The War against Japan* (Annapolis, Md., 1982).

The interpretation given here of Nimitz's strategy for the Battles of Coral Sea and Midway is based on this author's book, *The First South Pacific Campaign: Pacific Fleet Strategy December 1941–June 1942* (Annapolis, Md., 1976). For carrier operations in general in early 1942, see also John Lundstrom, *The First Team: Pacific Naval Air Combat from Pearl Harbor to Midway* (Annapolis, Md., 1990). The best accounts of the Battle of Midway are Walter Lord's classic *Incredible Victory* (New York, 1967) and Robert J. Cressman, ed., "*A Glorious Page in Our History": The Battle of Midway 4–6 June 1942* (Missoula, Mont., 1990). Richard B. Frank's *Guadalcanal* (New York, 1990) is indispensable for that campaign. Among the studies of later campaigns, Thomas J. Cutler's *The Battle of Leyte Gulf, 23-26 October 1944* (New York, 1994) stands out.

CHAPTER
36

Commentary on RADM Raymond A. Spruance

By Thomas C. Hone

Original to this volume

To understand then-RADM Raymond A. Spruance, you need to start with his mentors, then-VADM William F. Halsey Jr., and ADM Chester W. Nimitz. The two more-senior admirals were very different individuals, as any reader of World War II histories knows. Halsey was aggressive professionally, energetic and demanding as a commander, and personally outgoing. He could be thought of—and was often portrayed as—the ideal "fighting admiral." By comparison, Nimitz was steady, quiet, and calm. But Nimitz's calm and personal warmth masked great determination—and also a great ability to foster excellence in his subordinates. Those serving under Nimitz often spoke of his very penetrating blue eyes. Those eyes—sharp, bright, but not hostile or cold—were a sign of one of Nimitz's gifts: his ability to perceive the strengths and weaknesses in others without disconcerting them.

The confidence that Halsey and Nimitz placed in Spruance is noteworthy. In an official letter to Admiral Nimitz prepared just before Halsey's carrier task force entered Pearl Harbor on 26 May 1942, Vice Admiral Halsey wrote, "Rear Admiral Spruance has consistently displayed outstanding ability combined with excellent judgment and quiet courage." He went on to write, "I have found his counsel and advice invaluable. From my direct close observation I have learned to place complete confidence in him in operations in war time," and "I consider him fully and superbly qualified to take command of a force comprising mixed types

Rear Admiral Spruance's early career was spent mostly in surface ships and engineering assignments. A student at the Naval War College in 1926–1927, he returned there to teach and to study from 1935 until the spring of 1938. He spent the next two years in command of the battleship *Mississippi* and then was made commandant of the 10th Naval District and—a year later—also commander of the Caribbean Sea Frontier. Appointed a cruiser division commander in September 1941, he was Rear Admiral Halsey's surface ship commander when Halsey commanded the Pacific Fleet's initial carrier task force in early 1942. Spruance was promoted steadily after Midway—to Admiral Nimitz's chief of staff and then deputy. He commanded the Central Pacific Force in 1943 and the Fifth Fleet in 1944–1945, leading joint forces that captured the Gilbert, Marshall, and Mariana Islands, and then Iwo Jima and Okinawa. After the war, he commanded the Pacific Fleet and then served as president of the Naval War College.

U.S. Naval Institute Photo Archive

and to conduct protracted independent operations in the combat theater in war time."[1] This was high praise, indeed. Nimitz added to it by telling Spruance that he wanted Spruance as his chief of staff after the Midway operation was over.

But what Spruance had wanted when the Navy Department had promoted him to rear admiral was command of a battleship division, not command of cruisers and destroyers in a carrier task force. Spruance's commitment to the battleship force was both professional and personal. As his biographer Thomas B. Buell discovered, Spruance was deeply shaken on 8 December 1941 when he first saw the battleships damaged and sunk at Pearl Harbor—*Arizona* crumpled as if by a mighty fist; *Oklahoma* capsized, her superstructure jammed in Pearl Harbor's bottom; *West Virginia* burned and blackened by fires that had ravaged her as she settled upright in the harbor; *California* and *Nevada* filled with water after being torpedoed and bombed. But Spruance stayed grief stricken only a day and only in the presence of his wife and daughter. As Buell found, Spruance "had recovered his poise and equilibrium" by the next day.[2] This ability to impose calm *on himself* in the face of disaster or uncertainty is one of the characteristics that apparently appealed strongly to both Halsey and Nimitz.

Another such characteristic was Spruance's knowledge of naval aviation. Before Midway, there were senior aviators who believed that Spruance lacked a thorough understanding of naval aviation because he had never trained as a pilot or commanded a carrier. But in a 1971 letter to biographer Buell, Robert J. Oliver, Spruance's flag lieutenant at Midway, noted, "Spruance had a keen interest in all components of Naval Aviation. He studied all the air tactical instructions, bulletins, and news letters he could get his hands on. . . . He wanted to know in detail everything that was going on. He inquired into every phase of carrier operations. He informed himself of the military characteristics of every type of aircraft in the fleet. He was particularly interested in the younger pilots and never missed an opportunity to pick their brains. [LT Charles R. Ware], my classmate and a pilot in [Scouting Five], who we fished out of the drink on the Marcus raid, asked me, 'How in the hell does that man know so much about Naval Aviation?'"[3]

Spruance's performance at Midway showed that the confidence in his leadership and judgment expressed by both Halsey and Nimitz was justified. On boarding the *Enterprise,* Halsey's flagship, Spruance had to relieve misgivings on the part of Halsey's staff. It was true that Halsey had praised Spruance to his staff, but what was the quiet "battleship admiral" really like? Having served as a civilian on an admiral's staff, I know first hand how important it is for a new senior officer to both "break the ice" and at the same time communicate his expectations to a staff he has largely inherited. Spruance was able to do this, just as Nimitz had done it when he took command of the Pacific Fleet. However, Spruance also had to make it clear to Rear Admiral Fletcher—one of the few flag officers who really had experience in carrier warfare—that he was a competent and loyal subordinate. Finally, Spruance had to keep his mind on what really mattered and not become distracted by the details of task force operations.

Admiral Nimitz had taken advantage of the operational factors of time, geography, and force. Nimitz had given Fletcher and Spruance the most ships he could reasonably muster, especially the *Enterprise, Yorktown,* and *Hornet.* Nimitz had also pushed as many aircraft as possible to Midway so that Midway could serve as a stationary aircraft carrier. Based on determined and creative code-breaking and traffic analysis, Nimitz had been able to inform his subordinates when the *kidō butai* would appear, and he had positioned TF-16 and TF-17 where they could ambush the oncoming Japanese. It was up to Spruance and Fletcher to specifically locate the *kidō butai* and destroy or severely damage it.

Fletcher and Spruance appear to have had little choice in what they did—that is, to throw as much of their carrier aviation as possible at the Japanese at the earliest opportunity. The best admirals in both navies knew that striking first with carrier airpower gave the attacker a great advantage. But to gain that advantage, an admiral's task force had to find the enemy first and then mount a coordinated strike that combined torpedo and dive bombing attacks. Much could—and did—go wrong, on both sides, to impede finding and attacking the enemy. The opponent's carriers had to be discovered, then identified, and then attacked. Once the attacking squadrons had been launched on their way, each task force had to protect itself and steam to a rendezvous point, recover returning planes, and then quickly prepare a second strike if that were necessary.

If Spruance had learned anything from Halsey's February 1942 raids on the Marshall Islands and Wake, and from the April mission to launch B-25s against Tokyo, it was that many things could go wrong. Good planning was not enough. Task force commanders had to have a nice sense of timing and the ability to calculate risk. They also had to keep an accurate image of the battle in their heads. Their staffs could and did plot suspected and actual enemy contacts, but the commanders had to abstract from this information a picture that told them when to attack, where to send their attacking squadrons, and when to avoid the enemy.

Spruance showed that he understood this when he went aboard the *Enterprise* carrying a "rolled-up twenty-inch-square maneuvering board [a paper form containing a compass rose and a distance scale], fastened by a paper clip." As biographer Buell noted, Spruance was "never without it. . . . He would use it to make the most important decision of the Battle of Midway."[4] That decision was when to launch his first and most important air strike at the *kidō butai.* As Spruance noted, "As soon as I got the contact report of the attacking [Japanese] groups headed toward Midway from the northwest, I turned TF 16 towards where we estimated the Japanese carriers would be when our attack groups would reach them. This was based on the assumption that they would continue towards Midway at 25 knots. I speeded up to 25 knots and made preparations to launch aircraft when we got within striking distance. I felt we must strike their carriers before they could launch a second attack on Midway."[5]

His next decision was just as demanding as his first: when to launch the remaining planes against the *Hiryu* on the afternoon of 4 June. Spruance made one major error. He held strike aircraft on the flight decks of the *Enterprise* and *Hornet* when he knew that planes from the remaining Japanese carrier were searching for his force. Fortunately for Spruance, fortune smiled on his command. The *Hiryu*'s strike aircraft attacked the *Yorktown* and did not find his two carriers, while a *Yorktown* scout bomber found the Japanese. Spruance promptly ordered strikes by the aircraft waiting on the flight decks of his two carriers. They found and attacked the fourth enemy carrier, but their attack left the *Hiryu* burning and did not sink it.

That left Spruance with another dilemma. Should he pursue the retiring Japanese at night in order to make sure of the fourth enemy carrier at dawn on 5 June? Spruance chose not to do that. As he explained after the battle,

> We had to keep moving because of the possible presence of enemy submarines. Our primary mission was still to prevent the capture of Midway. We did not know whether the enemy would continue with that task, or whether the loss of his three carriers, and the damage we had inflicted on the fourth, would cause him to give up the attempt. Should I continue steaming west, with a view to overtaking and engaging the enemy? If I did this, we would run the risk of a gun engagement during the night with possible superior forces, at a time when our two aircraft carriers could not operate, and would be a source of weakness rather than strength to us. The Japanese were believed to have two fast battleships with their carrier force. The Japanese were reputed to be well trained in night gunnery and in night destroyer attacks.[6]

So Spruance decided "to steam to the eastward instead." Once he felt clear of any pursuing Japanese surface forces, he turned back to the west. As he said later, "I was uncertain whether the enemy would attempt his landings on Midway on 5 June. I wanted to be within air supporting distance of Midway at daybreak so as to be able to furnish air support to its defenders."[7] After Midway, Spruance was criticized for not being more aggressive. As it happened, his decision was correct, but no one knew for sure at the time. In facing the critics and to deal with his own doubts, Spruance had to impose the calm on himself that was his trademark.

Once it was clear on 5 June that the Japanese invasion force was withdrawing, Spruance realized that "I had to decide on my next objective. I took this to be the sinking of the damaged fourth carrier. During the middle of the forenoon I received a report from an aircraft from Midway that [the fourth carrier] had been sighted steaming to the northwest at ten knots. We steamed to the northwest at 25 knots, all the rest of the day, with frequent launchings and recoveries of our CAP—the wind usually light and in the wrong direction. Late in the day I received a report from a Midway based aircraft which indicated an enemy carrier and a weather front a considerable distance ahead on our course. I ordered *Enterprise* and *Hornet* to send out available dive bombers armed with 500 lb. bombs to search ahead on our course and to attack any targets. All they sighted was one ship, variously reported as a destroyer or cruiser. This they attacked but did not damage."[8]

Spruance was cautious in pursuing the Japanese. As he explained to a member of his staff, "I will not expose this force to attack by shore-based aircraft. Therefore I will not pursue within range of shore-based air power."[9] Before the battle, Spruance had told his flag lieutenant, "I have written orders to meet and defeat the Japs. My oral orders are not to lose my force."[10] The need to preserve his force guided Spruance's thoughts and actions throughout the Battle of Midway.

CHAPTER

37

Harsh Lessons

By John B. Lundstrom

Black Shoe Carrier Admiral (Annapolis, MD: Naval Institute Press, 2006): chap 19 The Battle of Midway II, pp. 299, Conclusion 508, 511, 514

Despite a few farsighted individuals, the question of carrier air coordination remained largely unrecognized even after the fiasco at Midway. When Fletcher returned to Pearl he found an urgent request from Nimitz seeking his personal views on carrier tactics "in light of the Coral Sea and Midway actions." No one could claim more carrier battle experience. Following the lead of Ted Sherman [the *Lexington*'s captain at Coral Sea], Fletcher fervently advocated the carriers be concentrated at least in pairs in the same task force and within the same screen. Nearly everyone else, starting with [Admiral] King, stuck with the old concept of single-carrier task forces and some degree of separation, although after Midway [CAPT Miles] Browning also remarked to the "great advantage" of a two-carrier task force. Fletcher argued that only multi-carrier task forces provided the air strength required for effective attack and defense, as well as for the searches that circumstances often compelled the carriers themselves to make. Alone among the top carrier commanders, he stressed the necessity for coordinated strikes by air groups from different carriers, instead of the doctrinaire "wave attacks" that [RADM Aubrey] Fitch and Sherman employed in the Coral Sea. Fletcher desired to "present the maximum number of planes (particularly VF) to the enemy at one time" to "thin out enemy VF opposition" and "not give him the opportunity of

RADM Frank Jack Fletcher as a vice admiral in September 1942. Awarded the Medal of Honor for bravery under fire at Veracruz, Mexico, in 1914, Fletcher commanded destroyers, served as executive officer of the battleship *Colorado,* and attended the Naval War College in the 1920s. He applied for flight training in order to qualify as a carrier commander, but his eyesight did not meet the necessary standard. In 1935 he served as an aide to the secretary of the Navy. In 1937 he was captain of the battleship *New Mexico.* Promoted to rear admiral in 1939, Fletcher commanded a cruiser division in the Pacific Fleet in 1941. After the Japanese attack on Pearl Harbor, ADM Husband Kimmel, commander in chief of the Pacific Fleet, selected Fletcher to command the carrier and surface ship task force assigned to relieve besieged Wake Island. After that mission was cancelled, Fletcher was given command of TF-17, which was built around the carrier *Yorktown.* Fletcher exercised that command from the *Yorktown* until he had to leave her on 4 June 1942.

Navy Department, National Archives

attacking our incoming planes in piecemeal fashion." He did not understand that Japan had already effectively integrated air groups from different carriers—no one on the U.S. side did—but he certainly saw the possibilities. In that, Fletcher was far ahead of his time on the U.S. Navy side. . . .

The Evolution of an Image

The common perception of an historical figure is far more influential than reality itself. A sad example of that paradigm is Frank Jack Fletcher, an obscure rear admiral at the start of World War II who remained little known during that conflict despite his part in three naval victories in 1942. That year Admiral King restricted publicity of top naval commanders for security reasons. The only exception was Admiral Halsey, dubbed "Bull" by exuberant reporters. The curtain of anonymity started to lift in 1943 and soon national magazines regularly featured articles on celebrated admirals, notably not Fletcher. His most prominent coverage in the wartime press came that year in a piece on the Battle of the Coral Sea written by Fletcher Pratt, a breezy popular historian well connected to [the secretary of the Navy's] Office of Public Relations. Pratt quaintly described Fletcher, whom he evidently never met, as "an old sea dog out of Admiral Benbow's time," hardly a ringing endorsement in a modern technological war. More ominously, both Pratt and reporter Gilbert Cant completely omitted Fletcher in their 1943 accounts of Midway, but designated Raymond Spruance as the sole U.S. carrier commander in that battle. . . . In 1944 Pratt incorporated his articles, sans corrections regarding Fletcher, into the book *The Navy's War,* whose credibility [Navy] Secretary Knox's handsome forward further enhanced. Thus certain powers in Washington grudgingly allowed Fletcher public credit for Coral Sea (they could not plausibly give it to anyone else) but denied him any role in the ultimate triumph at Midway. . . .

[For the historians of World War II], All Fletcher had was memory, because he tragically retained *no* papers from his 1941–42 carrier commands. Everything prior to Midway, indeed all of his personal files from September 1939, went down in the *Yorktown*. . . .

An Evaluation

Displaying flexibility and nerve, Fletcher performed at Coral Sea, Midway, and even at Guadalcanal better than anyone could have reasonably anticipated. . . . In retrospect it appears Fletcher's well-measured style of command was actually the most appropriate for that particular time of peril, when the Pacific Fleet was outnumbered and operating on the tactical defensive even during its Guadalcanal counteroffensive. Cautious when necessary, Fletcher proved decisive when the situation called for it. . . .

It is fascinating to consider why Fletcher, a well-seasoned naval officer but carrier neophyte lacking a technical background in naval aviation, developed or at least recognized such advanced concepts for carrier employment. He also fostered the creativity that led, in particular, to the *Yorktown*'s remarkably effective performance. The fundamental reason is that Fletcher did not already think he knew it all. Thus he was particularly receptive to advice from the younger aviator leaders, who offered fresh, cutting-edge opinions based on the latest operational flying experience. That certainly was not always the case with many senior aviators, . . . who proved reluctant to discard years of hard-earned but obsolete aviation lore in favor of innovative new ideas.

CHAPTER

38

Enemy Carriers

By John B. Lundstrom

Black Shoe Carrier Admiral (Annapolis, MD: Naval Institute Press, 2006): chap. 17 The Battle of Midway I: "Give Them the Works", pp. 240–241, 254–255

Like Fletcher and Spruance, Vice Adm. Nagumo Chuichi, age fifty-five, was no naval aviator, but a surface warrior known as a particularly sharp and aggressive torpedo expert. Promoted to rear admiral in 1935, he led light cruisers in the opening stage of the China Incident, and in 1939 he rose to vice admiral in charge of the four *Kongo*-class fast battleships. Afterward, he served as president of the Naval Staff College. In April 1941 the IJN entrusted Nagumo, who had no previous aviation experience, with the First Air Fleet of carriers. Late that year he formed the *Kido Butai,* the operational command of six elite carriers that constituted the greatest concentration of naval aviation yet achieved. Nagumo won great success attacking Pearl Harbor, supporting the invasion of the Dutch East Indies, and in the Indian Ocean. By necessity like Fletcher and Spruance, he relied on the advice of his carrier experts. Unlike his U.S. Navy counterparts, Nagumo appears to have shown little interest in the actual mechanics of carrier air operations. It became increasingly apparent by Midway that he was out of his depth, worn down by the responsibility of commanding a force whose technical intricacies he had not mastered. Such passivity resulted from a system where top commanders almost invariably (Yamamoto a rare exception) decided in favor of staff recommendations, once the staff officers themselves reached consensus. Cdr. Genda Minoru, the brilliant air staff officer who largely planned the air portion of the attack on Pearl Harbor, and senior strike leader Cdr. Fuchida Mitsuo,

The *Hiryu*'s dive-bombers and torpedo planes struck the *Yorktown* twice on 4 June, but dive-bombers from the *Enterprise* and *Yorktown* dealt the *Hiryu* terrible retribution, striking the forward part of the carrier with four 1,000-pound bombs, leaving the *Hiryu* a smoking wreck. B-17s from Midway and Hawaii also attacked the carrier, though none of their bombs hit her. Though the *Hiryu* continued to steam west and north at nearly thirty knots, her crew could not contain the fires that were burning her out, and after midnight on 4 June she lost power. Rear Admiral Yamaguchi Tamon, commander of Carrier Division 2, refused to leave the *Hiryu*. Captain Kaku Tomeo stayed with him. Yamaguchi ordered the destroyer *Makigumo* to torpedo the carrier. After doing so, the *Makigumo* left the scene with survivors, but the *Hiryu* stayed afloat long enough for several dozen other survivors to cast a cutter adrift and spend fourteen days drifting alone, until they were found by the U.S. Navy's seaplane tender *Ballard*. This photo of the *Hiryu* was taken on 5 June by a plane from the small carrier *Hosho*, scouting ahead of Admiral Yamamoto's three battleships.

U.S. Naval Institute Photo Archive

who executed that plan in flawless fashion, exerted an overconfident influence on Nagumo. The chief of staff was Rear Adm. Kusaka Ryunosuke, a non-aviator who nevertheless captained two carriers. He refereed the debates and served as conciliator. At Midway illness slowed Genda, and Fuchida did not fly because of a recent appendectomy. Their incapacity contributed to a lack of decisiveness by Nagumo in the top level of command.

Nagumo's first order of business on 4 June was to mount his Midway strike and dawn search. [One hundred eight planes] from all four carriers assembled with an ease that again demonstrated the marvelous coordination between carrier divisions and air groups that was far superior to the U.S. Navy's. Because each carrier only launched a portion of her strength as a single deck load, takeoff and assembly went quickly. Yet the downside of such cooperation in the face of opposition was that all four carriers were committed to the eventual recovery of the Midway strike. . . . The dawn search did not go as well. . . . [T]he cruiser planes scheduled for north of Midway were tardy. . . . Even worse, Nagumo's staff committed the key blunder of assigning too few planes to such a wide expanse of ocean. . . . Nagumo ignored that the Midway strike was going in a day late and that the Americans were already aware of the approach of at least part of the invasion force.

Such slackness reflected Nagumo's strong confidence that he had surprised Midway. Even so, he tucked a card up his sleeve, actually in the hangar decks of the four carriers. In the unlikely event the [dawn] search discovered U.S. ships, he readied a second wave of 101 aircraft . . . that could surely handle anything that might turn up. This contingency rose from Combined Fleet orders as a precaution should U.S. carriers already be off Midway. No one in the 1st *Kido Butai* seriously believed that would happen. . . .

The "Grand Scale Air Attack"

At 0830, . . . confirmed carrier opposition caught Nagumo in a dilemma. At that point he would need time, because of the need to spot and warm up planes, even to mount a partial strike. [Rear Admiral] Yamaguchi had no doubt what Nagumo should do and had not hesitated to tell him. Valid reasons existed for Nagumo to follow his advice, not the least of which was to get in a carrier strike as soon as possible. Prospects for a fighter escort, though, were sparse. Kusaka and Genda vehemently disagreed, and they swiftly swayed Nagumo into postponing any second attack. The carrier bombers that Yamaguchi was spotting up on deck had yet to be armed and warmed up before launch. That process might take a half hour. In the interval some or even many Midway attackers might ditch before flight decks were again open to receive them. Thus Nagumo resolved to land the Midway strike as soon as possible, then recycle the combat air patrol, regroup his task force, and complete the rearming. His "grand scale air attack" of seventy-seven strike aircraft . . . and fighter escorts should be ready to depart in about two hours. Nagumo and the staff must have judged that any real danger to the carriers in the meantime was minimal.

The risk of losing many of the Midway first attackers to the sea evidently was the overriding factor in the decision to delay the second strike. Kusaka later declared, and Genda and Fuchida concurred, that they also worried that the precipitous strike Yamaguchi recommended could only have a few escort Zeroes. A strong fighter defense could overwhelm a small escort and shred the bombers just the way their own combat air patrol ground up the enemy. This particular excuse almost certainly arose from hindsight to justify the decision that ultimately decided the course of the battle. In fact the staff assigned only a dozen fighters (three from each carrier) to accompany the reorganized "grand scale air attack." That hardly squares with their supposed concern over defending U.S. fighters. Instead, Nagumo and his advisors perceived the situation as sufficiently favorable not to force them to commit an unbalanced attack. The second strike could wait until everything was ready to go. The methodical Kusaka distrusted precipitate actions, preferring "a concentrated single stroke after sufficient study and minute planning." He and ex-fighter pilot Genda felt fully confident their own superb Zeroes, rapidly reinforced by the former Midway escort, would annihilate whatever the bumbling Americans might throw at them. Fuchida reflected their optimism. "It was our general conclusion that we had little to fear from the enemy's offensive tactics." . . .

At 0830 Nagumo directed Yamaguchi to "prepare for second attack" by arming his carrier bombers with 250-kilogram semi-armor-piercing bombs. With the [U.S.] air attacks from Midway tailing off, he reassembled his task force and turned into the slight wind to recover the fuel-starved Midway attackers. At 0837 the *Akagi* and *Kaga* began landing aircraft. The *Hiryu* and *Soryu* followed suit after arming their carrier bombers and striking them below in the upper hangar decks. Three carrier attack planes ditched, and destroyers swiftly rescued the crews. At 0917 with most of the first wave snugly on board, Nagumo changed course northeast (070 degrees) at thirty knots. . . .

Nagumo radioed Yamamoto and Kondo at 0855 to report the enemy force of one carrier, five cruisers, and five destroyers discovered 240 miles north of Midway. "We are heading for it." . . . By 0900 Nagumo anticipated unleashing his great air strike in ninety minutes. . . . In the meantime [Petty Officer First Class Yoji] Amari [flying cruiser *Tone*'s No. 4 reconnaissance seaplane] radioed that he was homeward bound, but then, about 0840, unexpectedly placed two additional cruisers northwest of the main [U.S.] body. . . . During his brief withdrawal Amari stumbled across TF-17 while the *Yorktown* launched her strike. . . . Amari conscientiously stayed on station despite dwindling fuel until after 0940, but in the interval he gave his superiors no additional information.

In retrospect [Petty Officer First Class Yoji] Amari's failures to develop his contacts deeply harmed the Japanese cause. Had he come through promptly and clearly with word of U.S. carriers (which certainly were nearby), Nagumo might have attacked them using whatever planes were at hand. . . . That blow might not have won the battle for Nagumo, but it certainly could have increased the cost to the Pacific Fleet.

CHAPTER 39

Mitscher and the Mystery of Midway

By Craig L. Symonds

Naval History, June 2012: pp. 46–52

Compelling evidence (and its absence) suggest the *Hornet*'s CO deliberately filed a misleading report on his air group's puzzling 'flight to nowhere' in the pivotal battle.

Just a handful of veterans of the Battle of Midway—virtually all of them now in their 90s—survive as we mark the 70th anniversary this summer of that stunning naval victory. The subject of scores of books and movies, the decisive showdown has been studied and debated exhaustively. Yet even seven decades on, some lingering questions continue to perplex historians.

Five years ago in these pages, Ronald Russell, webmaster of the Midway veterans' online site (www.midway42.org), and author of the thoughtful and respected volume *No Right to Win*, noted the glaring discrepancies between Captain Marc "Pete" Mitscher's official report on the battle—particularly the actions of the air squadrons of the USS *Hornet* (CV-8) on 4 June 1942—and the recollections of most of the pilots who flew off the *Hornet* that day. Russell wrote correctly that the discrepancies left students of the battle wondering about "what actually happened to all of those aviators on that epic day." While it may be impossible at this remove to resolve the mystery with certainty, it is the purpose of this article to suggest a possible answer.

The origins of the puzzle stretch back to the commissioning of the new-construction *Hornet* [CV-8] in March 1942. The newest American carrier, the *Hornet* did not even have sufficient time to qualify most of her pilots as she steamed south from Norfolk to the Panama Canal, then up the U.S. West Coast to Alameda, California. There the planes of her air group were struck below, to the hangar deck, so she could take on board 16 Mitchell B-25 bombers for an Army Air Forces raid on Tokyo led by Lieutenant Colonel "Jimmy" Doolittle. Naturally, pilot training had to be suspended while the *Hornet* was thus encumbered, and only after Doolittle and his fellow pilots took off did the *Hornet* resume normal carrier operations. Given that timetable, the *Hornet* had not been able to participate in any of the early American raids against Japanese outposts in the Marshall Islands and elsewhere. The Battle of Midway was therefore her first action against an enemy force.

On 28 May 1942, the *Hornet* left Pearl Harbor in company with her sister ship, the *Enterprise,* for a rendezvous nearly 1,500 miles to the north, a location optimistically code-named Point Luck. Cryptanalysts under Commander Joseph Rochefort, working in the dark, air-conditioned basement of the 14th Naval District headquarters in Honolulu, had determined that the Japanese were embarking on a major operation to seize the two-island atoll of Midway, and Admiral Chester Nimitz had decided to send his carrier force there in the hope of springing an ambush.

An Incorrect Assumption

The crucial role of the code-breakers in the Battle of Midway is well known—often even overstated. Some students of the battle have asserted that Rochefort and his colleagues were able to provide Nimitz and the other senior American planners with a copy of the Japanese order of battle. That however, was not the case, which is particularly important in assessing the role of the *Hornet* air group in the subsequent battle. While Nimitz *did* know that the Japanese were sending four carriers—plus supports and escorts—to attack Midway, the available intelligence did *not* tell him how the Japanese would deploy those four carriers—a point to bear in mind. We know now, of course, that all four ships operated together as a single task force—the Mobile Striking Force, or *Kidō Butai.* But at the time, Nimitz and the other key decision-makers assumed that the Japanese would operate those four carriers in two separate groups.

The source of that assumption is unclear, but it may well be something as simple as a case of mirror-imaging: The United States operated its three carriers in two task forces (TF 16 and TF 17), so it perhaps seemed quite likely to the Americans that the Japanese would do the same. Evidence of this assumption is in Nimitz's initial orders to the task force commanders and the commanders on Midway. In those orders, Nimitz suggested that "one or more [of the enemy] carriers may take up close-in daylight positions" for the attack on Midway, while "additional carrier groups" operated against American surface forces. In the briefing that Mitscher's intelligence officer, Lieutenant Stephen Jurika, gave to the pilots on the *Hornet* the night before the battle, Jurika told them "there were at least two carriers, two battleships, several cruisers and about five destroyers in the attack force which would attempt to take Midway" and that "the support force some distance behind contained the rest of their forces."

Those assumptions were reinforced at 0603 on 4 June when a PBY Catalina out of Midway reported the first sighting of the enemy: two carriers and two battleships, 180 miles north of the atoll. Two carriers! Where were the others? Forty-five minutes later, Rear Admiral Frank Jack Fletcher, the senior American officer afloat, sent a message (which Mitscher monitored) to the commander of TF 16, Rear Admiral Raymond Spruance, to remind him: "Two carriers [are] unaccounted for." It is important to remember those assumptions in considering what happened next.

A Curious Lack of Documents

At 0705, the *Hornet* and the *Enterprise* began launching aircraft. By prearrangement, the *Yorktown*—the third U.S. carrier at Point Luck—would hold her strike force back to await further news—presumably information about those "missing" two carriers. By 0800, all the planes from the *Enterprise* and the *Hornet* were aloft. The *Enterprise* planes flew to the southwest on a bearing of approximately 239 degrees True, toward the coordinates sent in by the PBY two hours earlier. But what about the *Hornet*'s planes? Which way did they go? That turns out to be a complicated question.

For starters, there is a gaping hole in the official record concerning the activities of the *Hornet*'s air group on 4 June. Though all unit commanders were required to submit official written reports after each action, there is only one official report from the *Hornet*, written by—or at least signed by—Pete Mitscher. Stamped "Secret" and dated 13 June 1942, it is sufficiently detailed in its description of events, but it is not accompanied by a group commander's report, or reports from any of the squadron commanders. The absence of a report from the torpedo squadron (VT-8) is easily explained: Torpedo Eight from the *Hornet* was wiped out in its attack on the *Kidō Butai* that morning; only one pilot survived, Ensign George Gay. Though he was debriefed, and much later wrote a personal memoir, Gay never wrote an after-action report. There is no explanation, however, for the absence of reports from any of the three other squadrons.

In the one report that does exist—Mitscher's—he asserts that "The objective, enemy carriers, was calculated to be 155 miles distant, bearing 239° T[rue] from this Task Force; one division of 10 VF [fighters], Squadron Commander in charge, was sent with 35 VSB [bombers] and 15 VTB [torpedo planes]. . . . " It is noteworthy that Mitscher uses the passive voice: the range and course bearing "was calculated"—by whom he does not say. Similarly, the strike force "was sent" and while he does not specifically say that it was sent on that bearing of 239 degrees, that is certainly implied. (Of course passive voice was—and is—common in Navy parlance. Even today, officers do not make requests, instead their chits read: "It is requested that . . . "—as if the request existed independently of the author.)

Mitscher's 13 June report continues: "They [the pilots] were unable to locate the enemy and landed on board at 1727." Mitscher explains this by noting "about one hour after the planes had departed the enemy reversed his course and started his retirement." And it is true that the *Kidō Butai* turned from the southeast to the northeast at 0917 that day. As a result of that turn, Mitscher writes, the American pilots failed to spot the enemy and eventually returned to the carrier—those who could. Mitscher even included a map in his official report showing the air group flying on the 239-degrees-True course, and missing the Japanese carriers because they had turned north.

(Most) Pilots Tell a Different Story

For more than 50 years, students of the Battle of Midway took Mitscher at his word and described the *Hornet* air group as missing the Japanese because the American planes flew south of the target. But, As Ronald Russell noted in his February 2006 article, unofficial evidence, mainly from post-battle interviews, memoirs, letters, and other such sources, mostly (though not exclusively) indicate that the *Hornet* air group had not flown to the southwest on a course of 239, but to the west—on a course of 265 degrees.

That evidence comes mostly from the pilots themselves, who, in postwar oral interviews recalled that they had flown "westerly," as one put it, "almost due west," according to another, or more precisely (from yet another), "at 265 degrees." When one pilot, Troy Guillory, initially said that the air group flew "westerly," his interviewer suggested that he must be mistaken, that the course was to the southwest, at 239 degrees. No, said Guillory. "We went the wrong way to start with," and then, he said—pointing to the chart—"to the 265 line." Ensign Ben Tappan stated simply, "we were going west." The commander of the *Hornet*'s scouting squadron (VS-8), Lieutenant Commander (later Rear Admiral) Walt Rodee stated bluntly: "We took the bearing and the course they gave us. It was about 265. . . . It was almost due west." Rodee did not file an after-action report, but he did make note of the course in his flight log—which he kept. Finally, the radar operator on board the *Hornet* recalled tracking the air group as it flew away from TF 16, and said that as far as the CXAM radar could track the air group, it had flown outbound on a course of 265 degrees. Significantly, not all the pilots agreed. Ensign Clayton Fisher, who flew as wingman for the group commander on 4 June, claimed until his death in January 2012 that the air group flew southwest on a bearing between 235 and 240 degrees.

Explaining the discrepancy between Mitscher's report and the pilots' memories is difficult. The absence of any squadron reports from the *Hornet* is by itself suspicious, and encourages the conclusion that Mitscher's official report may well be in error. Not surprisingly, Spruance thought so, too. In his own report on the battle, he wrote, "Where discrepancies exist between *Enterprise* and *Hornet* reports, the *Enterprise* report should be taken as more accurate." That is an astonishing statement to make in an official report, and comes close to asserting that Mitscher's report was not to be trusted.

A Calculated Risk

To try to resolve this mystery, it is essential to re-examine what the Americans knew—or thought they knew—about Japanese intentions that day. Remember that most of the high command—including Mitscher—believed the Japanese were operating in two carrier groups: the one that had been sighted, and a second one, which was presumed to be operating 80 to 100 miles to the rear. Mitscher knew that the planes from *Enterprise* were going after the two carriers that the PBY had sighted and reported, and he may have harbored fears that even if that strike were successful the other two enemy carriers would remain untouched—and more important, that the element of surprise would be lost.

Pete Mitscher was the most senior U.S. Navy aviation officer afloat that day. Rear Admiral Bill Halsey, an aviator who was supposed to have commanded at Midway, was in the hospital. Captain George Murray, commander of the *Enterprise*, was Naval Aviator #22, and Spruance had designated him as tactical air officer for the strike. But Mitscher, who was Naval Aviator #33, had been selected for promotion to rear admiral, and his staff already was referring to him as "Admiral Mitscher." In Halsey's absence, Fletcher was the senior officer afloat, but neither he nor Spruance were aviators. It is easy to imagine that, in Mitscher's mind, it was up to him to ensure the proper coordination of the air strikes.

Mitscher knew there would be only one chance to effect surprise, and that once surprise was lost, the battle would become a tossup. If the *Enterprise* planes succeeded in surprising and sinking the two enemy flattops at the known coordinates, it is entirely reasonable to assume that Mitscher may have calculated the best use of the *Hornet*'s air group was to find and sink the two carriers that had not yet been sighted—but which presumably were operating 80 to 100 miles behind the other Japanese ships. In consideration of those factors, Mitscher may have told his air group leader, Commander Stanhope Ring, to take the entire air group to a position

80 miles behind the leading Japanese carriers. If one calculates that bearing from the *Hornet*'s position that morning, it turns out to be about 265 degrees.

If that is what happened, Mitscher apparently did not share the revised objective with any of the four squadron commanders—just with group commander Ring. That would explain why the commander of Torpedo Eight, Lieutenant Commander John Waldron, was so surprised—and then angry—when he was told the course he was to fly. He knew that a course of 265 would not lead them to the coordinates he had carefully plotted in the ready room that morning based on the location of the sighted Japanese carriers.

Broken Silence, Angry Words, and a Breakup

There are no official transcripts of the radio chatter that morning because everyone was supposed to be observing radio silence. The objective, after all, was surprise. But years later, many of the air group pilots recalled what they heard being transmitted, and their memories are revealing.

After the *Hornet*'s planes launched between 0700 and 0755 that morning, the bombers and fighters climbed to 20,000 feet while the torpedo planes flew almost three vertical miles below them at 1,500 feet. Though they all flew under radio silence, only about 15 minutes into the mission several of the pilots remembered John Waldron's voice coming through their headsets: "You're going the wrong direction for the Japanese carrier force." Ring was furious that Waldron had broken radio silence, and equally furious to be challenged on an open radio net—in effect, in front of the entire command. The next voice on the air was Ring: "I'm leading this flight," he snapped. "You fly with us right here." Waldron was not intimidated. "I know where the damned Jap fleet is," he insisted. Ring, even angrier, barked back: "You fly on us! I'm leading this formation; you fly on us." There was a brief silence before a final rejoinder came from Waldron: "Well, the hell with you. I know where they are and I'm going to them." Three miles below Ring, Waldron banked his plane to the left, heading southwest. His entire squadron went with him.

History tells us, of course, that Waldron was right. He did know where "the damned Jap fleet" was. And when he found it, his squadron was annihilated in a futile and hopeless attack against overwhelming odds. But meantime, what was happening with the rest of the *Hornet* air group? A half hour after Waldron departed, the Wildcat fighters accompanying the strike force began to run low on fuel and they, too, abandoned the mission, flying back toward the *Hornet* on a reciprocal course. None of them made it, for they had waited too long and failed to find the task force. All of them ran out of fuel and ditched in the ocean. Two lost their lives.

Soon after the departure of the fighters, some pilots in the bombing squadron (VB-8) recalled hearing another broadcast from Waldron: "Stanhope from Johnny One. Stanhope from Johnny One." There was no reply, but there were more messages from Waldron: "Watch those fighters!" and "My two wing men are going in the water." It was evident now that Waldron had indeed found the *Kidō Butai.* Soon after that, the planes from the *Hornet*'s bomber squadron, led by their CO, Lieutenant Commander Ruff Johnson, peeled off from the formation and turned south. Ring broke radio silence in an attempt to recall them, but they continued on, partly to look for the Japanese, partly to see if they could make it to Midway's airfield because Johnson doubted that his pilots had enough fuel left to make it all the way back to the *Hornet.* Eleven of them eventually landed on Midway; three went into the water out of fuel; and three managed to reach the *Hornet.*

Ring continued to fly west, now with just the scout bombers still in company. At 225 miles out—nearly 100 miles beyond the calculated range to the target—the scout bombers, too, left, low on fuel. Astonishingly, for a few brief moments Ring flew on by himself. Very soon, however, he gave up and turned. He flew back toward the *Hornet* completely alone—abandoned by his entire command. In the day's final tally, just 20 of the 59 airplanes that took off from *Hornet* that morning returned. Not one of them had dropped a bomb on an enemy ship.

The Case for Fudging an After-Action Report

The episode has gone down in the history of the Battle of Midway as "the flight to nowhere." As Mitscher noted laconically in his official report, "None of Scouting Eight or Bombing Eight made contact with the enemy. . . ." That much of Mitscher's report, at least, is true enough. But if the recollections of the pilots are accurate, much of the rest of his report is not. So we are still left with the puzzle of why Mitscher recounted a dramatically different story in his report. It can't be known for certain, but a very plausible explanation is that three considerations influenced Mitscher.

First, by the time Mitscher sat down to write that report nine days later, he knew that all four Japanese carriers had been operating as a unit, so that if he had, in fact, made an independent decision to send the entire air group to look for two of them elsewhere, that decision would now be revealed as—at the least—unwise. Second, by then Mitscher also knew most of the details of the several mutinous actions of the squadron commanders who, one-by-one, had defied orders and abandoned the group commander. If all that were reported officially, Mitscher would almost certainly have to file court-martial papers against each of them. Disobeying orders during a war patrol, after all, is mutiny.

Finally (and this may have been decisive) by 13 June when Mitscher wrote his report, it was very clear that the Americans had won an overwhelming victory at Midway—indeed, the greatest triumph in U.S. naval history. It simply would not do, then, to sully that achievement with a raft of posthumous courts-martial against men such as Waldron. So instead of filing mutiny charges, Mitscher wrote this: "Torpedo Eight, led by Lieutenant Commander John C. Waldron, U.S.N., was lost in its entirety. This squadron flew at 100 knots below the clouds while the remainder of the group flew at 110 knots climbing to 19,000 feet. Lieutenant Commander Waldron, a highly aggressive officer, leading a well-trained squadron, found his target and attacked. . . . [T]his squadron is deserving of the highest honors for finding the enemy, pressing home its attack, without fighter protection and without diverting dive bomber attacks to draw the enemy fire."

So Waldron was not a mutineer—he was a hero. Mitscher may well have asked himself what was to be gained by submitting a report that attacked the memory of the martyred Waldron or filing court-martial papers against any of the other squadron commanders. So instead Mitscher recommended all of them for medals, told those squadron commanders who had survived not to file reports, and submitted what he knew to be a false report.

Is that what happened? The best answer a responsible historian can offer now, 70 years later, is "probably." The historical quest is never-ending, however, and it is not impossible that one day additional material will come to light that will help explain further the enigma of the so-called flight to nowhere. In the meantime, how do we assess the actions and decisions of Marc Mitscher at Midway? Here was the man who, over the next three years, would command the Fast Carrier Task Force that led the American drive across the Pacific to Saipan, Iwo Jima, and Okinawa, and become known as "The Magnificent Mitscher." Should that assessment be modified based on the likelihood that he knowingly filed a false report about the Battle of Midway? Or given the circumstances of 13 June 1942, was his decision to gundeck the story of the flight to nowhere a reasonable one?

— AUTHOR —

Craig L. Symonds has taught at both the Naval Academy and the Naval War College. He is the author of *Decision at Sea: Five Naval Battles that Shaped American History* (2006) and *The Battle of Midway* (2011).

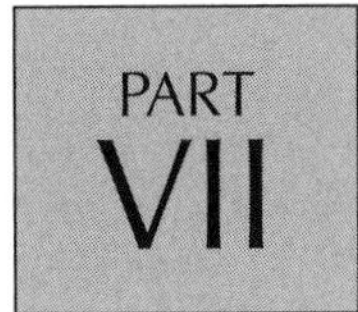

PART VII

The Code-Breaking

The story of the U.S. code-breaking before the Battles of Coral Sea and Midway has been oversimplified. Too many accounts of Midway tend to overlook the following: First, the fact that the 14th Naval District code-breakers (Pearl Harbor radio intelligence unit, or Station Hypo) had not warned Admiral Kimmel, Pacific Fleet commander in December 1941, that Pearl Harbor was about the be attacked and were therefore suspect in the eyes of senior Navy officers in Washington. The reasons for this "failure" can be found in Elliot Carlson's *Joe Rochefort's War* and RADM Edwin Layton's *And I Was There: Pearl Harbor and Midway—Breaking the Secrets* (Annapolis, MD: Naval Institute Press, 1985). The point to keep in mind is that then–Commander Rochefort and then–Lieutenant Commander Layton had to convince Admiral Nimitz that the earlier apparent failure was not their doing, and that they could organize intercepted messages and other pieces of intelligence to provide Nimitz with what he needed, which was a knowledge of where the Japanese were going to attack and when. They also had to provide a strong case that Nimitz could then show to Admiral King.

Second, code-breaking was not possible without enough intercepted radio messages for the cryptanalysts to work on. The code-breakers worked hand in hand with the traffic analysts. The latter studied which radio stations (on land and at sea) communicated with others in an effort to build a picture of Japanese forces and their movements. The traffic analysts also tried to identify specific Japanese radio telegraphers and then associate them with specific ships or shore stations. This work aided the cryptanalysts, who had to decide which intercepted messages to try to decrypt and then interpret. If there were only a few intercepted messages, that was one thing. But if there were many—hundreds, perhaps thousands—then the cryptanalysts needed help in deciding what messages to try to crack. So the ability of the intercept stations to pull in Japanese messages was a two-edged sword. Too few intercepts stymied both the traffic analysts and the code-breakers. Too many intercepts left the traffic analysts and the code-breakers with a serious sorting problem; they could be literally buried in intercepts.

Third, Station Hypo (Rochefort's command) was part of the 14th Naval District, which at the time of Pearl Harbor was headed by RADM Claude C. Bloch, who had been CominCh of the United States Fleet in 1939. The CominCh had four stars. If he left that post before retiring from the Navy, he returned to his permanent rank of rear admiral (two stars). So Admiral Bloch had been a rear admiral when he took command of the 14th Naval District. At the time of the Battles of Coral Sea and Midway, Station Hypo was under Bloch's control, and therefore it was essential that Commander Rochefort find a way to link his organization with the staff of Admiral Nimitz, the fleet commander, without threatening the chain of command of the 14th Naval District. The link was the close contact between Rochefort and Lieutenant Commander Layton. They created a direct phone connection and used it every day with Rear Admiral Bloch's approval.

Fourth, code-breaking in 1942 was still very much a matter of the insightfulness and painstaking hard work of individual cryptanalysts. But they were aided by the use of Hollerith cards manipulated on counter sorters. Information about Japanese intercepts was typed and punched into the cards, and machine operators ran the cards through electro-mechanical countersorters in efforts to establish relationships between elements in the messages. With the countersorters, analysts could build tables showing, for instance, that certain radio telegraphists always communicated with certain others, or that certain groups of code letters were always associated with messages sent from a shore headquarters to ships at sea. Tables could reflect "if . . . then" relationships: If ship A sent a certain form of message to a shore station B, then it meant that ship A had received instructions on where to steam and when to leave. That information might be collated with other similar pieces of information to indicate when a major element of the Japanese fleet was planning to sail. As you can imagine, Station Hypo created and stored thousands of Hollerith cards and the paper print-outs of the tables based on the data in those cards. However, these tables were no substitute for the work of the cryptanalysts—the code-breaking was not automated.

Fifth, code-breaking was almost always fragmentary. Messages were rarely decrypted without gaps in them. The task of the Station Hypo code-breakers and their Pacific Fleet intelligence analyst colleagues was to recognize meaningful patterns in the combined decrypted messages, the work of the traffic analysts, and the other pieces of collected evidence. Too often, the hard work—performed under great pressure and often around the clock—has been ignored on the assumption that "all it took" was finding the one message that would reveal the enemy's whole plan.

What Rochefort, Layton, and their colleagues did was extraordinary, and it was essential to keep it secret—absolutely secret. The secret was almost lost as the Battle of Midway was being fought, as "Freedom of the Press or Treason?" (chapter 42) shows.

CHAPTER
40

Code-Breaking before Midway

By Elliot Carlson

Joe Rochefort's War: The Odyssey of the Codebreaker Who Outwitted Yamamoto at Midway (Annapolis, MD: Naval Institute Press, 2011): chap. 22 Something Is Brewing, pp. 300–303, chap. 23 Five Days in May, pp. 307–312, 319

Hypo finally scored a breakthrough on 8 May. Rochefort's top traffic analysts . . . correctly associated Nagumo's First Air Fleet with key elements of the Second Fleet, most notably the fast battleships *Hiei* and *Kongo* and the cruisers *Tone* and *Chikuma,* still in Empire waters. The analysts called attention to what they believed was the reappearance of Nagumo's old striking force—the same *kido butai* that had slammed Pearl Harbor, now consisting of four carriers . . . , two battleships, two cruisers, destroyers, and other warships. A merging of Kondo's Second Fleet with Nagumo's *kido butai* would put under one umbrella the most formidable naval force the Imperial Japanese Navy had yet assembled. Rochefort brought this new information together and told his superiors at Pearl and Main Navy [in Washington] what he thought: "Something is brewing." . . .

As the Imperial Navy assembled its far-flung forces, . . . Japanese naval communications exploded. At first the increase seemed a blessing, as it gave analysts more traffic with which to work. But then the volume got ridiculous. . . .

Station Hypo now received somewhere between 500 and 1,000 intercepts per day, a sizable number but far fewer than the Japanese transmitted. . . . Hypo was translating or partially translating only about a quarter of all IJN messages then being transmitted. That may not have seemed like much, but under the circumstances it represented an astonishing feat. It proved to be enough.

As more and more intercepts poured into Hypo, the character of the basement changed once again. From a monastery the place turned into a pressure cooker. Rochefort set the tone. During the run-up to the Coral Sea engagement he had begun working twenty- and twenty-two-hour days, taking time off only to sleep an hour or two in a small room in a corner of the basement where he had a cot. . . .

Rochefort's core group . . . worked similar hours, settling into a routine they would observe through May and into June. . . .

Gradually life in the basement took on a surreal quality. The only reality was the basement itself, the world of codebreaking. The outside world, the war itself, receded. . . . The problem was time. . . .

Staying awake was almost as much of a problem as solving JN-25(b). Rochefort recalled people using amphetamines. . . .

[LCDR Thomas G.] Dyer took both uppers and downers. "I couldn't keep awake sitting at my desk," he recalled. I complained about that, so [my doctor] gave me some Benzedrine sulfate. I would take that in the morning and Phenobarbital at night. They worked pretty well." . . .

Everything changed on 13 May. The day marked a turning point in the long-simmering debate over where the next Imperial Navy blow would fall. Before that day a fair case could have been made for any number of sites in the Pacific area, but after 13 May, reasonable grounds for doubting the main Japanese objective vanished.

On that day Hypo analysts decrypted, and Rochefort translated and interpreted, an Imperial Navy message pointing emphatically in one direction. The intercept left room for the Aleutians and Pearl Harbor only as secondary targets. It would take a while for this news to sink in; not all would accept it. Some would harbor doubts for weeks, but for those who examined Hypo's latest decrypt, there was now powerful evidence that the Japanese intended to invade two small islands 1,200 miles northwest of Pearl Harbor: the Midway Atoll.

The critical player in this discovery was an ordinary Japanese supply ship called the *Goshu Maru.* Since the outbreak of the war, she had plied the waters from Nagoya and Yokosuka on the Japanese mainland to Empire bases at Rabaul, Wake, and the Marshall Islands, ferrying fighter aircraft, aircraft engines, and spare parts. Early on Wednesday 13 May, while anchored at Wotje Atoll in the eastern Marshalls, the *Goshu Maru* received an important transmission from the commander of the Japanese navy's Fourth Air Attack Squadron, based in the Marshalls. [Hawaii's] radiomen intercepted the message and speeded it to Station Hypo, where it was decrypted and translated that afternoon by Rochefort and his analysts. The message told the *maru* to advance to Imieji, a small IJN base near Jaluit, "load air base equipment and munitions of the Imieji [sea plane unit] and proceed to Saipan."

Once there, the message made clear, the ship was to join the assembling occupation force—the by-now familiar term *koryaku butai.* It was then to "load its base equipment and ground crews and advance to Affirm Fox ground crews. Parts and munitions will be loaded on the *Goshu Maru.* . . . Everything in the way of base equipment and military supplies which will be needed in the K campaign will be included."

Two elements in the message jumped out at Rochefort: Affirm Fox, or AF, clearly a geographic designator, and the K campaign. . . .

Rochefort was satisfied. He had no doubts that AF stood for Midway. Nor did any other analyst in the basement. . . .

Rochefort didn't circulate that news instantly. There was always a lag of several hours between the arrival of an intercept by either teleprinter or jeep, its decryption and translation, and its release to the Navy's high command in Washington and at Pearl Harbor. Still, while the AF message was in raw form, intelligible but not fully translated and not ready for release, Rochefort knew he had something of the greatest importance. He knew what to do with it. . . .

He called [LCDR Edwin T.] Layton on their secure phone, realizing that Nimitz might require additional explanation. "I've got something so hot here it's burning the top of my desk." When Layton asked what it was, Rochefort told him what he had. "You'll have to come over and see it. It's not cut and dried, but it's hot! The man with the blue eyes [Nimitz] will want to know your opinion of it." . . .

The admiral was interested but, as luck would have it, tied up. He said he couldn't spare the time. But he did agree to send over to the basement his new war plans officer, Captain [Lynde] McCormick, a seasoned Navy officer who had served on battleships and commanded destroyers and submarines. McCormick would give Rochefort's material the hard-headed review Nimitz needed. He arranged to drop by the next morning, 14 May. . . .

Rochefort started out by giving McCormick a tutorial on traffic analysis, explaining how radio intelligence had captured the Imperial Navy changing its command structure and fleet arrangements to accommodate a massive invasion of Midway. He showed [McCormick] intercepts gathered during recent days—fragments of code and partial decrypts that fleshed out the picture he was painting. . . .

Rochefort walked McCormick through the *Goshu Maru*'s projected route—first stopping at Imieji, bringing on board air base equipment and munitions; proceeding to Saipan, loading supplies needed for the K campaign; joining the *koryaku butai* and advancing to AF. How did Rochefort know AF was Midway? "It was only logic," Rochefort said later. . . .

IJN transmissions following the 4 March raid [on Pearl Harbor] proved to be the clincher for AF as Midway. "The Japanese in their orders to the planes made mention of the fact that the Americans maintained a rather extensive air search from AF," Rochefort said. "So AF then had to have some airfield on it or seaplane bases and the only thing we had was, of course, Midway."

But if the case for AF was closed, as Rochefort believed it to be, much else about the Imperial Navy's fast-developing offensive remained unknown, including the two next most important facts about the operation: the date and time. . . . Nor did Rochefort and his analysts have, at least at this stage, an order of battle—a definitive lineup of the IJN forces that would be arrayed for the engagement. . . .

McCormick returned to CINCPAC headquarters convinced that Rochefort was correct about AF. He conferred with Nimitz. . . . On 14 May 1942, Nimitz became a convert to Hypo's Midway analysis. . . .

On Sunday evening, 17 May, at Pearl Harbor, CINCPAC received an "urgent and confidential" cable in the Navy's most secret flag officer's code. . . .

King was now comfortable with the Rochefort-Nimitz perspective. Aside from a detail or two, his thinking now closely paralleled Nimitz's: "Estimate that Midway attack may possibly be preceded by shipborne air raid on Oahu and that enemy intention includes effort to trap and destroy a substantial portion of the Pacific Fleet." . . . To blunt the IJN force, King recommended that Nimitz "make strong concentration Hawaiian area [and] employ strong attrition tactics and not repeat not allow our forces to accept such decisive action as would be likely to incur heavy losses in our carriers and cruisers."

— *AUTHOR* —

Elliot Carlson is a veteran journalist who has written for the *Wall Street Journal*, the *Honolulu Advertiser*, and *Newsweek*.

CHAPTER

41

America Deciphered Our Code

Translated by RADM Edwin T. Layton, USN (Ret.)

Proceedings, June 1979: pp. 98–100

Over the past twelve years, the war history room of the Japan Defense Agency has published about a hundred volumes covering the various Japanese army, navy, and air (naval and army) actions in the Pacific War.

Volume 43 of that *War History Series* is entitled "The Battle of Midway." Chapter 14, "Examination of the Failure of Our Operations," in a section entitled "3. America Deciphered [broke] our Code," describes the Japanese Naval Code D, and related matters. Pages 591–592 are presented here. Dates and time are Tokyo Standard Time Zone (–9). Comments by the translator are enclosed in double parentheses: ((. . .)).

Our Navy used many different codes/ciphers but an examination of their message texts indicates that the system most certainly broken was in all probability the Navy Code "D." Of all our regular codes, it was the one used principally for strategic matters. It was a five-digit mixed code made up in two volumes, one for sending and one for receiving, and was also provided with a separate table of five-digit random additives which, when applied in accordance with special rules for use with Code "D," completely altered the original code-test. Navy Code "D" was first placed in effect on 1 December 1940; Random Additive Table # 8 was put into use just before the start of the war, 4 December 1941.

Three other separate tables were also in use in conjunction with Code "D": (1) a Table of Grid Positions (in latitude and longitude), (2) a Table of Geographic Designators, and (3) a Table for Enciphering Dates (of events). The first of these used three *Kana* ((a syllabury representing the 50 basic sounds in the Japanese language: essentially the vowels A, I, U, E, and O alone or in combination following the consonants K, S, T, N, M, Y, R, and W)) plus two numerals. The initial *Kana* designated the selected 15 degree by 15 degree square (of the earth) of latitude and longitude, while the second and third *Kana* (using the 50 *Kana*) indicated the selected latitude and longitude within the above square, to the nearest 20 minutes; the two numerals further refined the designated position in the above 20-minute square to the nearest two minutes of latitude and longitude ((less than a two-mile square in the middle of the ocean)).

The second table, for geographic designators, consisted of two or three Roman letters, which were used to indicate a specific place, geographically; the first letter representing a common geographic entity (for example "A" represented "America," "P" stood for Japan's Mandated Islands) ((which they called their "South Sea Islands")); the second letter stood for a specific geographic place name; and if there was a third letter, that place was near the geographic place designated by the second letter (for example "PS" stood for Saipan, "PST" represented Tinian).

The third table was a different type, three-*Kana* table and was used for enciphering the date of an event or action; this table was arranged in *Kana* sequence ((analogous to our a, b, c . . . etc.)). Both these latter tables were used, without change, from the beginning of the war.

After the plain text of a message was written out, all the dates, grid locations, and geographic place names were then enciphered by using their respective tables, and this modified text of the message was then encoded into a series of five-digit code groups taken from the transmission volume of Code "D." Now, following the special rules for the use of the Random Additive Table with Code "D," another series of five-digit code groups were selected from the Random Additive Table and placed in sequence under each corresponding five-digit code group, and, using false addition—i.e., without carrying forward 10s—the final code text was arrived at, e.g.

A. Assume the text begins:	(("Enemy"	"Sighted"))	etc.,
B. Code text from Code "D"	52194	73442	etc.,
C. Random Additives from Table:	39682	44189	etc.,
Coded and Enciphered Message	81776	17521	etc.

Since the Random Additive Table consisted of 500 pages, each containing 100 random five-digit groups, the (false) addition of these additives to the code groups completely altered the original/modified code text of the original text, making it extremely complicated and very difficult to "break." It is said that our experts in cryptanalysis, and others connected with code and cipher matters, were unable to "break" it.

The Japanese Navy issued orders to replace Code Book "D" with Code Book "D-1" and to replace Random Additive Tables #7 and #8 with new Table #9 on 1 May 1942, although it is said that this had been originally planned for 1 April. According to the postwar statement of the officer in charge of code changes, this change in code could not be carried out because of the delays in distribution of the new code books, and that this change was made just before the sortie of the fleet for the Midway operation ((27 May 1942—Japanese "Navy Day"—the anniversary of Admiral Togo's victory in the Battle of Tsushima Straits, and the date the Japanese Carrier Striking Force sortied from the Inland Sea for Midway)). . . .

Breaking our code, even partially, undoubtedly increased the reliability of America's strategic estimates and gave them some definitive intelligence on our concepts of operations and furnished them with a substantial outline of our plans for operations in the future. There is no doubt that from early May onward a great many of our radio messages dealt with operational matters. As there is very little of that material now available, it is not possible to speculate as to which of those messages were broken, but subordinate forces undoubtedly communicated their intended movements to other forces concerned, based on the overall plan. There is no doubt that there were many radio messages concerning the "MI" ((Midway)) operation during the early days of May, but we have no reference material containing the geographic designators "AF" ((Midway)), "AO" ((Aleutians)) or "AOB" ((Kiska)); undoubtedly, there were radio messages concerning future reconnaissance operations by the ((auxiliary seaplane carrier/tender)). *Kimikawa Maru* and Submarine Squadron 1 that contained the geographic designators "AO" and " AOB." We have no radio files to show how the enemy confirmed "AF" to be Midway, but the diary of Commander Sanagi of the Naval General Staff contains the entry "MIDWAY IS SHORT OF FRESH WATER," and a radio message to that effect was indeed transmitted. ((This is apparently the author's answers [*sic*] to David Kahn's [*The Code Breakers*] and Walter Lord's [*Incredible Victory*] assertions of how U.S. intelligence learned in advance, that the Japanese objectives were Midway and Kiska.))

4. Our Intelligence Estimates (page 593)

Our navy was not able to break the American military's code(s); our intelligence appreciations and strategic estimates were primarily based on communications intelligence which was derived from enemy traffic analysis, call sign identification, direction-finder bearings, and the interception of plain language transmissions ((particularly those of aviators when airborne)). As an example, we could estimate when a strong American force sortied from port or was operating, because their air patrols in that area became intensified and expanded and many patrol planes' messages then came up on the air; we could also ascertain the general area of the enemy's intended attack because of their custom of stationing submarines in that general area, in advance of the planned attack.

However, it is said that since the beginning of the war, only a few of our many intelligence estimates based on communications intelligence really "hit the mark," and our navy's confidence in them was, therefore, relatively low.

— *AUTHOR* —

RADM Edwin T. Layton, a Japanese linguist, spent three years in the American embassy in Tokyo before World War II as assistant naval attaché. In December 1940, he was selected as ADM Husband E. Kimmel's combat intelligence officer, and he served in that role under ADM Chester Nimitz, ADM Kimmel's successor.

CHAPTER

42

Freedom of the Press or Treason?

By Grant Sanger, M.D.

Proceedings, September 1977: pp. 96–97

On 7 June 1942, *The Chicago Tribune* published an article entitled "Navy Had Word of Jap Plan to Strike at Sea." Identical articles, with different headlines, appeared the same day in the New York *Daily News* and Washington *Times-Herald.* At the time these newspapers comprised what was called the McCormick-Patterson empire.

For those readers under 30, the United States was at war with Japan; the Battle of Midway was still on; and the USS *Yorktown* (CV-5) was still afloat.

An investigation revealed that the article was written by a *Tribune* correspondent, Stanley Johnston, and filed from Honolulu. There had been a serious error when, some months before, he had not been asked to sign accreditation papers as a war correspondent attached to the Navy. This freed him from submitting for censorship everything he wrote.

It was fairly obvious to those who read the article carefully that a Japanese naval code had been broken. (U.S. Naval Intelligence called it JN-25-C.)

All of this is not new, but . . . at least three different authors have asked, and at the same time have told us, how Stanley Johnston did it!

On 9 July 1971, on the "Op-Ed" page of *The New York Times,* Clayton Kirkpatrick, editor of *The Chicago Tribune,* wrote that Johnston's "remarkably accurate deductions," from recent experiences in the Battle of the Coral Sea (3–6

May 1942), enabled him to tell readers in great detail the complex Japanese plan of attack on the Aleutians and Midway Island! Also, he returned to Chicago to write the story!

Then-Commander Edwin T. Layton, senior intelligence officer for the Pacific Fleet in 1942, placed Stanley Johnston in USS *Saratoga* (CV-3) which was just emerging from the San Diego repair yard and was rushing to help in action at Midway. In a U.S. Naval Institute "Oral History," Rear Admiral Layton relates that someone posted on the wardroom bulletin board a dispatch from Admiral Nimitz which revealed Japanese Admiral Isoroku Yamamoto's operation plan for the attacks on the Aleutians and Midway Island. It was there Stanley Johnston acquired his information!

Philip Knightley, in his book, *The First Casualty* (Harcourt Brace Jovanovich, 1975), finds Stanley Johnston in a naval transport en route to California. Somehow he put all the pieces together while the Battle of Midway was in progress after his arrival in Chicago.

So much for revisionist historians.

Back in Washington was Secretary of the Navy Frank Knox, a former publisher of *The Chicago Daily News,* who had no love for Colonel Robert R. McCormick, publisher of *The Chicago Tribune.* The wheels of law were set in motion, and on 7 August 1942, the U.S. Attorney General, Francis Biddle, announced that a Grand Jury would be convened in Chicago to investigate the facts of Johnston's article.

William D. Mitchell was chosen to head the government's legal staff. He was the first U.S. Solicitor General to become Attorney General, having been appointed to the former position in 1925 and the latter in 1929.

For five days, the editors of the three McCormick-Patterson newspapers and Stanley Johnston were called to testify.

In March 1959, this author was fortunate to meet the late Adlai Stevenson. I asked him what he knew of the Stanley Johnston article since he had been a special assistant to Secretary Knox from 1941 to 1944. Stevenson said that Stanley Johnston told the Grand Jury that when he abandoned the mortally wounded USS *Lexington* (CV-2) in the Coral Sea, on 4 May 1942, he was picked up by a motor whaleboat from the USS *New Orleans* (CA-32), along with 580 others. After dropping the survivors in Noumea, the *New Orleans* proceeded to Pearl Harbor, where she arrived on 26 May 1942. Being a war correspondent, Johnston had free run of the ship and was not deposited in Noumea.

One day while going to the bridge, he passed through the captain's cabin, where an open message lay on the desk. Johnston told the Grand Jury he did not touch the message, but memorized its content. This was the basis for his article.

Rear Admiral Theodore S. Wilkinson, then Director of Naval Intelligence, used his influence and power to prevent any naval officer from appearing before the Grand Jury. Hence, the jury knew nothing about the breaking and using of a Japanese naval code. William D. Mitchell, therefore, had to tell the press on 20 August 1942 that "no violation of the Espionage Act had been disclosed."

On 31 August 1942, Representative Elmer J. Holland stated on the floor of the House of Representatives:

> A bill of indictment means a public trial, Mr. Speaker. A public trial means public testimony. And public testimony in a court of law, with skilled counsel representing the defendants, means that military secrets, however vital, must be revealed if they are relevant to the defense of those accused.
>
> It is public knowledge that the *Tribune* story, published also in the New York *Daily News* and the Washington *Times-Herald,* tipped off the Japanese high command that somehow our Navy had secured and broken the secret code of the Japanese Navy.
>
> That is a priceless advantage in war—to know your enemy's plans through your knowledge of his code.
>
> Three days after the *Tribune* story was published, the Japs changed their code.

We now know that whatever changes the Japanese made in their code JN-25-C were neither major nor severe, for we continued to read successive generations of that code to the end of the war.

Clayton Kirkpatrick, in the aforementioned article in *The New York Times,* wrote, "The *Tribune* has never wavered in its conviction that the controversial story violated no law and that publication was consistent with a newspaper's privileges under the First Amendment. Only a distortion of history could support the insinuations that the newspaper violated national interests."

One might well ask, "Where were the Japanese spies?" If there were any in the United States in the summer of 1942, they would not or did not read *The Chicago Tribune,* New York *Daily News,* Washington *Times-Herald,* or the *Congressional Record!*

At the end of the war, the Statute of Limitations had expired, and no further legal action was desirable or possible. However, I agree with the late Judge Thomas D. Thacher, Solicitor General 1930–1933, that if the Navy had seen fit to present evidence to the Chicago Grand Jury in August 1942 on the background of how we got Admiral Yamamoto's plan of operation, those responsible for the article would have been indicted for treason.

Treason is defined in Article III, Section 3 of the U.S. Constitution as follows: "Treason against the United States, shall consist only in levying War against them, or in adhering to their Enemies, giving them Aid and Comfort. No Person shall be convicted of Treason unless on the Testimony of two Witnesses to the same overt Act, or on confession in open Court."

— *AUTHOR* —

Dr. Grant Sanger served in the Navy during World War II, rising to the rank of commander. After the war, he joined the staff of the Columbia Presbyterian Medical Center as a professor of clinical surgery.

PART VIII

Assessments of the Battle

Was Midway the beginning of the end of the IJN? Did the battle doom that great navy to ultimate defeat? Or was Midway just the beginning of an American effort to roll back the Japanese from their initial conquests and break through their island defenses? Did Midway have strategic implications for the war beyond the Pacific? Do we really understand the battle from a strategic perspective?

Was the U.S. victory at Midway a matter of luck as well as a matter of sound planning, proper training, and intelligent decisions? Can the battle be analyzed quantitatively, or was the outcome an accident? How can we know?

This last part deals with these questions. Its selections invite the reader to take a stand—to evaluate the evidence and decide just what role the Battle of Midway and the U.S. victory there played in World War II. It also invites the reader to consider how the U.S. Navy can best commemorate the Battle of Midway. What—if anything—does that long-ago battle mean for the men and women of the Navy today and in the future? What should it mean? Answering those questions is a fitting way to end the U.S. Naval Institute's story of the Battle of Midway.

CHAPTER

43

Foreword to *Midway, The Battle That Doomed Japan, The Japanese Navy's Story*

By ADM Raymond A. Spruance, USN (Ret.)

Proceedings, June 1955: pp. 658–659

Admiral Spruance wrote his foreword for *Midway, The Battle That Doomed Japan, The Japanese Navy's Story* by Mitsuo Fuchida and Masatake Okumiya (Annapolis, MD: Naval Institute Press, 1955) while en route from the Philippines, where he had served as U.S. ambassador since 1952.

It is always interesting and instructive after a naval operation or battle to try to get as complete a picture as possible from the enemy's point of view. During the Battle of Midway the "fog of war" was fairly thick, in spite of the excellent intelligence we had prior to it. For instance we were not sure of the fate of the [*Hiryu*] until a number of days after her sinking, when our Midway search located and rescued a boatload of survivors from her engine rooms. Similarly, the identity and the fate of the *Mikuma* were in doubt for some time. The last we knew of the *Mikuma* was when we photographed her late on the afternoon of 6 June, as she lay disabled and dead in the water, with survivors on her bow and stern. The next morning she had disappeared when one of our submarines investigated the area. The fact that Admiral Yamamoto with seven battleships, one carrier, cruisers, and destroyers was operating to the northwestward of Midway was not known to us for several months after the battle.

Midway, The Battle That Doomed Japan, The Japanese Navy's Story is a most valuable historical contribution to our knowledge of Japanese naval planning and operations, from the months leading up to the outbreak of war through the first six months of the war itself.

In reading the account of what happened on 4 June, I am more than ever impressed with the part that good or bad fortune sometimes plays in tactical engagements. The authors [Fuchida and Okumiya] give us credit, where no credit is due, for being able to choose the exact time for our attack on the Japanese carriers when they were at the greatest disadvantage—flight decks full of aircraft fueled, armed and ready to go. All that I can claim credit for, myself, is a very keen sense of the urgent need for surprise and a strong desire to hit the enemy carriers with our full strength as early as we could reach them.

Two other points may be of interest in reading the Japanese account of Midway. One is our retirement to the eastward for some hours during the night of 4–5 June. The situation toward sundown on 4 June was that Admiral Fletcher's afternoon search from *Yorktown* had located and reported *Hiryu;* then *Yorktown* had been disabled by two torpedo hits from *Hiryu*'s second attack; and finally *Enterprise* and *Hornet*'s planes had knocked out *Hiryu.* After *Enterprise* and *Hornet* had recovered aircraft, I decided to retire to the eastward so as to avoid the possibility of a night action with superior forces; but to turn back to the westward during the night, so that at daylight we would be in air supporting distance of Midway, in case the enemy were to attack there. The Japanese did order a night attack.

The second point concerns what occurred on 6 June, the third and last day of the battle. I had desired to chase and to inflict as much damage as possible on the retreating enemy. We knew, however, that the Japanese had strong air forces on Wake waiting to garrison Midway after its capture. I had decided in advance that I would keep outside of the 700 mile circle from Wake to avoid attack by these forces. When the day's action on 6 June was over—one search mission, three attack missions, and one photographic mission—we were short of fuel, and I had a feeling, an intuition perhaps, that we had pushed our luck as far to the westward as was good for us. Accordingly, we turned back to the eastward and headed for the oiler rendezvous which Admiral Nimitz had set up for us. Had we continued on to the westward during the night of 6–7 June, we would probably have run foul of Admiral Yamamoto and his superior Japanese forces the next morning.

Our success at the Battle of Midway was based primarily on the excellent intelligence which enabled Admiral Nimitz to exercise to the full his talent for bold, courageous, and wise leadership. He recalled Task Forces 16 and 17 from the South Pacific and, with no time to spare, had them lying in wait to the northeast of Midway. He disposed his available submarines to the northwestward of Midway. He strengthened the defenses of Midway itself with Marines, artillery, and aircraft, and instituted air searches over the critical areas. He sent forces to the Aleutians.

Admiral Fletcher, Commander Task Force 17, was also in overall command of Task Forces 16 and 17 and played a very important part in the battle. The *Yorktown*'s air group did splendid work as a unit until their ship was disabled, and after that the individual aircraft recovered by *Enterprise* and *Hornet* continued in the fight for the following two days.

I feel sure that all of us who took part in the Battle of Midway, as well as those who have studied it, will enjoy and profit by reading this Japanese account. The authors are to be congratulated on the research they have done and the book they have written.

CHAPTER 44

Underappreciated Victory

By James Schlesinger

Naval History, October 2003: pp. 20–23

This is an edited version of the remarks of former Secretary of Defense James Schlesinger to an audience whose members were commemorating the sixty-first anniversary of the Battle of Midway. The October 2003 issue of the U.S. Naval Institute's *Proceedings* magazine features an interview with Dr. Schlesinger.

As we honor those who turned the tide of World War II with a victory over ostensibly overwhelming force at the Battle of Midway in 1942—61 years ago—too few of us understand the battle's world-historic significance. It is essential, therefore, for us to go forth and proselytize.

I continue to be puzzled over the fact that it comes as something of a revelation to many people that this battle played such a crucial strategic role for the war in Europe. So the question before us is: Why is Midway not recognized as the crucial battle for the West in World War II, just as Stalingrad is recognized as a crucial battle for the Soviet Union? The comparative neglect of Midway is a great historical puzzle and, in a sense, a great injustice.

In relation to what British Prime Minister Winston Churchill and others called Grand Strategy, Midway was far more than a decisive naval victory. It was far more than the turning of the tide in the Pacific war [*sic*]. In a strategic sense,

Midway represents one of the great turning points of world history. And in that role, the battle remains underappreciated.

Consider the Grand Strategy of the Allies, which Churchill naturally preferred and President Franklin D. Roosevelt was eager to endorse. It was, quite simply, to deal with Adolf Hitler and with the German threat in Europe first. It had been embraced shortly after the Japanese attack on Pearl Harbor, at the Arcadia Conference. President Roosevelt clearly recognized and acted on the conviction that the Third Reich was the greater menace. Dramatic as the Japanese advance after Pearl Harbor had been, it was into slightly developed colonial regions—to be sure, those possessing rubber and tin. Yet, at its base, it was far less dangerous than Hitler's continuing advance, crushing and then organizing the industrial nations of Europe, while to that point almost entirely obliterating far more formidable resistance. But it was Japan that had attacked the United States, and it was Japan on which the anger of the American people had focused.

Though Churchill could almost automatically concentrate on Europe, it required considerable courage for President Roosevelt to carry through on the Grand Strategy. Germany's declaration of war on the United States on 8 December 1941 provided a small opening. Yet, had it not been for Midway, President Roosevelt could not have persevered with a Europe-first policy. Public opinion would not have allowed it. Indeed, even after Midway, he paid a substantial political price. In the mid-term election of 1942, the Democrats lost 44 seats in the House of Representatives, barely retaining control, with comparable losses elsewhere. In a subsequent poll of all the Democratic congressional candidates, the principal reason given for the debacle: "frustration" and fury at Roosevelt's Germany-first strategy, which translated into failure to punish the Japanese more aggressively for Pearl Harbor.

Nonetheless, despite the inclinations of the public, President Roosevelt recognized that the larger threat lay elsewhere, and he was prepared to pay the domestic political price for that larger national objective, defined by his Grand Strategy.

Consider the overall military situation in spring 1942. Japan was on a roll. The Philippines had fallen, including the final outposts of Bataan and Corregidor. The Japanese had swept through the Malay Peninsula from French Indochina, and on 15 February the supposedly "impregnable fortress" of Singapore had fallen to numerically inferior Japanese forces. The Dutch East Indies had been captured. Japanese forces were advancing into Burma and threatening India. Even Australia appeared to be a target. U.S. naval forces, significantly weakened by the attack at Pearl Harbor, appeared vastly inferior to the armada that Japan was gathering to advance eastward in the Pacific toward Midway—then possibly to the Hawaiian Islands or even to the U.S. West Coast. Additional Japanese victories would have made it politically impossible for President Roosevelt to continue to pursue the Grand Strategy of Europe-first.

Then came Midway. Through an extraordinary combination of the skill and courage of our pilots, splendid intelligence, prudent risk-taking by our commanders that paid off, and sheer good luck, the apparently inferior U.S. forces were victorious. This victory occurred despite inferior aircraft, ineffective torpedoes, the substantial absence of backup surface ships, and our overall numerical inferiority. The rest is well known. Four Japanese carriers had been sunk, confirming the dictum of Otto von Bismarck: "[T]he Lord God has special providence for fools, drunkards, and the United States of America." The Japanese offensive had been blunted. The Japanese fleet turned back toward the home islands, their opportunity for victory lost forever. President Roosevelt could then execute his Grand Strategy, with all that was to imply regarding the condition of postwar Europe.

After Midway, the United States could, to the chagrin of General Douglas MacArthur, turn its primary attention back to the European theatre. After the stunning surrender of Tobruk, which appeared to jeopardize both Cairo and the Suez Canal, President Roosevelt thus could accommodate the somewhat distraught Churchill's request for 300 of the new Sherman tanks to bolster the defenses in Northeast Africa, ultimately leading to the victory at El Alamein. The Battle of the Atlantic gradually turned with the steady improvement in antisubmarine warfare, thereby helping to ease the shipping shortage. By the fall, Operation Torch, the landings in North Africa, initiated offensive operations that ultimately led to the destruction of Field Marshal Erwin Rommel's Afrika Korps. The invasion of Sicily soon followed, succeeded by the invasion of Italy and eventually the landings in Normandy.

Had these events not taken place or been much delayed, it is possible the Soviet Union would not have survived. But if it had, and succeeded in its march westward, the face of postwar Europe would have been vastly different. Soviet forces would have deployed farther to the west. Germany likely would have been occupied in its entirety. The West's foothold in Europe would have shrunk, perhaps dramatically. The ability of France and Italy to survive communist pressures, precarious as it was in 1947, would have been much reduced. In brief, it was Midway, a battle in the distant Pacific, that shaped the face of postwar Europe.

Despite its crucial historic role, Midway gets scarcely more attention in our history books than the War of 1812 naval battles on Lake Champlain or Lake Erie—let alone the scant attention Europeans have paid to it. Let us reflect on a few other notable battles that turned the tide of history.

In 480, B.C., Athens had fallen to the Persian army, but Athens had in a sense survived in the form of its 200 naval vessels that Athens, prodded by Themistiocles, an early apostle of naval construction, had created. On 28 September in the straits of Salamis, before the very eyes of the Emperor Xerxes, the combined Greek naval force delivered a devastating blow, sinking some 200 Persian ships, with the loss of only 40 of their own. Xerxes, as Herodotus describes, had wanted to rule Europe as well as Asia. Fearing an attack on its bridges over the Hellespont, the Persian army largely withdrew. Greek (and European) civilization had been preserved. Indeed, begging pardon for a lapse from political correctness, Europe had been saved from Oriental Despotism. It was a naval battle that decided the fate of a civilization, a turning point in history.

Each year, the English-speaking world celebrates Trafalgar. Yet, it is not clear that even in the absence of victory England would not have survived. Midway, at a minimum, was the most decisive naval victory since Trafalgar, and perhaps the most strategically decisive victory since Salamis.

What of the crucial battles here in the United States? The Revolutionary War Battle of Yorktown is, of course, celebrated appropriately. Yet, after the Battle of the Capes, Yorktown was but the frosting on the cake, an almost inevitable triumph. The Battle of Saratoga, by contrast, is seen rightly as the turning point of the Revolution.

One is no doubt obliged to speak also of the Civil War Battle of Gettysburg. Yet, while Gettysburg may have been the high-water mark of the Confederacy, the outcome of the war was never much in doubt. Just recall the remarks of that military logistician, Rhett Butler, at the beginning of *Gone With the Wind,* when he rebukes some Southern hotheads by pointing to the overwhelming industrial domination of the North.

Then why, if Midway had such world-historic strategic significance, has it received so much less attention than it deserves? A recent documentary supposedly detailing the Pacific War, produced by Steven Spielberg and Stephen Ambrose, moves smoothly from Pearl Harbor to island hopping in the western Pacific, with scarcely a mention of Midway. How could such a momentous victory come to be overshadowed? There are, I believe, three prominent reasons.

First, the Europeans are quite naturally even more Eurocentric than we are. For them, the crucial battle for the European theater had to be in the European theater itself and not some remote spot in the Pacific. There is still little sense in Europe of what a vast enterprise the war in the Pacific was. El Alamein continues to be celebrated in the United Kingdom. Similarly, the Battle of the Bulge is celebrated annually here. But the outcomes of both those battles were almost foreordained by the balance of forces.

Moreover, the most prominent, indeed almost the canonical, history of World War II was written by Winston Churchill himself. And where would Churchill look? Not to some purely American engagement in the distant Pacific. Midway is mentioned only in Churchill's six-volume history, with no indication of how it shaped the outcome in Europe.

Second, Midway always has lain in the shadow of D-Day, which occurred two years later, but which has an anniversary that coincides with Midway in the calendar year. D-Day, which was truly touch-and-go, deserves all the attention it has received. But it should not come at the detriment of Midway itself. For without Midway, there would have been no D-Day on 6 June 1944, with all that that implies about the condition of postwar Europe.

Third, it is also in a sense the fault of the U.S. Navy itself. The Navy (take no offense) is both too shy in blowing its own horn and too complacent. Naming a carrier after a battle, for example, is considered so high an honor that nothing more needs to be said.

Midway may be the victim of intraservice politics or more exactly, intertribal fights. If one glorifies what was so dramatically a carrier victory, it might be interpreted to the detriment of the surface navy and/or the submarine force. So tact required a relatively discreet silence. Thus, regarding the crucial significance of Midway in world history, more than the submarine force has been the "Silent Service."

Our British allies perennially have demonstrated a masterly touch in displaying, not to say marketing, their armed forces and their accomplishments. Go to London. See the centrality of Trafalgar Square in the city. Observe that obelisk for Admiral Horatio Nelson towering over the Square. It all provides a setting and reinforcement for the annual celebration of the naval battle itself. By contrast, Farragut Square in Washington is a very dim competitor. And where, pray tell, is Midway? It is, of course, the Midway, a part of Chicago, named after the 1893 World's Fair—or a nearby airport, a transition point halfway across the United States.

Now hear this! It is time to go forth and proselytize and underscore the world-historic role of Midway. The battle and its veterans deserve no less.

— *AUTHOR* —

Dr. Schlesinger served as secretary of defense, director of the Central Intelligence Agency, secretary of energy, and commissioner on the Hart-Rudman Commission on National Security.

CHAPTER 45

The Great Midway Crapshoot

By Lee Gaillard

Proceedings, June 2004: pp. 64–67

From the perspective of the events two years later at the Marianas Turkey Shoot, the U.S. victory at the Battle of Midway—including the sinking of the Japanese carrier *Akagi*—was anything but a sure thing.

—

For poet T. S. Eliot, April may have been the cruelest month, but for the Imperial Japanese Navy, it was June. First was the disastrous defeat of 4 June 1942 at Midway. Then, two years later, came the humiliating 19 June air engagements off the coast of Saipan, a debacle now known as the "Marianas Turkey Shoot." And this is not to mention fleet losses in the Philippine Sea in the days following.

But far more than the Battle of the Philippine Sea and its Turkey Shoot subset (which historian Samuel Eliot Morison called "the greatest carrier battle of the war"), the earlier Battle of Midway is the contest that triggered crucial tectonic shifts in the balance of naval power in the World War II Pacific Theater, its strategic and historical significance overshadowing Jutland's and matching that of Actium, the Armada, and Tsushima. British military historian John Keegan considers Midway "the greatest naval victory of all time."

Yet, even though it reversed the course of the war in the Pacific and shaped the outcome of those air battles off Saipan two years later, Midway itself was in fact a real crapshoot in which luck played a major role.

The *Nautilus* was a large submarine, displacing almost four thousand tons when submerged. She was 371 feet long, armed with two 6-inch guns, and able to fire torpedoes from four tubes forward and two aft. As a part of TG-7.1 at Midway, she twice attacked Japanese ships on 4 June and was depth charged both times. Her great length and size made her slow to maneuver under water, but despite this handicap her skipper, LCDR William H. Brockman Jr., persisted in stalking Japanese ships until he had to surface to recharge his ship's batteries on the evening of 4 June.

U.S. Naval Institute Photo Archive

Fast Forward: The Turkey Shoot

D-Day for the invasion of Saipan (Operation Forager) was 15 June 1944, just nine days after the Normandy landings. Lieutenant General Yoshitsuga Saito, trying desperately to keep U.S. Marines from breaking out of their beachhead, was told to hold on and that help was coming—a large fleet commanded by Vice Admiral Jisaburo Ozawa. Convinced this was Japan's last chance to annihilate the U.S. Pacific fleet, Admiral Soemu Toyoda had ordered Ozawa to implement Operation A-GO immediately and accomplish what Japan had failed to do two years earlier at Midway.

As at Midway, the number of surface combat ships involved was staggering: 167. This time, however, the inverted odds favored the United States. What chance did Vice Admiral Ozawa and Rear Admiral Sueo Obayashi have against a massive U.S. fleet that outnumbered the Japanese not only in each ship category, but also two to one overall in both ships and aircraft? It was a fleet protected by F6F Hellcats instead of F4F Wildcats, incorporating 15 aircraft carriers (including 6 of the new 27,000-ton *Essex* [CV-9] class) and 7 battleships (among them two of the recently launched 45,000-ton *Iowa* [BB-61] class). Commanding the fleet were Admiral Raymond A. Spruance and Vice Admiral Marc Mitscher. A U.S. victory should never have been in doubt, even before first contact.

On 19 June, Ozawa launched four separate air attacks against the U.S. ships and lost 346 planes and pilots in huge air battles off the coast of Saipan. This was not to mention those previously destroyed in astute U.S. pre-invasion sanitizing air sweeps against supporting airfields on Guam, Rota, Iwo Jima, and Chichi Jima. Such unprecedented destruction of aircraft in just a few hours quickly earned this engagement the sobriquet, Marianas Turkey Shoot. By the end of the Battle of the Philippine Sea two days later, Japan had lost 480 aircraft, two oilers, three heavy cruisers, and three more carriers (the *Shokoku*, *Hiyo*, and the new *Taiho*). The navy that had begun World War II as the dominant force in the Pacific was mortally wounded.

These staggering Japanese losses represented part of an already steepening death spiral that had its origins at Midway. For Admiral Chuichi Nagumo and General Saito, the situation was too much. Following the fall of Saipan and defeat in the Battle of the Philippine Sea, they committed suicide; Prime Minister General Hideki Tojo resigned shortly thereafter.

The insurmountable challenge that had confronted Ozawa on 19 June was that by 1944, U.S. aces rotated home for combat flight training duty had in turn produced a cadre of superbly trained carrier pilots. Japanese aviators, on the other hand, were increasingly inexperienced, hamstrung by an inflexible military leadership insistent on keeping top pilots at the front. As attrition took its toll of skilled veterans, depleted ranks were filled by recent flight school graduates with rudimentary and inadequate combat skills. On that June morning off Saipan 60 years ago, Hellcat pilots scrambling to intercept incoming waves of attackers were astounded to see Japanese flight leaders tightening loosely strung formations, "giving on-the-job training to amateurs—in combat."

Such ominous symptoms had surfaced two years earlier when the fleet carrier *Zuikaku* could not participate in the Battle of Midway because replacements for pilots recently lost during the Battle of the Coral Sea were not yet combat ready. Even so, Tokyo refused to acknowledge that its improperly focused pilot training program contributed indirectly to the Imperial Navy's disastrous defeat on 4 June. Significant additional pilot losses at Midway, along with the sinking of four fleet carriers, severely degraded Japanese carrier capability in the months following, especially at the Turkey Shoot.

Midway as Turning Point

Therefore, despite higher aircraft losses registered in the Turkey Shoot and the Battle of the Philippine Sea, Midway stands as World War II's pivotal engagement in the Pacific. Had there been any trend before Midway, it was one of Allied defeats and continued Japanese expansion. With the Battle of the Coral Sea having set the stage, Midway reversed the course of the Pacific war [*sic*].

At this early point in the conflict, however, a U.S. victory was by no means assured. Although broken Japanese naval codes had provided critical advance knowledge, U.S. naval forces at Midway were still the underdogs. Excluding both navies' Aleutian detachments, the U.S. fleet was outnumbered two to one. It was a matter of 132 Japanese combat ships versus roughly 50 U.S. ships. Against these significant odds on 4 June 1942, the United States lost the carrier *Yorktown* (CV-5), the destroyer *Hammann* (DD-412), 147 aircraft, and 307 lives.

But for Japan, in its first naval defeat in 350 years, the losses were catastrophic: 275 aircraft, one cruiser (*Mikuma*), 3,500 lives, and four indispensable fleet carriers (*Akagi, Kaga, Soryu,* and *Hiryu*). Perhaps more devastating than the destruction of these essential carriers was the sudden elimination of the crucial core of Japan's elite naval pilots. They, too, could not be replaced, and their inexperienced successors subsequently became machinegun fodder for Hellcat pilots in the Turkey Shoot.

Thus, strategic control of the entire Pacific campaign passed to the United States and its allies. With the *Akagi*'s flight deck blasted minutes earlier by U.S. dive-bombers and the Japanese carrier already an inferno of blazing fuel and exploding munitions, perhaps Commander Minoru Genda phrased it best. On the bridge, he turned to his friend, Commander Mitsuo Fuchida. "Shimatta," he said. "We goofed." It was perhaps the most notable understatement of World War II.

The Crapshoot Factor

For his part, in an interview about Midway after the war, Admiral Spruance admitted: "We were shot with luck." Although it was a saga of preparation, tactical intuition, and courage, this stunning victory for Spruance and Rear Admiral Frank J. Fletcher could well be labeled the Great Midway Crapshoot.

True, one cannot forget cryptanalysts painstakingly cracking top-secret Japanese JN-25 naval codes and forecasting the exact date of the impending Midway attack. And no one can discount the courage of Torpedo Squadron 8 pilots, without fighter escort, boring in low against Japanese carriers, only to be annihilated by antiaircraft fire and defending Zeroes. Not one torpedo hit. Not one plane returned—"a gallant but useless sacrifice," Admiral Frederick C. Sherman wrote in 1950. Then, incorporating advice from Captain Miles Browning, Spruance risked launching pilots early and at extreme range, hoping to catch Japanese carriers recovering their Midway attack aircraft, their decks full of planes, fuel lines, and bombs as they rearmed. He did.

But much also hinged on random events and unintended consequences—what today might be called Chaos Theory. Therein lies the "crapshoot factor": luck. For example, on their way from Pearl Harbor to the secret staging area northeast of Midway, U.S. carriers were never spotted by Japanese picket submarines. Why? Because Imperial Headquarters refused to listen when Commander Shojiro Iura had strongly urged that Submarine Squadron 5's eight obsolescent subs be replaced with faster, more modern types for their Midway screening mission. The resulting extensive refurbishment, following a long deployment in southern waters, delayed departure for Midway "well past their scheduled date," and once under way, they were slow. When they arrived on station, U.S. carriers had passed.

Consider also the special blue-tipped .50-caliber explosive bullets B-17 Flying Fortress crew members, newly arrived on Midway, had shown to PBY Catalina gunners. The latter brought six of them on patrol to test against Japanese planes. Only because pilot Ensign Jack Reid had been begged to extend the patrol a little longer for this very purpose on 3 June could he report sighting the lead Japanese transport group just as he decided to return to base.

Furthermore, at crucial moments Japanese radios either were misused or did not work. Admiral Isoroku Yamamoto, in the new 64,000-ton battleship *Yamato* to the rear of Vice Admiral Nagumo's strike force, foolishly maintained radio silence, failing to transmit the PBY discovery of their transports and subsequent B-17 bombing runs. Nagumo proceeded as if his strike force were still undetected.

Then engine trouble and catapult problems caused a half-hour delay in the launch of Japanese scout planes from the cruisers *Tone* and *Chikuma.* In addition, an inoperative radio prevented another reconnaissance aircraft from reporting full U.S. carrier strength until after its pilot had landed on the *Hiryu* 20 minutes too late, with the carriers *Kaga, Soryu,* and *Akagi* already in flames.

Earlier, west of Midway, the USS *Cuttlefish* (SS-171) lurked submerged. Ira Dye, then a young ensign, was officer of the deck in the conning tower "and through the periscope saw the big group of planes go by that turned out to be our B-17s on their way to fruitlessly attack the Japanese." Indeed, during our first strikes against the invasion fleet, Midway-based B-26s and B-17s had attacked its carriers and cruisers (the B-17s from as high as 20,000 feet), dropping 322 bombs in the process. Not one hit. But, significantly for the outcome, gunfire and smoke from this futile fracas attracted attention of the USS *Nautilus* (SS-168), one of the largest submarines in the U.S. fleet. Approaching submerged, her periscope wake was spotted, and the *Nautilus* was driven deep by the destroyer *Arashi*'s depth charges.

Now out of formation, the *Arashi* raced to rejoin her group. Overhead at 14,000 feet, Lieutenant Commander Wade McClusky and his SBD Dauntlesses were lost and low on fuel. Through a fortuitous break in the clouds, he sighted the destroyer's wake and shrewdly matched his course with the *Arashi*'s. Minutes later he was over the Japanese carriers.

The Zeroes still were down low, having just slaughtered our defenseless torpedo planes and their pilots, whose sacrifice thus proved to be far from "useless." Selecting targets, McClusky and his pilots winged over into screaming 70° dives. And the rest, so the cliché goes, is history—naval, in this case.

Some say luck occurs when preparation meets opportunity; others cite beneficial unintended consequences. Both are right, of course. Just as Lieutenant Colonel James H. Doolittle's daring carrier-launched B-25 raid against Japan in April caused minimal damage but unexpectedly catalyzed Yamamoto's Midway operation, so at Midway a "fruitless" B-17 mission indirectly triggered an event sequence that would doom Nagumo's carriers. And numerically identical submarines played ironically parallel roles: just as the *Nautilus* (SS-168) and her periscope wake unwittingly lured the destroyer *Arashi,* forming an absolutely crucial link in the causal chain that led to three carriers' destruction, so did the Japanese submarine *I-168* destroy a U.S. carrier. On 5 June [6 June by the Japanese calendar], Lieutenant Commander Yahachi Tanabe fired his Model 89 torpedoes (with their smaller 649-pound warheads) to sink the destroyer *Hammann* and provide the coup de grace for the wounded *Yorktown.*

That evening, after the main encounter, the cruisers *Mikuma* and *Mogami* were detached to bombard Midway's runway, thus preventing land-based aircraft from taking off to attack the retreating Japanese fleet. Spotting and quickly turning to avoid the USS *Tambor* (SS-198), however, they collided in the dark. Damaged, they limped after their fleet, stragglers, easy prey for U.S. dive-bombers that pounced the next day, sinking the *Mikuma* and badly damaging the *Mogami.*

About the Clouds

Although complicating navigation and refueling operations, a weather front had—as at Pearl Harbor—cloaked the Japanese fleet's approach to Midway. Remnants of that same front then separated U.S. torpedo planes, dive-bombers, and fighter escorts, rendering them vulnerable to defending Zeroes as they bore down on Nagumo's strike force. On the other hand, those broken clouds lingering at 9,000 feet also evoked Commander Fuchida's postwar lament that Japanese "carriers had no time to evade because clouds hid the enemy's approach until he dove down to the attack." Then it was too late.

But what if Tokyo had listened to Commander Iura? What if there been no blue-tipped bullets, no catapult problems, no radio failures, no futile B-17 foray, and no clouds? Pick one, any one. It was a real crapshoot. And "if the battle had gone the other way," Admiral Fletcher emphasized later, "things would really have been in a hell of a mess in the Pacific."

— *AUTHOR* —

Mr. Gaillard's articles and reviews have appeared in *20th-Century Literature, Defense News,* the *Chicago Tribune,* the U.S. Naval Institute's *Proceedings,* and other journals and publications in the United States.

CHAPTER 46

Comment and Discussion: The Great Midway Crapshoot

By CAPT Chris Johnson, USN (Ret.)

Proceedings, July 2004: p. 10; also see L. Gaillard, *Proceedings,* June 2004: pp. 64–67

The account of the Battle of Midway has been a favorite of mine, but the way Mr. Gaillard tells the story, I hardly recognize it anymore. Luck? Crapshoot? It might look that way from a cold, academic point of view, but for those who have seen much of their life through binoculars on the bridge of a ship, laying the credit for victory at the foot of fortune is an exceedingly shallow way of explaining something much more heroic.

For much of my career as a surface line officer and aspiring tactician, I read and reread the major accounts of this battle and associated biographies with great professional interest. I have thought extensively about Wade McClusky's actions that day, and the concept of luck never crossed my mind. I see courage, fortitude, perseverance, and the willingness to listen to that inner voice that speaks to us in times of doubt and confusion. If McClusky had been an MBA, he would surely have analyzed his fuel state and returned home to fight later that day. And to believe that he simply saw a Japanese destroyer racing through the water and decided to follow is too trivial an explanation: Navy men know that these ships race through the water for a hundred different reasons, only one of which is to regain station. Something more simply had to be guiding him that day.

This is not an easy case to make in an over-rationalized society that worships fact-based reasoning and spreadsheets. I believe, however, that those who have served at sea know that intuition and instinct are powerful mental resources that frequently leap over logic and reasoning to provide compelling answers, often when things seem most desperate and confused. Sometimes we call that luck, probably because we don't know how to describe it to those who have not been in our footsteps.

The events surrounding Midway are indeed full of miscues, coincidences, and apparently random events—good and bad—but no more than occur in any fleet exercise. They were neither crucial nor extraordinary; they were the characteristic vicissitudes we have come to expect and to deal with. But what was extraordinary were the many acts of undaunted courage and unswerving determination to win that characterized the entire campaign, including Admiral Chester Nimitz's willingness to believe his cryptologists' analysis; his decision to give a cruiser sailor command of the carrier force; Admiral Raymond Spruance's decision to launch his raid early and at maximum range; and McClusky's unwillingness to give up when all seemed murky and very confused.

At the darkest hour of the Pacific War, at the very point of a spear that absolutely could not fail, McClusky refused to give in; he pressed on until he got a clue that in turn prompted the intuition to turn north. If you call that luck, then you don't begin to understand what the U.S. Navy does for a living, or how it has achieved such greatness with everyday American men and women like Wade McClusky.

— AUTHOR —

CAPT Chris Johnson was captain of *USS Vandegrift* (FFG-48) and the director of the Prospective Commanding Officers Course at the Surface Warfare Officer School in Newport, Rhode Island. After retiring from the Navy, he joined the Northrop Grumman Corporation.

CHAPTER

47

A Tactical Model of Carrier Warfare

By CAPT Wayne P. Hughes Jr., USN (Ret.)

Fleet Tactics, Theory and Practice (Annapolis, MD: Naval Institute Press, 1986): chap. 4 World War II: A Weaponry Revolution, pp. 93–97

A Tactical Model of Carrier Warfare

The model of carrier warfare compares with the Lanchester-Fiske model of gunnery in several ways. Fiske [commander, later admiral] envisaged a mutual exchange of salvos that would erode the residual strengths of both sides simultaneously. His purpose was to show the cumulative effectiveness of superior firepower, the dominance of a small advantage if the advantage could be exploited with coherent maneuvers, and the disproportionately scanty damage the inferior force would inflict, no matter how well it was handled tactically. . . .

The gunfire model of simultaneous erosive attrition does not work for the World War II carrier offensive force. That force is best represented as one large pulse of firepower unleashed upon the arrival of the air wing at the target. If, as was common, the second carrier force also located the first and launched its strike, simultaneous pulses of firepower would be delivered from both fleets. If the second carrier fleet did not find the first in time, it would have to accept the first blow. By then it would probably have located the first force and, if there were any attack capacity remaining, it would strike back.

To calculate damage from an air attack it is necessary to figure the defender's counterforce as the combination both of active defense (fighters and [anti-aircraft] strength) and passive defense (formation maneuverability and carrier survivability).

The *Neosho* and her sisters were high-speed tankers based on civilian designs. The *Neosho* was at Pearl Harbor on 7 December 1941, but was not attacked by the Japanese. Through the spring of 1942, the *Neosho* played an important part in sustaining U.S. carrier forces. Here, members of her crew struggle to complete an at-sea refueling of the *Yorktown* in early May. The *Neosho* was attacked and severely damaged by Japanese carrier aircraft at the Battle of the Coral Sea. She was sunk by a U.S. destroyer on 10 May 1942 after her survivors had been rescued.

Navy Department, National Archives

In the Pacific, effective carrier-based air attack ranges were comparable, 200 to 250 nautical miles, and neither side could outrange the enemy's carrier aircraft. So in carrier battles, the crucial ingredients were *scouting effectiveness* and *net striking power.* Scouting effectiveness came from many sources: raw search capability, including organic and land-based air reconnaissance; submarine pickets; intelligence of every kind; all enemy efforts to evade detection; and, not to be overlooked, the planning skill of the commander and his staff. Net striking power was made up of raw numbers of attacking bombers and fighter escorts, reduced by the active and passive defenses and the relative quality of material and personnel on both sides.

For our purposes now, scouting effectiveness will be determined simply by asking who attacked first or whether the attacks were simultaneous. As for striking effectiveness—damage inflicted—the crucial question is the value of a carrier air wing's strike capacity. Of course there is much room to examine tradeoffs in practice between attack aircraft used for scouting or attacking and fighters used for escort or [defensive combat air patrol]. These were problems air staffs had to deal with. I need not introduce them in detail here.

For the moment I will assume (not unreasonably, as we will see) that in 1942 one air wing could on balance sink or inflict crippling damage on one carrier and that cumulative striking power was linear: two carriers were about twice as effective as one and so could sink or cripple two. A very rudimentary table of outcomes after the first strike can be constructed for three cases: (1) the equal or superior force A attacks first; (2) the inferior force B attacks first; or (3) A and B attack together.

Table 4–1. First Strike Survivors (A/B)*

	Initial Number of Carriers (A/B)				
	2/2	4/3	3/2	2/1	3/1
(1) A strikes first	2/0	4/0	3/0	2/0	3/0
(2) B strikes first	0/2	1/3	1/2	1/1	2/1
(3) A and B strike simultaneously	0/0	1/0	1/0	1/0	2/0

*It is immaterial here whether the nonsurvivors are sunk or out of action. But later we will take survivors to mean carriers with operational flight decks and viable air wings.

If we allow the survivors of the initially superior but surprised force A to counterattack, the final outcome is:

Initial force (A/B)	2/2	4/3	3/2	2/1	3/1
Survivors (A/B)	0/2	1/2	1/1	1/0	2/0

It may be inferred from reading the views of naval aviators at the time that they believed a carrier air wing would sink more than one enemy carrier on the average. It is pretty clear that U.S. aviators thought the thirty-six dive-bombers and eighteen torpedo bombers that comprised an air wing at the outset of the war would sink or put out of action (achieve a "firepower kill" on) several carriers with one cohesive strike. They estimated that the enemy could do the same. They were obsessed with the need to get at the enemy first, and we need not accept their optimism to see the enormous advantage of striking first.

The picture gets interesting when the results for B, the inferior force, are perused. If both sides attack together B cannot win, but compared with its performance in the [CDR Bradley] Fiske model of continuous fire B does well—the enemy, while winning, can suffer severely. Even more instructive are the numbers when B successfully strikes first. Unlike B in Fiske's continuous-fire model, here B can be outnumbered 1:2 and establish the basis of future equality if he can attack and withdraw safely. He can be outnumbered 2:3 and establish the same after-action equality even if A is able to counterattack after absorbing the first blow. Evident as all this may be, to note it is crucial. . . .

Before proceeding we should roughly calibrate attacker effectiveness by reviewing [two of] the four carrier battles of 1942. . . .

For 1942 (not later) we will assume that:

> The carrier-air-wing effectiveness of every carrier on either side was equivalent.
>
> The defensive features of every carrier and its escorts on either side were equivalent.
>
> Japanese carriers physically separated should be counted. Deliberately or inadvertently they served as decoys and absorbed U.S. attention and air assets.

I indicate who attacked the enemy main force first. To compute theoretical results I show the results of all attacks, including diversionary actions, in the proper sequence. Although they do not enter into the calculations, initial and surviving *aircraft* strengths are also shown.

The Coral Sea, May 1942

On 7 May the U.S. force (the *Lexington* and the *Yorktown*) sent a major strike against the little Japanese force covering the invasion force (the small carrier *Shoho*) and sank the carrier. On 8 May the U.S. force and the Japanese striking force (the *Shokaku* and the *Zuikaku*) struck simultaneously. The *Lexington* was sunk; the *Yorktown* suffered minor damage. The Japanese *Shokaku* suffered heavy damage; the *Zuikaku*, not found by U.S. aircraft, survived undamaged.

Theoretical Survivors:	After 7 May	After 8 May
A Japan	2	0
B United States	2	0
Battle Synopsis:	Initial Forces	Actual Survivors
A Japan	2.5 CVs/ 146 aircraft	1 CV/ 66 aircraft
B United States	2 CVs/143 aircraft	1 CV/77 aircraft

NOTES: The small Japanese carrier *Shoho* is counted as one-half. The *Yorktown,* though damaged, is counted as surviving. She fought at Midway. The *Shokaku* suffered heavy damage and is not counted as a survivor. This battle was marred tactically by very poor scouting on both sides.

Midway, June 1942

The U.S. force (the *Yorktown, Hornet,* and *Enterprise*) successfully surprised the Japanese striking force (the *Kaga, Akagi, Soryu,* and *Hiryu*) on 4 June. Most of the circumstances are well known, but many have not noted that the island of Midway served in effect as a highly significant decoy. After the successful U.S. surprise attack, the Japanese counterattacked, and then the surviving U.S. force reattacked.

Theoretical Survivors:	After U.S. attack	After Japanese attack	After U.S. reattack
A Japan	1	1	0
B United States	3	2	2

Battle Synopsis:	Initial Forces	Actual Survivors
A Japan	4 CV/272 aircraft	0 CV/0 aircraft
B United States	3 CV/233 aircraft	2 CV/126 aircraft
. . .		

Resolution of Tactical Problems

What insight do these rough and ready comparisons yield . . . ?

1. *The tactical formation.* The first problem was whether to give each carrier its own screen or to put two or more carriers inside a common screen of escorts. The Japanese used single-carrier formations at Coral Sea. But at Midway they were forced by a scarcity of escorts to double up (in 1942 Yamamoto still believed that carriers would protect battleships, not the converse). . . .

   The decision to put two or more carriers in one formation depended on the effectiveness of the defense.

2. *Dispersal or massing?* . . . In 1942 the problem lay with the Japanese commanders, who were required to cover an invasion or reinforcement in all four of the big carrier battles. Their motives were mixed, for the Japanese also sought to draw out and defeat the U.S. Fleet. Admiral Nimitz, appreciating his inferiority, was not going to risk his fleet unless forced to do so. . . . Yamamoto must have believed, as American and Japanese naval aviators did, that a successful surprise attack by two big carrier air wings would destroy more than an equal number of the opposition. One carrier, it was thought, could sink two or three carriers clustered together, and therefore massing two or three units against one risked three units and gained nothing. If this was Yamamoto's rationale, then he was thrice confounded.

Code breaking gave the United States too much strategic intelligence. Air search radar gave too much tactical early warning. And, from the evidence, it can be said that the destructive power of a carrier air wing was not sufficient to justify the anticipation of a two-for-one effectiveness potential. . . .

3. *Offensive vs. defensive firepower.* . . . As the war progressed, the U.S. Navy strengthened carrier defenses. . . . Thus defensive considerations came to dominate and the destruction of aircraft became, all too subtly, more significant than the destruction of carriers.

4. *Daytime vs. nighttime tactics.* . . . As early as the Battle of the Coral Sea the Japanese tried a night attack. But it was surface night action that they continually sought. In three of the four 1942 carrier battles, the Japanese detached gunships to find U.S. carriers. Owing to American prudence or luck, the Japanese never succeeded in forcing an engagement. . . .

5. *Dual objectives.* . . . In 1942 . . . Strategic imperatives drove Yamamoto's tactics. Why were the Japanese caught at the Battle of the Coral Sea with a striking force of merely two carriers? It was because Yamamoto was in a hurry. His carriers were all busy. . . .

Yamamoto split his carriers for the Midway operations because he was in a hurry and his motives were mixed. With two geographical objectives, Midway and Kiska/Attu, he had to cover two invasion forces. . . . He need not and should not have squandered effort in the Aleutian sideshow, which drew away two small carriers. It was right, however, not to wait for the repair of his damaged carriers. By all reasonable estimates there could have been at most two carriers plus Midway's aircraft facing him. If he had waited thirty days more, the *Yorktown*'s wounds would have been healed, the *Saratoga* would have joined up, and in another thirty days the *Wasp* would have arrived from the Atlantic.

— AUTHOR —

CAPT Wayne P. Hughes has served as a professor of operations research at the Navy's Postgraduate School and as Dean of the Postgraduate School's Graduate School of Operational and Information Sciences. His most recent book on tactics is *Fleet Tactics and Coastal Combat* (2010).

CHAPTER

48

Midway: The Decisive Battle?

By Geoffrey Till

Naval History, October 2005: pp. 32–36

Admiral Heihachiro Togo's victory at Tsushima was clearly in Admiral Isoroku Yamamoto's mind when the Combined Fleet sailed from Kure on Tsushima, or Navy, Day, 27 May 1942. Just a coincidence? I think not. It should be remembered that Yamamoto was at Tsushima, was badly wounded in the leg, and lost two fingers of his left hand there. "When the shells began to fall above me," he said, "I found I was not afraid." Likewise, Chester Nimitz talked with Togo shortly after the battle, insisted on attending his funeral in 1927, and played a leading part in the re-establishment of Togo's shrine in Tokyo after World War II. As for Togo himself, he clearly had Vice Admiral Lord Nelson in mind when he signaled the fleet: "The existence of our Imperial country rests on this one action. Every man of you must do his utmost." And Togo's battle flag flew again from the carrier *Akagi* for the attack on Pearl Harbor 36 years later.

All in all, it is hard to avoid the conclusion that, for professional sailors, preparing for and pursuing the glorious and decisive battle was what naval warfare and maritime strategy was basically all about. It is a central part of the naval faith.

Decisive?

But what, exactly, is a decisive battle? One could say that it was decisive if it decided the outcome of a war on land or at sea. Obviously, there is plenty of room

On the afternoon of 4 June, Vice Admiral Kondo Nobutake, commander of the Japanese forces assigned to occupy Midway, ordered Rear Admiral Kurita Takeo, leading Cruiser Division 7, to send four heavy cruisers on a high-speed run to bombard Midway with their 8-inch guns. Their goal was to finish the task that the Japanese strike aircraft from the *kidō butai* had begun. Accordingly, Kurita steamed at high speed through the night, and he did not learn that his bombardment mission had been cancelled until he was ninety miles from Midway. Withdrawing at high speed, Kurita's cruisers encountered the American submarine *Tambor* on the surface. In attempting a high-speed turn away from the submarine in the dark, the cruiser *Mogami* collided with her sister the *Mikuma*. Both ships were damaged, but the *Mogami*'s crushed bow limited her speed to twelve knots. Rear Admiral Kurita ordered the *Mikuma* to stay with the *Mogami*, and the two ships steamed for safety, trying to get beyond the reach of U.S. aircraft. Marine Corps scout bombers from Midway found the two cruisers first, on 5 June, but did not sink either. That same day, B-17s from Midway also attacked the pair, but both cruisers escaped without serious damage. Worse was to come on 6 June, when dive-bombers from both the *Hornet* and the *Enterprise* assailed the cruisers, leaving the *Mikuma* sinking and the *Mogami* severely damaged. The close-up photo shows the crew of the *Mikuma* in the process of abandoning ship. Thanks to first-rate damage control, the *Mogami* made it back to Japan.

U.S. Naval Institute Photo Archive

for interpretation here—usually the degree of decisiveness lies in the eye of the beholder.

Certainly the decisiveness and indeed the very character of a battle may appear very different to the historian in the comfort and safety of retrospection than it does to the participant for whom it might well have been a life-changing or indeed a life-ending event. Even for the participants, the battle may have seemed very diverse. Their outlook and their interpretation of events will usually depend on who they were, where they were, and what they were doing.

In historical circles there is something of a vogue for the kind of history that seeks to tell later generations what it was like to be there—to recapture, if you will, the experience of battles like Trafalgar, Tsushima, or Midway. What such books reveal, however, is that there is no such thing as the experience of

Midway—instead we have experiences, in the plural, that reflect the manifold viewpoints of the participants. Battle is an intensely private affair that often has huge consequences for them as well.

These days, however, the notion of decisive battle has become rather unfashionable, in some circles at least. It is thought misleading, simplistic, and sometimes dangerous. Some argue, for example that this preoccupation takes sailors' minds off other things that need doing, possibly more urgently. Here, the argument goes that by focusing so much on getting ready for the Battle of Jutland, the Royal Navy took its eye off the humdrum business of protecting shipping against U-boats. These days, too, there are many other things that navies, and indeed military forces generally, need to be doing apart from fighting battles. Perhaps especially in regard to current events, we may need to be reminded of Napoleon's observation: "To conquer is easy, to occupy hard—to conquer is nothing, one must profit from one's success." It has led to widespread fears that some of us in the West are so absorbed by the need to win battles that we are neglecting the need to win the peace afterward as well—even though this, the end-state, is what should justify the whole business in the first place.

Decisive battles are also out of favor because all too often they are not decisive—in the sense that even great victories do not necessarily decide the outcome of conflict at sea, let alone on land. Trafalgar—surely the archetype of devastating naval victory in that Nelson destroyed two-thirds of the allied battlefleet—did not end the Napoleonic wars. Napoleon reversed its strategic effect a few weeks later at Austerlitz, and the war carried on for another decade.

Even at sea, the French were able to conduct a dangerous and ferocious war on trade and to compete with the British in a score of minor naval campaigns around the world. They also managed in effect to reconstruct their battlefleet. By 1813 Napoleon had another 80 line-of-battle ships in commission. In the 12 years before Trafalgar the British lost 87 warships to the French; in the ten years afterward they lost another 61. Arguably, Jutland actually made things worse for the British, because the Germans effectively abandoned their battlefleet pretensions and focused instead on U-boats, which turned out to be much more dangerous.

Problems in achieving decisiveness also derive from the increasing scale of naval warfare, especially in the 20th century. At Tsushima, the Japanese sank such a high proportion of the Russian fleet that virtually nothing was left to fight another day, and, in the time available, the Russians could not hope to replace their losses. But this was very unusual. British strategist Sir Julian Corbett called it "perhaps the most decisive and complete naval victory in history . . . not in our most successful war had we obtained a command of the sea so nearly absolute as that which Japan now enjoys." He wondered whether anyone would ever have such uncontrolled sway ever again.

Normally, only a portion of the adversaries' main fleets encounter each other in battle. The grander the physical scale of the war the more likely it is that fleets will be dispersed rather than concentrated, divided geographically and intent on different tasks in different areas. The usual pattern therefore is not of the single decisive battle but of a sequence of more or less indecisive battles that become decisive over a period when their results are added together. This is the reason why in the 20th century we discovered the key: the so-called "operational" level of war, where the focus was on winning campaigns through the delivery of a beneficially cumulative sequence of battles. Against this criterion, it is perhaps hard to conceive of any single battle in a monumental conflict like the [*sic*] World War II being decisive.

Part of a Sequence

So, against all this, how does Midway stack up?

In terms of losses there can surely be no argument. The Japanese lost four fleet carriers, some two-thirds of their air striking force (about 250 aircraft together with a large number of irreplaceable aircrew), and two heavy cruisers. More important, perhaps, they lost their aura of invincibility. For all these reasons Nimitz claimed it as "the greatest battle since Jutland."

But there is danger here. After Jutland, one British admiral complained that the press was inclined to score the battle as though it were a cricket match. But victory is better defined not by ships lost or captured but by what it makes possible. The point is that what happens afterward is the issue.

Midway was not decisive in the sense that everything after it was easy sailing. Four months later during the ghastly Solomons campaign, Nimitz summed it all up on 15 October 1942: "We are unable to control the sea. The situation is not hopeless, but it is certainly critical. . . . " That was partly because this was a different kind of close-quarter war in the narrow seas of the Slot, often at night, and partly because even after Midway the correlation of naval, air, and Marine forces between the Japanese and the Allies that were relevant to the situation was still dangerously close. The result was a grueling series of perhaps 50 closely fought surface and air skirmishes and battles in support of the Marines on Guadalcanal. Arguably it was the naval battle of Guadalcanal, 11 to 15 November, that really decided the issue of the Solomons campaign. "It would seem," said President Franklin D. Roosevelt, "that the turning point in this war has at last been reached." Which implies, of course, that Midway was not the turning point—it was merely a part of a cumulative sequence of operations that started in the Coral Sea and ended in the Slot.

Together, the effect of this campaign was fundamentally to change the nature of the war in the Pacific. At Coral Sea, Midway, and Guadalcanal, Japan's advance to a defensive perimeter that it might hold against the returning Allies was stopped. The captured papers of one Japanese officer contain the perceptive and prophetic comment: " . . . [T]he success or failure in recapturing Guadalcanal Island and the vital naval battle related to it, is the fork in the road which leads to victory for them or for us."

After these battles, the tide turned and the Allies moved up the Solomons chain toward Rabaul and down the Kokoda Trail in New Guinea. Afterward, the strategic movement was toward Japan not away from it. "The real war," said Japanese Prime Minister General Hideki Tojo a little later, "is just beginning."

Japan Had Already Lost

But there is another even more substantial argument that seems to cut away at the individual significance of Midway—namely that in strategic terms, the Japanese were already defeated by the time the battle was fought.

The Japanese suffered from a series of critical weaknesses that made strategic failure against the United States highly probable—almost inevitable. Most obviously, they had a romantic view of war that paid far too much attention to the concept of glorious victories for the emperor and too little, for example, to the mundane business of protecting the merchant shipping on which their empire absolutely depended. Relations between the army and navy were so bad they made Nimitz and Army General Douglas MacArthur look like close co-workers in comparison. The Japanese navy lacked rational decision- and policy-making systems and had a permanent penchant for dispersing their forces rather than concentrating them at vital points. This was particularly evident at Midway and was based in large measure on monumental failures in intelligence and consequent assumptions that their adversary would cooperate in his own destruction. They had too little appreciation of the need, on the one hand, to accumulate sufficient stockpiles of strategic materials and, on the other, to establish a method to replace losses in key personnel—especially pilots and aircrew—and important classes of warships.

Even more substantially, and as Yamamoto himself pointed out, the United States was superior in industrial resources. Once these were effectively mobilized, the Japanese would find themselves confronting a military-industrial power that would out-produce any losses in materiel the Japanese could inflict and dwarf Japan's productive capacity. For each major warship the Japanese built after Midway, the Americans built 16. The Japanese built another seven carriers before the war ended; the Americans more than 100. The Americans produced 300,000 aircraft by August 1945; the Japanese rarely managed 12,000 a year, and the quality of those aircraft and the skill of the men flying them dropped off significantly—so much so that the Japanese logically concluded that since they were unlikely to return from their missions anyway, they might as well be turned into kamikaze pilots. In this calculus, the Japanese were bound to lose in the end. To quote Winston Churchill on the later stages of the battle of the Atlantic, "All the rest was merely the proper application of overwhelming force."

War as Business or as Art?

What was basically at issue, it could be argued, were two styles of war, as exemplified perhaps by the nature of the key decision-makers on both sides at the strategic and operational level. On the American side, there was the relentless Admiral Ernest King arguing for a Pacific-first priority and the cool rationalism of Admirals Nimitz and Raymond Spruance.

On the Japanese side, by strong contrast, operational policy emerged from a miasma of compromises and unquestioned assumptions. In Japanese planning, a key role was played by Captain Kameto Kuroshima, the so-called "God of Operations" who produced his plans after long sessions meditating naked in his cabin, drinking heavily, chain-smoking, and burning incense. His inspirational role was very much in the tradition of the medieval warrior-monk Musashi. He never washed and perhaps unsurprisingly never married but exerted a tremendous mystic influence over later generations of Japanese, including Yamamoto himself. Musashi derived his concept of strategy from his sword-fighting expertise in one-on-one duels; perhaps it was partly because of this and their general reverence for the man that the Japanese tended to treat the concepts of war, campaign, battle, and victory as though they all meant the same thing. It was a style of war beyond Western concepts of good sense, and surely it was bound to fail.

The result of all this has been described by one perceptive analyst in these words: "The U.S. Navy regarded men and machines as interchangeable parts and battle as a managerial exercise, to be embarked upon with a strict eye on profit and loss, while the Japanese saw it as an art form in which will and élan were the decisive elements." Putting this all together, the conclusion seems inescapable. Midway merely accelerated a process that was inevitable, and so hardly counts as a war-changing event.

But this approach is surely overdrawn, for war is not simply a matter of profit and loss, of industrial superiority, and of more efficient decision-making systems. All history suggests that those who think of victory as achieved simply through the accumulation of overwhelming superiority in numbers and weaponry are often shown to be mistaken. After all, both at Trafalgar and Midway the strongest side on paper actually lost.

A Necessary Victory

Of course this can be explained by such factors as better training, intelligence, and luck, but there is also another crucial human, political, and moral dimension to it all. An interesting observation is that Midway was indeed a decisive event, for without it, Roosevelt would have found it impossible to hold the line against those who wanted a reversal of priorities between the European and the Pacific theaters of war. A success at Midway was necessary in order to satisfy the American public's need for retribution after Pearl Harbor. Without it, and still more after a defeat at Midway, the American contribution to the war in Europe, and indeed in the Atlantic, would have to have been reduced in scale and delayed in time—with enormous if incalculable consequences. Midway, in short, was a necessary victory. Losing it could have been decisive in ways impossible to predict, but for moral and political reasons not that closely related to the materiel situation before and after.

Finally, victories do not always go to the side with the largest forces or the best weaponry. In fact Midway was not won by the superior side from either point of view. It was three American carriers against four Japanese, and the odds would have been even worse had the Japanese disposed their forces more wisely. What mattered, at the successive decisive points of the battle, was the individual skill, the fighting determination of people, and the straightforward, self-sacrificing heroism of individuals such as Lieutenant Commander John Waldron, who led his squadron of Devastators from the *Hornet,* or Ensign Albert Earnest, who got his aircraft home with his turret gunner dead, his radioman unconscious, his controls wrecked, and more than 70 hits on his aircraft. The sum of actions like this produced not only narrow tactical and operational results in terms of ships sunk and aircraft shot down, but achieved a crucial moral effect for the United States and its allies.

To summarize, we should not commemorate the undoubted victory at Midway merely as a single battle, important in itself. Nor should we base our view on Midway simply on a comparison of ships sunk or aircraft shot down on both sides. Nor, even, should we remember the battle as what was in effect the U.S. Navy's first-ever large-scale fleet engagement, important though that was. Instead we should recognize Midway as an inspiring symbol of a decisive campaign that started in the Coral Sea and ended at Guadalcanal. And so when we remember the brave men who served at Midway, we should also remember the equally brave ones who went before and came after them in that grand and war-reversing campaign.

— AUTHOR —

Dr. Till was dean of academic studies at the British Joint Services Command and Staff College and was a visiting scholar at the U.S. Naval Postgraduate School, Monterey, California, and the foundation chair in military affairs at the U.S. Marine Corps University, Quantico, Virginia. He is author of *Airpower and the Royal Navy 1914–1945, Seapower: A Guide for the 21st Century,* and *Maritime Strategy and the Nuclear Age.* This article is adapted from a speech presented at the Navy's 2005 Battle of Midway Commemorative Dinner.

CHAPTER

49

Descending in Flame

By Mark R. Peattie

Sunburst, The Rise of Japanese Naval Air Power, 1909–1941 (Annapolis, MD: Naval Institute Press, 2001): chap 7 Descending in Flame, pp. 174–175

First, it must be said that the nature of the Japanese defeat [at Midway] has been frequently misunderstood. In strategic terms, there is little doubt that it was a momentous reversal in the tide of Japanese conquest in the Pacific, but it was not the "Battle that Doomed Japan." In material terms, the destruction of four fleet carriers . . . was, of course, a stunning loss, but other carrier hulls were on the slipways or being completed. One estimate is that the navy lost some 228 aircraft at Midway, but at this point in the war the navy was not suffering severe shortfalls in aircraft production.

Nor is it apparent that the defeat caused catastrophic losses to trained aircrews, the most precious element in Japanese naval aviation. . . .

[C]areful sifting of the evidence in recent years has shown that in fact only about 110 Japanese fliers died at Midway (most of them from the *Hiryu*), no more than a quarter of the carrier aircrews the navy had at the start of the battle. American aircrew losses were actually greater than those of the Japanese, if Marine Corps aviators from Midway Island itself are included in the tally. Surprisingly, moreover, the morale of Japanese pilots seems to have been higher than ever after the battle. They were unimpressed by the combat skills of their American adversaries, and the superiority of their own skills seemed confirmed by the fact that they had crippled an American carrier. Nor did Japanese aircrew performance fall off sharply after Midway. In interviews after the war, Japanese navy men contended that the high quality of the navy's air arm continued through at least the fall of 1942. In fact, the really serious aviation personnel losses at Midway were those of skilled aircraft maintenance crews, who accounted for perhaps twenty-six hundred of the three thousand shipboard personnel who went down with the four carriers.

CHAPTER

50

Midway: The Story That Never Ends

By Thomas B. Allen

Proceedings, June 2007: pp. 62–67

On the sixty-fifth anniversary, we are still finding out what happened at Midway in the sky and sea in late spring 1942.

Few World War II battles illustrate the rewriting of history better than the Battle of Midway. First news of that key engagement came on 6 June 1942, only two days after Admiral Isoroku Yamamoto, commander-in-chief of the Japanese Combined Fleet, launched an attack on the U.S. base at Midway, two small islands that form a coral atoll about 1,300 miles northwest of Hawaii. If news reports are the first drafts of history, then the 6 June story in the *New York Times* was a succinct example of that adage. The story, datelined Washington, began: "The capital received tonight official word that United States forces were scoring a crushing victory over Japanese naval units in the greatest air-sea battle fought thus far in World War II." Admiral Chester W. Nimitz, commander-in-chief of the Pacific Fleet, added in a communiqué dated 6 June: "Pearl Harbor has now been partially avenged."

Then, on Sunday, 7 June, the *Chicago Tribune* published its own version of the battle under a bank of headlines:

Jap Fleet Smashed By U.S. 2 Carriers Sunk At Midway
Navy Had Word Of Jap Plan To Strike At Sea
Knew Dutch Harbor Was A Feint

At Midway, the *New Orleans* was part of the screen for the carriers *Enterprise* and *Hornet* (TF-16). Sister ship *Astoria* became Admiral Fletcher's emergency flagship after the *Yorktown* was bombed on 4 June. The first year of the war for the *New Orleans* was filled with action. The ship was caught at Pearl Harbor on 7 December 1941 under repair and without power but was not seriously damaged. At the Battle of the Coral Sea (8 May), the crew of the *New Orleans* saved 580 members of the crew of the sinking carrier *Lexington.* After Midway the *New Orleans* screened the carrier *Saratoga* in the waters near Guadalcanal, escorting her to Pearl Harbor after the carrier was torpedoed on 31 August. The *New Orleans* was herself torpedoed and lost her bow at the Battle of Tassafaronga on 30 November 1942, but her crew kept her afloat and got her back to Pearl Harbor. After repairs in the United States, the *New Orleans* served out the rest of the war in the Pacific.

U.S. Naval Institute Photo Archive

The story also appeared in the *New York Daily News,* the *Washington Times-Herald,* and four other Midwestern newspapers associated with the *Tribune.* Somehow, the *Tribune* knew far more than the Navy had revealed. The story gave the names of 4 Japanese carriers, 2 battleships, 2 heavy cruisers, and 12 destroyers, seemingly lifted from a secret Navy document. Two headline phrases—Navy Had Word and Knew Dutch Harbor Was A Feint—suggested that the United States had some way of learning about Japanese operational plans. The *Times-Herald*'s headline was more explicit: "U.S. Knew All About Jap Fleet. Guessed There Would Be A Feint At One Base, Real Attack At Another."

Midway Was Main Objective

Part of the massive, two-pronged Japanese force had sailed to the Aleutians and bombed Dutch Harbor, site of a U.S. naval base on the island of Unalaska. The Japanese also landed troops on Attu and Kiska, an operation that the Navy did not confirm until 12 June. Japanese strategists believed that the two simultaneous

The new submarine tender *Fulton* at Pearl Harbor in May 1942. The *Fulton* carried the *Yorktown*'s survivors to Pearl Harbor after the Battle of Midway. The first of a new and larger class of submarine tenders authorized in 1938, the *Fulton* was commissioned in 1941. In this photo, a submarine is moored alongside the tender. The *Fulton* could repair and replenish submarines at forward bases and offer food, showers, and other support to submarine crews. She was the ideal ship to return the *Yorktown*'s survivors to Pearl Harbor.

Navy Department, National Archives

attacks would lure U.S. carriers to their doom, but no U.S. carriers went to the Aleutians, and the *Tribune* story obligingly provided the Japanese with a reason: The Navy knew Midway was the main objective.

The *Tribune* story did not say the Navy had broken Japanese naval codes. But the suggestion was so strong that Secretary of the Navy Frank Knox, former publisher of the *Chicago Daily News*, immediately contacted the *Tribune* and other newspapers. Without telling the editors why, Knox asked them to halt further coverage of the story. Knox's action was not enough for Admiral Ernest J. King, commander-in-chief of the U.S. Fleet. Infuriated at the leak, he ordered an investigation. Thus began the long campaign to protect a momentous secret.

The Leak

The leak investigation quickly established how the *Tribune* had obtained its information. The USS *Lexington* (CV-2) had been sunk on 8 May in the Battle of the Coral Sea. Among the survivors was Stanley Johnston, a *Tribune* war correspondent. Johnston and many other survivors were taken aboard the transport USS *Barnett* (AP-11), which was bound for San Diego. He probably shared a cabin with his friend, Commander Morton T. Seligman, executive officer of the *Lexington*.

At sea, Johnston read a decoded intelligence bulletin, transmitted on 31 May. It described the order of battle of the Japanese fleet heading for Midway. Whether Johnston saw the bulletin with or without Seligman's permission was never determined. When investigators compared the bulletin to the *Tribune* story, they were stunned to discover that the description of the Japanese fleet was an "almost verbatim" copy of the bulletin. The message containing the bulletin had been transmitted through communications channels available to other ships, which were expected to ignore traffic not addressed to them. *Lexington* officers, including Seligman, served as watch-standers on the *Barnett* and probably routinely decoded the message, although it had nothing to do with the *Barnett*.

The information in the bulletin had been gleaned from the decoded intercepts that had shaped Nimitz's strategy. Intelligence officers at Pearl Harbor had learned of the existence of a massive Japanese fleet and had deduced its probable objectives: Midway and the Aleutians. Analysis of the intercepts had produced a recommendation about the best place to assemble an attack. All of this work was now at least indirectly revealed by the *Tribune* story.

That story had its origin in Chicago, where Johnston headed after disembarking in San Diego. When he began writing his account of the Coral Sea battle, he mentioned to his editor, J. Loy "Pat" Maloney, that he also had some exclusive information about Midway. He would not reveal his sources. Maloney rewrote Johnston's Midway story, attributing unofficial information to "reliable sources in the Navy Department" and "naval intelligence." He also put a fake Washington, D.C., dateline on the story and did not add a byline.

Walter Winchell versus Robert McCormick

The next mention of Midway secrets was far more worrisome to the code breakers. On 5 July, gossip columnist and radio star Walter Winchell mentioned the Coral Sea and Midway battles and, in his staccato voice, excitedly added: "When the history of these times is written, it will be revealed that twice the fate of the civilized world was changed by intercepted messages." Two days later, in his column "On Broadway" in the *New York Daily Mirror,* Winchell attacked Colonel Robert R. McCormick, publisher of the *Tribune,* saying he "allegedly printed the lowdown on why we won at Midway—claiming that the U.S. Navy decoded the Japs' secret messages." There had been no mention of "secret messages" in the *Tribune* story. But Winchell added that gossipy touch, and the fact that he was a lieutenant commander in the Naval Reserve buttressed his authority.

Secretary Knox, under pressure from Admiral King and Navy intelligence officers, asked Attorney General Francis Biddle to prosecute the *Tribune* and Johnston under the 1917 Espionage Act. But, fearing disclosure of code-breaking secrets in an espionage trial, the Department of Justice quietly closed the case.

Pearl Harbor code breakers believed that the damage had already been done. A key code, Japanese Fleet General-Purpose System, was changed on 15 August, only two months after an earlier change. Other alterations were made in "virtually all Japanese codes and ciphers," and it took cryptanalysts nearly four months of around-the-clock work to crack the new version and once again penetrate the Japanese navy's operational radio traffic.

By the end of June the U.S. Navy had announced the full toll of Japanese losses: four aircraft carriers and a heavy cruiser sunk, two destroyers and a cruiser damaged. The major American loss—the sinking of the USS *Yorktown* (CV-5)—was not officially disclosed until September. Even after the war ended in 1945, many details of the battle of Midway were still hazy and basically known only from an American perspective.

Winchell was right. History some day would hail the code breaking as a crucial contribution to victory in the Pacific. But it would take a while for history to reveal that contribution.

Morison: No Reference to Code Breaking

In May 1942, Samuel Eliot Morison, a distinguished professor of history at Harvard, at the suggestion of his friend, President Roosevelt, had been commissioned a lieutenant commander in the Naval Reserve and given the mission of writing the World War II operational history of the U.S. Navy as a seagoing historian-eyewitness. He was serving in the Atlantic during the battle of Midway, but he later sailed with Pacific Fleet forces in operations from Guadalcanal to the Marianas.

When he returned to Harvard after the war, he continued to work on his 15-volume *History of United States Naval Operations in World War II.* In his richly detailed account of Midway (first published in Volume V in 1949), he did not mention the code-breaking, writing only, "Intelligence fed him [Nimitz] a fairly accurate account of Japanese plans and preparations, deduced from various bits of information from a variety of sources." In a tenth-anniversary article in 1952, Morison still made no reference to the intercepts and code breaking.

The Truth, 25 Years Later

Captain Roger Pineau, a Japanese language specialist who assisted Morison, knew about the Navy's cryptographic success. But even when he realized Morison was not getting the cryptographic secrets of Midway (or Pearl Harbor), Pineau had to remain silent. He "eventually arranged officially for Morison to be let in on the secret—but he could never write about it." Not until 1967, in Walter Lord's classic book, *Incredible Victory*, did the public begin to learn about the code breakers' role in the battle.

That knowledge seemed to make the Midway story complete: Nimitz, responding to what would be an extraordinarily accurate intelligence analysis, had sent his three carriers—the *Hornet* (CV-8), *Enterprise* (CV-6), and *Yorktown*—to a rendezvous point for an attack on the Japanese fleet. The intelligence analysts' prediction—that aircraft from four Japanese carriers would attack Midway—came true, beginning at 0553 on 3 June when radar on Midway spotted Japanese aircraft 93 miles to the northwest. Twenty Marine F2A-3 Buffalo and six F4F Wildcat fighters flew to intercept the Japanese. Fifteen Marine fighters were shot down and seven damaged. Two Zeros were knocked out. The Japanese bombers got through under severe antiaircraft fire. Seven planes went down, and the attack leader radioed the carriers: "There is need for a second attack wave." Torpedo-carrying planes from Midway—six Navy-piloted TBF-1 Avengers and four Army Air Forces B-26 Marauder bombers—attacked the carriers. Every released torpedo missed.

No One Came Back

Two damaged B-26s survived, along with one Avenger piloted by Ensign Bert Earnest. Shells from Japanese Zeros killed his gunner. Other shells knocked out the hydraulic system and elevator wires. A shell fragment hit the other crewman. A bullet tore through Harry Ferrier's baseball cap and grazed his scalp, knocking him out. Somehow [Earnest] regained control of the plane. Earnest had no compass, but he saw black smoke rising from Midway. He headed that way. With 70-odd holes in his plane, he skidded in for a landing, "I waited for the other people to come back," Earnest said. "But no one came back." Every other Avenger was shot down, and all the other men were killed. He earned a Navy Cross for his attack on the Japanese and a second for managing to fly his riddled plane back to Midway. He was awarded a third Navy Cross later in the war.

Meanwhile, a Japanese search plane reported "what appears to be ten enemy surface ships" about 200 miles from the Japanese carriers. At almost the same moment, the *Hornet* and the *Enterprise* began to launch their aircraft toward what they believed to be two Japanese carriers. The *Hornet*'s 15-plane Torpedo Squadron Eight flew into a swarm of Zeros and an inferno of antiaircraft fire. The Japanese defenders wiped out the squadron. The only survivor of 30 men was Ensign George H. Gay, whose riddled plane cart-wheeled into the water with the radioman-gunner dying and Gay wounded. A PBY Catalina rescued him on 5 June.

Torpedo bombers kept coming in at low levels. As Norman Polmar points out in *Aircraft Carriers:* "Of the 41 carrier-based torpedo planes that had attacked the Japanese ships only four survived the massacre. . . . But the disastrous attack of the three torpedo squadrons was the final event leading to the conditions that made possible the destruction" of the Japanese carriers.

While Zeros and antiaircraft crews concentrated on the torpedo planes, Douglas SBD Dauntless dive bombers from the *Enterprise,* far overhead, went into steep dives over two Japanese carriers, the *Akagi* and *Kaga.* SBDs from the *Yorktown* dived on a third, the *Soryu.* Within minutes, the three Japanese carriers were aflame and doomed. The fourth carrier, the *Hiryu,* had only hours to live. She, too, would be destroyed by dive bombers, but she had already launched dive bombers that had mortally damaged the *Yorktown.*

Jammed Japanese Flight Decks?

Accounts of the battle, beginning with the first published Navy version, usually say that the Japanese carriers' flight decks were jammed with fully fueled and armed planes when the American dive bombers tipped over and dropped their bombs. Pilots diving on the carriers did see some planes on the flight decks. Most of them were defensive aircraft—fighters assigned to combat air patrol. But writers on the battle assumed that offensive aircraft were crowding the decks. That assumption was based on two entangled decisions by Vice Admiral Chuichi Nagumo, commander of the carrier striking force.

Nagumo had ordered a second attack on Midway, and so aircraft that returned from the first attack had to be refueled and rearmed, along with other aircraft assigned to the second strike. But, reacting to the search plane report that a U.S. carrier was within striking distance, Nagumo ordered that the Midway-bound aircraft be rearmed: The bombs for an attack on ground targets had to be replaced by torpedoes and armor-piercing bombs for an attack on ships.

Recent Revisionism

The next revision of the Midway story has taken up the crowded-deck issue and the question of Nagumo's decision, reexamining what a recent chronicler of the battle, Dallas Woodbury Isom, called the "standard scenario": A "befuddled" Nagumo "refuses to accept the reality of the situation, 'dithers,' and then in a series of blunders throws away any chance he had of countering the American carrier threat." The Japanese, Isom wrote in the *Naval War College Review,* did not make "idiotic mistakes, as is commonly implied." According to Isom's view, Nagumo assumed he could not make a quick, effective attack with what he had available: unescorted dive-bombers.

Isom essentially accepted the crowded-decks aspect of the "standard scenario," inspiring criticism from a new set of Midway writers, also writing in the *Naval War College Review.* They pointed out that aerial photographs "show no strike planes on deck, only a handful of fighters." In reality, they wrote, the rearming and most of the refueling was done on hangar decks below the flight decks.

Both Isom and his critics followed up the *Review* articles with books that use Japanese sources and change the traditional American perspective. Isom's book, *Midway Inquest,* [was] published by the University of Indiana Press in June 2007. *Shattered Sword,* by two of the *Review* critics, was published in 2005.

The two books are unlikely to be the final accounts of Midway, one of the most analyzed battles of World War II. An annotated bibliography of books, periodicals, videos, and Web sites related to Midway is already 110 pages long.

— *AUTHOR* —

Mr. Allen has written or cowritten thirty-four books on a vast array of subjects, from espionage to exorcism. Among the many publications where his work has appeared are *National Geographic Magazine, Smithsonian, Military History Quarterly, American History,* the *Washington Post, New York Times Magazine, Washingtonian, Naval History,* and the magazine *Proceedings.*

CHAPTER
51

Identifying *Kaga*

By Jonathan Parshall, with Anthony Tully and David Dickson

Proceedings, June 2001: pp. 48–52

In September 1999, undersea explorers located some intriguing wreckage on the bottom of the Pacific near Midway Atoll. The question was, exactly what had they found? To answer that, a team of web-enabled historians was asked to help, and its members confirmed the identity of one of the more exciting underwater archaeological finds of recent years. . . .

The Battle of Midway remains one of the most crucial and widely studied battles of World War II. Any truly new find there would be of considerable importance to the historical record and would increase our understanding of the battle. . . .

[I]n February 2000, [the undersea exploration firm Nauticos provided] us with both video and still photography of a large piece of wreckage lying 17,000 feet below the surface of the Pacific. . . .

The wreckage [was] a portion of a ship's side plating. The piece once had been a relatively flat section of the ship's side structure. This was confirmed in the video footage, which also showed a porthole in the piece. Attached to what would have been the top of the structure [were] two semicircular platforms of equal diameter. The platforms, as was typical of Japanese carriers, [were] supported by large cantilevered braces that met the ship's side some 15 feet below the platform. . . .

A second mosaic . . . partially showed the backside of the artifact, which at one time would have been on the interior of the ship. It showed a stairway, presumably coming down from the level of the machinegun galleries, leading into the interior of the vessel. These two mosaics, and the video footage, comprised the basic evidence we had available to pinpoint the ship's identity. . . .

The telemetry information . . . [gave] the diameter of each of the two semicircular tubs as approximately 14 feet. This was too large a tub for a fire-control director mount, and too small for a 5-inch mount (which would have been some 22 feet across), but matched the diameter of the tubs used for twin 25-mm antiaircraft mounts. Both tubs had a section of walkway appended to them of some eight to ten feet in length, one leading forward, the other leading aft. This meant that the structure once had comprised the middle part of a machine-gun gallery, with walkways fore and aft leading to other gun or fire-control mounts.

Even more intriguing was the wreckage attached to one of the gun tubs. On closer examination, this turned out to be a landing-light array (*chakkan shidoto*—landing guidance lights). These arrays (usually four to a ship) were used to help Japanese pilots establish the proper glide slope during a landing approach, very similar to modern carrier landing aids. The design of such arrays varied from ship to ship, but generally comprised a triangular supporting arm structure atop which were either two or four rectangular colored lights (either green or red). The arm itself was hinged at the base, and was provided with cables at the apex, so it could be stowed flush with the ship's side when not in use or cranked out perpendicular to the flight deck during flight operations. The structure attached to the chunk fit this description nicely. Though it had crumpled on impact, the array was well defined structurally. One of the landing lights even had survived the descent to the seafloor, and the rigging cables still trailed from the end of the arm. . . .

The Japanese lost four aircraft carriers at the Battle of Midway: the *Akagi, Kaga, Soryu,* and *Hiryu.* Of these, the *Hiryu* was not a candidate for our investigation because she was sunk far to the north of Nauticos's search area. The other three vessels, however, were lost in relative proximity to each other. . . . [W]arship sinking locations often are inaccurate. In the heat of battle, it is difficult to fix a position precisely. In fact, it is not uncommon for ships of the same formation to record their positions differently. [Moreover], the exact Japanese formation at the time of the U.S. dive bomber attack at 1020–1025 on 4 June 1942 still is a hotly debated issue. Exact course and speed information for the three victims after the attack also is very sketchy. Very little is known of the tracks these ships took during the late morning as they staggered and drifted, all three ablaze, toward their final resting places that evening. Consequently, we had to be open to the idea that the wreckage could have come from any of the three ships. . . .

[Evidence, however, pointed to the *Kaga.*] Limited as the photographic record of the *Kaga* is, it turned out that there was one superb overhead shot of her. Taken in April 1941 by a Japanese aircraft, it shows the *Kaga*'s flight deck in great detail. Indeed, the resolution of the photograph was good enough that we even could make out the support spars for the safety nets hung along the side of the flight deck. And almost immediately, as we studied the starboard gallery, we saw a thick white line emanating from the outermost point on one of the two forwardmost tubs—the landing-light array. . . . Finally, here was positive evidence to support all the negative evidence that had eliminated the rest of the *Kido Butai.* Nauticos had indeed found the *Kaga*. . . .

The main question to be answered now is how and when did the chunk get blasted from the *Kaga*'s side? The sheer size of the artifact suggests a rather powerful explosion tore it from the ship. But was this explosion one of the initial 500- and 1,000-lb bomb hits (one of which landed no more than 40 feet away), a result of induced explosions during her day-long fire, or a relic of her sinking? . . .

Nauticos hopes to return to the Midway battlefield to find the *Kaga*'s main wreck sometime in the not-too-distant future. Hopefully, finding the main wreck will not be overly difficult, given that there now is a positive data point from which to work. Finding the *Kaga* doubtless will increase our knowledge of how the Japanese carrier force fought and died that day, and help complete the record of one of the most important naval engagements in history.

For further information, consult www.combinedfleet.com.

— AUTHORS —

Jonathan Parshall is a senior business analyst for a web-development firm. Anthony Tully is information systems manager for a professional technical recruiting company. David Dickson is corporate counsel for an insurance company. Jonathan Parshall and Anthony Tully are co-authors of *Shattered Sword, The Untold Story of the Battle of Midway* (2005).

CHAPTER
52

Book Review of Peter C. Smith, *Midway: Dauntless Victory: Fresh Perspectives on America's Seminal Naval Victory of World War II*

(Barnsley, South Yorkshire, UK: Pen and Sword Books, 2007)

Reviewed by CWO Ronald W. Russell, USNR (Ret.)

Naval History, August 2008: p. 68

Naval history students and scholars might rightly wonder why anyone at this late date would attempt yet another full-scale rendition of the Battle of Midway. Surely, it's a story that has been adequately told by now. But prolific British author Peter Smith's latest book not only retells the familiar story, it does so to a depth that is rarely, if ever, seen. He largely eschewed the battle's time-honored and well-worn references, instead undertaking original research into official archives in both the United States and Japan as well as extensive first-person interviews with Midway veterans in both countries. The result is an account of the battle that may somewhat resemble other volumes in style but definitely not in scope.

The book is literally crammed with detailed footnotes (indeed, some pages are little else) that immensely expand the narrative. The first appearance of virtually every notable Midway personality, even some of the minor players, is accompanied by a lengthy biographical footnote. Other notes and tables give an abundance of detail on the ships, aircraft, and squadrons engaged at Midway, including listings of every pilot and aircrew that launched from the atoll and from the American carriers on every combat sortie. Smith projects far beyond the battle with expansive segments concerning Midway's impact on numerous other nations, Allied and Axis, and how it was perceived by still others. Additionally, he has drawn on his 38 years as a military researcher and author to present perspectives that won't generally be found in other works on this topic, particularly the earlier ones.

Regrettably, *Midway: Dauntless Victory* has some fundamental flaws that prevent this otherwise remarkable book from being ranked among the best of class. Smith's "fresh perspectives" are just his personal opinions, and while they are exhaustively researched and should resonate well with almost anyone, an informed reader will find several passages that are quite vulnerable to debate, if not outright correction.

Examples include the author's views concerning the controversial flight of the USS *Hornet* (CV-8) air group, and how the battle might have evolved differently had Vice Admiral William Halsey been at the helm of Task Force 16 instead of the "black-shoe" Rear Admiral Raymond Spruance. Most troubling of all, though, are certain judgments Smith makes that smack of tabloid journalism rather than scholarly history.

His evaluation of Rear Admiral Frank Jack Fletcher's air search prior to the battle—"which, naturally, had seen nothing whatsoever"—is pointlessly arrogant. He alleges that "many respected critics and some veterans" have branded John Lundstrom's *Black Shoe Carrier Admiral* (Naval Institute Press, 2006), a detailed account of Fletcher during the 1942 carrier battles, as "highly biased and one-sided." But his only evidence of such criticism is a single quote from one veteran who wasn't at Midway. Smith selectively ignores the numerous favorable reviews Lundstrom's book has earned, and those "many respected critics" are apparently all anonymous.

Finally, Smith's book suffers from an inordinate number of simple typographical errors and structural gaffes. A few inconsequential mistakes of that kind can be excused in any work of similar magnitude, but the sheer number of them in this one turns what should be a minor imperfection into a much too noticeable defect. Embarrassing miscues like saying a ship made a 360-degree turn in order to reverse course, or footnote citations that take the reader to the wrong footnote should have been fixed in the editing process. (After publication, the author made it known that problems of that sort will be corrected in any subsequent reprint of the book.)

While such negatives do tarnish an otherwise impressive volume of wartime history, they are easily lost in its scope, which is richly detailed and mostly accurate. It should make a worthy addition to any naval history library providing the reader can look past the structural errors and some of the author's arguable assertions.

— AUTHOR —

Mr. Russell, a retired operations manager and technical writer in the telecommunications industry, is the author of *No Right to Win: A Continuing Dialogue with Veterans of the Battle of Midway* (Lincoln, NE: iUniverse, 2006). He is editor for the Battle of Midway Roundtable, an association of veterans, historians, and others with a strong interest in the battle.

CHAPTER
53

Midway Is Our Trafalgar

By CDR Brian Fort, USN

Proceedings, June 2006: pp. 62–66

History is a force. It can push us to success if we learn its lessons, or it can pull us to doom if we fail to heed them. No one understood this better than Alfred Thayer Mahan. In his classic *The Influence of Sea Power Upon History 1660–1783,* he used the history of Britain's Royal Navy to address the enormous impact of controlling the seas.

His logic was clear. Britain secured its world prominence by transporting and trading in vast quantities of raw materials provided by its colonies under protective cover of its navy. Dominion over the oceans provided easy access to sources of wealth, because trade went mostly uninterrupted. The impact of that dominance became the strategic cornerstone for navalists and the naval arms race of the early 20th century.

Influence clearly served Mahan's purpose; not only did sea power influence history, but history would indeed have a profound effect on sea power, as well. By treating the wars of the time span he covered as purely maritime conflicts, he was able to use history as a force to help shape doctrine that modernized navies prior to and after World War I.

Unfortunately, naval history's force and influence on sea power in the United States today is weak, unfocused, and, sadly, too often ignored. Sounding this alarm, Dr. John Hattendorf, the Ernest J. King Professor of Maritime History at the Naval War College, wrote in the Spring 2003 *Naval War College Review* about the U.S. Navy's tendency "to ignore the value of and advantages to be found in historical insight." In the December 2004 *Proceedings* he wrote: "Present historians have a difficult time learning what our service is doing today, and our achievements may never be known to future generations."

The bottom line is that the Navy simply does not appreciate its history and is therefore not well positioned to learn from it today or tomorrow. Short-term corrective action and plans for a long-term vision are needed now. A comparison between the Royal Navy's annual commemoration of the Battle of Trafalgar and the U.S. Navy's attempt at an annual commemoration of the Battle of Midway is a case in point. The U.S. Navy's negligence in celebrating the annual anniversary of Midway, Fleet-wide, is the single most egregious example of its failure to embrace its own history.

The Royal Navy and the Battle of Trafalgar

Consider Trafalgar. On 21 October each year, every Royal Navy command, afloat or ashore, in conflict or at peace, honors the immortal memory of Vice Admiral Lord Horatio Nelson and the triumph of the Royal Navy over the combined French and Spanish fleets at the 1805 Battle of Trafalgar. Typically, mess dinners celebrate the victory. Many U.S. Navy Sailors, officers and enlisted, have attended such dinners as guests of the Royal Navy, and everyone comes away from these events with tremendous respect and admiration.

The 2005 Trafalgar anniversary was distinctive, marking the bicentennial of the battle and of the death of Nelson. Navies from around the world turned out for a multitude of celebrations, including a Fleet Review off Portsmouth, England, at Spithead. What is distinctive about Trafalgar and the death of Nelson is that they are two historic events immortalized not only within the Royal Navy, but also by the British populace at large, the most obvious monumental testaments being Trafalgar Square and the Nelson Column. Centrally located in London, the square, with its iconic column, is one of the most recognized places in the world, taking center stage every year during New Year's Eve celebrations. Of particular note here, no one had to tell the British about the importance of Nelson's victory at Trafalgar, and no one had to tell the Royal Navy to honor its significance annually.

The U.S. Navy and the Battle of Midway

Now, consider Midway. A dedication stone inscription by historian Walter Lord at the National World War II Memorial in Washington, DC, puts the Battle of Midway in its proper context: "They had no right to win. Yet they did, and in doing so they changed the course of a war . . . even against the greatest of odds, there is something in the human spirit—a magic blend of skills, faith, and valor—that can lift men from certain defeat to incredible victory." Add to that remarks by former Secretary of Defense James R. Schlesinger at a dinner to recognize the 61st anniversary of the battle at the Army and Navy Country Club in 2003, and you have the definitive context for placing Midway among other crucial turning points in world history:

> Then came Midway. Through an extraordinary combination of the skill and courage of our pilots, splendid intelligence, prudent risk-taking by our commanders that paid off, and sheer good luck, the apparently inferior American forces were victorious. This victory occurred despite the inferiority of our aircraft, the ineffectiveness of our torpedoes, the substantial absence of backup surface ships, and our overall numerical inferiority. You know the rest! Four Japanese carriers had been sunk. It all confirmed the dictum of Otto von Bismarck: "[T]he Lord God has special providence for fools, drunkards, and the United States of America." The Japanese offensive had now been blunted. The Japanese fleet turned back toward the Home Islands and the opportunity for victory had been lost forever. Roosevelt could now execute his Grand Strategy, with all that was to imply regarding the condition of post-war Europe.

So, with this remarkable historical backdrop, how are the U.S. Navy and the American people memorializing this turning-point battle? America has no equivalent of Trafalgar Square, and there is no American Nelson. Only three modest memorials commemorate the Battle of Midway, one placed on Sand Island of the Midway Atoll in 1995, another placed on the grounds of the U.S. Naval Academy just more than a year later, and a third opened in 2001 at Chicago's Midway Airport Terminal. Were it not for the extraordinary efforts of the International Midway Memorial Foundation (IMMF), the Naval Academy Class of 1942, and the Chicago Department of Aviation, it is unlikely any of these unassuming memorials would even exist.

Unfortunately, because the Navy Reserve Officer Training Corps is the Navy's major commissioning source, only a relatively small percentage of officers will ever see the Academy's memorial, and only an extremely small percentage of the general public will ever visit Midway and see the memorial there. While Midway Airport sees considerable traffic, its memorial is really more of an exhibit than a memorial.

Influenced by the first two memorial initiatives, then-Chief of Naval Operations (CNO) Admiral Jay Johnson attempted to take another step toward instilling historical esprit de corps into the Fleet through release of a message titled *Naval Heritage*. In it, the CNO cited preserving and building on naval heritage as a Fleet goal, indicating the Navy's date of birth, 13 October 1775, and the date of the Battle of Midway, 4 June 1942, should be celebrated annually. Less than a year later, Vice CNO Admiral Donald Pilling released a follow-up message specific to

Midway commemorations, and the Naval Historical Center added Midway Night dining information to its Web site. The vision of a Fleet-wide commemoration of Midway through an annual Midway Night dinner along the lines of the Royal Navy's Trafalgar Night dinner, however, has not come close to reality.

How is this still possible, and how was it possible that the 50th anniversary commemoration of the Battle of Midway included no formal monument to the battle? How is it possible today that so few U.S. Navy Sailors have participated in celebrations honoring Midway and remain unaware of the battle's significance in the context of world—much less Navy—history?

While there may be many reasons why Midway has not garnered proper historical respect and recognition, Dr. Schlesinger gave three summations in his previously mentioned speech: (1) British Prime Minister Winston Churchill's Eurocentric canon on World War II, (2) Midway amidst the shadow of the D-Day invasion at Normandy, and (3) lack of recognition within the U.S. Navy itself.

Added to this could also be that, because recognition of Midway has been so passive in the past, memorializing it today might seem somewhat forced. And while victory at Trafalgar quelled the immediate English fears of the threat of invasion from Napoleon, the victory at Midway, although recognized as having turned the tide of the war in the Pacific, still left the U.S. Navy with tremendous challenges to ensure the ultimate defeat of the Imperial Japanese Navy.

With respect to Admiral Johnson's naval heritage initiatives in general, like many ideas that begin with the right intentions, naval heritage has since been fundamentally diminished by relegating it to the realm of a few questions on rating examinations and in warfare qualification standards and subsuming it to the environment of Navy general military training. This effectively kills any real value associated with naval heritage training. Nothing demonstrates this last point more clearly than a review of the 12 training topics for 2006, which include not a single stand-alone naval heritage topic, even though the Navy Education and Training Center conveniently labeled all 12 as part of the naval heritage subject area. These include topics such as sexual assault, personal financial management, and grievance procedures, to name only a few. This is a poor excuse for naval heritage training.

Of positive note, however, are a few outstanding examples of Midway Night celebrations and naval heritage being done right. For example, Naval Air Station Jacksonville held a Midway Night dinner on 4 June 2005 that was co-sponsored by the Navy League of Mayport and the Greater Jacksonville United Services Organization. More than 400 attended the event, including 22 Midway veterans, then-CNO Admiral Vern Clark, and the mayor of Jacksonville.

The U.S. Navy and the Battle of Trafalgar

Notwithstanding such examples, echoes of the chairman to the Secretary of the Navy's Advisory Subcommittee on Naval History's warning—that for too long the Navy has viewed history as "someone else's problem"—can still be heard loud and clear throughout the Fleet. Along these lines, a blatant and globally visible example of the U.S. Navy's failure to use naval history to its advantage was its level of participation in and recognition of the importance of the Royal Navy's 2005 Trafalgar Bicentennial Fleet Review.

On 28 June 2005, 167 ships from some 35 countries participated in the review at Spithead. The invitation to participate in this 600-year-old tradition provided the U.S. Navy an excellent opportunity to take part in one of the most significant maritime and historical events of a lifetime. Just as shameful as the U.S. Navy's failure to embrace the historical significance of Midway was the fact that its participation in the review was limited to a single warship, USS *Saipan* (LHA-2). Owing to the requirements of the war on terrorism, no U.S. Navy aircraft carrier participated, leaving the French carrier *Charles de Gaulle* as the largest warship.

Adding to this lack of historical perspective, the press release from Commander, Naval Forces Europe/Commander, U.S. 6th Fleet, noting *Saipan*'s participation, failed to capture the significance of the event, blandly noting that "Participating in the celebrations provides the U.S. Navy in Europe the opportunity to promote theater security cooperation through pursuit of shared diplomatic goals and military readiness." Not only was this not a theater security exercise, but no mention was made of the importance of the Battle of Trafalgar, the leadership example of Nelson, or the importance of an enduring maritime legacy to a nation's history.

The point here is certainly not to denigrate the men and women of *Saipan*, who looked magnificent on the deck as they passed before the Queen of England on the reviewing ship, nor any of the Sailors stationed in the United Kingdom who participated in Trafalgar bicentennial events. And it is particularly not the intent to criticize the Sailors on board 6th Fleet ships who could not participate because of current operations. The point is that for an International Fleet Review of this significance, which was planned with as much lead time as this one was, the U.S. Navy should have sent an aircraft carrier and at least one escort.

Short-Term Recommendations

Laying out a set of complaints is simply that—a set of complaints. Therefore, following are some simple recommendations:

- Uniformed and civilian senior leadership must be actively involved in annual Midway Night commemorations. There are more ships, submarines, squadrons, and naval stations than there are flag officers and senior executive service officials. There is no excuse for invitations not to go to every member of the U.S. Navy's senior leadership each year for Midway Night events. If not already scheduled, commanding officers and executive officers must direct a Midway Night celebration be added to their command calendars now.

- U.S. Navy public affairs officers must go on a naval heritage frontal assault. They need not be overly creative. Start by getting permission to reprint the words of Dr. Hattendorf, Dr. Schlesinger, and Walter Lord regarding the importance of the Battle of Midway and the value of naval heritage.
- Truly incorporate naval heritage training in officer and enlisted basic training. Don't waste time re-inventing the wheel. Copy the Marine Corps model. It works.
- Send historians to sea. Get historians involved in the process at sea. Get Sailors involved with historians.
- Do whatever it takes to have the U.S. Navy Memorial in Washington, DC, opened on Sundays. Half of weekend tourists miss the opportunity to see naval heritage in operation.

One recent bright spot on the naval heritage horizon is the U.S. Naval Institute's introduction in 2004 of an annual Applied Naval History Conference that has begun to attract active-duty panelists and audience and those of us who are naval history enthusiasts but don't have history degrees. Its cosponsors include the U.S. Naval Academy history department, which will resume its biannual Naval History Symposium for academic purists.

A Vision

Although the CNO's naval heritage message is now more than five years old, Fleet-wide commemoration of the Battle of Midway through annual Midway Night dinners will not happen overnight, nor will a Midway equivalent of Trafalgar Square, with statues of the great naval commanders, appear on the Capitol Mall [*sic*] tomorrow.

First, the message of the importance of naval heritage must continue to reach many audiences, in many venues, and in many forms. We cannot afford to miss opportunities to promote it. For those who truly believe in the significance of the Battle of Midway and the importance of honoring naval heritage, long-term goals to achieve something as spectacular as the Trafalgar celebrations must be bold and visionary.

An example of the possibilities for one such vision exists in Washington today. Restoration of the capital city's southeast corridor along the Anacostia River waterfront is being planned around a new baseball stadium to house the Washington

Nationals professional baseball team. Conveniently, the metro [*sic*] stop that will bring fans to the new ballpark is the Navy Yard stop. What if a monument to the Battle of Midway were also built in this revitalized neighborhood? What if this development simply became known as the Washington Midway, second only to the Mall in attracting tourists to the nation's capital? What if we could combine America's pastime with America's naval heritage to recognize the turning-point Battle of Midway and the fact that our history would be substantially different if not for this great victory?

History is indeed an extremely powerful force. A century ago Mahan's dissertation about the influence of sea power on history set in motion the course of events that led to the status the U.S. Navy enjoys in the world today. It is the history, though, before and after Mahan, from Trafalgar to Midway, and history as yet unwritten, that must be recognized, studied, articulated, respected, and prepared for because of the nature of its influence on sea power. The Royal Navy has provided the example, in honoring the Battle of Trafalgar, that the U.S. Navy should follow to appropriately memorialize the most decisive naval battle in its own history.

— *AUTHOR* —

Commander Fort [was] serving on the Joint Staff J7 [in June 2006]. He is an avid naval history enthusiast and future commanding officer afloat.

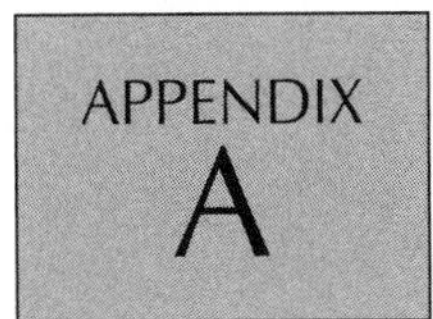

USS *Enterprise* Action Report, 8 June 1942

The following report from the captain of the *Enterprise* (CV-6) is interesting if only because it gives today's reader a sense of the intense activity on the ship on 4 June 1942. Between 0906 and 2034 (using the times given in the report), the *Enterprise* launched and recovered two major strike groups, nine defensive CAPs (and two fighters of the tenth CAP), and recovered thirty-three fighters and scout bombers from the *Yorktown*.

Between 1244 and 1247 eight fighters of her third CAP left the *Enterprise*. That was one fighter launched about every twenty-two seconds. At 1255 the fighter escort for the first attack group began returning. They were all recovered within twenty minutes, and then the flight deck had to be cleared as the eight fighters of the ship's second CAP landed (between 1316 and 1329). As each plane landed, the barrier protecting aircraft already parked on the forward part of the flight deck was lowered and the plane that had just landed was pushed over the barrier wires and the barrier was raised. This is why recovering planes took longer—about ninety seconds per plane versus the twenty to twenty-five seconds per plane during launch operations.

In the three minutes between 1337 and 1340, the *Enterprise* launched the eight fighters of her fourth CAP, and soon her attack group's bombers returned. They were taken on board by 1410, and the next (fifth) CAP of eight Wildcats began leaving the deck at 1433. Two minutes after they had gone, two dive-bombers from the *Yorktown*'s strike group landed on the *Enterprise*, and more came soon after—seven between 1442 and 1448, and ten more between 1451 and 1459.

In effect, the *Enterprise* was an extraordinarily busy airport, but with one major difference. Once a plane landed safely, it taxied forward to join others shielded by the wire barrier. Once a number of planes had landed, the barrier was lowered and they were moved to the rear of the flight deck, refueled, and rearmed—or taken below on one of the ship's elevators. The area forward of the barrier could get crowded very quickly, and that created both an obstacle to launching further strikes and a target for enemy planes.

What the following report does not discuss is the huge amount of physical labor expended by the ship's flight deck crew—folding and unfolding the wings of aircraft, arranging them on the flight deck, and shoving them into position. They had to do this quickly so the armorers could load the returned aircraft with bombs and machine-gun bullets and the crew members responsible for refueling the planes could gas them up. It should not come as any surprise that the flight deck crewmen—as well as the plane handlers in the hangar deck below—were exhausted by the evening of 4 June.

The fighter pilots were also worn out by the need to fly off the *Enterprise,* maintain their readiness in their positions in the CAP over the carrier, and then land on the ship's relatively small flight deck—not once, but several times during the day. The *Enterprise* was a "fighting machine" on 4 June, and her crew performed splendidly, but like any machine she ran down. That is what readers of this report must keep in mind.

CV6/A16–3/(60-Br) (0133) U.S.S. ENTERPRISE
At Sea, June 8, 1942

From: The Commanding Officer

To: The Commander-in-Chief, U.S. Pacific Fleet.

Via: Commander Task Force Sixteen (Rear Admiral R. A. Spruance, U.S. Navy)

Subject: Battle of Midway Island, June 4–6, 1942, Report of.

References: (a) Articles 712 and 874, U.S. Navy Regulations, 1920. . . .

I. PRELIMINARY

1. On the afternoon and evening of June 3, 1942, the general situation prior to the battle was as follows (times throughout are Zone plus 10): Task Force Seventeen and Task Force Sixteen had previously rendezvoused in the general vicinity of "Point Luck," approximately 350 miles northeast of Midway Island and were operating in that area closing Midway during darkness and opening during the day, remaining east of the longitude of Midway. Both Task Forces had completed fueling to capacity and the oilers despatched [*sic*] to their rendezvous. The Senior Officer present Afloat and Officer in Tactical

Command was in YORKTOWN. The two task forces were separated but were within visual contact. They were operating independently but generally conforming in their movements. At 2150 course was changed to 210 deg. T. toward a 0630, June 4, rendezvous (31 deg. 30 min. N; 176 deg. 30 min. W) designated by Commander Task Force 17. At 1812 a radio message from Flight 312 to Radio Midway was intercepted "2 enemy destroyers 2 cargo vessels course 020 speed 13."

2. At 2000, June 3, 1942, ENTERPRISE, Flagship of Commander Task Force 16 was in position 33 deg. 16 min. N, 175 deg. 46 min. W, in the center as guide of Cruising Disposition 11-V, axis 270 deg. T, course 100 deg. T, speed 15 knots and zigzagging according to Plan Number 7. Wind south 9, clouds cumulus 7, visibility 30, sea smooth.

3. The following significant messages were received during the night of June 3–4:

   a. At 0447—from Flight 44 to Radio Midway "large enemy forces bearing 261 deg. T, distance 500 course 080 speed 13 x ten ships."

   b. At 0734—from Flight 58 to Radio Midway "enemy carriers."

   c. At 0753—from Flight 58 to Radio Midway "many planes heading Midway bearing 320 distance 150."

   d. At 0803—from Flight 92 to Radio Midway "2 carriers and battleships bearing 320 deg. distance 180 course 135 speed 25."

   e. At 0807—from Commander Task Force 17 to Commander Task Force 16 "proceed southwesterly and attack enemy carriers when definitely located."

II. THE ACTION

June 4, 1942. Wind SE 5, clouds cumulus 4, visibility 50, sea smooth.

Time

0906—Commenced launching attack group of 33 VSB, 14 VT, 10 VF. 15 VSB armed with one 1000 lb. bomb each. 12 VSB armed with one 500 lb. bomb and two 100 lb. bombs each. 6 VSB armed with one 500 lb. bomb each. 14 VTB armed with torpedoes.

1015—Type 97 enemy twin-float seaplane sighted bearing 180 deg. T, distance 72,000 yards. Combat Patrol failed to find this plane although radar and lookouts confirmed its position.

1129–1132—Launched 8 VF for second Combat Air Patrol.

1145–1152—Landed first Combat Patrol 8 VF.

1202—Commander ENTERPRISE Air Group sighted Japanese Force composed of 4 CV, 2 BB, 4 CA, 6 DD.

1220—VT commenced attack; probably one hit on CV.

1222—VSB commenced dive bombing attack; two (2) CV badly damaged with many direct bomb hits, left in flames. Position of enemy force, Lat. 30 deg. 05 min. N, Long. 178 deg. 50 min. W.

1244–1247—Launched 8 VF for Third Combat Patrol.

1255—Commenced landing VF escort.

1316–1329—Landed second Combat Patrol 8 VF.

1337–1340—Launched 8 VF, fourth Combat Patrol.

1405—20 enemy planes reported bearing 310 deg. coming in. (Attack on YORKTOWN followed).

1410—Completed landing attack group.

1433–1435—Launched 8 VF, fifth Combat Patrol.

1437–1438—Landed 5-B-3 and 5-B-16 (YORKTOWN planes). YORKTOWN pilot reported YORKTOWN in bad shape. Heavy smoke seen from YORKTOWN.

1442–1448—Landed 5-B-7, 5-B-8, 5-B-9, 5-B-10, 5-B-12, 5-B-14, 5-B-15 (YORKTOWN planes).

1451–1459—Landed 5-F-2, 5-F-3, 5-F-8, 5-F-21, 5-B-4, 5-B-5, 5-B-6, 5-B-11, 5-B-13, 5-B-17 (YORKTOWN planes).

1504–1505—Landed 5-F-10, 5-F-15 (YORKTOWN planes).

1539–1541—Launched 6 VF, sixth Combat Patrol.

1547–1559—Landed third and fourth Combat Patrol, 16 VF.

1610—VF shot down seaplane tracker 50 miles south of our force.

1645—Received message from YORKTOWN scout, "1 CV, 2 BB, 3 CA, 4 DD, 31 deg. 15 min. N, 179 deg. 05 min. W, course 000, speed 15."

1730—Commenced launching second attack group composed of 24 VSB. 11 VSB armed with one 1000 lb. bomb each. 13 VSB armed with one 500 lb. bomb each.

1742–1752—Landed fifth and sixth Combat Patrols 10 VF. 6-F-12 Mach. Warden missing and reported to have landed in water out of gas. Also landed 3 VF and 3 VSB from YORKTOWN. Landed 6-S-16 from Attack Group.

1835—Combat Patrol (6-F-1 shot down 4-engine enemy seaplane).

1842–1846—Launched 12 VF for ninth Combat Patrol.

1850–1852—Landed 5 VF of seventh Combat Patrol. Also landed 1 VF and 4 VSB from YORKTOWN.

1905—Attacked Japanese Force composed of 1 CV, 2 BB, 3 CA, 4 DD, position Lat. 31 deg. 40 min. N, Long. 179 deg. 10 min. W. Left 1 CV and 1 BB severely damaged and mass of flames.

1928–1930—Landed 2 VF of eighth Combat Patrol and 1 VF from YORKTOWN.

1958–2005—Launched 20 VF for tenth Combat Patrol.

2008–2034—Landed 20 VSB of Attack Group. (3 did not return). Landed 9 VF of ninth Combat Patrol. Landed 2 VF of tenth Combat Patrol.

2034—Completed landing attack group.

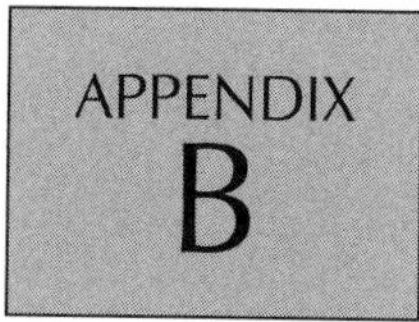

APPENDIX B

RADM R. A. Spruance's Letter of 8 June 1942 to RADM F. J. Fletcher

United States Pacific Fleet
Flagship of Commander Carriers

June 8, 1942

Dear Fletcher,

Thank you very much for your message which the *Balch* relayed to us this morning.

You were certainly fine to me all during the time the two task forces were operating together under your command, and I can't tell you how much I appreciate it.

It was tough luck that the *Yorktown* had to stand those two attacks. We tried our best to close you after the first attack, but it seemed that every mile we made toward you in between air operations was more than lost when we had to launch and recover.

If it had not been for what you did and took with the *Yorktown*, I am firmly convinced that we would have been badly defeated and the Japs would be holding Midway today. As it is, I think their ears will be pinned back for some time to come.

I am enclosing a copy of a personal letter I am sending in to the Commander-in-Chief. It should give you some idea of our operations during those three days.

Good luck until we are both in port at the same time and can talk things over.

Sincerely,

R. A. Spruance

APPENDIX C

Aircraft Names

USN Aircraft	USN Aircraft Names	IJN Aircraft	USN Code Names
F4F-3 & F4F-4	Wildcat (fighter)	A6M2 Type 0 fighter	Zero
SBD-2 & SBD-3	Dauntless (bomber)	D3A1 Type 99 bomber	Val
TBD-1	Devastator (bomber)	B5N2 Type 97 bomber	Kate
PBY	Catalina seaplane	E13A seaplane	Jake
TBF-1	Avenger (bomber)	E8N2 seaplane	Dave
SB2U-2 & SB2U-3	Vindicator (bomber)	D4Y1 bomber	Judy

Notes

Part I. Midway Anthology

1. Ministry of Defence (Navy), *War with Japan*, vol. 2, *Defensive Phase* (London: HMSO, 1995), 130.

Chapter 1. *Akagi,* Famous Japanese Carrier

1. Statement to the press, Washington, DC, November 1, 1944.
2. Secret War Speech in the House of Commons, April 23, 1942.
3. [The *Nautilus* had actually attacked the *Kaga*. As Robinson points out, the torpedo that hit the *Kaga* did not explode.]

Part III. The Battle

1. Jonathan Parshall and Anthony Tully, *Shattered Sword, The Untold Story of the Battle of Midway* (Washington, DC: Potomac Books, 2005), xi.

Chapter 23. "Flags" at Midway

1. Peter Karetka provided the author with copies of his notes and other documents, some of which appear on his website, http://www.geocities.com/karetkamidway/.
2. Weise's words come from an account he wrote and sent to Kareta. He was also interviewed by the author for the *National Geographic* article cited above.
3. Karetka obtained the information about Tanabe and I-168 from Noritaka Kitazawa of the Military History Department of Japan's National Institute for Defense Studies.

Chapter 29. Lost Letter of Midway

1. Spruance reported that: "*Hornet* dive bombers failed to locate the target and did not participate in this attack (of 4 June). Had they done so, the fourth carrier could have been attacked and later attack made on *Yorktown* by the carrier prevented."
2. Lisle A. Rose, *The Ship That Held the Line* (Annapolis, MD: Naval Institute Press. 1995), p. 158.
3. Theodore Taylor, *The Magnificent Mitscher* (New York: W. W. Norton & Co., 1954), p. 142.

4. Primary Midway histories include: Samuel Eliot Morison's multi-volume *History of United States Naval Operations* in *World War II* (Boston, MA: Little, Brown and Company, 1949) with Volume IV devoted to Coral Sea, Midway, and Submarine Actions; Gordon W. Prange, *Miracle at Midway* (New York: McGraw Hill, 1982); Walter Lord, *Incredible Victory* (New York: Harper & Row Publishers, 1967); Thomas B. Buell, *The Quiet Warrior, A Biography of Admiral Raymond A. Spruance* (Annapolis, MD: Naval Institute Press, 1987); John Lundstrom, *The First Team: Pacific Naval Air Combat from Pearl Harbor to Midway* (Annapolis, MD: Naval Institute Press, 1984); and Rose's *The Ship That Held the Line*.
5. Rose, [*Ship That Held*], p. 85.
6. Morison, [*Naval Operations* in *World War II*], Vol. IV, p. 91.
7. Ibid., p. 109.
8. Lord, [*Incredible Victory*], p. 141.
9. Ibid., p. 139.
10. Rose, [*Ship That Held*], p. 141.
11. Ibid., p. 142.
12. Lord, [*Incredible Victory*], p. 270.
13. Morison, [*Naval Operations* in *World War II*], Vol. IV, p. 149.
14. Prange, [*Miracle at Midway*], p. 342.

Part IV. The End of the Battle

1. See Clark G. Reynolds, *Admiral John H. Towers, The Struggle for Naval Air Supremacy* (Annapolis, MD: Naval Institute Press, 1991), 398–399.
2. See John Lundstrom, *Black Shoe Carrier Admiral* (Annapolis, MD: Naval Institute Press, 2006), 282–283 and 289–290.
3. Interview, VADM Lloyd M. Mustin, 16 January 1973, Interview no. 12; transcript at U.S. Naval Institute, 476.

Part V. The Official Report of the Battle

1. Walton L. Robinson, "*Akagi*, Famous Japanese Carrier," U.S. Naval Institute *Proceedings* (May 1948), 579–595. This essay is the first selection in the anthology.

Chapter 36. Commentary on RADM Raymond A. Spruance

1. Thomas B. Buell, *The Quiet Warrior, A Biography of Admiral Raymond A. Spruance* (Annapolis, MD: Naval Institute Press, 1987), 135.
2. Ibid., 109.
3. Letter from CAPT Robert J. Oliver, USN (Ret.) to LCDR Thomas B. Buell, USN, 5 August 1971, p. 5. The letter is in the Buell papers in the Naval War College Archives.
4. Buell, *Quiet Warrior*, 142, and the accompanying footnote.
5. VADM E. P. Forrestel, USN, *Admiral Raymond A. Spruance, USN, A Study in Command* (Washington, DC: Government Printing Office, 1966), p. 43.
6. Ibid., p. 50.
7. Ibid., pp. 50–51.
8. Ibid., p. 52.
9. Ibid., p. 53.
10. Letter from Oliver to Buell, 5 August 1971, p. 7.

Selected Bibliography

The literature on the Battle of Midway is huge. Some of the best examples of that literature are in this anthology. However, if you need more material, these are references that I recommend, along with the reasons I recommend them.

Agawa, Hiroyuki. *The Reluctant Admiral: Yamamoto and the Imperial Navy.* Tokyo: Kodansha, 1979.

Admiral Yamamoto is still something of an enigmatic figure. This book was the first to go behind the image of the admiral in search of his true character.

Buell, Thomas B. *The Quiet Warrior: A Biography of Admiral Raymond A. Spruance.* Boston: Little, Brown, 1974, and Annapolis, MD: Naval Institute Press, 1987.

An excellent study of Admiral Spruance.

Cressman, Robert. *That Gallant Ship: U.S.S. Yorktown.* Missoula, MT: Pictorial Histories, 1985.

This large-format paperback has excellent photographs of the Yorktown, *her aircraft before and during World War II, and her personnel. It also contains accurate summaries of her combat experiences.*

Dulin, Robert O. Jr., with William Garzke Jr., Charles Haberlein Jr., Robert Egan, David Mindell, and William Jurens. "The Loss of the USS Yorktown (CV 5), A Marine Forensics Analysis." Society of Naval Architects and Marine Engineers, 1999 Annual Meeting Preprints.

An expedition funded by the National Geographic Society and headed by oceanographer Robert Ballard located the sunken Yorktown *near Midway in June 1998. The authors of this paper are specialists in ship design and operations. The paper compares the official Bureau of Ships War Damage Report No. 23 (on the* Yorktown*) prepared during World War II with what an examination of the actual wreck reveals.*

Evans, David C., and Mark R. Peattie. *Kaigun: Strategy, Tactics, and Technology in the Imperial Japanese Navy, 1887–1941*. Annapolis, MD: Naval Institute Press, 1997.

This thorough study provides the institutional, social and political context for the development of the IJN that went to war in 1941.

Friedman, Norman. *U.S. Aircraft Carriers, An Illustrated Design History*. Annapolis, MD: Naval Institute Press, 1983.

If you wish to understand why carriers such as the Enterprise *were designed the way they were, you must consult this book.*

Layton, Edwin T., with Roger Pineau and John Costello. *And I Was There: Pearl Harbor and Midway—Breaking the Secrets*. New York: William Morrow, 1985, and Annapolis, MD: Naval Institute Press, 2006 (Bluejacket Books ed.).

Layton describes his cooperation with CDR Joseph Rochefort in working out the date and direction of the Japanese attack on Midway. This book is best read in parallel with Elliot Carlson's Joe Rochefort's War, *which was used as a source for this anthology.*

Mrazek, Robert J. *A Dawn Like Thunder, The True Story of Torpedo Squadron Eight*. Boston, MA: Little, Brown, 2008.

This is a very moving account of the aviators who flew in the squadron in 1942.

Morison, Samuel Eliot. *History of United States Naval Operations in World War II*, vol. 4, *Coral Sea, Midway and Submarine Actions, May 1942–August 1942*. Edison, NJ: Castle Books, 2001.

Morison's account set the standard for the U.S. Navy's side of the Battle of Midway for two generations.

Parshall, Jonathan, and Anthony Tully. *Shattered Sword, The Untold Story of the Battle of Midway*. Washington, DC: Potomac Books, 2005.

This book brought the fruits of Japanese scholarship to an American audience that had relied too long on Captain Mitsuo Fuchida's Midway: The Battle That Doomed Japan. *The product of years of research,* Shattered Sword *showed what extensive communication among Japanese and American investigators facilitated by the World Wide Web could do for naval history.*

Polmar, Norman. *Aircraft Carriers: A Graphic History of Carrier Aviation and Its Influence on World Events*. New York: Doubleday, 1969.

The author brings his great knowledge of aircraft carriers and the navies that have operated them to bear on the many campaigns in which carriers have been used.

Reynolds, Clark G. *The Fast Carriers: The Forging of an Air Navy*. New York: McGraw-Hill, 1968.

This is a classic study of the development of the carrier force of the U.S. Navy. It begins before World War II and traces the struggles of the carrier aviators to defeat their Japanese opponents.

Reynolds, Clark G. "The U.S. Fleet-in-Being Strategy of 1942." *Journal of Military History* (January 1994): 103–119.

This essay concisely lays out Admiral King's approach to the Pacific War in the first months of 1942.

Smith, Douglas V. *Carrier Battles: Command Decision in Harm's Way*. Annapolis, MD: Naval Institute Press, 2006.

Smith provides an overview of key carrier battles in World War II. A very handy reference.

Tillman, Barrett. "Douglas TBD: The Maligned Warrior." *The Hook* 18 (Special Issue, August 1990): 18–31.

This is an excellent article covering the development and operations of the TBD "Devastator." Tillman notes that the Devastator's torpedo, the Mk. 13, restricted TBD tactics because it had to be dropped at a height no greater than fifty feet and at a speed no greater than 110 knots. The numbers for the Nakajima B5N (Kate) were a drop speed of no more than 260 knots and a drop height of more than double that of the U.S. plane.

Wildenberg, Thomas. *Destined for Glory: Dive Bombing, Midway, and the Evolution of Carrier Airpower.* Annapolis, MD: Naval Institute Press, 1998.

This book is less about Midway and very much about the history of dive-bombing in the U.S. Navy before World War II. Where did dive-bombing come from? This book will tell you.

Willmott, H. P. *The Barrier and the Javelin: Japanese and Allied Pacific Strategies, February to June 1942*. Annapolis, MD: Naval Institute Press, 1983.

Willmott gives the reader an assessment of the two sides that came to blows over Midway. What were their respective strategies? Willmott explains them.

Index

About the Editor

Thomas Hone is a former senior executive in the Office of the Secretary of Defense and a former member of the faculty of the Naval War College. He is the author or co-author of three books on naval administration and innovation, the co-author of a book on the Navy between World War I and World War II, and an award winning author of articles and essays on naval and military affairs. He resides in Arlington, Virginia.

The Naval Institute Press is the book-publishing arm of the U.S. Naval Institute, a private, nonprofit, membership society for sea service professionals and others who share an interest in naval and maritime affairs. Established in 1873 at the U.S. Naval Academy in Annapolis, Maryland, where its offices remain today, the Naval Institute has members worldwide.

Members of the Naval Institute support the education programs of the society and receive the influential monthly magazine *Proceedings* or the colorful bimonthly magazine *Naval History* and discounts on fine nautical prints and on ship and aircraft photos. They also have access to the transcripts of the Institute's Oral History Program and get discounted admission to any of the Institute-sponsored seminars offered around the country.

The Naval Institute's book-publishing program, begun in 1898 with basic guides to naval practices, has broadened its scope to include books of more general interest. Now the Naval Institute Press publishes about seventy titles each year, ranging from how-to books on boating and navigation to battle histories, biographies, ship and aircraft guides, and novels. Institute members receive significant discounts on the Press's more than eight hundred books in print.

Full-time students are eligible for special half-price membership rates. Life memberships are also available.

For a free catalog describing Naval Institute Press books currently available, and for further information about joining the U.S. Naval Institute, please write to:

Member Services
U.S. Naval Institute
291 Wood Road
Annapolis, MD 21402-5034
Telephone: (800) 233-8764
Fax: (410) 571-1703
Web address: www.usni.org

Midway from the northwest. One carrier had been reported among the ships west of Midway, but this contact was not verified. It is possible that the Japanese had five carriers off Midway and that the fifth one moved from the west to the northwest for the engagements of the fourth of June, but there is no clear evidence yet to bear to this.

Before dawn on 4 June PBY's took off from Midway continuing their invaluable scouting that contributed so greatly to the success of the action. Sixteen B-17's were dispatched by Commanding Officer, Midway, to attack the enemy transport force to the westward. At 0545 the most important contact of the battle was made. A PBY reported many planes heading for Midway 150 miles distant on bearing 320; 7 minutes later another PBY sighted 2 of the enemy carriers and many other ships on the bearing, distant 180 miles, coming in at 25 knots on course 135.

All serviceable planes at Midway were in the air before 0600 (except for 3 SB2U spares); 6 Navy TBF and 4 Army B-26 armed with torpedoes, and 27 Marine dive bombers were dispatched to strike the enemy carriers. The B-17's proceeding westward were also diverted to the carriers. Midway radar picked up the enemy planes and, at 0615, 14 of the 27 fighter planes available made contact 30 miles distant with 60 to 80 dive bombers (possibly a few of these were twin-engined horizontal bombers) and about 50 fighters. Severe fighting continued as long as our fighters were in the air, which was not long for most of them against these odds, accentuated by the poor maneuverability of these planes. Of the 27 fighters available, 15 were lost and 7 severely damaged. Statements from 9 of the 11 surviving pilots show that they shot town a total of 3 Japanese Zero fighters and 8 Aichi Type 99 dive bombers. Survivors believe the total number destroyed by all the fighter planes was probably 8 zero fighters and 25 dive bombers.

The first bomb hit Midway at about 0633 from horizontal bombers. Dive bombing and strafing continued for about 17 minutes. Considerable damage was done to nearly all structures above ground, the most serious at the time being the destruction of the power plant on Eastern Island. Little damage was done to the runways, the Japanese apparently leaving these intact for their own anticipated use. The anti-aircraft batteries shot well, downing 10 planes and, with the fighters, damaging many more, so that our returning airplanes reported "large numbers of enemy planes down on the water and falling out of formation."

The B-26's found their targets, 2 CV, about 0710 and made a most gallant attack. This is likewise another historical event, and, it is hoped, one soon to be repeated under better conditions—our Army's first attack with torpedo planes. Heavy fighter concentrations were encountered; 2 of the 4 planes did not return; one was shot down before launching his torpedo, and possibly the other, though it is said to have attacked and in pulling out touched the flight deck of the target before crashing into the sea. Both of the 2 planes that did return were so badly shot up by the terrific fighter and AA fire encountered that they were unserviceable. Survivors had no time to observe results but approaches were such that it is believed probable that one torpedo hit.

The TBF's made a similarly gallant attack almost simultaneously with the B-26's and against an equally determined and overwhelming number of fighters. At least 2 of them were shot down before they could launch torpedoes. Only one badly shot-up plane returned. The pilot could not tell what happened to the remainder of his unit or how the attack fared. A B-17, on reconnaissance, reports seeing one of the planes make a hit. Although the TBF is a well armed plane, it is obvious that it cannot go through fighter opposition without fighter protection.

At 0755 a group of 16 Marine dive bombers, under Major L. R. Henderson, U.S.M.C., made a gallant glide bombing attack on one of the carriers in the Striking Force. The planes had been received too recently for training in dive bombing, so the Commander chose this less effective and more hazardous method of attack because it permitted lower pullouts. His and 7 other planes were shot down by overwhelming fighter opposition. The 8 planes that did return were badly shot-up, one having 210 holes. The target, probably the *SORYU,* was hit 3 times and left afire.

Soon afterward, at about 0820, the 11 SB2U Marine bombers from Midway made a glide bombing attack on a battleship, likewise against heavy fighter attack. Two hits are reported. When last seen the battleship was smoking and listed.

The B-17 unit of 16 planes, under the Commanding Officer of the 431st Bombardment Squadron, Lt. Col. W. C. Sweeney, U.S.A., who led each flight he made in an outstanding manner, was directed to change its objective from the Transport Force to the carriers. Promptly and with skillful navigation the planes proceeded, picked up the enemy fleet on bearing 320° about 145 miles from Midway, and at 0814 began attacking from 20,000 feet, each plane carrying 8 500-pound demolition bombs. Results were reported as a total of 3 hits on the carriers present, possibly 2 carriers hit with heavy smoke from one; carriers still maneuvering and operating normally. Since only one carrier was reported smoking, this was probably the same one, *SORYU,* the Marine dive bombers had set afire a few minutes earlier with 3 hits.

The Midway Forces had struck with full strength, but the Japanese were not as yet checked. About 10 ships had been reported damaged, of which 1 or 2 AP or Ak [*sic*] may have sunk. But this was hardly an impression on the great force of about 80 ships converging on Midway. Most of Midway's fighters, torpedo planes and dive bombers—the only types capable of making a high percentage of hits on ships—were gone, and 3 of the Japanese carriers were still either undamaged or insufficiently so to hamper operations.

This was the situation when our carrier attack began. Task Force 16 and 17, ready about 200 miles to the northeast of the Japanese carriers, had intercepted the first contact reports by the Midway scouts. At about 0700 launching commenced